Chinese Language, Thought, and Culture

Photo by Louis M. Green, 1988

DAVID S. NIVISON

Critics and Their Critics

VOLUME III

Chinese Language, Thought, and Culture

NIVISON AND HIS CRITICS

EDITED BY

Philip J. Ivanhoe

Foreword by
Patrick Suppes

OPEN COURT
Chicago and La Salle, Illinois

$$\boxed{\textit{Critics and Their Critics}}$$

The front cover photograph of David S. Nivison was taken in 1962 by William McCullough in the Rinrokaku Bookstore across the street from Tokyo University. Nivison is shown contemplating the 1936 Commercial Press typeset edition of the *Collected Works of Zhang Xuecheng*, which he subsequently purchased.

Library of Congress Cataloging-in-Publication Data

Chinese language, thought, and culture : Nivison and his critics / edited by Philip J. Ivanhoe.
    p.   cm. — (Critics and their critics ; v. 3)
    Includes bibliographical references and index.
    ISBN 0-8126-9318-3 (pbk. : alk. paper)
    1. China—Civilization. 2. Philosophy, Chinese. 3. Nivison, David S. I. Ivanhoe, P. J. II. Nivison, David S. Selections. 1996. III. Series.
DS721.C5173   1996   96-12392
951—dc20   CIP

CONTENTS

Foreword by Patrick Suppes vii

Introduction xi

Biography xvi

Contributors xvii

Acknowledgments xx

Note on Transcription xxi

Part One

1 Toward a New Pronominal Hypothesis of *Qi* in Shang Chinese 3
Ken-ichi Takashima

2 Zou and Lu and the Sinification of Shandong 39
Edwin G. Pulleyblank

3 Micro-Periodization and the Calendar of a Shang Military Campaign 58
Edward L. Shaughnessy

4 The Mean in Original Confucianism 83
Kanaya Osamu

5 Women in the Life and Thought of Zhang Xuecheng 94
Susan Mann

6 Zhang Xuecheng Versus Dai Zhen:
A Study in Intellectual Challenge and Response in Eighteenth-Century China 121
Yü Ying-shih

7 Beyond Post-Modernism 155
Henry Rosemont, Jr.

8 Duty and Virtue 173
Chad Hansen

9 A Villain in the *Xunzi* 193
Donald J. Munro

10 Xunzi on Moral Motivation 202
David B. Wong

11 What Should Western Philosophy Learn from
    Chinese Philosophy?   224
    Bryan W. Van Norden

12 "Existentialism" in the School of Wang Yangming   250
    Philip J. Ivanhoe

PART TWO

Replies and Comments   267
    David S. Nivison

PUBLISHED WORKS OF DAVID S. NIVISON   342

INDEX   349

FOREWORD

David Nivison came to Stanford in 1948 as an acting instructor in Chinese in the Department of Asiatic and Slavic Studies. Prior to this time he had graduated from Harvard with a major in far eastern languages, served for three years in the United States Army from 1943–1946 as a translator of Japanese, and begun graduate work at Harvard. While holding various positions at Stanford in the early 1950s he completed his Ph.D. at Harvard in 1953 and in the fall of that year became an instructor in Chinese and Philosophy at Stanford. After his one-year appointment, which ended in 1954, he received a Fulbright Research Fellowship for study in Japan in 1954–1955 and then returned to Stanford as a Lecturer in Philosophy from 1955–1958, a position that gave him considerable freedom to teach what he wanted and continue research. In 1959 he was appointed Associate Professor of Chinese and Philosophy at Stanford, and he continued as a tenured member of the Stanford faculty until his retirement in 1988. Beginning in 1974 he became Professor by Courtesy in the Department of Religious Studies. In 1983 he was appointed the Walter Y. Evans-Wentz Professor of Oriental Philosophies, Religions, and Ethics, and in connection with this Chair, a member of the faculty in the Departments of Philosophy, Asian Languages, and Religious Studies. During his many years as a faculty member at Stanford, David split his time on a regular basis between the Department of Philosophy and the Department of Asian Languages, and in the later years the Department of Religious Studies. He was active in all three of these departments both intellectually and administratively.

As can be seen from this brief academic history, David originally concentrated his intellectual energies in the study of Far Eastern languages. His interest in philosophy began to be serious in the early 1950s. In the winter of 1952 he audited my Intermediate Logic course. To develop his teaching skills in philosophy, he took charge of the sections in Elementary Logic in the fall of 1955, and then gave the lectures himself in the spring of 1956. Moreover, in 1952–1953 he had a faculty research fellowship from the Ford Foundation for study in philosophy at Stanford and Harvard; one of the highlights of that fellowship was auditing Quine's Philosophy of Language course at Harvard. In those early years, he also attended several courses of Donald Davidson's and was a continual participant in Davidson's graduate seminar in philosophy from 1956 until the early 1960s when Davidson left Stanford for Princeton.

Apart from this brief summary of how David developed his interest in philosophy, what is important to note is the central role he played over many years in the Department of Philosophy in the teaching of a variety of courses in Chinese philosophy, as well as courses in elementary logic, philosophy of history, and Marxist ethics. The philosophy department was indeed fortunate to have such a distinguished scholar of Chinese intellectual thought continually engaged in the academic life of the department, even when he was carrying a substantial load in other areas. But there is more to it than I have yet expressed. I remember in the late 1960s reading some of the reviews of his extraordinarily well-received book, *The Life and Thought of Chang Hsüeh-ch'eng*, and I thought, it is very clear that David is becoming one of the few distinguished American scholars of Chinese intellectual thought in what we would consider the early modern period. Not long after that, however, he began a course of research that took him in a new and surprising direction. He began research on ancient Chinese inscriptions as he became engrossed in the problem of a more accurate dating of early Chinese chronology.

From his interest in Chinese chronology and ancient Chinese inscriptions, he was led to what has turned out to be a deep and continuing interest in ancient Chinese astronomy, a subject in which after many years he is just beginning to publish, for example, in his work on the origin of the Chinese lunar zodiac. Even more surprising is that after he saw an exhibit of pre-Columbian work at the National Gallery in Washington D.C., he saw immediate parallels between Aztec and ancient Chinese astronomy. He has since proceeded to learn much about Aztec astronomy, even to study the Aztec language and to attend a variety of conferences on astronomy in Mesoamerica. I can remember when he told me about his ideas about Aztec astronomy about ten years ago. It was like other conversations I have had on many occasions with David. I always learn something that I did not know before, and often in a very enlightening way.

I now want to turn to a survey of David's surprisingly wide-ranging administrative services at Stanford. Already in 1962 he served as Acting Head of the Department of Asian Languages for several months, and then served as the first Director of the Stanford Center for Chinese Studies in Taipei, Taiwan. In 1969–1972 he served as Chairman of the Department of Philosophy which, in my own judgment, was the most difficult period to be a Chairman in the modern history of Stanford. This was a time of student riots and problems between students and administration in universities throughout the world. I can remember that David spent one night in 1970 in his office in order to protect the Department of Philosophy building from attack. This is only one of several occasions during this tense period when a Chairman was called upon to have strength of character far beyond that ordinarily thought of as a requirement for the position. David was fortunately the best possible choice as chairman during this period. He also served in 1970–1972 as a faculty member on the Judicial Council, which handled a series of tense and difficult disciplinary cases. The faculty members on this committee were often verbally attacked publicly by students during this period. He served again as Chairman of the Department of Philosophy for the academic year 1975–1976 and was Acting Chairman of the Department of Asian Languages for 1985–1986. He served on numerous other committees at Stanford, too numerous to mention, and in particular on committees of all three departments of which he was a member during the last years of his academic appointment.

Outside of Stanford David has also had an active role in a variety of organizations, but I want to mention especially, as a measure of his esteem among philosophers, that he was elected President of the Pacific Division of the American Philosophical Association for 1979–1980.

David's long-term interest in Mencius, Confucius, and central problems of what we would term Chinese moral philosophy continues, but now he is as interested in ancient Chinese astronomy and even its relation to Aztec astronomy. Although I was surprised at this shift, I was not as surprised as I might have been, because I have known for a long time about David's strong interest in one of the famous outstanding problems of number theory, namely, does there exist an infinite number of twin primes, that is, prime numbers p such that both p and p+2 are prime? He did not solve the problem, which is still open, but I know that he did spend, at various times, a lot of time thinking about it and trying various approaches to a proof. Anyone who has thought hard about the twin prime problem is bound to find logic easy to learn, and I guess we could even generalize this to ancient astronomy. As I said already, every time that I see David I learn something new. I would not want to predict in what direction his intellectual energies will next be focused.

Patrick Suppes
Stanford, California

INTRODUCTION

When David S. Nivison retired from Stanford University in 1988, a conference was held to mark the occasion. On the opening day of the conference, Albert E. Dien gave an elegant and incisive introduction in which he described the general trajectory of Nivison's work. He noted, among other things, that Nivison began his career by working on the late Qing philosopher of history Zhang Xuecheng.[1] Qing intellectual history and philosophy occupied much of the early part of his career. During this period, Nivison also worked on more contemporary material, producing an important work on the relationship between Chinese Marxist thinkers and the Confucian tradition.[2] Then began a steady and determined drive *back* to the earliest periods of Chinese history. He worked on early Qing thinkers and problems and spent considerable time on the Ming philosopher and moral teacher Wang Yangming. Certain problems in Wang's moral philosophy, involving issues of motivation and agency, led Nivison to skip across centuries, and focus concerted attention on the late Zhou philosopher Mengzi. This in turn led him to pursue a wide-ranging study of pre-Qin moral philosophy.

Nivison's pursuit of several nagging grammatical puzzles encountered in his teaching of old Chinese, such as the problem of "modal *qi* 其," led him to seek David N. Keightley's instruction in reading Shang and early Zhou inscription texts. This led to articles and papers on linguistic problems and to the study of Shang and Zhou concepts of *de* 德 ("moral virtue, power, or charisma"). This work, in turn, led him to exploit astronomical details and dates in inscriptions and in old texts, such as the supposedly fake *Bamboo Annals*, to reconstruct exact chronology far into the Chinese past. Revolutionary discoveries have resulted from these inquiries, by Nivison and by others; and in reaching those that are his own, Nivison acknowledges a debt for the stimulation of vigorous debate with his colleagues: on linguistic problems, especially with Ken-ichi Takashima, David N. Keightley and

Paul Serruys; on the *de* problem, especially with Keightley; and on astronomy and chronology, notably with Edward L. Shaughnessy and David W. Pankenier, who have made remarkable discoveries themselves.

Nivison's work thus extends over vast spans of Chinese history and across a wide range of different interests. This breadth and variety is reflected in the different essays found in the present volume. One finds such impressive diversity even when one looks at Nivison's work within a highly specific field such as philosophy.[3] I would like to suggest, however, that there is "a single thread" running through all of Nivison's work. Whether he is working on an explicitly philosophical topic such as *akrasia* in Mengzi's moral philosophy or presenting his latest research on the semantics and grammar of oracular inscriptions, Nivison is always thinking *philosophically*. I mean by this that no matter what else he may be doing, on another level he is always *thinking about his thinking*. Two examples may suffice to make my point.

The present volume contains an essay by Ken-ichi Takashima on the modal particle *qi* 其 in Chinese oracle bone inscriptions, which reflects a rich and extensive exchange going back many years between Keightley, Takashima, and Nivison. Indeed, Keightley was the one who first drew Nivison into the difficult and fascinating field of oracle bone inscriptions. In the course of their most recent exchange, Nivison raised a methodological issue that illustrates the kind of concern that I maintain runs through and unites all his work. Nivison challenged what at first glance looks to be a self-evident principle in linguistics: that every difference in language reflects a difference in meaning. In the specific case that they were discussing, it would seem that the best theory about the use of the character *qi* will explain the differences in *each individual instance* of its appearance. However, Nivison points out—and he is surely right—that some differences make no difference. That is to say, in certain cases, the presence or absence of *qi* has no consequence whatsoever for the meaning of the sentence. Of course, there are other cases, theoretically perhaps quite rare, where the use or absence of *qi* is absolutely critical. But in either of these cases and in all cases, what linguistic theory seeks to explain are not individual instances, but general *classes* of usage. In the same way, while there is an obvious difference between the sentences "It will rain tomorrow" and "It is going to rain tomorrow," they often mean *exactly* the same thing. This of course in no way implies that there are no cases in which the choice between "will" and "is going to" is a difference with a profound difference. Throughout his career, Nivison's attention to methodological issues of this sort has served to focus attention not only on the texts being interpreted but on our methods and theories of interpretation as well.

My second example concerns Nivison's work on dating, part of his larger study of early Chinese calendars.[4] Specifically, it concerns Nivison's theory that during the Western Zhou the regular practice was to begin the official calendar for a given King with what is actually the third year of his reign. In devising this theory and in arguing and providing evidence for its support, Nivison has relied upon a sophisticated understanding of issues in both the philosophy of science and the philosophy of history. Here again, Nivison's work has shown us that it is impossible to understand someone else's projects and practices without first taking account of our own: our methodological assumptions, standards of evidence, and criteria of truth.

Nivison's primary innovations concern how one understands the nature of explanation in general and historical explanation in particular. There has been a fairly recent revolution in the philosophy of science that is largely a reaction to the idea that there is some unified discipline called "science" which applies "laws" to individual situations and circumstances and thereby "derives" certain results. The opposing view is that such an attempt to replace a cause-and-effect narrative of *events* with one of logical inference from certain *premises* distorts the true nature of explanation. Explanations are not simply arguments, they are narratives based upon certain law-like assumptions about the way the world works.

Historical explanation has its own unique character, because the phenomena which history seeks to explain are special: history is an account of the *actions of human beings*. In order to explain why people acted as they did, the historian must understand not only the material circumstances in which historical events took place but also the intentions, plans, and methods of reasoning of the people involved in these events.

Much of Nivison's work on dating events in early Chinese history relies upon the theoretical insights described above. By way of contrast, most of the people working in this area think that one must argue *from* certain established facts *to* particular, rather limited, conclusions and refuse to consider arguments that do not follow a similar structure and logic. For without "hard facts" and deductive arguments, they insist, one is simply engaging in wild speculation. Nivison however began by supposing that certain information, specifically certain dates in texts like the *Bamboo Annals,* which many scholars had regarded as unreliable myth, was in fact accurate and reliable. He then speculated about what kinds of beliefs and practices might have combined with certain circumstances and events in order to yield the dates we presently find in these sources. This required him to postulate practices like the two-year mourning period between the reigns of Western Zhou kings and the subsequent ignorance of this convention, on the part of Chinese scholars during late antiquity. These hypotheses led him to look for confirmation in places where earlier he would not have known to look; as a result, he has been able to produce significant evidence to support his theory. What is more, it enabled him to explain why we find certain systematic errors in dating in sources from late antiquity. Nivison's work in this area provides a powerful example of inference to best explanation.

The concept of inference to best explanation, to be sure, is no one's personal property. It has a venerable history; arguably its ancient ancestor is the hoary concept of a hypothesis that seeks to "save the phenomena." It is ably demonstrated in the writings of others who work in this field. One example is Shaughnessy's contribution to the present volume. Another, as Nivison has pointed out,[5] is Pankenier's "Mozi and the Dates of Xia, Shang, and Zhou".[6] Nivison's contribution has been to show clearly that this form of argument is required for any successful work on very ancient material, which will often seem to be too "thin" to work in interesting ways.

Here and in the previous case, Nivison's philosophical approach has allowed him not only to contribute to the accumulation of knowledge in different fields but, more importantly, to improve the ways these fields are worked. In the process, he has done some very interesting philosophy.

Most of the remaining essays in this volume are explicitly philosophical in nature; half are by scholars who are themselves philosophers by trade. But I submit that this interest is not restricted to these authors or their works, as I have shown in the two cases discussed above. All of the contributors in this volume are on some level engaged in philosophical reflection about their respective projects. They are thinking about thinking: about what they bring to and how they go about their own intellectual work. This underlying concern is the "one thread" uniting the essays in this volume and running throughout the life and thought of David S. Nivison.

Philip J. Ivanhoe
Stanford University
January 1994

NOTES

1. The primary result of this work was his book *The Life and Thought of Chang Hsüeh-ch'eng* (Stanford University Press, 1966). For a complete list of other works on this topic and from this period, please see the bibliography of Nivison's works included in the present volume.

2. "Communist Ethics and Chinese Tradition," first appeared in *The Journal of Asian Studies* 16, no. 1 (November 1956): 51–74. It subsequently appeared in partial and full reprints (see bibliography for details and complete citations).

3. Bryan W. Van Norden has done a masterful job selecting and editing a volume of essays, *The Ways of Confucianism: Investigations in Chinese Philosophy,* which focus on Nivison's most philosophical work. This collection is also available through Open Court Press and can be read as a companion to the present work.

4. The example I will describe here is from Nivison's "The Dates of Western Chou," *Harvard Journal of Asiatic Studies* 43, no. 2 (December 1983): 481–580.

5. "Forum" response to critics, *Early China* 15 (1990): 162.

6. *Early China* 9–10, (1983–1985).

BIOGRAPHY

David Shepherd Nivison was born in Farmingdale, next to Gardiner, Maine, on the seventeenth of January 1923. His younger brother, William, (Rear Adm., U.S. Navy, retired) was born on 12 July 1924. Their father, William Nivison, was born in Guardbridge, Scotland, in 1884, emigrating in 1905 to Maine, where he eventually became superintendent of a paper mill in Gardiner. In 1940 he was transferred to Mobile, Alabama; later he returned to Gardiner where he died, in 1944. Their mother, née Ruth Robinson, was a niece of the poet Edwin Arlington Robinson. Before her marriage in 1921, she served as a nurse in the Grenfell Mission in Newfoundland and Labrador. Born in Farmingdale in 1890, she died in Saratoga, California, in 1971.

On 11 September 1944, David Nivison married Cornelia Green, whose father and grandfather had been professors of law. The Nivisons have lived in Los Altos, California since 1952. There are two daughters, Louise (1947) and Helen Thom (1949), and two sons, David Gregory (1956) and James Nicholas (1959).

Nivison attended public schools in Farmingdale and Gardiner, and was valedictorian of his class in Gardiner High School in 1940. Entering Harvard that year, he majored first in Classics, later in Far Eastern Languages. Entering the Army in January of 1943, he joined a group recruited by Edwin O. Reischauer, and worked three years as a translator of Japanese. Returning to Harvard, he graduated in 1946 *summa cum laude.* He earned both the M.A. (1948) and Ph.D. (1953) at Harvard in Far Eastern Languages, working primarily with J. R. Hightower, L. S. Yang, William Hung, Edwin O. Reischauer and John K. Fairbank. His dissertation, directed by Hightower and Yang, was "The Literary and Historical Thought of Chang Hsüeh-ch'eng (1738–1801)."

Joining the faculty of Stanford University in 1948, during the next forty years he taught both old Chinese and various subjects in philosophy. A description of his service to the university and to the field of philosophy, by his long-time colleague and friend Patrick Suppes, is included as the forward to this volume. Among many academic distinctions, he was elected to the Harvard chapter of Phi Beta Kappa in 1943 and has held fellowships from the Harvard-Yenching Institute, the Ford Foundation, the Fulbright Administration, the American Council of Learned Societies, and the Guggenheim Foundation. In 1967, he was awarded the Prix Stanislas-Julien, Institut de France (Academie des Inscriptions et Belles-Lettres) for his book *The Life and Thought of Chang Hsüeh-ch'eng*. His offices in professional societies have included the presidencies of the Western Branch of the American Oriental Society (1971–1972) and of the Pacific Division, American Philosophical Association (1979–1980). In 1983, he was appointed by Stanford University the first Walter Y. Evans-Wentz Professor of Oriental Philosophies, Religions, and Ethics. He retired in 1988 and has devoted himself in recent years primarily to his interests in ancient Chinese astronomy, dating, inscriptions, and calendar studies.

CONTRIBUTORS

KEN-ICHI TAKASHIMA studied at Sophia University in Tokyo and the University of Washington in Seattle (M.A., 1967, Ph.D., 1973). He is Professor of Chinese and Japanese in the Department of Asian Studies, University of British Columbia in Vancouver, Canada. From 1988 to 1990 he taught at the University of Tokyo. His publications include: *A Concordance to Fascicle Three of Inscriptions from the Yin Ruins* and *Studies in Early Chinese Civilization: Religion, Society, Language, and Palaeography* (co-author, Michiharu Ito; forthcoming).

EDWIN G. PULLEYBLANK is Professor Emeritus of Asian Studies in the University of British Columbia. He holds degrees from the University of Alberta (B.A. 1942), and the University of London (Ph.D. 1951). He taught at the School of Oriental and African Studies, University of London (1948–1953) and from 1953 to 1966 was Professor of Chinese in the University of Cambridge. His publications include *The Background of the Rebellion of An Lushan* (1955), *Middle Chinese* (1984), *Lexicon of Reconstructed Pronunciation in Early Middle Chinese, Late Middle Chinese and Early Mandarin* (1991) as well as articles on Chinese history and linguistics in academic journals and other collective works.

EDWARD L. SHAUNGHNESSY is Associate Professor of Chinese at the University of Chicago. Educated at the University of Notre Dame (B.A. in Theology, 1974) and Stanford University (M.A. and Ph.D., Asian Languages, 1980 and 1983), he is the editor of the journal *Early China* and author of *Sources of Western Zhou History: Inscribed Bronze Vessels*, as well as various articles on the cultural history of Bronze Age China and on Chinese classicism.

KANAYA OSAMU is Professor Emeritus of Chinese philosophy at Jokoku University in Japan. He was taught by Takeuchi Yoshio and specialized in the history of ancient Chinese thought. He is the author of numerous books and articles and several Japanese translations of classical Chinese texts. Among his books are *A Study of the History of Qin and Han Period Thought* and *A Study of the 'Guan Zi'*. His work on classical Chinese texts includes his well-known translation, of the *Analects*, and *Mencius*.

SUSAN MANN is Professor of History at the University of California, Davis. She received her M.A. (1966) and Ph.D. (1972) degrees at Stanford University, where she was a student of David S. Nivison. She is the author of several articles and a book (*Local Merchants and the Chinese Bureaucracy, 1750–1950*, 1987) on the history of merchants and trade organizations in late imperial China. Her recent studies of the history of women in Qing times have appeared in *The Journal of Asian Studies, Late Imperial China*, and in numerous anthologies. She has just completed a book on women in eighteenth-century China.

YÜ YING-SHIH received his B.A. from New Asia College (1952) and his Ph.D. from Harvard in History and Far Eastern Languages (1962). He has taught at Harvard and Yale and since 1987 as the Michael Henry Strater University Professor of East Asian Studies and Professor of History at Princeton University. His publications include: *Trade and Expansion in Han China* (1967), *Fang Yizhi (1611–1671): His Last Years and His Death* (1972), *Dai Zhen and Zhang Xuecheng, A Study in Mid-qing Intellectual History* (1976), *Religious Ethic and the Merchant Class in Early Modern China* (1986; Japanese tr., 1991), *Chinese Intellectuals and Chinese Culture* (1987), and *Early Chinese History in the People's Republic of China* (1981, editor and principal author). He has also published numerous articles in Western, Chinese, and Japanese learned journals.

HENRY ROSEMONT, JR. studied at the Universities of Illinois (B.A., 1962), and Washington (Ph.D., 1967) and did post-doctoral work at MIT and the University of London. He is Professor of Philosophy at St. Mary's College of Maryland, and Consulting Professor at Fudan University in Shanghai, where he taught 1982–1984 and 1993–1994. His most recent publications are *Chinese Texts and Philosophical Contexts: Essays Dedicated to Angus C. Graham*, *A Chinese Mirror*, and with Daniel J. Cook, *G.W. Leibniz: Writings on China*.

CHAD HANSEN is Reader in Philosophy at the University of Hong Kong. He received a B.A. from the University of Utah (1966), and Ph.D. from the University of Michigan (1972). He has taught at the University of Pittsburgh, University of Michigan, U.C.L.A., Stanford, the University of Hawaii, and for thirteen years at the University of Vermont, where he was elected University Scholar in 1991. He is the author of *Logic and Language in Ancient China* (1983) and *A Daoist Theory of Chinese Thought* (1992). He has written articles for *Philosophy East and West,* the *Journal of Chinese Philosophy, Journal of Asian Studies,* and for various encyclopedias and edited collections.

DONALD J. MUNRO teaches at the University of Michigan. He is an associate of the Center for Chinese Studies, a Professor of Chinese in the Department of Asian Languages, and a Professor of Philosophy. He is the author of a trilogy of books on Chinese philosophy: *The Concept of Man in Early China, The Concept of Man in Contemporary China,* and most recently, *Images of Human Nature: A Sung Portrait.* He has given the Evans-Wentz Lectures at Stanford, the Fritz Lecture at the University of Washington, the Gilbert Ryle Lectures at Trent University, and the John Dewey Lecture at the University of Vermont. He is a former Ford Foundation Fellow, Guggenheim Fellow, and ACLS Fellow, and has done research in both Taiwan and the People's Republic of China.

DAVID B. WONG received degrees from Macalester College (B.A., 1971) and Princeton University (Ph.D., Philosophy, 1977). He is Professor and Chairman of the Department of Philosophy at Brandeis University. He is author of *Moral Relativity* (1984) and of articles appearing in *The Encyclopedia of Ethics* and journals such as *The Philosophical Review, Midwest Studies in Philosophy, Ethics, The Journal of Chinese Philosophy,* and *Philosophy East and West.*

BRYAN W. VAN NORDEN received his B.A. from University of Pennsylvania (1985) and his Ph.D. from Stanford (1991). His work appears in *The Journal of Chinese Studies, The Journal of Asian Studies, The Journal of Chinese Philosophy,* and the *International Philosophical Quarterly.* He has also contributed several entries on Chinese philosophy to *The Cambridge Dictionary of Philosophy.* He has been a lecturer at Stanford University, a visiting Professor at the University of Vermont, and is now an Assistant Professor of Philosophy at Vassar College.

PHILIP J. IVANHOE received his B.A. (1976) and his Ph.D. (1987) from Stanford University. His articles have appeared in such journals as the *Journal of the American Academy of Religion, The Journal of Religious Ethics, Philosophy East and West, The Journal of Chinese Philosophy,* and the *International Philosophical Quarterly.* He is the author of *Ethics in the Confucian Tradition; The Thought of Mencius and Wang Yang-ming* (1990) and *Confucian Moral Self-Cultivation* (1993). He is currently an Assistant Professor in Philosophy and Religious Studies at Stanford.

ACKNOWLEDGMENTS

I would like to thank Henry Rosemont Jr. both for suggesting and promoting the present project and for contributing to it. Without his encouragement and support, this volume would not have been realized. I would also like to thank Open Court for undertaking and supporting this work. In particular, I would like to thank Kerri Mommer for her patience and guidance.

Paul Kjellberg, Bryan W. Van Norden, and Mark A. Csikszentmihalyi provided helpful comments on several of the essays included here and on the introduction. I would also like to thank each of the authors for their excellent contributions and for their patience with me as editor. They made this process as painless and productive as it can possibly be.

Philip J. Ivanhoe
Stanford, California

NOTE ON TRANSCRIPTION

The articles in the present volume employ the *pinyin* romanization system. Chinese names or terms in quotations from other works have been converted to *pinyin* whenever they appear in the essays or in their subsequent notes. However, in order to facilitate locating cited works, the names of works and their authors have been left in their original romanization.

Transcription Conversion Table

Pinyin	*Wade-Giles*
b	p
c	ts', tz'
ch	ch'
d	t
g	k
ian	ien
j	ch
k	k'
ong	ung
p	p'
q	ch'
r	j
si	szu
t	t'
x	hs
you	yu
yu	yü
z	ts, tz
zh	ch
-i (zhi)	-ih (chih)
zi	tzu

PART
ONE

Toward a New Pronominal Hypothesis of *Qi* in Shang Chinese

Ken-ichi Takashima

For more than twenty years I have had the privilege of knowing Professor David Nivison; on occasion, my work has been the object of his criticism as his has been of mine—the two of us never seem to be able to agree on certain major issues.[1] The present paper, however, is different, in that even though our perspectives and assumptions are not in perfect consonance,[2] there just may be some issues about which Nivison and I once disagreed, but where we now are more in agreement. The scholarly issues involved are quite thorny ones: (1) the possibility that *qi* in the Shang oracle-bone inscriptions (hereafter abbreviated as "OBI" or, when we wish to focus more on their linguistic aspect, as "OBL") might have been used as an anaphoric pronoun; (2) the possibility that *qi* might have been used as a subordinate sentence marker of the embedment type,[3] and (3) the possibility that *qi* might have been used as a function word representing what amounts to the "subjunctive mood" in traditional grammar. All of these possibilities are closely connected, so that the acceptance of any one of them may entail the acceptance of them all.

The single most serious obstacle to exploring the above-mentioned possibilities is that for these usages, unlike the rich corpus of inscriptions available for testing my separate theory that *qi* is a modal and aspectual particle in the OBL, we are faced with a relatively small number of examples upon which to make our judgment. But, as we shall see in section 2, there are a few striking examples and some consistent patterns of occurrence which suggest that the possibilities may just be borne out.

First, however, as a background to section 2 where I address the pronominal hypothesis, it is necessary to present the gist of my interpretation that *qi* functions as a kind of adverbial particle, conveying a variety of modal as well as aspectual meanings.

1.   The Modal and Aspectual Theory of *Qi*

1.1 The Nature of Modal Qi

One major controversy surrounding *qi* is whether or not it conveys a sense of uncertainty or certainty. Most specialists have taken the former interpretation, while the single, most consistent advocator of the latter interpretation has been Nivison (e.g., 1971a, 1992, 1992a, 1992b). Only Serruys (1972; 1974, 94, n.8) reacted against the interpretation that *qi* conveyed a sense of uncertainty (Takashima 1970; 29–32), and had the following to say about the matter:

> *Qi* does not express primarily "uncertain feelings" but a definitely certain judgment and opinion, *viz.* that the proposition carrying the particle *qi* represents the "less desired alternative," and the English "perhaps, may be" does not seem to account for the real meaning implied by absence and presence of *qi* in certain opposite sentences.

This interpretation is similar, though not identical, to Nivison's in that *qi* is used in statements of firm intent as in the following example:

(1)   余其作邑.   *Qianbian* 4.10.6
"I *will* found a settlement here." (Nivison 1992, 7)

Nivison argues as follows:

> The objector would interpret it "I will perhaps found a settlement (here)." He wants the line to mean, "I intend to found a settlement here, but I am uncertain whether I should do so." But what it *says* is, "I *will* found a settlement here," i.e., I hereby announce my intention to do so—for the purpose of conducting a divination test. The announcement *is* tentative, but the tentativeness is *not* expressed in the language used. The tentativeness is revealed only in the fact that the *sentence* is a *charge* in a divination rite.

Although Serruys did not provide a translation for the inscription just quoted, his rule of "undesirable *qi*" (1974, 25)[4] would lead one to interpret it as "I might (*qi:* but would rather not) found a settlement here."[5] It follows that to Serruys, the *qi* might be translatable as "might," but it does not express any meaning of uncertainty, conveying instead a clear preference on the part of the king for not building a settlement. The illocutionary force of Nivison's understanding and that of Serruys' are thus completely opposite to each other. They cannot both be right. And, then, there is of course the third possibility against which Nivison was reacting: "I will perhaps found a settlement" or "I might found a settlement," expressing a genuine uncertainty as to the wisdom of carrying out the project.

In order to be able to decide which, if either, of these rival interpretations is the correct choice, we need to examine the inscription in a context greater than that in which it is found. First, we need to pay attention to the left or right placement of the inscription on the bone—something which is not always easy to establish for small fragments. We also need to interpret each divinatory charge in the context of the greater inscription, for this might indicate whether the content of the charge would or would not have been something the Shang really desired. The latter has the danger of imposing upon the Shang our own notion of what is "good," which may not necessarily have been regarded as "good" by the Shang themselves. But there are examples which, when placed in a larger context, are quite suggestive.

Example (1), cited above, occurs on a fragmentary piece of bone, and it is probable that it had occurred in a context such as the following:

(2A) 壬子卜爭貞我其作邑帝弗左若. (R)   *Bingbian* 147(1)

Crack-making on the *renzi* day [49], Zheng tested: We will found a settlement, (for) Di will not oppose (but) will approve.

(2B) 癸丑卜爭貞勿作邑帝若. (L)   *Ibid.* (2)

Crack-making on the *guichou* day [50], Zheng tested: (We) should not found a settlement, (for) Di will approve.

It is generally agreed among specialists that the semantically positive charge, that is, positive or desirable to the Shang, was carved on the right side of a shell (R), and the semantically negative or undesirable charge was carved on the left (L). Keightley (1978; 51, n. 124) provides the following charge pair as illustrating a preferred distribution of *qi* in the semantically negative:

(3A) ↓貞子〔啇〕亡〔疾〕. (R) *Zhuihe* 292
>Tested: Zi Shang shall have no sickness.

(3B) ↑子啇其有疾. (L) *Ibid.*
>Tested: Zi Shang might have sickness.

Although (3A) is grammatically negative and (3B) positive, (3A) is inscribed on the R and (3B) on the L side of the shell. I agree with Keightley's characterization that "since Zi Shang was an ally and perhaps a member of the royal family, his possible sickness was undesirable, . . . the inscription was carved on the left side of the shell."

Now if we examine (2A) and (2B), we find that (2A) occurs on the "desirable R" and (2B) on the "undesirable L" and that *qi* occurs on the R but not on the L. The literal application of Serruys' rule would be that (2A) was undesirable to the Shang, i.e., the Shang didn't want to found a settlement. This is not impossible, but it is unlikely for three reasons: for one, the reason clause[6] which follows 我其作邑 says specifically that Di will not oppose such an undertaking but will approve of it, indicating a clear intention, if not wish, that the Shang had the desire to perform this action. To be sure, the negative counterpart (2B) says the opposite, so it cancels the force of the first argument—almost, but not quite, when one considers the second reason, which is that (2A) and (2B) are followed by the ensuing divinations:

(4A) ↓癸丑卜爭貞我宅茲邑大賓帝若. (R) *Bingbian* 147(3)
>Crack-making on the *guichou* day [50], Zheng tested: We will take up residence in this settlement and conduct a great entertainment ritual, (for) Di will approve.

(4B) ↑癸丑卜爭貞帝弗若. (L) *Ibid.* (4)
>Crack-making on the *guichou* day [50], Zheng tested: Di will not approve.

In (4A) it is clear that the Shang contemplated the next move after the founding of a settlement—taking up residence and conducting an (ancestral) ceremony there. Again, (4A) is inscribed on the R; Di not approving in (4B) was undesired, and so was inscribed on the L. The third reason, which may not be totally unequivocal, is that sentence parallelism suggests that the degree of modality of *qi* be taken as equal, except that *qi zuo* is positive and *wu zuo* 勿作 'don't build' is negative. That is, because *wu* is a modally strong prohibitive negative, it is matched, as pointed out by Nivison and Keightley (1993, 35), with an equally strong modal word. I would maintain this interpretation is applicable to *qi* in (2A), but not to the same in (3B), for it is difficult to think that the Shang expressed a strong statement such as "Zi Shang *shall* have sickness." In terms of the degree of modality, then, I suggest that *qi* behaves in such a way as to change its modal force at will.

As far as can be established, I find that the "desirable R" and the "undesirable L" placement of the inscriptions is, on the whole, not violated[7] (so much so, in fact, that one can conjure up the *yin* and *yang* forces at work in the OBL). It thus seems prudent to interpret examples (1), (2A), (3A), and (4A) as representing the desired alternative to the Shang.

As seen in the above examples, the placement of *qi* is observed on both sides of a shell expressing a possibly strong intention as in (1) and (2A), as well as a not so strong "possibility" of Zi Shang succumbing to illness as in (3B). (I will later argue that it is not so much the "possibility" which is at issue here as the diviner's "wish" [sc. *qi*] that Zi Shang *not* succumb to illness.) Examination of as many examples as could be mustered reveals that where the verb is characterized as having an element of human will, symbolized as "+will," *qi* is invariably associated with the "intention" and "wish" scale of modality, and that where the verb is characterized as having no element of will, symbolized as "−will," *qi* is associated, at least on the surface, with the "possibility" and "certainty" scale of modality. The +will verb, in other words, is controllable, and the −will verb is uncontrollable. The verb *zuo* 作 'make' in (1), (2A) and (2B), and the verb *zhai* 宅 'reside' in (4A) are +will and controllable, while *you* 有 'have, there is' as used in (3B) is −will and uncontrollable. *Qi*, when combined with these verbs, moves on the modal scales of "intention/wish" and of "possibility/certainty." I would suggest that it means "certainly, definitely,"[8] as well as "perhaps, may be." One must decide case by case. The prognostication portion of (5A) below shows a case of the use of *qi* operating on the modal scale of the decidedly "wish" side, which amounts to optative:

(5A) ↓甲辰卜殼貞奚來白馬·王占曰其來· (R)   *Bingbian*
157(11)

> Crack-making on the *jiachen* day, Que (?) tested: Xi shall bring white horses. The king, having prognosticated, said "Lucky. May (Xi) be going to bring (them)."

(5B) ↑甲辰卜殼貞奚不其來白馬· (L)   *Ibid.* 157(12)

> Crack-making on the *jiachen* day, Que (?) tested: Xi may not be going to bring white horses.

The verb 來 *lai* 'bring (< lit. cause to come)' in the above examples is inflected as −will or uncontrollable from the Shang point of view. But it is clear from the prognostication portion of (5A) that the king wished Xi to contribute white horses. That is, the modal *qi* here incorporates the +will feature of what was presented as the −will nature of the verb *lai*. The king wanted to transform the uncontrollable into the controllable. The meaning here is clearly one of wish or hope. This is essentially what Nivison (1978a) argued, and I agree (cf. also Takashima 1973, 191).

Now apply this meaning to the same *qi* in (5B). We cannot translate this as "Xi will hopefully not bring white horses" or anything like this. We would have to work within the modal scale of "possibility/certainty," and more on the side of possibility. Thus, my proposed translation reads "Xi may not be going to bring white horses," expressing in this case a genuine uncertainty on the part of the diviner. It is awkward to understand *qi* here as meaning "definitely." By contrast, however, it is not totally out of the range of the intention side of the "intention/wish" scale to translate the same *qi* as "definitely" or "certainly" in (1) and (2A). If the modality of *qi* is operating on the epistemological scale of both "possibility/certainty" and "intention/wish," and the distribution of *qi* is split between both the "desirable R" and the "undesirable L," *qi* must be responding not really to its own intrinsic meaning, but to some sort of stimulus which must be located outside the confines of "sentence grammar." I have come to hold the view that the modal *qi* responds to the intricacies of what linguists and logicians call "presupposition." According to Lyons' (1977, 2.762) characterization of presupposition,

> To investigate and formalize the presuppositions of different kinds of questions is one of the central concerns of erotetic logic . . . . Another is to decide what constitutes a valid answer to a question. That these parts of the logic of questions are interconnected will be clear from the fact . . . that either to assert or to deny the presupposition of a question is to fail to answer it. But there are other ways in which one can respond to a question without answering it . . . . Responses may be appropriate or inappropriate; and answers, complete or partial, constitute but one of the subclasses of appropriate responses.

Without wishing to get involved in the controversy of whether the charges in the Shang OBI were questions or not (but cf. e.g., Nivison 1982, 1989; Takashima 1988–1989, 1989), we could adopt a heuristic approach by taking Lyons' characterization of the presuppositions underlying different kinds of charges.

Let us examine a set of examples in which *yu* 'rain', modulated by *qi,* was desired by the Shang:

(6A) ⩗（辛亥卜內貞）翌癸丑其雨. (R)   *Bingbian* (154[2]) + 153[13]

Crack-making on the *xinhai* day, Nei tested: On the following *guichou* day [50], it shall be going to rain.

(6B) ⼘辛亥卜內〔貞〕翌甲寅其雨. (L)   *Ibid.* (154[2]) + 153(14)

Crack-making on the *xinhai* day, Nei tested: On the following *jiayin* day [51], it shall (?) be going to rain.

(6C) 〔王〕占曰癸其雨.三日癸丑允雨.   *Ibid.* 154 (3)

The king, having prognosticated, said, "On a *gui* day, it shall be going to rain." (Or: "May it be going to rain on a *gui* day.") (In) three days, on the *guichou* day it indeed rained.

(6C) confirms that the charge in (6A), inscribed on the R, was desired. In these examples, we seem to be dealing with a presumption on the part of the diviner and the king—in that they were in a position to be able to expect rain to fall on the days specified (cf. Keightley 1993, 26). *Qi*, in other words, represented their presupposition that the rain was indeed forthcoming. The answer to the unasked hypothetical question, "Will it be (*qi*) raining?," would have been "Yes, it shall be going to rain." I interpret the modality of *qi* in this context to be marked +will operating on the "wish" side of the "intention/wish" scale. This is superimposed on the basically uncontrollable event of raining. For a controllable verb such as *zuo* 'make', *qi* modalizes it on the scale of "intention/wish" where the presupposition and the surface form match.

On the other hand, when negation is involved as in (5B) 奚不其來白馬 'Xi may not be going to bring white horses', the presupposition to the hypothetical question "Will Xi not bring white horses?" would take a different form: "No, my [= diviner's] formulation of not bringing white horses should be rejected." *Qi* in (5B), occurring on the L, responds to that presupposition. Here, too, we see the modality of *qi* being superimposed on the uncontrollable and eventive verb *lai* 'to bring'.

According to the interpretation just presented, *qi* is used to either affirm or deny the diviner's presumption that the oracle would respond in a certain specific way. But it is possible that the analytic framework allowed in my scheme, where either Yes or No was the answer to be expected, may quite possibly be too narrow and con-straining. Since I characterized the modality of *qi* as operating on the scale of "possibility/certainty" and "intention/wish," there is no reason for me not to allow the fluctuation of modality in the diviner's presup-position of Yes or No itself. That is, as it were, "Perhaps yes," "Definite-ly yes," and so on almost *ad infinitum*. In fact, I believe this to be the nature of modality. So, to formalize this usage is not easy, and if attempted (as I did in Takashima 1993, sec. 2.3.6), there are bound to be problems and the result may be greeted with some skepticism. But we must begin somewhere, and if we do so by considering examples such as (5B) 奚不其 來白馬 and (6A) 翌癸丑其雨, it is quite possible that *qi* in (5B) had a strong modality of "No," and that *qi* in (6A) had a strong modality of "Yes."

1.2 The Aspectual Qi

Linguists recognize the existence of the aspectual character of a verb as either "grammaticalized" or "lexicalized" (Lyons 1977, 2.706). The English progressive aspect with such a meaning as "be +V-ing" (e.g., I am writing now) is grammaticalized. And apart from certain subclasses of English verbs (i.e., stative verbs) which do not occur in the progressive aspect (e.g., "know," "have," "belong," etc.), verbs with a dynamic meaning occur in this grammaticalized pattern. While the modern Chinese progressive aspect can be grammaticalized (e.g., by the attachment of *zhe*), classical Chinese generally expresses the aspectual meanings through the use of particles, and is thus lexicalized. In the case of Shang Chinese—and possibly Zhou Chinese as well—I would like to propose that there is what I call the "anticipative" or "prospective" aspect, lexicalized (or represented) by *qi*. Furthermore, partly because the anticipative/prospective aspect interacts with the system of negatives which are also aspectual in character (Takashima 1988), I also wish to reserve, in my repertory of the aspectual description, the term "mutative" in the sense of "being transformed into something."

In his discussion of the prospective aspect of English and Russian, Comrie (1976, 64) defines it as follows:

> Perfect is retrospective, in that it establishes a relation between a state at one time and a situation at an earlier time. . . . one might equally well expect to find prospective forms, where a state is related to some subsequent situation, for instance *where someone is in a state of being about to do something.*

The italicized portion should easily be adopted to cases where the subject is not necessarily human, leading us to the equally valid aspectual interpretation of "prospective forms, where a state is related to some subsequent situation, e.g., the weather is in a state of turning to rain." It goes without saying that rain can be negated, notably by the stative/eventive negative of *bu* 不. The expression *bu qi* is, then, a realization of near aspectual concord or agreement, because "stative/eventive" and "prospective" are different only in their relationship to a subsequent situation.

In connection with this, it is interesting to note that Graham (1983, 68) says "there is a change of state which makes it suitable to translate [*fu* 弗] by 'no longer'," and he further speculates that "*fu* in the *Documents* is what might be called a 'prospect closing' negative, in contrast with the 'prospect opening' modal *qi* 其." While this deserves further study in classical Chinese, there is at least one instance of the combination "*fu* + *qi*" in the *Documents* (*SSTJ* 33/0223), and more examples than can easily be counted in the OBL (cf. Takashima 1985a, 483–89). One would therefore think that if *qi* embodies, as is quite possible, the "prospect-opening" aspect, it should not be contrasted with the "prospect-closing" negative *fu*. I have suggested that *fu*/*pjət, a non-modal *p-type negative in the OBL, is indeed a negative used to negate a non-stative/non-eventive verb (Takashima 1988). Because I used a binary analysis in 1988, this non-stative/non-eventive verb is equivalent to, or paraphrased as, the "mutative" verb. Thus, *fu qi* is a combination which should yield a general meaning of "mutatively prospective," i.e., the prospective aspect is superimposed on something being transformed into something else, stated negatively in this case.

For the negation of a stative and eventive verb, either *bu*/*pjəg 不 or *wu*/*mjəg 毋 is used. For details of my argument with examples, I must refer the reader to Takashima (1988). On page 125 I characterized them as meaning "be +V-ing, not so much in its progressive aspect but as in its eventive or happening aspect." I think we can improve upon this interpretation even further on the basis of Comrie's discussion of English aspect (Comrie 1976, 64). He says:

> Typical English expressions of prospective meaning are the constructions *to be going to, to be about to, to be on the point of,* as in *the ship is about to sail, the ship is on the point of sailing*—both of which describe the ship's present state relative to some future event, with these constructions an imminently future event—and *the ship is going to sail,* where there is again a present state related to a future event, but here without any implication of imminent futurity.

What we find in the OBL is that the stative/eventive verb is also accompanied by a temporal adverb (e.g., 今夕其雨 "This evening it *qi* rain"), so that we would want *qi* to have such a meaning as "to be going to," rather than "to be about to" or "to be on the point of"—though I do not wish to abandon the latter meanings, should the context require them. Thus, 今夕其雨 should be rendered "It shall be going to rain this evening." Applied to the negative (as in our example "[R]"

不其雨 in note 7), we also need to take the modality and presupposition into account, yielding an accurate, albeit perhaps trite, translation of "It will perhaps not be going to rain" (sc. presupposition: "No, it will rain"). In my translations of the inscriptions with *qi* cited so far, I have reflected this aspectual interpretation of the word.

2.   The Pronominal Hypothesis of *Qi*

The more vexing problems than the modal and aspectual ones sketched in section 1 above (more elaborate and full treatment can be found in Takashima [1993]) concern what may be called the pronominal hypothesis of *qi*. As known to many in the field of early Chinese studies, it is David Nivison who has continued to do research in this area, first as a problem in classical Chinese, and then in the inscriptional language of the Shang and Zhou periods (Nivison 1968, 1971, 1971a, 1991, 1992, 1992a, 1992b). I myself once dubbed this the problem of trying to account for the use of the same graph in two different functions, one modal and the other pronominal, in classical Chinese, while seeking their origins in the OBL (Takashima 1970). The problem was so daunting that after three years I withdrew my claim of the same-origin hypothesis of the "two" *qi*'s (Takashima 1973, 267–305). It is in a way ironic that Nivison was instrumental in my change of view which had, in substance, agreed with his. So after all of these years, what is new? The inscriptional material available for our studies is about the same and there have been no dramatic methodological advances. But the way we look at the inscriptions is new—at least in my own case—and Nivison makes his arguments more airtight and sophisticated than before. Sometimes, however, examples can speak more powerfully than this little linguistic game of mine (though I play this very seriously) or the philosophico-logical argumentation of Nivison. We need to look at the inscriptions more straightforwardly than before.

2.1 Qi *as Anaphoric Pronoun*

Let us begin with an observation of Nivison's (hereafter abbreviated as "N") best examples:

(7A)   ↓貞有虎.   (R)   *Bingbian* 366(1)

N (1992, 11): "Testing: There will be tigers."

N (1992a, 9): "There are (going to be) tigers."

Takashima (T): (Same as N [1992], except that the modality of "wish" should be assigned to the verb *you*, leading to a translation "There shall be tigers.")

(7B)　↑貞亡其虎.　(L)　*Ibid.* (2)

N (1992, 11): "Testing: There will not be the (supposed) tigers."

N (1992a, 9): "There are none of the/these tigers (in question)."

T: (Same as N[1992a].)

In (7B), which occurs on the left (L) side of the plastron, the pre-verbal, modal *qi* theory does not fair well, for it occurs before the noun *hu* 'tiger'. Other similar examples have *lu* 鹿 'deer' (*Bingbian* 286 [2] and [4]) or other animals in the same position where *hu* occurs, thus leaving no question as to the nominal interpretation of what follows *wang qi*.

Nivison (1992, 12) criticizes my previous treatment of taking *qi* in cases like (7B) as a post-posed particle acting on the preceding verb (first put forth in Takashima [1970, 13–15] and repeated, without satisfaction, in Takashima [1973, 268–69; 1988a, 657, n. 1; 683, n. 25]). He points out that my "'way out' is impossible. Always, *qi* is to be grouped with the *following* word or phrase . . . ." I agree. One might entertain the possibility that the verb *you* "there is; have" has been omitted after *qi*. This would mean that (7B), for example, had the underlying structure, **wang qi you hu*, from which *you* was deleted because of redundancy (*wang*, though a negative, entails the meaning of *you*). Such a transformational operation seems just as unsatisfactory as the one I assumed in 1970: that the surface *wang qi hu* was derived from **qi wang hu* by transformation. Not only are both hypotheses untestable, the deletion of *you* after *wang*—considered here mainly in deference to the more normal pattern of *wang qi* + V—produces a highly eccentric underlying structure in the context of (8B): **wo wang you huo* "we have not have misfortune". Even the staunchest Chomskyan might be brought up short by such a grotesque agglomeration. On the other hand, as Shen Pei (1992, 168) has also pointed out, *qi* in this position behaves like other adverbs such as *yi* 亦 'also' and *xiang* 詳 'specifically' (cf. Takashima 1973, 389–92). The *yi* occurs after the negative *bu* and *wang* (*Heji* 22258, where *ji* 疾 'illness; suffer from illness' occurs as object). The *xiang* occurs after the negatives *bu, wù,* and *wang* (*Tunnan* 994, where a nominalized VP, *qin* Tufang 擒土方 'capture the Tufang', occurs as object). *Qi* also occurs after the negatives *bu, fu, wú,* and *wang*—more frequently than one cares to count in the OBL. It would therefore seem justified in considering *qi* to belong to a class of adverbs like *yi* and *xiang*. But if so, could one expect to have an adverb before a "pure" noun? Just changing "adverb" to "particle" will not do (cf. also Nivison 1971, 12). The most straightforward interpretation, therefore, is what Nivison has been saying all along: *qi* is, in fact, used as a pronoun having anaphoric reference.

If it is as simple as that, it would not have met with such consistent resistance by specialists. There are also problems with such a straightforward interpretation. Let us reconsider one problem I myself raised for Nivison (and for Keightley's earlier version of 1992) in Takashima (1992, 5):

> While the hypothetical demonstrative *qi* in the *wang qi yu* 亡其雨 may work in the sense that *qi* refers back to the positive *you yu* 有雨, it does not work in the following pair, in which *qi* appears in the positive counterpart:
>
> (8A) ↓貞我其有禍.   (R)   *Bingbian* 3 (11)
>> Tested: We might be going to have misfortunes.
>
> (8B) ↑貞我亡禍.   (L)   *Ibid.* (12)
>> Tested: We will have no misfortunes.
>
> The only way the demonstrative or pronominal interpretation of *qi* can work is by assuming that the negative statement was made first, and that *qi* in the positive statement refers to the non-occurrence of the *huo* being divined about—a rather bizarre situation.

This still seems to be a difficult problem to explain. Even if we can in fact assume that (8B)—which we should now characterize as a semantically positive or desirable alternative to the Shang—was uttered first, why do we not have *我有其禍? There are quite a few inscriptions in which the object of the verb *you* is *huo*, but the order is invariably *qi you huo.*

Perhaps there is a basis for the non-occurrence of **you qi huo.* A possible reason, which may turn out to be quite simple, is that the Shang didn't *want* to say *you qi huo,* even though they could have.[9]

Recall that in section 1 I interpreted *qi* as a modal and aspectual particle: the modality operated on the scales of "possibility/certainty" and
"intention/wish," further involving the presupposition of the speaker
to deny or affirm it (with varying degrees of modality), and the aspectual character involved the "anticipative/prospective/mutative" meanings. When applied to the use of *qi* in (8A), we can say that for the
Shang the *prospect* of having misfortunes was a possibility. But it was
inscribed on the "desirable R" side, so the presupposition of the diviner in this case must surely be one which denies it: "My [= diviner's]
formulation of us having the possibility of misfortunes is to be rejected." The modality of the diviner's rejection must have been a rather
strong "No." It is, therefore, difficult to assign the modal *qi* in (8A)
such a "certainty" sense as "definitely." That would be sacrilegious. I
have thus chosen a weaker sense of "might," but "perhaps" will also do.
Now, if (8A) had been expressed as *我有其禍, we would *lose* all the
analyses provided in section 1, because *qi* is no longer the modal or
aspectual particle; it would have to be treated as simply pronominal.

Another problem that needs addressing is the order of utterance in
the divinatory charges. We need to determine which of two inscribed
sentences in a charge pair was *said* first. (Here the question of which
was *written* first is not necessarily crucial.) The order of utterance is
important particularly for charges such as (7A) and (7B) on the one
hand, and (8A) and (8B) on the other. In the former, (7A) *must* be
considered to have been uttered first for the pronominal *qi* hypothesis
to be valid. In the latter, however, it should be noted that (8A) does
not depend on the order of utterance for the modal and aspectual *qi*
theory to be valid (for this theory *is* based on the syntax *wo qi you huo*
rather than **wo you qi huo*). However, the order of utterance becomes
relevant to the degree of the modal force which one can assign to *qi* in
the context of presuppositions associated, as discussed in section 1.1,
with the "desirable R" and "undesirable L" placement.

Concerning this problem of the order of utterance, Nivison (1992,
13) makes the following observation:

> Serruys' observation, accepted as a rule by Keightley, that *qi* marks the
> less desired alternative in a *duizhen* pair may be accidentally right most
> of the time: normally the desired alternative is tested first; *qi* in the
> alternative is thus acting on an idea already introduced, which is
> implicitly being referred back to as "old information."

Keightley (1992, 23–26) picked up this "old information" hypothesis for *qi* and developed his "delimiting *qi*" hypothesis, which he subsequently withdrew (1993). But his conclusion, cited below, is a fair characterization of the problems involved.

> In short, placement alone cannot tell us which charge in a charge-pair was divined first. Any conclusion about the delimiting use of *qi* that depends on determining which charge was primary must depend upon the assumption, not always testable, that the desirable charge was the one that the diviner first proposed to the shell (and, of course, on the additional assumption that we can determine Shang preferences). These considerations do not invalidate the "old-new" hypothesis but they make it impossible to test in every case.

I would add to this, however, that there are inscriptions which, when placed in larger context, can suggest to us which charge was desirable to the Shang. The examples selected so far in this paper (i.e., [1], [2A], [3A], [4A], [5A], [6A], [7A], [8B]) are all those, which in my judgment, represent the desirable alternatives. Used with caution, therefore, Nivison's assumption is acceptable as a working hypothesis.[10] In the case of (7A) and (7B), it seems natural to assume that the Shang wanted to get tigers, and if so, (7A) was uttered first.

If the pronominal *qi* is indeed considered acceptable, Nivison's (1992b, 8) second best example (though not translated by him) is no longer a puzzle. It is pronominal, pure and simple:

(9)   更寅卜王余燎于其配.   *Yingguo* 1864

Crack-making on the *gengyin* day, the king [tested]: I will make a burnt-offering to his mate.

Unfortunately, since the piece on which this inscription occurs lacks a fuller context, we don't know to which ancestral spirit *qi* may have referred.[11] But the inscription is authentic and clearly inscribed.

2.2 Qi *as Subordinator*

The use of *qi* as subordinator of what may be referred to as the "embedment" type or "finite clause" type (cf. Quirk et. al. 1980, 832–33) was first suggested by Chang Tsung-tung (1970, 117, n. 1) and taken up by Serruys (1974, 57–58), though neither has developed this analysis any further than what is cited below.

Chang: [Qi] fungiert hier als subordinierende Partikel und steht
für das Subjekt des Nebensatzes. [Example to follow shortly.]

Serruys: Among these [referring to sentences in which *qi* is treated
as subordinator of "if," "when," and the like] must be counted the
cases where the *qi* clause *follows* the main verb . . . . The most striking
case of *qi* functions is the . . . quite exceptional pattern *wang qi* 亡其
as for instance in 亡其雨: "there will be no rain" (*qi*, less desirable
alternative) . . . . The hypothesis presented to explain this exception is
simply that *wang* is treated as a main verb "not have" followed by what
is really an object clause, and that *wang qi yu* literally means "not have
[chance] that it might rain." (N.B. No analysis of the pattern *wang qi*
+ N is provided.)

The aim of this subsection is to advance the *qi*-as-subordinator
hypothesis even further than what is quoted above. But first, working
separately from Chang Tsung-tung and earlier than Serruys whose
views were just quoted, Nivison (1971a, 18–19) also had the seminal
idea that the clause after *wang qi* should be analyzed as "nominalized."
He says that *qi*

as verbal adjective, where no subject is thought of (where there is no
restriction with regard to agent) will yield a definite descriptor translatable (if necessary) as the/that (process, act of . . .), (For, obviously,
"this X which there is," i.e. "definitely existing X," just means "this X.")
One would assume that there must be certain idiomatic contexts generating this attributive-demonstrative use of the verb of definite existence [here Nivison is assuming *qi* to be a "verb of definite existence"]
. . . . The contents "亡其 + nominalized verb" . . . , "亡其 + noun"
. . . are obvious candidates.

This analysis, an important aspect of which (i.e., "the verb of definite
existence" for *qi*) I still find hard to accept, is further developed by
Nivison (1992, 10–11), idem (1992a, 9), and idem (1992b, 3ff.). Since
the gist of these three papers is more or less the same (but stated a little differently), I shall quote from one here:

N (1992, 10–11): My . . . theory is that *qi* is (1) a verb of strong asser-
tion: "it is the case that . . . ," or "this will be, namely . . . " (of uncontrollable happenings); speaker "will make it the case that . . . " (of controllable actions); (2) an adverb, "definitely;" and (3) a verbal
adjective amounting to "the" (which would indicate definite existence

or occurrence). Before a noun it might amount to "the . . . in question," and even "his . . . ," etc.; and before a verb it could in its "adjective" phase convert the verb into a verbal noun, "the . . . -ing." Before a
verb-phrase or sentence it could thus create a noun phrase: "the fact
that . . . ," or simply "that . . ."

It is this last point of Nivison's theory that I would like to follow up,
except that I do not start with his assumption (of which he himself is
unsure) that *qi* is a verb.[12] I start with the apparent fact, as presented in
section 2.1, that *qi* is used as a pronoun.

Let us first look, then, at Chang Tsung-tung's example, quoted in
the beginning of section 2.2:

(10)   已未貞王其告其從亞侯.   *Cuibian* 367

    Chang: Am Tage Jiwei wurde das Orakel befragt: "Soll der König eine
rituelle Mitteilung darüber machen, daß er in Begleitung des Fürsten Ya
in den Krieg ziehen wird?"

    T: On the *jiwei* day tested: The king shall be going to perform the
announcement ritual (that he) follow Ya Hou. (More smoothly: "The king
shall be going to announce his [intention to] follow Ya Hou.")

Chang's comment applies to the second *qi* in (10); he translated it
as "daß er." I think he is (almost) right. Here we are looking at the
same *qi* as observed in section 2.1, except that 其從亞侯 is the
object clause or, if we use the terminology of Quirk et. al. (1980,
832–34), the "finite clause object." However, noticing that *qi* in (7B)
and (9) is used more like "possessive, attributive" as it is in classical
Chinese, the more literal translation should be "The king shall be
going to announce *his following Ya Hou*." And, if we also apply, as we
should, the aspectual interpretation of *qi,* we obtain "The king shall be
going to announce his (intention) to follow Ya Hou." The first occurrence of *qi* is modal and aspectual, as discussed in section 1 and
reflected in my translation, and the second should be analyzed the
same except that *qi* also functions anaphorically.

The freedom gained by us to analyze *qi* in this way will lead us to
find a respectable number of examples of this type. Some typical cases
include the following:

(11)   丁卯貞其告于父丁其獸一牛.   *Cuibian* 374

On the *dingmao* day tested: The king shall be going to announce to Fu Ding his (intention) to keep [> set aside for sacrificial use?][13] one ox.

(12) 辛未貞今日告其步于父丁一牛,在秘. *Ninghu* 1.346

On the *xinwei* day tested: Today the king will announce to Fu Ding his (intention) to go on foot (the announcement ritual to be carried out by the sacrifice of) one ox. It was at Mi (we) did the crack-making.

These examples embody the structure in which the finite clause object comes under the scope of the performative verb *gao* 'to make the ritual announcement, to announce' which was normally carried out by the king (Takashima 1988a, 680–83). The surface realization of this is in (10), whereas in (11) and (12) it is not realized. It can, however, be supplied. There are also examples in which the second clause may not come under the scope of the verb in the first clause, as in the following:

(13) 王其田其告妣辛王受祐. *Xucun* 2.769

As for the king's going to hunt [or: When the king is going to hunt], he shall be going to announce it to Bi Xin. The king shall receive blessing.

(14) 未貞王其令望乘歸其告〔于〕祖〔乙〕一牛父丁一〔牛〕. *Cuibian* 506 (rejoined to yield a fuller context in *Hebian* 334)

On . . . *wei* day tested: As for the king's going to order Wang Cheng to return [or: When the king is going to order Wang Cheng to return], he shall be going to announce it to Zu Yi (with the sacrifice of) one ox (and to) Fu Ding (with the sacrifice of) one ox.

It might be possible to interpret the second *qi* clauses in (13) and (14) *as if* there were not the first; that is, the second *qi* clauses were simply successive activities proposed for the oracle. If we allow for this possibility, then there would not be any need to construe *qi* as having any anaphoric reference. The reasoning that underlies this analytical possibility is that we have not yet assigned any anaphoric function to *qi* in its first occurrence; we have been interpreting it as being modal and aspectual. Is this interpretation all that there is to know about the function and meaning of *qi*? The answer is "No, most likely not."

It is quite possible to interpret that *qi* occurring after *wang* 'king' in (13), (14), and indeed in many other examples where *qi* follows after a noun has, in fact, the anaphoric function of a genitive nature. One could explore this possibility on theoretical grounds, but I shall appeal here to some comparative materials taken from the *Shangshu* and the *Shijing*. Even though they will not *prove* that the OBL had worked in the same way, they are highly suggestive of such, and we can discern some historical changes that might have taken place.

(15)　王若曰‚孟侯‚朕其弟‚小子封. . . . .（康誥）
　　　(*SSTJ* 29/0056)

　　　"The king spoke thus: Oh you leading prince, my younger brother,
youngster Feng! . . ."

Karlgren (1950a, 39)

(16)　王其德之用祈天永命.（召誥）　(*SSTJ* 33/0602)

　　　"May the king [by the virtue's use =] by means of [his] virtue pray for
Heaven's eternal mandate."

Karlgren (1950a, 51)

(17)　孺子其朋. 孺子其朋往.（洛誥）　(*SSTJ* 33/0209)

　　　"The young son's associates! The young son's associates, go!"

Karlgren's translation (1950, 52) modified

(18)　王命作册逸祝册‚惟告周公其後.（洛語）
　　　(*SSTJ* 33/0730)

　　　"The king gave order to *zuoce*, Yi, to recite a brevet in order (for him)
to announce Duke of Zhou's successor [sc. in Lu]."

Karlgren's translation (1950, 55) modified

There are more examples of this type where *qi* occurs between two nouns, the first noun (often a topic) followed by what should be analyzed not as a modal particle but as a genetivized anaphoric-pronoun *qi*.[14] Thus, the second noun following *qi* is really the one that is attributed by *qi*. In the *Shijing* we also find examples such as:

(19)　彼其之子‚不與我戍申. . . . .（揚之水等）
　　　(*H-Y* 15/68/1,2,3; 17/80/1,2,3; 22/108/1,2,3; etc.)

　　　"That person there [sc. my wife], she is not with me keeping guard at
Shen . . ."

Karlgren (1950, 46)

(20) 築室百堵,西南其戶,爰居,爰處,．．．．（斯干）
      (*H-J* 42/189/2)

  "He builds a house of a hundred *du* measures; to the west and the
  south are its doors; and then he will live and dwell . . .."

                                          Karlgren (1950, 130)

(21) 誰謂爾無牛,九十其犉．．．．（無羊）(*H-J* 42/190/1)

  "Who says that you have no cattle? Ninety are those which are seven
  feet high . . .."

                                          Karlgren (1950, 131)

(22) 我彊我理, 南東其畝.（信南山）(*H-J* 5/210/1)

  "We draw boundaries, we divide them into sections; running towards
  the south or running towards the east are the acres."

                                          Karlgren (1950, 164)

I am aware of no scholar of the *Shijing* who has proposed that *qi* functions anaphorically in these examples, but because *qi* is flanked by two
nouns, the genitivized-anaphoric-pronoun theory would explain this
use most cogently. If we adapt the same interpretation for the pattern
"descriptive adjective (predicate) + *qi* + N" (cf. Yang and Hé 1992,
487), as did Yu Min (1949, 79), we have literally hundreds of examples
in the *Shijing*.

  If the above analysis of the genitive-pronominal *qi* in the *Shangshu*
and *Shijing* holds true, it is reasonable to assume that it also had a similar function in stages of language earlier than that represented in the
Shu and the *Shi*. Nivison (1991, 15) quotes the use of *qi* in the phrase
朕宗君其休 "my ancestral lord's grace" in the second *Diao sheng
gui* 琱生毀 bronze inscription of Western Zhou (cf. Shirakawa 1970,
633). He ends with a parenthetical comment "Compare 'John his
book', for 'John's book' in earlier English," and this hits the mark
exactly. There is, of course, a plethora of Western Zhou bronze inscriptions in which *qi* appears as the cliché "May the sons and the grandsons forever treasure and use this vessel," but in addition to Nivison's
example we find more instances of *qi* being used genitive-pronominal-
ly (Chou Fa-kao 1975, 6.2819 <0057>, 2823 <1183>, 2824 <1224>,

2832 <2897>, 2832 <2921>). There is no question about this use in the Western Zhou bronze inscriptions.[15]

Returning now to the OBL, the situation is slightly different in that, although *qi* is still to be construed as a genitive pronoun, it does not occur between two nouns (cf. Takashima 1984, 255–57). Instead, it predominantly occurs after a noun—which is optional—and before a verb. Here I find myself substantially agreeing with Nivison (1992b, 4):

> "*Qi*" . . . could be used (my theory goes) as an adjective, nominalizing the verb or verb-phrase that follows, so that the *noun-phrase* "*qi* X(ing)" refers to the "X(ing)," actual or hypothetical, that would have been asserted by the *sentence* "*qi* X." The resulting idiom is a quasi "that" clause that functions as a subordinate clause (just as the form "subject *zhi* verb *ye*" does in later Chinese), the commonest use being as a conditional clause. But "conditional *qi*" and "modal *qi*" are merely transforms of each other: "*qi wei geng ji*" means "(as for the case of its being on a *geng*-day =) if it is on a *geng*-day, it will be fortunate." The component "*wei geng*" can be exposed and resumed by "*qi*" (now "modal"), giving "*wei geng qi ji*," which means exactly the same thing—i.e., "as for its being on a *geng*-day, in this case it will be fortunate."

I take issue with two points, one minor and one not. The minor point is terminological: I wish to avoid "adjective" for the use of *qi*, even though it is in a way adjectival—lest one lose the important feature of referentiality in *qi*. The not-so-minor point I question is Nivison's claim that 其隹庚吉 means exactly the same as 隹庚其吉.[16] In the former, the modal and aspectual *qi* are modulating the copula *wei* 'to be', whereas in the latter the same *qi* is modulating *ji* 'to be auspicious, lucky'. If one translates them, the former means "It may turn out to be a *geng* day [< lit. 'may be going to be . . .'] that is auspicious," and the latter, "It is a *geng* day that may turn out to be auspicious." The illocutionary message of the two may be the same, but their modality and aspect are appreciably different. Furthermore, if one applies the subordinating *qi* hypothesis I am now advancing, 其隹庚吉 embodies a structure consisting of the NP (其隹庚) and VP (吉), whereas (其吉) embodies a different structure of the VP (隹庚) + NP (其吉). The latter, of course, is commonly referred to as a "cleft sentence" (cf. Lyons 1977, 2.598; Takashima 1990, 38).

Apart from these comments on Nivison's formulation, everything else is acceptable: *qi* has a nominalizing effect, entailing a quasi "that" clause which functions like "subject *zhi* verb *ye*" in classical Chinese. In fact, *zhi* in the OBI is also pronominal, meaning "this, that," and its later development into a genitive marker parallels the case of *qi*. The only difference is that in this stage of the OBL, *qi* is already genitive-pronominal. The translations I have provided for the representative examples in this section ([10]–[14]) have reflected all the analyses presented so far. I shall, however, make one final comment upon the significance of the structural difference I pointed out for (13) and (14), i.e., the second clauses which have *qi*, but which do not come under the scope of the verb in the first clauses. If a sentence (e.g., 王其田其告妣辛) has this structure, it is possible to interpret the first clause as dependent meaning "when + V$_1$," or "V$_1$-ing." Otherwise, we should interpret the second clause as being dependent with the meaning "that he/she/it/they." It is also possible to analyze these first clauses as having been deliberately taken out of the scope of the verb in the second clauses. If so, one could interpret them as topical, in the objective case. We could then maintain a consistent analysis of *qi* clauses as meaning "X's V-ing," so that in (13), for example, "the king's hunting" was topically preposed as the object of the verb *gao* "announce." This analysis seems more attractive than assigning a dependent meaning of "when + V1" in (13) and (14). However, in other contexts, the "when + V2" interpretation may well be more appropriate.

2.3 Qi as "Subjunctive Mood"

Strictly speaking, the heading I give to this last section, "Subjunctive Mood," is a misnomer. This traditional name should be used when the choice of modality is determined entirely by syntactic dependency, rather than by independent semantic criteria. That is, the modality is determined by the character or type of the sentence itself, and, in a complex sentence, by its relation to the main clause on which it is dependent. It is widely known, for example, that in French the indicative and subjunctive forms of the verb appear to be in complementary distribution, because in certain contexts the subjunctive form is required regardless of the speaker's attitude regarding what he says.

We are taught that we cannot say "Je ne pense pas qu'il *vient*," where *vient* is the indicative form; we must say instead "Je ne pense pas qu'il *vienne*," *vienne* being the subjunctive form. The sentence involves "negation," implying (very roughly) a modal quality of "doubt, subjectivity, or hypothesis" which can be defined more precisely in terms of the modal scales of "possibility/certainty," "intention/wish," and "obligation/necessity." (This last scale is something I have not discussed in this paper.) In any event, let us keep in mind that the subjunctive *vienne* is predictable, but as I discuss below, the use of *qi* is not dictated wholly by surface grammar, but partly by grammar and partly by semantic criteria. It is a kind of hybrid.

I should like to approach this subject by reconsidering example (7B) in section 2.1. Contrary to the interpretation put forward by Nivison which I have accepted, it came to my attention that Shen Pei (1992, 169) offered the speculation that *wang qi* was formed analogically from the ubiquitous pattern "Neg + *qi* + VP" "(是由'不／弗／毋＋其＋VP'句類推而成的")". His opinion is not very convincing, because we also get the pattern in which *qi* precedes, though infrequently, nearly all the negatives in the OBL. Thus, the real task is to account for their differences. Let us first examine an example in which *qi* precedes the negative verb *wang*:

(23)　王占曰吉隹其亡攻，舌占其值. *Bingbian* 77 (2)

　　　The king, having prognosticated, said, "Lucky. It [= omen] means (that [the Fang]) will not, in fact [< have no occasions to], be going to make a (successful) attack; it should be (that) Shé is to straighten [the Fang]."[17]

This inscription occurs on exactly the opposite side of (24), below:

(24)　貞方弗戈我史. *Ibid.* 76 (3)

　　　Tested: The Fang will not harm our emissaries.

Here the subject is the Fang, a group hostile to the Shang, so that the king's prognostication in (23) is undoubtedly a response to (24). In fact, the above example occurring on this shell constitutes a set of related inscriptions (*chengtao* 成套) with *Bingbian* 386, from which particularly significant inscriptions are quoted below:

(25A) ↓貞我史亡其攻. (R) *Bingbian* 386 (9)

   Tested: Our emissaries will not, in fact [< have occasions to], be going to make a (successful) attack [against the Fang].

(25B) ↑貞我史有攻. (L) *Ibid.* (10)

   Tested: Our emissaries will, in fact, make a (successful) attack [against the Fang].

Provided as we are with a fuller context such as the above, we can be reasonably sure that *qi* in (23) does refer to the Fang. It is pronominal, and genitive at that. This explains the reason why *qi* occurs before the VP, *wang gong* 亡攻, because *qi* is preceded by the explanatory copula *wei*, turning 其亡攻 into an embedded sentence. Thus, the expression 隹其亡攻 literally means "it means [< is]/his going to/have no (occasions)/to attack." On the other hand, in (25A) the syntactic order of *wang qi gong* 亡其攻 is required because the main verb is *wang*, and the subject is *wo shi* 我史 'our emissaries'. Thus, *qi* in this structure should be analyzed as resuming the subject, *wo shi*, and further genitivizing the embedded verb *gong*. Literally translated, this should be: "(As for) our emissaries, (they) shall have no (occasions of) their going to make a (successful) attack [against the Fang]." Furthermore, if one takes into account the presupposition theory of *qi*, one obtains that because (25A) is inscribed on the "desirable R," *qi* implies a strong "No" in the sense of: "Our emissaries, on the contrary, will be going to make a successful attack against the Fang."

   Once we accept this genitive-pronominal function of *qi* as valid, we can begin looking at the inscriptional language with different analytical perspectives than what we have been schooling ourselves in for a long time. It just so happens that example (23) contains another use of *qi* as a genitive-pronoun, namely, in 舌 盅 其 值.[18] Following what I have just done for the two other sentences, this sentence should be literally translated: "As for Shé it should be (that) s/he is to straighten [the Fang]." Syntactically, this sentence is to be compared with 王 盅 出 值 (*Bingbian* 22[7]) 'It should be (the act of) taking the field to straighten that the king does'. In the latter there is no hedging in the modal implication of the king's action. That is, the modality of the verb *zhi* is unmarked (probably coming within the scope of *hui* 'it should be'), and the anaphora is not materialized (sc. *王叀出其值). On the other hand, the use of *qi* in 舌叀其值 suggests not only the genitive-pronominal function, but also the aspectual character as well. However, it is not clear whether it also suggests the existence of modal meanings. The reason is that the *qi* in this context is almost predictable. Given the subject Shé, to which *qi* anaphorically refers, *qi* occurs in the syntactic position determined by the prescriptive copula *hui* 'it should be'. Therefore, the modality associated with *qi* seems overridden by that associated with *hui* (i.e., operating on the modal scale of "obligation/necessity"). This is a case of the "subjunctive mood" characterized in the beginning of this section. But one cannot say that *qi* is dictated wholly by grammar, because the aspectual character of *qi* is left unaccounted for. It is difficult to think that the aspectual character of "prospect" could be determined by a copula, whether it be a descriptive one of *wei*, or a prescriptive one of *hui*. (Here, I shall not get into the area of the possible "stative-aspectual" nature of the copulas.)

Now if my analysis for the string 舌叀其值 is correct, it should be applicable, *mutatis mutandis*, not only to 隹亡其攻 in (23) but also to 亡其攻 in (25A). In the former, I argued that the copula *wei* is free of, or unmarked for, modality (Takashima 1990). Because 亡其攻 is syntactically embedded in such a modally neutral copula as *wei*, one is not bound by the constraints experienced in the case of 舌叀其值. In fact, the king's prognostication in (23) as a response to the diviner's charge in (24), "The Fang will not harm our emissaries," strongly suggests his presumption that the Fang "will not indeed be going to make a successful attack (against our emissaries)."[19] So here the modal *qi* is "flexing its muscle," as it were, reflecting the strong wish of the king. *Qi*, in this sense, is not predictable, and thus the subjunctive-mood analysis does not apply. It goes without saying that the aspectual character of *qi* should also be recognized, as it is not predictable. Finally, 我史亡其攻 should be analyzed, in a way similar to 舌叀其值, as a structure embodying a kind of hybrid "subjunctive mood." On the one hand, one can predict the pronominal *and* modal *qi* to occur in this position because, as already mentioned, *qi* refers to *wo shi* 'our emissaries', and at the same time it gets embedded by the main verb *wang*, which, as my theory dictates (see notes 16 and 18), produces an emphatic effect. This emphatic effect can easily be interpreted in terms of the modal scale of "possibility/certainty," with the weight moving more to the certainty side. It is in this sense that *qi* is predictable, thus qualifying itself as a case of "subjunctive mood." But then, its aspectual character cannot be accounted for by such syntactic dependency.

3. Closing Remarks

It is obvious throughout this paper that Nivison's contribution to the study of *qi* is enormous. Without it, I could not have developed my theory of the modal and aspectual *qi*, nor the pronominal hypothesis of *qi* as found in the preceding pages.

Apart from several points of detail where Nivison and I differ, our greatest difference is that, while Nivison starts his inquiry on the assumption that *qi* was originally a verb, I start mine on the observed fact that *qi* is to be recognized as a pronoun present in the Shang OBL. If one speculates upon even earlier stages of the language, it is not impossible to derive the anaphoric use of *qi* from the aspectual meaning of the anticipative/prospective/mutative "to be going to, to be about to," rather than from the modal meanings of "possibility/certainty," "intention/wish," and "obligation/necessity." That is, the modality can easily be thought of as being closely related to subordination, condition, or syntactic dependency in general, whereas aspect—because it captures the state of a verb—has the potential of being referred to. Reference is just to that aspect of a verb. However, I have avoided such speculation. Instead, I have appealed to empiricism in this paper: there are quite a few striking examples in which one is encouraged to see the genitive-pronominal use of *qi* already in Shang Chinese. I might add that this hypothesis will make it much easier to interpret how the modal (and perhaps also aspectual) *qi* could have had the same origin. But while Nivison (1992a, 11) concluded "we must recognize *already in Shang Chinese* uses of the same word *qi* as a modal and as in effect a demonstrative adjective," I would simply reverse the order of "modal" and "demonstrative adjective."

NOTES

1. On the controversy involving the use of the verb you 屮／又／有 in pre-classical Chinese, Nivison (1971a, 1977, 1978, 1991, 1992, 1992a) has maintained that the verb can be used pronominally, while I have not (Takashima 1978, 1980; Takashima and Itō 1996). On the interpretation of the word zhen 貞 and its related problems, we also have disagreements (Nivison 1982, 1989; Takashima 1988–1989, 1989). These are only a couple of the things that have been published, and it goes without saying that there have been many personal exchanges characterizable as critical of each other's work. However, I consider myself very lucky to be able to study in Nivison's company, and feel very grateful to the unfailingly helpful and gentlemanly way in which he has always responded.

2. Nowhere have the differences in our assumptions been more clearly brought out than in Nivison (1992b, 1), where he takes issue with my explicit statement in Takashima (1988a, 688) that my conclusions are "based on the fundamental assumption that whenever the form differs there must be some underlying semantic motivation." Nivison argues that in a homely example in English, "It will rain tomorrow," there is no difference in meaning between this statement and "It is going to rain." I disagree. There are a number of studies in the field of English linguistics available in which specialists are concerned precisely with the difference between such examples as Nivison provided. For example, Comrie (1976, 64–65) has the following to say about it:

> It is important to appreciate the difference between these expressions of prospective meaning and expressions of straight future reference, e.g. between *Bill is going to throw himself off the cliff* and *Bill will throw himself off the cliff*. If we imagine a situation where someone says one of these two sentences, and then Bill is in fact prevented from throwing himself off the cliff, then if the speaker said *Bill will throw himself* off the cliff, he was wrong, his prediction was not borne out. If, however, he said *Bill is going to throw himself off the cliff*, then he was not necessarily wrong, since all he was alluding to was Bill's intention to throw himself off the cliff, i.e. to the already present seeds of some future situation, which future situation might well be prevented from coming about by intervening factor.

As it turns out, the problem of the use or non-use of *qi* is very much related to such an aspectual nature as that to which Comrie draws our attention, as well as to the range of modal meanings associated with *qi*. I shall sketch them in section 1.

3. Regarding the claim made, for example, by Serruys (1974, 48–57), that *qi* is a clear marker for subordination of the "dependent clause + main clause" type (such as may be expressed by "if" or "when"), I have taken the contrary position as discussed in Takashima (1977). See also Takashima (1993, section 2.3.4).

4. To quote from Serruys' own work:

We find that the presence or absence of *qi* is a sign of very clear contrasts between two different kinds of oracular propositions: presence of *qi* marks the proposition or the alternative among possible courses of action, which is considered less desirable, less preferred, often positively feared and resorted to only if really unavoidable. This rule applies regardless of whether the proposition is expressed in negative or affirmative sentences.

The above is often referred to as "Serruys' rule of undesirable *qi*."

5. Consider, for example, Serruys' own translation (1974, 33) provided for the following inscription:

↓丙辰卜串串貞敓羌· (R)

    "At divination on Ping-ch'en day, Chung tests (the proposition): we might [*ch'i:* but rather not] beat the Ch'iang." *Bingbian* 7(1)

↑貞于庚申伐羌· (L)

    "Coming to Keng-shen day we shall sacrifice [i.e., behead] a Ch'iang." *Ibid.* (2)

I should also point out that in the more recent work of Serruys (1985), he consistently takes *qi* as a verb meaning "to expect." This, in my judgment, has more problems than his earlier modal *qi* formulation. See also note 12.

6. For a study showing that the second clause is to be interpreted as a reason clause, I refer the reader to Chow Kwok-ching (1982, 171–87). Keightley (1978, 66, n. 44 [citing Nivison]; 77–79; 1992, 5; 1993, 50–51) also interprets it similarly.

7. Keightley (1978, 51, n. 124) finds an exception to this in *Bingbian* 235(1) and (2), translations of which are mine:

(R) ↓己卯卜殼貞不其雨·

Crack-making on the *jimao* day, Que [?] tested: It will not perhaps be going to rain.

(L) ↑己卯卜殼貞雨·王占曰其雨隹壬·壬午允雨·

Crack-making on the *jimao* day, Que [?] tested: It shall rain. The king, having prognosticated, [said], "(The day on which it) is, hopefully, going to rain is a *ren* (day)." On the *renwu* day it indeed rained.

The grammatically negative charge at the R is, however, semantically positive or desirable to the Shang because "not rain" was intervened by *qi* "undesirable" (if one takes Serruys' rule), thus rain was desired. But the charge at the L, with its accompanying prognostication and verification, suggests that rain was also desired—yet it was placed on the left. Exactly the same phenomenon is observed in *Bingbian* 3(11) and (12), which I discuss later in section 2.1 (my [8A] and [8B]).

8. If one characterizes this a bit more colorfully, one obtains what Keightley (1993, 33–34) called the "executive use of *qi*" which he finds often used in the inscriptions by the Li-group diviners of Period II. But that is only accidental and is not reflective of how the language worked in the Shang.

9. As Shen Pei (1992, 166) has noticed, there are quite a few examples of the pattern "*you* + *qi* + NP" as in the following:

(1)   戊戌卜貞有其疾·

Crack-making on the *wuxu* day, tested: There will be such illness. *Heji* 21045

(2)   癸亥卜王貞有其降禍·

Crack-making on the *guihai* day, the king tested: There will be (a possibility that Di) might send down misfortunes.   *Heji* 21300 (= *Jiabian* 3827)

N.B. Another *you qi jiang* expression occurs on a fragmentary piece of *Yicun* 713.

(3)   辛亥卜王〔貞〕余有其令·

Crack-making on the *xinhai* day, the king [tested]: I will have such orders [?]/I will, in fact [<have occasions to], issue an order [?] *Heji* 40823

(4a) 癸酉卜有其 ...

   Crack-making on the *guiyou* day: There will be such .... *Heji* 2060

(4b) 癸酉卜亡其 ...

   Crack-making on the *guiyou* day: There will be no such .... *Ibid.*

10. If I am correct in interpreting the following passages from the Jin Teng chapter of the *Shangshu* (chapter 26) as representing Zhou scapulimantic charges (Takashima 1989, 46), then the positive and the desirable charge, (A), must have been uttered first:

(A) 爾之許我，我其以璧與珪，歸俟爾命. (*SSTJ* 26/0181)

   "If you grant me my wish [sc. that the king may recover], I will with the *bi* jade disc and the *gui* tessera return and wait for your order [sc. to be called away by death]."

                                                    Karlgren (1950a: 35)

(B) 爾不許我，我乃屏璧與珪. (*SSTJ* 26/0191 for *bu*)

   "If you do not grant me my wish, I will shut up the jade disc and the tessera [i.e. no more function as officiant in sacrifice]."

                                                                    Ibid.

This, of course, does not prove the Shang practice, but suggests a better alternative for us to maintain the hypothesis first suggested by Nivison (1992, 13). As a Shang example clearly illustrating which of the charge pairs was uttered first, we have the following:

(A) ↓貞侑犬于父庚劉羊.

   Tested: Offer dog(s) to Fu Geng (and) cut open sheep.

Bingbian 12(7)

(B) ↑貞祝氐之，疾齒鼎龍.

   Tested: (If) the prayer-master brings them [= dogs and sheep] on, the ailing teeth will certainly improve. *Ibid.*

In the above pair, (A) must have been uttered first because the word *zhi* 'them' in (B) must refer to the dog(s) and sheep in (A). Another excellent example is found in our sentences (2A) and (2B) which, in terms of placement and the positive/negative polarity, satisfy the requirements of a charge pair *except* for the fact that (2A) was uttered on the *renzi* day and (2B) on the following day.

11. Judging from the fact that it is a Period I piece, it is possible that *qi* here referred to the consort of Huang Yin 黃尹 who appears frequently as a recipient of the burnt-sacrifice. The use of Huang Shi 黃奭 as in 貞于黃奭燎 'Tested: To Huang's consort we will make a burnt-offering' (*Bingbian* 122[8]) is suggestive. There are two problems with this interpretation. One is that the consort of the ancestors is normally expressed, as in the above example, by the word *shi* 奭 (there are different interpretations for this, but all agree that it refers to a consort). Another is that the word *pei* 配 is also used as a ritual verb of some kind. In (9), however, the use of *yu* 于 'to' compels us to take *qi pei* as a nominal term.

12. My analysis presented in section 1 will make it clear that we are dealing with an adverb-like word, since there is *always* a verb which carries the main semantic load of a sentence. *Qi* does not occupy the kernel of a sentence; it is auxiliary at best. More discussion on this point is found in Section 2.3.5 of Takashima (1993).

13. The palaeograph 獸, which I transcribed as *shou* 獸 'to hunt; to keep', follows Guo Moruo (1965, 58b). Normally, *shou* means "to hunt," but 獸一牛 'to hunt one ox' is quite unnatural, because "one ox" is singled out as though it were a category or class, which it does not seem to be. I have taken this graph to have stood for the word *shou* 守 'to keep, guard' (see also *S:* 446.2).

14. Other examples are *SSTJ* 14/0210 (先王其訓), 24/0534 (于帝其訓), 27/0521 (民養其勸), 34/0815 (天其澤), some of which have already been discussed by Yu Min (1949, 79–80) (though not all of his examples are susceptible to interpretations different from what he has proposed).

15. Keightley (1993, 53) cites the cliché mentioned above from the famous Qiu Wei *gui* (裘衛殷) bronze inscription of the Western Zhou: "衛其子 子孫孫永寶用" taken from Shaughnessy (1991, 87), repeating Shaughnessy's translation "May Wei's sons' sons and grandsons' grandsons

eternally treasure and use (it)." I briefly mentioned (6 January 1994) my recent ideas on the genitive-pronominal *qi* to Derek Herforth, who quickly pointed out Keightley's case as another sample to add to my list. (Shaughnessy's translation of "may" for this cliché is correct for wrong reasons, but I shall refrain from getting into them here.)

16. Nivison's claim here is a critical response to my fundamental assumption that "whenever the form differs there must be some underlying semantic motivation," mentioned in note 2. I still uphold this assumption, thus requiring me to respond to his criticism.

17. For a theory proposing that the *you/wang* + VP pattern produces, in effect, a kind of emphasis, I refer the reader to Takashima (1988a). The graph normally transcribed as *she* 舌 is commonly used as a sacrificial verb of some sort, but it is also used as the name of an officer. It is accompanied in *Yibian* 8892 with the epithet *duo* 多 (which is comparable to *bai* 百 as in *baigong* 百工 'hundred artisans' in the Zhou). It is possible that the graph I transcribed here as *zhi* 値 'to straighten' may have stood for the word *de* 德 meaning "to display one's *de* to . . . , i.e., 'show the flag' and build up royal prestige, relying on his *de* and not actually using force," an interpretation proposed by Nivison (1977–1978, 53).

18. For the semantic interpretation of "N_1 + *hui* + N_2 + VP" which represents 舌 击 其 値, cf. Takashima (1990, 53–54).

19. Note that the emphatic theory of the *you/wang* + VP pattern (see note 17) works quite well in a contextual discourse-analysis such as the kind being pursued here.

ABBREVIATIONS

I have used standard abbreviations for various collections of oracular inscriptions. Full citations for these can be found in Keightley (1978, 229–31). The only source not included there is *Heji* (for *Jiaguwen Heji*). See Guo Moruo and Hu Houxuan (1978–82).

BIHP *Bulletin of the Institute of History and Philology* (= *Lishi yuyan yanjiusuo jikan* 歷史語言研究所集刊). (Taibei: Academia Sinica)

BMFEA　　*Bulletin of the Museum of Far Eastern Antiquities* (Stockholm)

EC　　*Early China* (The Annual Journal of the Society for the Study of Early China). (Institute of East Asian Studies, University of California, Berkeley)

H-Y　　*Harvard-Yenching Institute Sinological Index Series*

JWGL　　*Jinwen gulin* 金文詁林. (See Chou Fa-kao under references.)

MS　　*Monumenta Serica*

S　　*Inkyo bokuji sōrui* 殷墟卜辭綜類. (See Shima Kunio under references.)

SSTJ　　*Shangshu tongjian* 尚書通檢. (See Gu Jiegang under references.)

TP　　*T'oung Pao*

YJXB　　*Yanjing xuebao* 燕京學報.

REFERENCES

Chang, Tsung-tung. 1970. *Der Kult der Shang-Dynastie im Spiegel der Orakelinschriften.* Weisbaden: Otto Harrassowitz.

Chou, Fa-kao (Zhou Fagao) 周法高, ed. 1975. *Jinwen gulin* 金文詁林. 16 vols. Compiled by Cheung Yat-shing (Zhang Risheng) 張日昇. Tsui Chee-yee (Xu Zhiyi) 徐芷儀, Lam Kit-ming (Lin Jieming) 林潔明. Hong Kong: Chinese University of Hong Kong Press. (Abbreviated as *JWGL*.)

Chow, Kwok-ching 周國正. 1982. Aspects of Subordinative Composite Sentences in the Period I Oracle-Bone Inscriptions. Ph.D. dissertation. Vancouver: University of British Columbia.

Comrie, Bernard. 1976. *Aspect: An Introduction to the Study of Aspect and Related Problems.* Cambridge: Cambridge University Press.

Graham, Angus C. 1983. "Yún 云 and Yuē 曰 as Verbs and Particles." *Acta Orientalia* 44: 33–71.

Gu, Jiegang 顧頡剛, ed. *Shangshu tongjian* 尚書通檢. 1966. Reprint. Taibei: Chinese Materials and Research Aids Service Center, Inc.

Guo, Moruo 郭沫若. 1965. *Yinqi cuibian kaoshi* 殷契粹編考釋. Kaoguxue zhuankan jiazhong di shi'er hao 考古學專刊甲種第十二號. Beijing: Kexue Chubanshe 科學出版社. (Originally published in Tokyo: Bunkyū-dō, 1937.)

Guo, Moruo, ed., Hu, Houxuan, ed.-in-chief 郭沫若,胡厚宣. 1978–82.

Jiaguwen Heji 甲骨文合集. 13 vols. Shanghai: Zhonghua Shuju. (Abbreviated as *Heji*.)

Karlgren, Bernhard. 1950. *The Book of Odes.* Reprinted from the *BMFEA*, nos. 16 and 17.

———. 1950a. *The Book of Documents.* Reprinted from the *BMFEA*, no. 22.

Keightley, David N. 1978. *Sources of Shang History: The Oracle-Bone Inscriptions of Bronze Age China.* Berkeley and Los Angeles: University of California Press.

———. 1992. "Shang Charges and Prognostications: The Strong and the Weak?" Paper presented to the 25th International Conference on Sino-Tibetan Languages and Linguistics; Berkeley, 15 October.

———. 1993. "Certainty and Control in Late Shang China: Modal *Qi* in the Oracle-Bone Inscriptions." Typescript, 28 July.

Lyons, John. 1977. *Semantics.* 2 vols. Cambridge: Cambridge University Press.

Nivison, David S. 1968. "So-called 'Modal Ch'i' in Classical Chinese." Paper presented to the American Oriental Society, Annual Meeting, Berkeley, 19 March.

———. 1971. "Modal *Ch'i* 其 and Related Expressions in Chinese of the Chou and the Early Empire." Paper presented to the American Oriental Society, Western Branch Meeting, Santa Barbara, 27 March.

———. 1971a. "A New Analysis of 'Modal Ch'i' 其, and a Suggestion for a New Theory of the Archaic Chinese Demonstrative and Indefinite Substitutes." Manuscript with *Addenda et Corrigenda.* 41 pp.

———. 1977. "The Pronominal Use of the Verb *Yu* (*giŭg 出, 入, 㞢, 有) in Early Archaic Chinese." *EC* 3: 1–17.

———. 1978. "Reply to Professor Takashima." *EC* 4: 30–36.

———. 1978a. "The Grammar and Theology of the Shang King's 'Crack Reading'." Paper presented at the Annual A.O.S. Meetings, Toronto, 12 April.

———. 1978–79. "Royal 'Virtue' in Shang Oracle Inscriptions." *EC* 4: 52–55.

———. 1982. "The 'Question' Question." Paper prepared for the International Conference on Shang Civilization, Honolulu, Hawaii, 7–11 September.

———. 1989. "The 'Question' Question." *EC* 14: 115–25. (The 1982 paper contains an appendix which is not reproduced in the *EC* article.)

———. 1991. "Notes on 'Notes'. A Reply to Paul Serruys." Manuscript, December.

———. 1992. "A New Attempt on 'Modal *Qi*': Another Note on Serruys' 'Notes'." Manuscript, January and September.

———. 1992a. "'Modal *Qi*' in Shang and Early Zhou Chinese." (Typescript dated 15 July.) Paper presented to the 25th International Conference on Sino-Tibetan Languages and Linguistics, Berkeley, 15 October.

———. 1992b. "'Modal' *Qi:* Statement for the Sino-Tibetan Workshop." 25th International Conference on Sino-Tibetan Linguistics, Berkeley, 15 October.

Quirk, Randolph, Sidney Greenbaum, Geoffrey Leech, Jan Startvik. 1980. *A Grammar of Contemporary English.* Revised edition. Burnt Mill: Longman Group Ltd.

Serruys, Paul L-M. 1972. "[Review of] *Der Kult der Shang-Dynastie im Spiegel der Orakelinschriften: Eine paläographische Studie zur Religion im archaischen China* (Wiesbaden: Otto Harrassowitz, 1970)." Typescript; published as Serruys 1974.

———. 1974. "Studies in the Language of the Shang Oracle Inscriptions." *TP* 60 nos. 1–3: 12–120.

———. 1985. "Notes on the Grammar of the Oracular Inscriptions of Shang." *Contributions to Sino-Tibetan Studies.* Ed. John McCoy and Timothy Light, 204–57. Leiden: E.J. Brill.

Shaughnessy, Edward L. 1991. *Sources of Western Zhou History: Inscribed Bronze Vessels.* Berkeley, Los Angeles, Oxford: University of California Press.

Shen, Pei 沈培. 1992. *Yinxu jiagu buci yuxu yanjiu* 殷墟甲骨卜辭語序研究. (Ph.D. dissertation, Beijing University, 1991). Taibei: Wenjin Chubanshe 文津出版社.

Shima, Kunio 島邦男. *Inkyo bokuji sōrui* 殷墟卜辭綜類. Revised edition. Tokyo: Kyūko Shoin 汲古書院 1971. (Abbreviated as *S.*)

Shirakawa, Shizuka 白川靜. 1970. *Kimbun tsūshaku* 金文通釋. Hakutsuru Bijutsukan-shi 白鴻美術館誌, no. 29. Kobe: Hakutsuru Bijutsukan. (*Kimbun tsūshaku*, no. 1 was published in 1962 and no. 56, last issue, in 1984).

Takashima, Ken-ichi 高嶋謙一. 1970. "Amphibolous Ch'i 其 in the Bone Inscriptions of the King Wu Ting Period." Typescript. 48 pp.

———. 1973. Negatives in the King Wu Ting Bone Inscriptions. Ph.D. dissertation. Seattle: University of Washington.

———. 1977. "Subordinate Structure in Oracle-Bone Inscriptions: With Particular Reference to the Particle *Ch'i.*" *MS* 33 (1977–1978): 36–61.

———. 1978. "Decipherment of the Word *Yu* 出又有 in the Shang Oracle-Bone Inscriptions and in Pre-Classical Chinese." *EC* 4: 19–29.

———. 1980. "The Early Archaic Chinese Word *Yu* in the Shang Oracle-Bone Inscriptions: Word-Family, Etymology, Grammar, Semantics and Sacrifice." *Cahiers de Linguistique Asie Orientale*, no. 8: 81–112.

———. 1984. "Noun Phrases in the Oracle-Bone Inscriptions." *MS* 36 (1984–1985): 229–302.

————. 1985a. *Yinxu wenzi bingbian tongjian* 殷墟文字丙編通檢. (*A Concordance to Fascicle Three of Inscriptions from the Yin Ruins*). Taibei: Institute of History and Philology, Academia Sinica.

————. 1988. "Morphology of the Negatives in Oracle Bone Inscriptions." *Computational Analysis of Asian and African Languages,* 113–33. Tokyo: National Inter-University Research Institute of Asian and African Languages and Cultures.

————. 1988a. "An Emphatic Verb Phrase in Oracle-Bone Inscriptions." *BIHP* 59, part IV: 653–94.

————. 1988–89. "An Evaluation of the Theories Concerning the Shang Oracle-Bone Inscriptions." *The Journal of Intercultural Studies,* nos. 15 & 16: 11–54.

————. 1989. "Indai teiboku gengo no honshitsu" 殷代貞卜言語 の本質. *Tōyō Bunka Kenkyūsho Kiyō* (Tokyo Daigaku) 東洋文 化研究所紀要（東京大學）(*The Memoirs of the Institute of Oriental Culture,* University of Tokyo) 110: 1–165.

————. 1990. "A Study of the Copulas in Shang Chinese." *The Memoirs of the Institute of Oriental Culture* (University of Tokyo), no. 112: 1–92.

————. 1992. "On the Particle *Qi.*" Typescript, 24 May.

————. 1993. "The Modal and Aspectual Particle *Qi* in Shang Chinese." Paper prepared for the International Symposium on Ancient Chinese Grammar, University of Zürich, Switzerland, 21–25 February.

Takashima, Ken-ichi, and Itō, Michiharu. 1996. *Studies in Early Chinese Civilization: Religion, Society, Language, and Palaeography.* 2 vols. Hirakata: Kansai Gaidai University.

Yang, Bojun and He, Leshi 楊伯俊, 何樂士. 1992. *Gu Hanyu yufa ji qi fazhan* 古漢語語法及其發展. Beijing: Yuwen Chubanshe 語文 出版社.

Yu, Min 俞敏. 1949. "Hanyu de '*qi*' gen Zangyu de *gji*" 漢語的「其」 跟藏語的 *gji. YJXB* 37: 75–94.

Zou 邹 and Lu 魯 and the Sinification of Shandong[1]

E. G. Pulleyblank

The archaeological discoveries of the last hundred years have transformed our knowledge of early China. The simple, unilinear, legendary beginnings recorded by Sima Qian—which attributed the creation of Chinese civilization to the work of ancient sage rulers, culminating in the founding of the first dynasty, Xia 夏, around the end of the third millennium B.C.E., followed by Shang 商 and Zhou 周, around the end of the second millennium—have been replaced by a much more complex picture of a variety of neolithic cultures stretching back as far as the seventh millennium out of which bronze age civilization did indeed emerge around the time traditionally associated with the first dynasty. The discovery of the Shang oracle bones has verified the real historical status of the second dynasty, even though many problems still remain in the interpretation of these documents from a linguistic point of view and many new problems have arisen and keep arising about the nature of the society that created them and its relation to what came before and what came after. It is in the long-lasting Zhou period, however, that the problems of reconciling the traditional historical records, so much more abundant than for earlier times, with the expanded picture that has been created by archaeology, really become acute. It is at this time that China as we know it, the China that forms the focus of national and cultural identity for nearly a quarter of the world's population, takes shape and emerges into the full light of day.

How can we reconcile the cultural diversity in prehistoric China as revealed by archaeology with the high degree of cultural uniformity that has characterized Chinese civilization in historical times? The traditional story is of a single people, the Chinese, creating the arts of civilization, surrounded and threatened at every stage by other peoples at a lower level of development. Such an ethnocentric attitude is not at all unusual. It is very much like that of the Greeks to the *barbaroi*, that is, 'the babblers', the lesser breeds that could not even talk properly. In the case of the Chinese, however, it was continually reinforced through much of their history by the absence of competing literate civilizations near at hand to challenge the assumption. The Greeks did know about the Egyptians and the Phoenicians and even had legends attributing specific cultural advances to contacts with these more ancient peoples. The Chinese by contrast were isolated from such direct influences until the first contacts with Western Asia and India in the Han dynasty and even after that remained insulated from them to a very considerable extent by the difficulties of communication. Yet when we look at the evidence that is emerging out of the ground, it becomes obvious that the uniquely dominant Chinese culture that we know in historical times was not a single growth with only one prehistoric root but had multiple prehistoric sources.

The complexities of Chinese prehistory began to be revealed in 1922 with the discovery of the painted pottery culture associated with the site name Yangshao in Henan, followed in 1930 by the discovery of the very different black pottery culture at Longshan in the northeast. This seemed to tie in with the theory developed about the same time by Fu Sinian (1933) from the analysis of traditional sources of an east-west division in early China between the Yi 夷 on the eastern seaboard from Hebei and Shandong southward and the Xia 夏 in Henan, Shanxi and Shaanxi. When it was found, however, that at some localities Longshan remains overlay earlier Yangshao remains, it was argued that Longshan was not independent but had developed out of Yangshao. This theory, which was, in effect, a return to the monogenetic picture of Chinese civilization of China's traditional self-image, was propagated in the West during the sixties and seventies in the influential summations of Chang Kwang-chih. Other more recently discovered cultures that he grouped together under the term Longshanoid could be regarded as intermediate between Yangshao and Longshan, manifestations of the same civilizing impulse spreading from a single heartland in the valleys of the Wei and Yellow Rivers. The same idea was enthusiastically taken up by Ho Ping-ti in *The Cradle of the East* (1975).

By the time of the conference on the Origins of Chinese Civilization organized by David Keightley at Berkeley, California, in 1978 (the conference volume did not appear until 1983), it was clear even to an outsider like myself that the increased knowledge provided by recent excavations in many parts of China had made such a simplistic picture quite impossible to sustain. Since I am not an archaeologist, I shall not try to sum up all the complexities that have replaced it. The picture that emerges, for example, in recent publications by Elizabeth Huber (1983, 1988), Wu Hung (1985) and Keightley himself (1987) does, however, bear a strong resemblance to that sketched by Fu Sinian over half a century ago.[2] That is, it opposes two main cultural complexes, one in Northwest China and the western part of the Central Plains and one along the East Coast from the Gulf of Bohai to Zhejiang, each with numerous local variants such as Laoguantai, Dadiwan, and Banpo in the West and Hemudu, Majiabang, and Dawenkou in the East, flourishing independently from the sixth millennium onward. In many ways it would seem that the East Coast cultures were initially more advanced in many ways than those to the west. According to Keightley (1987, 94), "By the fourth and third millennia, one sees East Coast traits beginning to intrude in both North China and the Northwest, so that the true northwest tradition reaches its fruition during the third millennium in Gansu and Qinghai while fading away in the region of the Central Plains and even in the Wei River valley . . .. [T]he emergence of Shang culture in the Central plains (ca. 2000 B.C.E.) owes much, though not all, to this infusion of elements from the east."

Keightley's argument for the importance of the eastern contribution to the beginnings of Chinese civilization is based not only on the chronology of the westward spread of eastern cultural elements but also on an analysis of various cultural traits that he finds manifested in the material products of the East Coast cultures, particularly the ceramics. He emphasizes the componential character of typical Eastern vessels, requiring measurement and planning, as opposed to the holistic designs of the Yangshao pots, where the emphasis is on surface decoration, and he suggests a link between the organizational skills manifested by such Eastern products and the mind-set that we think of as 'Confucian' in later times. He finds similar traits in Eastern mortuary practices and also suggests a correlation between the attitudes revealed by Eastern artefacts and the Shang script. He notes that the earliest wrought-metal working began in the northwest (with, one might add, probable connections with the aeneolithic cultures of the western steppes) but adds that when the new discovery reached the Central Plain, bronze vessels soon began to be cast using techniques adapted from the proto-piece-mould technology of the Eastern potters. It is an interesting case, persuasively argued with much illustrative detail.

There is, however, a paradox lurking behind this reconstruction of China's prehistoric past. If, as Keightley suggests, Chinese writing, that most unique symbol of Chinese civilization, has its roots in the neolithic cultures of the eastern seaboard, we should expect that the Chinese spoken language also came from the northeast. As Fu Sinian clearly understood, however, when he labelled the two contending parties in early China as Xia and Yi, the historical tradition unequivocally points in the opposite direction. Xia is not only the name of the first dynasty. It is also one of the earliest names by which the Chinese referred to themselves in contrast to other peoples. The other name, Hua 華, which has also played this role from early times to the present day, is probably related to Xia. It has never been the name of a dynasty but its geographical connections are definitely western, as are the traditional associations of the name Xia. There would be no real problem if one could say that the ancient inhabitants of the eastern coastal regions, though different in culture, were of the same ethnic background, speaking a closely related proto-Chinese language. As Fu Sinian pointed out, however, in Shang and early Zhou times the eastern coastal regions were known as the territory of the Yi, whom the Chinese regarded as aliens, not part of the Zhu Xia 諸夏. What Keightley's scenario for the development of Chinese civilization seems to imply, therefore, is that much of its technological basis and ideological structure was not the work of the Chinese themselves but was borrowed from others who were not Chinese, at least by the labels, presumably based on language, that the Chinese themselves used at the time to define ethnicity. I don't pretend that I can resolve the paradox and provide a neat and satisfying account of the complementary roles of West and East in Chinese origins. What I want to do in this paper is to discuss from the point of view of a historian and linguist one revealing case history from the Spring and Autumn Period of the way in which the Western Xia and Eastern Yi were still in the process of merging at that comparatively late date and to try to draw some tentative conclusions about what this may mean for the linguistic and ethnic background of the prehistoric cultures that lay behind them.

The state of Zou 鄒 is probably best known as the home state of Mencius. It was a close neighbor of Confucius' home state, Lu 魯, and shared Lu's reputation as a center for Confucian learning (*Zhuangzi* 33/9). The site of its capital has been identified archaeologically at Jiwangcheng 紀王城, about 10.5 km south of present Zouxian 鄒縣 under Zouyi 鄒嶧 mountain (Li Xueqin 1985, 144), which in turn is only about 20 km south of the ancient capital of Lu at Qufu 曲阜. In Mencius' day Zou still maintained its independence and could engage in armed conflict with its northern neighbor (*Mengzi* IB/12), though neither was a match for any of the seven great powers that contended for supremacy in the Warring States period (*Mengzi* IA/7). It was not a major player in the interstate conflicts of the Spring and Autumn period either but because of its proximity to Lu it is frequently mentioned in the *Chunqiu*, where it is referred to, however, by a different name, Zhulü (or -lou) 邾婁. The bisyllabic form appears in the *Gongyangzhuan*, and also in the 'Tangong' section of the *Liji*, but is abbreviated to Zhu 邾 in the *Guliangzhuan* and *Zuozhuan*.

Zou, EMC[3] tʂuw, and Zhu, EMC truǎ, are phonetically similar. Both come from the same Old Chinese rhyme group. The relationship between the initials is, however, more complicated. Both tr- and tʂ- have a feature of retroflexion which looks suspiciously as if it were related to the initial l-, from earlier *r-, of the second syllable, but tr- and tʂ- are not initials that usually interchange in *xiesheng* series. Initial tr- interchanges in Middle Chinese with dental stops and palatals, cf. *zhu* 朱 EMC tɕuw < *t-. Initial tʂ-, on the other hand, interchanges with dental sibilants. Compare Zou 陬 EMC tʂuw, with *qu* 取 EMC tsʰuǎ' as phonetic, the name of the village in Lu from which Confucius is said to have originated, which is a homophone of Zou 鄒, sometimes written with the same character, and, no doubt, just a variant writing of the same word.[4] The variability in the spelling of the word and especially the alternation between monosyllabic and disyllabic forms strongly suggest the transcription of a non-Chinese word. There was also another related state in the Chunqiu period known as Little Zhu(lü) 小邾婁, also called Ni 倪 or 郳, located south of Zou.

The non-Chinese name is consistent with other evidence that Zhu(lü)/Zou was regarded even late in the Spring and Autumn period, at least for polemical purposes, as an Yi 夷 state, not one of the Zhu Xia, the Chinese states that constituted the original patrimony of the Zhou dynasty. It has long been recognized that in early Zhou times the Yi 夷 'barbarians' who were one of the principal enemies of both Shang and early Zhou were not found merely in the Huai river region but extended north through Shandong.

A key question is the language of the Yi and its relation to Chinese. It has often been maintained in the past by both Chinese and Western scholars that the so-called 'barbarians' with whom the Chinese contended in early times, at least those to the south and east, were of the same basic linguistic stock as the Chinese, differing only in their relative degree of civilization. This was, for instance, the view of Henri Maspero and, more recently, Ho Ping-ti concluded, "It is highly probable that from time immemorial the differences among [the various cultures out of which historic Chinese culture coalesced] were dialectal rather than linguistic" (1975, 352). I have argued elsewhere (1983) that such an assumption is both inherently improbable in the light of what we know of the surviving 'minority peoples' in China at the present day and unsupported by the ancient evidence. Admittedly we have no direct evidence about the Yi language. There is no evidence that they ever developed a script of their own and the best we can hope for is to find traces in nomenclature, particularly of place names such as Zhulü/Zou, concealed in Chinese transcription. In my 1983 paper I drew attention to another such place name, namely Mie 蔑 (written Mo 眜 in the *Gongyang zhuan*) or Gumie 姑蔑, a place in Lu where the Duke of Lu and the ruler of Zhulü performed an oath-taking ceremony in the first year of the *Chunqiu,* 722 B.C.E., and which was also the scene of an event recorded in the *Zuozhuan* under the 12th year of Duke Ding, 498 B.C.E. The identical disyllabic place name, Gumie, occurs in *Guoyu* 18 referring to a place in Yue 越; called Taimo 太末 in Han and located near present Longyou 龍游 county in Zhejiang. I showed that, in addition to the coincidence in the name, in the eighth century C.E. there was a temple at Longyou, then called Longqiu 龍丘, in honour of King Yan 偃王 of Xu 徐, the legendary hero of the Yi people, and that this suggested an ancient connection between the Yi and the Yue peoples. Li Xueqin has argued on archaeological as well as textual grounds that the Huai valley and the lower Yangtze including, among others, the states of Xu, Wu, and Yue, constituted a distinct cultural sphere extending south to the South China sea and southeast to Taiwan (1985, 14 and 189 ff.).

As I and others have shown, there are good reasons for thinking that the language of Yue was related to that of modern Vietnam. The name Vietnam is, of course, just Southern Yue and there is a continuity in its application to the non-Chinese peoples of the eastern seaboard from Zhejiang down as far as Hanoi from Qin and Han times to the present. It is now accepted that Vietnamese, though much altered by its long contacts with Chinese, as well as with the Tai languages of South China and Southeast Asia, belongs genetically to the Austroasiatic family, which includes Khmer and Mon, as well as various tribal languages. In support of the idea that Austroasiatic languages were once found much farther north than at present are clear traces that have been found of very early Austroasiatic loanwords in Chinese. The word *jiang* 江, EMC kaɨwŋ < *kráɥŋ 'river', referring especially to the great river of central China, the Yangtze, is undoubtedly the same as Vietnamese *sông* 'river', in which the initial retroflex initial [ʂ] comes from a *kr- cluster still found in Mon *kruŋ*, with cognates in other Southeast Asian languages (Shorto 1971, 61; cf. Pulleyblank 1966, 10). Other early loan contacts between Chinese and Austroasiatic, as well as evidence of an Austroasiatic substratum in colloquial Min dialects, in territory known as Min Yue in Han times, have been proposed by Mei and Norman (1976).

This should mean that the Yi too spoke an Austroasiatic language. I suggested in my 1983 paper that the syllable *gu-*, also found in Gusu 姑蘇, the ancient name for the capital of Wu at modern Suzhou 蘇州, might be a separable element, perhaps meaning 'great' like Tai *in Taimo.* I should now like to suggest that the second syllable -mo, 末／眜 EMC mat < *mát, may conceal the Austroasiatic word for 'eye', Vietnamese *mát,* written Mon *mat,* etc. This would account for the 'eye' signific in the graph found in the *Chunqiu.*[5] One cannot, of course, lay too much stress on a speculative etymology of this kind but at least it is consistent with the accumulating body of other evidence that links the Yi with Yue and hence to present-day Vietnamese and other Austroasiatic languages of Indo-China.

My main interest in the present paper is, however, in the political status of Zhulü. At the oath-taking in 722 its ruler is referred to in the *Chunqiu* as Yi fu 儀父 where Yi is his style (*zi* 字) and *fŭ* (EMC puă') is not the word *fù* (EMC buă') 'father' but an honorific title used for nobles of lesser rank than rulers of the *zhuhou* states. The *Zuozhuan*, which identifies him as Ke, Viscount of Zhu, 邾克子, explains the term *fŭ* by saying that he had not yet received the [Zhou] king's mandate: 未王命也. At a second oath-taking with the Duke of Lu in 695 (seventeenth year of Duke Huan) he was still referred to as Yi fu but when he died in 678 (sixteenth year of Duke Zhuang) he was called Ke, Viscount of Zhulü. According to Du Yu's 杜預 commentary, this was because meanwhile he had received the king's mandate at the request of Duke Huan of Qi. Duke Huan became ruler of Qi in 685 and within a few years proceeded to establish himself as the first hegemon, *ba* 霸, presiding over the *zhuhou* lords as representative of the Zhou king.

Why did Qi show such solicitude for the small state of Zhulü? Neither the *Zuozhuan*, nor the other two ancient commentaries to the *Chunqiu*, nor any of the later commentaries that I have looked at offer any explanation but I think it is not hard to guess at the answer. Zhulü had previously been a dependency of Lu, one of the *fuyong* 附庸 states with which Lu was endowed when it was established for the descendants of the Duke of Zhou as an outpost of Zhou power in the territory of the Yi after the conquest of Shang. As it says in the Odes, "And so he [the King] appointed the Duke of Lu to be lord in the east, giving him mountains and streams, lands and fields and attached states (*fuyong*)" (*Shijing* 300; translation of B. Karlgren). Maspero thought that *fuyong* meant sub-enfeoffment on the European model. Creel, who doubted that "the Kings would have set up feudal lords with the intention that they be attached to others" (1970, 323), suggested that *fuyong* were the result of the conquest of one state by another rather than an institution created by the Zhou kings. He stressed the lateness of the ode in question and suggested that it was a piece of boasting on the part of a later Duke of Lu.

Creel's puzzlement is quite understandable if one thinks of the Zhou 'feudal system' as parcelling out of land within already settled Chinese territory. It takes on quite a different complexion if we think of it as a colonization process by which the Zhou conquerors established their rule among an alien population. We do not have to suppose that the *fuyong* states were established (*jian*) by the Zhou kings in the same sense as the *zhuhou* states were enfeoffed. They must have been the existing non-Chinese communities which retained their traditional political organization but now had to pay tribute and serve their new overlords. The original *zhuhou* were mostly, if not all, kinsmen belonging to the royal Ji 姬 clan or to clans linked to it by marriage such as the Jiang 姜 with whom the Zhou rulers had regularly intermarried before the conquest, or the Zi 子 of Shang, with whom there had also been a preconquest marriage alliance. Their ties of kinship were assumed to give them a vested interest in upholding the authority of the Zhou king. The ode cited above goes on to tell of how the Dukes of Lu had fought against and brought to submission alien peoples on all sides, among whom the Yi of the Huai and the Southern Yi are specially mentioned. Also mentioned as a Lu possession is Mount Yi 繹 (= 嶧) under which lay the capital of Zou. No doubt much of this is retrospective boasting and not to be taken as literal history but it probably reflects quite faithfully what the Dukes of Lu believed to be their mission as inheritors and defenders of the Zhou conquest.

By the seventh century the military strength of Lu had greatly diminished and Qi had taken over the mantle of leadership in the northeast. Moreover, attached states such as Zhulü must have been becoming increasingly sinicized and less and less distinguishable in language or customs from their overlords. To recognize them as members of the Zhu Xia family had the advantage of removing them from the category of hereditary enemies and allowing the Zhou inheritors to concentrate their attention on defence against the still unregenerate 'barbarians' more on the periphery of the Chinese world. From the point of view of Qi, detaching *fuyong* states from Lu had the further advantage of weakening its immediate rival in the Shandong region.

The references to Zhu(lü) in the *Chunqiu* and its commentaries make it clear that Lu remained conscious of the fact that it had once held Zhu(lü) as a dependency long after the latter had been raised to independent status. An interesting episode that illustrates Lu's sensitivity on this score occurred in the twenty-third year of Duke Zhao (519). A body of men who had been walling an outlying town of Zhulü was ambushed while returning to the capital by people of Lu and several men were killed. Zhulü complained to Jin, which at that time held the

presidency over the Zhou states. Jin seized a minister of Lu who had
come as an envoy and sought to confront him with a minister of Zhu
and so try the case between the two states. The Lu envoy refused to be
put on trial on the grounds that according to the ancient rules of
Zhou the minister of one of the regular states should rank with the
ruler of a lesser state and that, furthermore, Zhu was an Yi state.

One alleged aspect of 'Yi-ness' of Zhulü that has attracted some
attention is the custom of carrying out human sacrifice at the altar of
the god of the soil (*she* 社). Under the sixth month of the nineteenth
year of Duke Xi (641) the *Chunqiu* laconically reports that Zhulü
seized the Viscount of Ceng 鄫 and sacrificed him (yong zhi 用之).
The *Zuozhuan* amplifies the story, stating that the "Duke of Song made
Duke Wen of Zhu sacrifice the Viscount of Ceng [whose crime apparently was that he had failed to appear on time at an oath-taking ceremony presided over by Song] at the Cisui 次睢 altar of the soil, wishing thereby to attach the Yi of the east" (宋公使邾文公用鄫子
于次睢之社。欲以屬東夷). Yu Weichao 俞偉超 (1973; see also
Li Xueqin 1985, 151) argues on the basis of this episode and other evidence that the practice of human sacrifice at the altar of the soil was
an Yi custom inherited through the Shang dynasty and one that, moreover, persisted locally at the very same place, Cisui, as late as the third
century of the present era. Certainly we know that human sacrifice was
a regular practice in Shang times and it is plausible to suppose that
Song, whose rulers were descended from the Shang royal line, might
have preserved this tradition. That it was a custom that Shang owed to
an Yi component in its make-up is an interesting possibility. The written language of Shang was undoubtedly Chinese but if, as the Zhou
people believed, Shang was preceded by Xia, it is possible that the
Shang rulers were originally Yi who had adopted the Chinese written
language, and presumably other features of their state culture from
their Chinese predecessors, while retaining many of their own cultural
practices. The Zhou conquest would then be a reassertion of Xia political dominance. As for the barbarity of the custom of human sacrifice,
which Yu attributes to its barbarian Yi origin, one must point out that,
even if regular Zhou states normally used animal victims in the sacrifices at the altar of the soil, they not infrequently followed what seems
to us the equally barbarous custom of sending human victims to the
grave at the death of an important person (*xun* 殉).

One would like to know much more about the actual process by which the assimilation of Yi states like Zhulü into the Xia-Zhou polity took place. One can surmise that not only power politics but also marriage politics (and of course the two things were very much connected) played a major role. The second ruler of Zhu after Ke, presumably his grandson, who had the posthumous title Wen Gong 文公, had two wives, the first of whom was from Jin 晉 with the surname Ji 姬 and the second of whom was from Qi 齊 with the surname Jiang 姜. He had thus made marriage alliances with the two most prestigious clans of the Zhou. As I suggested in my 1983 paper, there is good reason to think that in the ruling aristocracy of preconquest Zhou the Ji and Jiang were intermarrying moieties. The mother of the legendary founder of the Zhou rulers and therefore of the Ji 姬 clan, Houji 后稷, was called Jiang Yuan 姜嫄. The consort of Dan Fu 亶父, the grandfather of King Wen, was Tai Jiang 太姜 celebrated in *Shijing* 237 and 240. There is abundant evidence that intermarriage between the Ji and the Jiang continued as a frequent pattern after the conquest.[6] It was not exclusive even before the conquest, however. The mother of King Wen, Tai Ren 太任, is said in *Shijing* 236 to have come from Yin-Shang 殷商. Later, Ren was the surname of a number of *zhuhou* princes, including the rulers of Chou 疇 and Zhi 摯, and Ode 236 also says that Tai Ren came from Zhi. What this means precisely in terms of Tai Ren's relationship to the royal house of Shang, which in Zhou times had the surname Zi 子, is not clear but what does seem obvious is that the marriage link with Yin-Shang was important as one element in Zhou's legitimacy. The ode reads, in Karlgren's translation:

> Shedding brightness below,
> Majestic on high,
> Heaven is difficult to rely on;
> It is not easy to be king;
> The lawful heir of the Yin on the throne of Heaven
> Was not permitted to embrace the four quarters.
>
> The lady Zhong Ren of Zhi
> Came from that[7] Yin-Shang,
> She came and married in Zhou;
> She became bride in the capital;
> And so together with Wang Ji
> She practised the virtue;

Tai Ren became pregnant
And bore this Wen Wang. . . .

The same ode also refers to King Wen's consort, who it says came
from Shen 莘. Elsewhere she is called Tai Si 太姒. Shen is said to
have been a small state in Shaanxi, that is, the homeland of the Zhou
dynasty, and the surname Si was regarded in Zhou times as that of the
house of Xia, predecessors of Shang. This marriage too was no doubt
regarded as strengthening the claims of Zhou to be the legitimate
rulers of the Chinese, that is, the Zhu Xia people.

In the post-conquest period the Zhou states not only gave women
as brides to other states but also received their women in exchange,
establishing an intricate web of kinship relationships. Information on
this subject is only given incidentally in the sources and is unfortunately very fragmentary. One example that is pertinent to the present
enquiry is that of Song Cao 宋曹 whose death is recorded in the
Zuozhuan under the twenty-third year of Duke Ai (472). She was the
daughter of the elder sister of Ji Gongruo 季公若 of Lu and the ruler
of Little Zhu 小邾 and the wife of Duke Yuan 元 of Song. Little
Zhu was located to the south of Zhulü and had the same Cao surname.
Her daughter, who would have had the surname Zi 子 of Song, was
married to Ji Pingzi 季平子 (see Zhao 25/1 ZZ), grandfather of Ji
Kangzi, who was in charge of affairs in Lu at the time of the record.

A sine qua non for entering into marriage relations with Zhou and
its principal feudatories was possession of a surname (*xing* 姓). This
was because of the rule of clan exogamy which forbade intermarriage
between those of the same surname no matter how remote the
assumed common ancestor in the male line was from the parties concerned, a rule that remained the basis for Chinese marriages until
modern times (though the 'surnames' to which the rule was applied
from the end of the Chunqiu period onward were no longer the
restricted set of clan names by which aristocratic women were called in
Zhou and Chunqiu times). In later historical works the Zhou system of
surnames is projected back to the legendary predynastic period but
there is also a respectable tradition that this rule of clan exogamy was a
specifically Zhou institution (*Liji* 14, 'Dazhuan'). Vandermeersch even
suggests that it was a new institution introduced by Zhou at the time of
the conquest. This is hardly likely. There seems to be every reason to

believe that it was already the practice within pre-conquest Zhou itself. It was its extension to the conquered territory that was the innovation. It seems to me, however, that Vandermeersch is probably right in claiming that the surname Zi 子 that was attributed to Shang in Zhou times and used by the rulers of its successor, Song, in the Chunqiu period was not used in this sense in Shang itself (1977, 1: 302).

It is even more likely that the surnames that we find attributed to states of 'barbarian' origin that were not originally part of the Zhu Xia were not part of the original Zhou system of clan names. By the end of the Chunqiu period, however, an elaborate system of genealogies had been created which linked even these names together with the Ji and Jiang and other early Zhou surnames. A full study of this process, for which the sources are fragmentary and conflicting, lies far beyond the scope of this paper. I shall simply refer to one important text, *Guoyu* 16, Zheng yu, in which the Cao surname of Zhulü and Little Zhulü, or Ni 倪／郳, is traced back to Zhurong 祝融 who was also the ancestor of the royal lines of other southern states, in particular, the Mi 羋 clan of Chu. Zhurong in turn was said to be descended from Zhuanxu 顓頊, one in the line of legendary predynastic *di* starting with Huangdi 黃帝, the ancestor of, among many others, the Ji clan, and his brother Yandi 炎帝, the ancestor of the Jiang clan.

There has, of course, been much study of these genealogies from the point of view of trying to recover a pristine Chinese mythology that has been distorted by Confucian rationalization and euhemerization. I don't want to deny the value of such studies but it seems to me that the extent to which these genealogies were deliberately created in the Chunqiu period with the political motive of incorporating originally non-Zhou peoples into the Xia-Chinese community needs to be given more attention than it has in the past. It was after all primarily the elite governing class in the various states, including those who originally belonged to the Zhou community and those who were being incorporated into it, who were interested in this process, which besides the establishment of marital and political ties involved the spread of literacy in Chinese and adoption of Zhou institutions and rites. The common people in the original non-Chinese states either followed their rulers or, in the case of the more peripheral states like Chu, were alienated and pushed into upland regions where some of them have survived to the present day as 'minority' peoples.

In conclusion, let me return to the question with which I began, the interplay of East and West in the formation of Chinese literate civilization. I have argued that the prehistoric inhabitants of the eastern seaboard, who were responsible for the remarkable neolithic cultures that Keightley and others see as the source of many of the characteristic features of Chinese civilization as we know it in historical times, were not Chinese in language but were linguistically akin to the present-day Austroasiatic speakers of Southeast Asia—the Vietnamese, Khmer, Mon, etc. The Chinese language, on the other hand, in all its varied modern forms, is genetically related to Tibetan, Burmese, and the many other languages in the uplands of Inner and South Asia to the west of China that constitute the Tibeto-Burman language family. The present geographical distribution of the two language families is quite consistent with the assumption that it is the Yangshao type cultures of the Central Plain and the Northwest that should be identified as proto-Chinese in language. If so, it surely means that writing must have been invented in the west and not on the eastern seaboard, as Keightley (1989) suggests.

Theoretically, of course, the proto-Yi could have invented a writing system which the proto-Chinese borrowed or imitated in the same way that after the Sumerians invented cuneiform writing the Akkadians adapted it to their very different language and the Elamites imitated it to create their own script. There is, however, no evidence that anything like this took place. Attention has been drawn to bird images associated with circles, possibly representing the sun, and crescents, possibly representing the moon, in the art of several of the neolithic cultures of the eastern seaboard (Wu 1985). These are indeed interesting for the possible connections they may have with later mythology associated with the east but there is no more justification for regarding them as proto 'writing' than for the similar speculations that have been inspired by the even earlier marks on Banpo pottery. As Keightley correctly states, one cannot speak of true writing until there is a demonstrable connection with the representation of spoken language, not just the use of pictorial or other iconic markings as (alas, no longer decipherable) symbols. In China this appears for the first time on the oracle bones and Shang bronzes. It is no doubt legitimate to assume that the bones give only a partial and perhaps late picture of what actually happened, since then, as later, most writing would have used perishable materials that has not survived. What seems very clear, however, from the phonetic elements embodied in the Shang script is that it was based on Chinese and nothing else (even if, as one suspects, there were already Austroasiatic loanwords in the Chinese of those days).

The virtual monopoly that the Chinese writing system enjoyed in East Asia in early times is one of the most striking contrasts to the situation in Western Asia and the Mediterranean basin (Pulleyblank 1983). One exception that really seems to be of the kind that 'proves the rule' is the so-called Ba Shu script (Li Xueqin 1985, 215–16) found on seals and bronze halberds of the Warring States period coming from the non-Chinese states of Ba and Shu on the upper Yangtse. Evidently a local non-Chinese script of Chinese inspiration that did not survive, it is too late to have any bearing on the original invention of writing in China. Since there were still independent Yi states in Shang times and even early Zhou, it is hard to believe that if they had developed a script for their own language before the invention of Chinese writing (in Xia ?), they would not have continued to use it. Perhaps there is still evidence buried in the ground that will force one to abandon this conclusion but meanwhile one can only assume that they remained illiterate until they were absorbed into the expanding Chinese polity.

What this seems to mean is that the westward spread of eastern cultural influences into the Central Plain and the Wei valley in the fourth and third millennia was not the result of a movement of people but of the adoption of eastern traits by the existing proto-Chinese inhabitants, who then went on to develop bronze-age civilization, including the invention of writing based on their own, Chinese, language, and proceeded to establish the first aggressive Xia state. It is conceivable that it is the period of interaction between proto-Xia and proto-Yi that is responsible for the fact that the Chinese language is markedly different in some of its typological features from its Tibeto-Burmese cousins. Tibeto-Burman languages generally speaking have an SOV word order, while Chinese, like Vietnamese, has the basic order SVO. One cannot, however, press the comparison with Vietnamese too far, since adjectives precede the noun in Chinese but follow it in Vietnamese (as they also do in Tibetan!). What seems clear is that, however much the stone age Yi people of the east contributed to the cultural amalgam of early China, it was the Xia people of the west who made the decisive innovations, the use of beaten and then cast metal and the invention of writing, that marked the transition from prehistory to history. The story of Zou and Lu gives a little glimpse of the process by which the Yi lost their identity and were absorbed into the expanding Chinese world. No doubt the cultural legacy which they inherited from their neolithic ancestors continued to make its contribution in an underground way. It may be no accident that Confucianism, which in the end became almost synonymous with Chinese high culture, took shape in the heartland of the prehistoric Yi. As a people, however, the Yi disappeared from history and their name came to mean simply 'barbarian'.

A further question that I shall not discuss here is whether there was some impulse from farther west at the beginning of the bronze age. The fact that the first traces of metal working are found in the Qijia culture in Gansu, which has other features that seem to relate it to the mixed pastoralism of the aeneolithic cultures of western Central Asia, is certainly suggestive (Huber 1988, 76 n97). So far, however, there is no concrete evidence that knowledge of writing could have been transmitted from Western Asia along with metal-working to provide the stimulus for that key invention for the transition from pre-history to history.

NOTES

1. This paper grew out of an exercise on sources for the pre-Qin period prepared for the Scandinavian Summer Course on Research Methods in premodern Chinese History held at the University of Oslo, Norway, in June 1990 and I should like to thank the organizers for their kind invitation which stimulated me to turn my thoughts in this direction. A preliminary version was later presented at the meeting of the Western Branch of the American Oriental Society at the University of Washington, Seattle, in October 1991. I am especially beholden to David Keightley, who was not present but has read two later versions of the paper and offered useful comments. I offer it now as a tribute to my old friend and colleague, David Nivison, who has done so much to elucidate the history of Shang and Zhou China.

2. In the fourth edition of *The Archaeology of Ancient China* (1986) K. C. Chang also abandons the unilinear concept and emphasizes the interaction of different neolithic cultures in the formation of Chinese civilization.

3. Reconstructions labeled EMC (Early Middle Chinese) are in accordance with the system published in Pulleyblank 1991, representing the form of standard language underlying the *Qieyun* of 601 C.E. Conjectural earlier forms are labeled with an asterisk.

4. Other variants are 郰 (*Lunyu* 3/15), 郰 (*Shiji* 47, Kongzi shijia), 騶 (*Hanshu* 28B, Dilizhi).

5. There is a variant Mei 眛, EMC məj^h; but Mo 眜, EMC mat, is certainly to be preferred. The *Jiyun* gives this character a reading EMC mɛt, homophonous with mie 蔑, but specifically refers to the passage in the *Gongyang zhuan* and it is likely that the reading was invented to account for the parallel. This is not necessarily justified. As negative particles *mie* 蔑, EMC mɛt, in the *Zuozhuan* and *mo* 末, EMC mat, in the *Lunyu* are equivalent to one another (Pulleyblank 1978). They may be dialectal variants of the same word, or 蔑 may have had a reading *mat as the negative particle, from which the word *mie* 'annihilate', EMC mɛt, differed by a prefix which was responsible for the fronting of the vowel in Middle Chinese. Note that 蔑 is phonetic in some words pronounced EMC mat such as 瀎 as well as in *wa* 襪 EMC muat 'stocking' which also lacks any evidence of fronting of the vowel. The negative particle was already obsolete in the late Warring States period and the reading of 蔑 in this sense may have been lost.

It should of course be noted that by coincidence *mat corresponds to the word for 'eye' in Austronesian as well as Austroasiatic. Compare Indonesian *mata* 'eye'. This would be consistent with another hypothesis that identifies the ancient Yue people as proto-Austronesian, suggested by some on the basis of archaeological connections with Taiwan. The seeming identity between the Austroasiatic and Austronesian words for 'eye' is a puzzle, since in other respects the two language families seem to be unrelated and the possibility of a very early loan of a word for such an essential part of basic vocabulary also seems remote. In any case the weight of the linguistic evidence is very much on the side of identifying the Yi and Yue as Austroasiatic.

6. To give just one example, a certain Wang Jiang 王姜, evidently one of the early Zhou queens, perhaps the wife of King Cheng, figures in a number of bronze inscriptions (Vandermeersch 1977, 1: 304).

7. Karlgren omits *bi* 彼 'that', which does, however, seem to be important to the sense.

REFERENCES

Passages from the *Shijing*, the *Chunqiu* and its commentaries, the *Mengzi*, and the *Zhuangzi* are cited according to the editions in the Harvard-Yenching Index series. For the *Guoyu* see the edition of Shanghai shifan daxue guji zhenglizu, Shanghai, 1978. For the *Liji* see *Liji zhengyi* in Shisanjing zhushu, Beijing: Zhonghua shuju, 1957. For *Shiji* and *Hanshu* see editions of the Zhonghua shuju. Beijing, 1957 and 1962.

Chang, Kwang-chih. 1986. *The Archaeology of Ancient China.* 4th ed., revised and enlarged. New Haven and London: Yale University Press.

Creel, Herrlee G. 1970. *The Origins of Statecraft in China.* Vol. 1: *The Western Chou Empire.* Chicago and London: University of Chicago Press.

Ho, Ping-ti. 1975. *The Cradle of the East.* Hong Kong, Chicago, and London: The Chinese University of Hong Kong and the University of Chicago Press.

Huber, Louisa G. Fitzgerald. 1983. "The Relationship of the Painted Pottery and Lung-shan Cultures." In David N. Keightley, ed., *The Origins of Chinese Civilization,* 177–216. Berkeley: University of California Press.

Huber, Louisa G. Fitzgerald. 1988. "The Bo Capital and Questions Concerning Xia and Early Shang." *Early China* 13:46–77.

Keightley, David N. 1987. "Archaeology and Mentality: the Making of China." *Representations* 18:91–128.

Keightley, David N. 1989. "The Origins of Writing in China: Scripts and Cultural Contexts." In Wayne M. Senner, ed., *The Origins of Writing.* Lincoln and London: University of Nebraska Press.

Li, Xueqin. 1985. *Eastern Zhou and Qin Civilizations.* Trans. K. C. Chang. New Haven and London: Yale University Press.

Mei, Tsu-lin and Jerry Norman. 1976. "The Austroasiatics in Ancient South China." *Monumenta Serica* 32:274–301.

Pulleyblank, E. G. 1966. "Chinese and Indo-Europeans." *Journal of the Royal Asiatic Society,* 9–39.

Pulleyblank, E. G. 1978. "Emphatic Negatives in Classical Chinese." In David T. Roy and Tsuen-hsuin Tsien, eds., Ancient China: Studies in Early Civilization, 115–36. Hong Kong: The Chinese University Press.

Pulleyblank, E. G. 1983. "The Chinese and Their Neighbors in Prehistoric and Early Historic Times." In David N. Keightley, ed., *The Origins of Chinese Civilization,* 411–66. Berkeley: University of California Press.

Pulleyblank, E. G. 1991. *Lexicon of Reconstructed Pronunciation in Early Middle Chinese, Late Middle Chinese, and Early Mandarin.* Vancouver: University of British Columbia Press.

Shorto, H. L. 1971. *A Dictionary of the Mon Inscriptions from the Sixth to the Sixteenth Centuries.* London: Oxford University Press.

Vandermeersch, Léon. 1977–80. *Wangdao ou la Voie Royale: Recherches sur l' Esprit des Institutions de la Chine Archaique.* 2 vols. Paris: Ecole Française d'Extrême-Orient.

Wu, Hung. 1985. "Bird Motifs in Eastern Yi Art." *Orientations* 16, no. 10:30–41.

Yu, Weichao 俞偉超. 1973. "Tongshan Qiuwan Shangdai shesi yiji de tuiding" 銅山丘灣商代社祀遺跡的推定. *Kaogu* 128: 296–98.

Micro-Periodization and the Calendar of a Shang Military Campaign[1]

Edward L. Shaughnessy

Over the last dozen years or so, David Nivison has been at the forefront of efforts to reconstruct the political chronology of ancient China, being best known in this regard for his seminal essay "The Dates of Western Chou."[2] One of the features of Nivison's chronological studies that elevates his reconstructions above so many other attempts has been his concern to integrate them within broader historical and historiographical analyses.[3] Inspired by Nivison's work, I will try in this paper to reconstruct the calendar of a military campaign during the Shang dynasty. While I will of course suggest how this reconstructed calendar might be correlated with an absolute chronology, my primary purposes will be to demonstrate a methodology and to illustrate one particular historiographical implication. I will also take advantage of the format of this volume to end with a problem. I will be delighted—and not the least bit surprised—if David Nivison provides an answer in his response.

Unlike Nivison's work on Western Zhou chronology, in which he has utilized a large number of bronze inscriptions extending over a period of 275 years, I will focus on a very small corpus of oracle-bone inscriptions that I believe were produced during a single six-month period. The inscriptions are in the form of divinations concerning military activities directed against certain western enemies of the Shang. Most of the inscriptions are typologically similar, being of the "Early" type of the Bin 賓 group inscriptions that date to the early or middle part of the reign of Shang king Wu Ding 武丁, though I will also have occasion to draw on inscriptions from the Li 歷 group. I will assume that readers of this study are familiar with recent advances made in oracle-bone periodization, and especially those with respect to the relationship between inscriptions of the Bin and Li groups.[4] To these advances in periodization I would like here to suggest a refinement that I term micro-periodization.[5]

Section One: Micro-periodization

Most Shang oracle-bone inscriptions, including especially those of the Bin group, begin with a notation of the day, written as one of the sixty days of the *ganzhi* 干支 cycle, on which the divination was performed. Some inscriptions also include a notation of the month, enumerated from one through twelve or, in the case of intercalary months, thirteen. Given the documented use of intercalation during the period covered by the Bin-group inscriptions, most scholars assume that the Shang month was based on the length of a lunation; and since a lunation averages about 29.5 days, most scholars further assume that the Shang month alternated between "long" months of thirty days and "short" months of twenty-nine days.[6]

With these assumptions, it is possible to determine parameters of thirty days for the first day of a month referred to by an inscription that contains both a day and month notation. For instance, if the day of the divination is *guihai,* day sixty in the sixty-day *ganzhi* cycle, then the first day of that month could not have been earlier than *jiawu,* day thirty-one, nor later than *guihai* itself. If two or more such dates that belong to the same calendar year can be similarly defined, then it may be possible to narrow these parameters considerably.

By way of illustrating the methodology of micro-periodization, let us examine a single oracle bone which contains five separate weekly (*xun* 旬) divinations (see fig. 1).

1a. 癸亥卜爭貞：旬亡囚. 一月

Crack-making on *guihai* (day 60), Zheng divining: "In the next ten-day week there will be no misfortune." First month.

1b. 癸未卜爭貞：旬亡囚. 二月

Crack-making on *guiwei* (day 20), Zheng divining: "In the next ten-day week there will be no misfortune." Second month.

1c. 癸卯卜．．．．旬亡囚．二月

Crack-making on *guimao* (day 40) . . . : "In the next ten-day week there will
be no misfortune." Second month.

1d. 〔癸〕卯．．．．貞：．．．．亡．．．．五月

Crack-making on [*gui-mao* (day 40), . . . divining: "[In the next ten-day
week,] there will be no [misfortune]." Fifth month.

1e. 癸未卜爭貞：旬亡囚．三日乙酉夕月出食．聞．
八月

Crack-making on *guiwei* (day 20), Zheng divining: "In the next ten-day
week there will be no misfortune." On the third day *yiyou* (day 22), in the
evening the moon was eclipsed. It was heard. Eighth month.

(*Heji* 11485 = *Jiabian* Photo 55; II. Bin)[7]

If we can assume that all of these inscriptions date to the same year,
and the fact that they are all found together on a single piece (generally referred to in oracle-bone studies as having a "same-piece relationship" [*tongban guanxi* 同版關係]) makes this a reasonable assumption, it is possible on the basis of the dates available to determine
almost exactly the calendar of that year. There are five dates present:
guihai (day 60) of the first month (#1a), which I propose to abbreviate
as 1/60, and 2/20 (#1b), 2/40 (#1c), 5/40 (#1d) and 8/20 (#1e). As
noted above, assuming that the Shang calendar did not permit a lunar
month to exceed thirty days in length, the date 1/60 requires that the
first day of this first month could only be between *jiawu* (day 31), thirty
days before day 60 (inclusive), and day 60 itself. I will express these
parameters as 1:31–60. In a similar fashion, the date 2/20 requires that
the first day of the second month be within the parameters 2:51–20.
Alternatively, we can also use this datum to determine that the third
month could not have begun before day 21 or after day 50, thus giving
parameters for the third month of 3:21–50 (the reason for considering
this alternative will become clear below). Similar analyses of the other
three data (2/40, 5/40, and 8/20) would give the three further parameters: 3:41–10, 5:11–40, and 9:21–50.

In order to compare the parameters of different months, it is necessary to convert all of them to a common month standard, the most

convenient of which is the first month of the year. Since, as noted above, lunar months apparently alternated regularly between "long" thirty-day months and "short" twenty-nine-day months, conversion to the parameters of a first month is most easily effected by counting in two-month fifty-nine-day intervals from the parameters of odd months. Since fifty-nine days is just one day less than the sixty days of a full *ganzhi* cycle, each such interval entails the increase (if moving back in time) of one day on either end of the parameter. Thus, for instance, the 3:21–50 parameters determined from the date 2/20 can be converted to first-month parameters of 1:22–51. The following table illustrates the steps in this type of analysis for each of the dates on this piece.

TABLE 1

#	Date	Month	First Month	Composite
1a	1/60	1:31–60	1:31–60	
1b	2/20	3:21–50	1:22–51	
1c	2/40	3:41–10	1:42–11	*1:42*
1d	5/40	5:11–40	1:13–42	
1e	8/20	9:21–50	1:25–54	

It can be seen that after having converted each of these data to a common standard, there is only one day that is common to each of the parameters, which is to say, that could be the first day of the first month: day 42. I will express this restricted or composite parameter as *1:42*.

We are fortunate in this case to have one other datum that can verify the extremely narrow parameters for the calendar of this year determined by this type of micro-periodization. #1e contains the record of a lunar eclipse on *yiyou* (day 22) of the eighth month. Since lunar eclipses occur only at the time of the full-moon, which is the fifteenth day of a lunar month, it is possible from this eclipse record to determine that the first day of this eighth month must have been *xinwei* (day 8).[8] If once again we count back from this date eight months, by alternating long and short months, as the following chart shows, we find that the first month of the year could only have begun on either day 41 or day 42 (allowing for the possibility that the first month of this year might be either short or long), almost exactly the result obtained by the micro-periodization analysis.

TABLE 2

Month		First Day	
1	41	42	
2		11	
3	40		41
4		10	
5	39		40
6		9	
7	38		39
8		8	

Having thus obtained suitably narrow parameters for the first day of the first month of this year, it would then be possible to compare these parameters with an almanac juxtaposing *ganzhi* day designations with new-moon days to determine which year or years might be compatible.[9] In the case of this year, the first month of which we have determined must have begun on day 42, several years between 1225 and 1175 B.C., the most likely fifty-year interval for inscriptions of the Bin group,[10] are possibly compatible: 1217, 1212, 1186, and 1181. It will be seen that these calendars repeat (approximately) after five years and (almost exactly) after thirty-one years, so that these correlations are sufficient only to narrow the number of possibilities. However, when other information is available, such as the eclipse record in this inscription (there having been an eclipse visible in Anyang in 1181[11]), such a narrowing of possibilities can be very important.

Section Two: The Calendar of a Shang Military Campaign

I believe that the series of inscriptions on #1 above provides a good illustration of the type of results that can be obtained when micro-periodization is used to examine fully dated inscriptions from a single calendar year. Of course, we are not always so fortunate to have such a series of inscriptions with same-piece relationship indicating that they belong to the same year. However, I believe this limitation can be overcome to some extent by comparing fully dated inscriptions whose contents pertain to a single highly individuated historical event. In this regard, I believe that inscriptions about military campaigns against particular enemies can be particularly important. When these inscriptions are typologically similar and when they refer to the same cast of characters participating in a campaign against the same enemy, I think we can assume that that campaign must have occurred within a relatively well-defined interval of time, rather than recurring intermittently throughout an extended period of time. If a sufficient number of fully dated inscriptions from a single such campaign can be collected, it should be possible to compare their calendrical notations and to derive from them a composite calendar of the year or years of the campaign.

The campaign that I propose to study is one of the best known of all Shang campaigns due to its mention in the display inscription on the first plastron illustrated in *Xiaotun dierben: Yinxu wenzi bingbian* 小屯第二本：殷虛文字丙編, until recently the premier publication of oracle-bone inscriptions (see fig. 2).[12] This inscription concerns a Shang attack against an enemy state named Xi 医.[13] It contains not only a preface and divination charge, but also a prognostication and verification indicating that the attack did in fact take place. The inscription reads in full:

2a. 癸丑卜爭貞：自今至于丁巳我戋 医. 王固曰：丁巳
　　我毋其. 戋；于來甲子戋. 旬虫一日癸亥圭弗戋；
　　之夕虫甲子允戋.

Crack-making on *guichou* (day 50), Zheng divining: "From today until *dingsi* (day 54), we will harm the Xi." The king prognosticated saying: "On *dingsi* we ought not to harm (them); on the coming *jiazi* (day 1), (we) will harm (them)." On the eleventh day *guihai* (day 60), Ju did not harm (them); that evening cleaving into *jiazi*, he really did harm (them).

(*Heji* 6834a = *Bingbian* 1; I. Bin)

Even though this inscription is extraordinarily detailed for a Shang oracle-bone inscription, it barely begins to answer such basic historical questions about this attack as when and where it took place, not to mention the more involved questions of how and why it developed. We are fortunate, however, that this piece was excavated from pit YH127 at Anyang, a pit that contained over seventeen thousand pieces of turtle shell. This provenance has allowed the editor of *Bingbian* and his colleagues to rejoin both entire plastrons and also sets of plastrons pertaining to the same divination topic. In the case of the inscription above, both of these types of rejoinings will prove important in setting out to answer some of the historical questions concerning it.

Heji 6834a (=*Bingbian* 1), on which this inscription is found, has been rejoined from ten different pieces into a virtually complete plastron. This one plastron contains twenty-two discrete inscriptions. Among these, the following three provide further information about the timing of this campaign and the figures, both Shang and non-Shang, involved in it.

2b.   庚申卜王貞：余伐不. 三月

Crack-making on *gengshen* (day 57), the king divining: "I will attack the Bu." Third month.

2c.   庚申卜王貞：雀弗其隻缶.

Crack-making on *gengshen* (day 57), the king divining: "Que will not expect to capture Fou."

2d.   乙丑卜㱿貞：子啇弗其隻缶.

Crack-making on *yichou* (day 2), Ke divining: "Prince Shang will not expect to capture Fou."

From these three inscriptions that share a same-piece relationship with that concerning the attack on Xi and that we can therefore assume were produced at about the same time, we learn that the Shang king contemplated attacks against two other entities, Bu 不 (presumably the name of a state) and Fou 缶 (the name of a leader of a state elsewhere [e.g., #7–8] referred to as Jifang 基方 [14]), and that he proposed that two important Shang commanders, Que 雀 and Prince Shang 子啇, lead these attacks. Furthermore, the inscription concerning the attack on Bu indicates that that particular divination took place in a "third month."

Another plastron (*Heji* 6830 = *Bingbian* 558) discovered in the same pit contains a display inscription very similar to that above (see fig. 3).

3.　壬子卜㲀〔貞〕：．．．．．戈𫎌．王固曰：吉；戈．
　　旬㞢三日甲子允戈．十二月

Crack-making on *renzi* (day 49) Ke [divining]: ". . . harm the Xi." The king prognosticated saying: "Auspicious; (we will) harm (them)." On the thirteenth day *jiazi* (day 1), (we) really did harm (them). Twelfth month.

(Heji 6830 = Bingbian 558; I.Bin)

Given the formal and calligraphic similarities, it seems clear that this inscription was produced at the same time as #2a above, both pieces presumably being members of a multi-plastron divination set.[15] This again confirms that an attack against Xi really did take place on a day *jiazi* (day 1), and adds the information that this divination occurred in a twelfth month.[16] While we can assume that this twelfth month of #3 was not too far distant in time from the third month of #2b, it is not possible to determine from just the inscriptions considered so far whether it came before or after it; i.e., whether the two dates belong to the same or adjacent calendar years. This must be determined before any micro-periodization analysis of the campaign can be attempted.

Fortunately, another plastron from YH127 (*Heji* 1027 = *Bingbian* 124) includes inscriptions concerning attacks against both Xi and Fou (the topic of #2c and #2d), with two of the inscriptions concerning Fou bearing "first month" dates.

4a.　戊午卜㲀：我韋 𫎌戈．

Crack-making on *wuwu* (day 55), Ke: "We will ram the Xi and harm (them).

4b.　己未卜㲀貞：缶不我𪇷族．一月

Crack-making on *jiwei* (day 56), Ke divining: "Fou will not capture our legions." First month.

4c.　己未卜㲀貞：缶其來見王．一月

Crack-making on *jiwei* (day 56), Ke divining: "Fou is expected to come to see the king." First month.

(Heji 1027a = Bingbian 124; I.Bin)

This might well suggest that the general campaign began with the attack on Xi in the twelfth month of one year, and then proceeded into the first months of the following year with attacks against Fou and Bu. Indeed, it would be tempting to forego the type of micro-periodization analysis outlined above and simply correlate the 12/49 date of #3 with the 1/56 date of #4b–c to conclude that the first day of the first month of this following year must have begun between days 50 and 56. Before jumping to this conclusion, however, several other inscriptions (including three more on pieces unearthed from pit YH127) provide more dates for the Shang campaign against Fou (some of them referring instead to the name of his state, Jifang) and thus for the calendar of this following year. I here translate these inscriptions in the order of their date notations.

5. 丁卯卜殻貞：王𡘙缶于蜀．二月

Crack-making on *dingmao* (day 4), Ke divining: "The king will ram Fou at Shu." Second month.

(Heji 6863 = Houbian 1.9.7; I.Bin)

6. 丁酉卜殻貞：王击 . . . . . 𡘙缶．三月

Crack-making on *dingyou* (day 34), Ke divining: "The king will let it be . . . who rams Fou." Third month.

(Jimbun 364; I.Bin)

7. 乙酉卜丙貞：子商弋 基方．三月

Crack-making on *yiyou* (day 22), Bing divining: "Prince Shang will harm the Jifang." Fourth month.

(Heji 6570 = Qianbian 5.13.1; I.Bin)

8. 〔辛〕卯卜殻貞：勿𪊽基方缶作郭，子商弋．三月

Crack-making on [*xin*]-*mao* (day 28), Ke divining: "We ought not ?? Jifang Fou's building a wall, for Prince Shang will harm (him)." Fourth month.

(Heji 13514a = Hebian 121; I.Bin)

9. 辛丑卜㱿貞：今日子商其𦥑基方缶哉. 五月

Crack-making on *xinchou* (day 38), Ke divining: "Today Prince Shang is
expected to net Jifang Fou and harm (him)." Fifth month.

(*Heji* 6571a = *Bingbian* 302; I.Bin)

Assuming that all of these Bin-group inscriptions with month notations from the first through fifth months (including also #2b) belong
to the same calendar year, it is possible to derive from them the following micro-periodization analysis.

TABLE 3

#	Date	Month	First Month	Composite
4b–c	1/56	1:27–56	1:27–56	
5	2/4	3: 5–34	1: 6–35	
6	3/34	3: 5–34	1: 6–35	
2b	3/57	3:28–57	1:29–58	1:31–35
7	4/22	5:23–52	1:25–54	
8	4/28	5:29–58	1:31–60	
9	5/38	5: 9–38	1:11–40	

As can be seen, the seven dates from these five months are all consistent with a calendar the first month of which would begin between
days 31 and 35. This consistency is satisfying, as are the relatively narrow parameters. However, we should also notice (as the following table
shows) that such a calendar would be consistent with the 12/49 date of
#3 for the preceding year if, and only if, that preceding year contained
an intercalary thirteenth month.

TABLE 4

#	Date	Month	First Month (of following year)
3	12/49	1:50–19	1:50–19
		13:50–19	1:19–48

We know, of course, that at the time of King Wu Ding, the Shang did
use end-of-year intercalary months, which a lunar-solar calendar

requires about twice every five years. Therefore, there is about a forty-percent chance that such a thirteenth month did intervene between the 12/49 date of inscription #3 and the 1/56 date of #4b–c. What is more, there seems to be historical evidence of this intercalary thirteenth month. This evidence is found in the Li-group inscriptions, the periodization of which has been hotly contested in recent years.

I will not attempt here to reprise the arguments surrounding the periodization of the Li-group inscriptions. I have been on record for more than a decade as supporting the revisionist periodization that regards them as contemporary with the Bin-group inscriptions, and believe that clear evidence of this contemporaneity can be seen when inscriptions of the two groups concern highly individuated events occurring on the same day. Qiu Xigui 裘錫圭 has already adduced several examples of this sort of contemporaneity.[17] To his examples I believe we can add the following Li-group inscription concerning an attack against Xi divined on a *guichou* (day 50) day of a twelfth month (i.e., the same day as inscription #2a cited above).

10.   癸丑卜：王韋 栖. 十二月.

Crack-making on *guichou* (day 50): "The king will ram Xi." Twelfth month.

(*Heji* 33083; I.Li; see fig. 4a)

True enough, the Xi of this inscription is written somewhat differently from that of the Bin-group inscription #2a (栖 as opposed to 㢴). But this sort of variation has always been common in writing the names of foreign states. Besides, in addition to the element 西 which both graphs share, the 刀丶 and 宀丷 elements by which they differ seem also to be semantically related, both indicating covers over heads. Thus, I think there is no question that the graphs refer to the same state and, further, that the divinations of the two groups refer to the same event.[18]

We know from inscriptions #2a and #3 that even though the king divined about the attack against Xi on *renzi* (day 49) and *guichou* (day 50), the Shang did not actually attack until the night of *guihai* (day 60) and early morning of *jiazi* (day 1). Another Li-group inscription, dated to *xinyou* (day 58) of a twelfth month, indicates that the king continued divining until just before this climactic attack. More important for the purposes of micro-periodization, this piece contains two other inscriptions, *both of which contain month notations of "thirteenth month."*

11a. 辛酉卜：王翌壬戌戋栖. 十二月.

Crack-making on *xinyou* (day 58): "The king on the next day *renxu* (day 59) will harm the Xi." Twelfth month.

11b. 才尤. 十三月.

. . . at You. Thirteenth month.

11c. 令㱿先, 氐侯步. 十三月.

Command Lin[19] to go forward, taking the archer-lord to walk. Thirteenth month.

(*Heji* 33082; I.Li; see fig. 4b).

These Li-group inscriptions would seem to prove that the year of the attack against Xi ended with an intercalary thirteenth month, just as the micro-periodization analysis of the eight dated Bin-group inscriptions given above had predicted. And if they do, then this argument by compossibility (the term is David Nivison's[20]) serves as compelling evidence for both the value of micro-periodization and also the contemporaneity of the Bin and Li group inscriptions. Whether or not the precise dating of these inscriptions that I will propose in the next section is accurate, I believe that just this one historiographical implication suffices once again to demonstrate the value of chronological studies.

Section Three: A Problem

David Nivison knows perhaps better than anyone else that when dealing with such topics as periodization and chronology new evidence can always surface to make one reconsider one's results. The case of the Shang campaign against Xi, Fou, and Bu is no exception.

In addition to the two Li-group inscriptions cited above concerning Shang attacks on Xi,[21] there is another fragment with several Li-group inscriptions, including one concerning a Shang attack on Fou and another concerning the figure Lin mentioned in inscription #11c above. Hsu Chin-hsiung 許進雄 transcribes these two inscriptions as follows:[22]

12a. 庚寅卜：韋缶于蜀戈又旅. 才.... 一月

Divining on *gengyin* (day 27): "We will ram Fou at Shu, and harm the right legion." At . . . First month.

12b. 甲午卜：王囟婁配.

Crack-making on *jiawu* (day 31): "The king will let it be Lin that he accompanies."

(*White* 1640; see fig. 4c)

If this transcription is correct, the 1/27 date of #12a would be inconsistent with the *1:31–35* parameters determined by the micro-periodization analysis above for the first month of the year of the Shang campaign against Fou. Does this mean that we should discard that analysis? I think not. David Nivison might agree that many scholars have shown too great a willingness to dismiss the results of chronological analyses at the first sign of inconsistency. Sometimes inconsistencies can lead to interpretive breakthroughs, as Nivision has so insightfully shown with the dual regnal calendars used by Western Zhou kings.[23] Here, too, I think the inconsistency of inscriptions #12a and #12b may well lead to a refinement of the micro-periodization analysis given above.

Before returning to that analysis, we might consider whether this new evidence is even pertinent. For instance, it is possible first that these inscriptions do not belong to the same campaign and calendar year. However, the coincidence between #12a and #5, the charges of both of which propose a "ramming" (*shun* 韋) attack against Fou at the same place, Shu 蜀, would seem to suggest that they ought to be contemporary. Second, it is also possible that this month notation is incorrect or should be read differently. In the rubbing, a vertical line appears above the horizontal line of the "one," and this might be construed as a *hewen* 合文 for "eleven." However, the Shang *hewen* for "eleventh month" consistently places the vertical stroke for "ten" alongside the graph for "month," and even though Li-group inscriptions rarely contain month notations of any kind, there is no evidence that Li-group scribes wrote *hewen* numerals differently from scribes of other groups. Moreover, Professor Hsu informs me that this vertical line was not visible when he inspected the bone recently.[24] Thus, I think we should probably assume that the month notation was indeed intended to refer to the first month. Third and somewhat along these lines, it is also theoretically possible that the scribe mistook or miswrote the month of the divination. However, I would also be reluctant to accept such an assumption; as David Nivison has pointed out, "The need to impute a mistake to an inscription ought to make one question one's own assumptions."[25]

One ought perhaps also to question the assumptions of others. Such questioning would lead to yet another alternative in the interpretation of this inscription—that the transcription is mistaken in terms of the division between the two inscriptions. In this case, Hsu Chin-hsiung seems to have assumed in his transcription of #12a that the "zai 才 Place-name" after "harm the right legion" is a kind of post-placed place notation akin to those common in the Huang 黃 -group inscriptions of Period V. However, I have not been able to find any analogous examples among Li-group inscriptions.[26] If this is not a place notation, it would be difficult to include it within the charge (i.e., "harm the right legion at . . .") since that charge already contains a locative yu 于, "at" (i.e., "ram Fou at Shu").

The transcription of this place-name may give some clue as to its syntactic association here. Although Hsu cautiously declined to give any transcription, enough of the graph remains to suggest that it is the same graph as the You 尤 of inscription #11b. And once we make this identification, we should note as well that #11c, which is obviously related to #11b, records a command to Lin, the same figure as mentioned in #12b, to lead a portion of the army:

"Command Lin to go forward, taking the archer-lord to walk." Thirteenth month.

In #12b, according to Hsu's transcription, the king proposes to accompany Lin. This divination charge seems to be akin to the formula in which the king proposes to "ally" (bi 比) with some military leader, a formula which is usually followed by a main clause proposing *to attack some enemy*. If here we were to read "down the page" past the *pei* 配, "to accompany," the clause "harm the right legions at You" would form a reasonable conclusion to this charge; i.e., "The king will let it be Lin that he accompanies to harm the right legions at You." While the positioning of this clause parallel to #12a would not seem to support this reading, the notoriously sloppy "page design" of Li-group inscriptions suggests that such parallelism ought not to be an overriding factor in distinguishing the inscriptional boundaries here.[27]

If this clause does belong to inscription #12b, as I would like to suggest, then the "first month" month notation must also belong to it. Dissociating this month notation from the *gengyin* (day 27) day notation of the preface of #12a eliminates the inconsistency between a putative 1/27 date of #12a and the *1:31–35* parameters derived from the other inscriptions from this campaign. Moreover, by now associating that month notation with the *jiawu* (day 31) date of #12b, the new datum 1/31 would actually serve to restrict those parameters to the single day *1:31*. This is such a precise result that the almanac correlating new moon and *ganzhi* days for the probable period of King Wu Ding's reign shows only the years 1215, 1210, and 1179 B.C. to be compatible. Much work remains to be done to determine all of the dates of that very important reign, but I would like to suggest that we might begin with the years 1211–1210 B.C. as the date of the Shang campaign against the Xi, Bu, and Fou.[28]

NOTES

1. Preliminary versions of this paper were presented at the Fortieth Annual Meeting of the Association for Asian Studies, San Francisco, 26 March 1988, and to the International Symposium on Xia Culture, Los Angeles, 23 May 1990. I am grateful to Professors Huang Tianshu 黃天樹 (Shaanxi Normal University), David N. Keightley (University of California, Berkeley), and Qiu Xigui 裘錫圭 (Peking University) for their comments on the various versions of this paper.

2. David S. Nivison, "The Dates of Western Chou," *Harvard Journal of Asiatic Studies* 43, no. 2 (December 1983): 481–580.

3. Particularly important in this regard is his article "Western Chou History Reconstructed from Bronze Inscriptions," in *The Great Bronze Age of China: A Symposium*, ed. George Kuwayama (Los Angeles: Los Angeles County Museum of Art, 1983), 44–55.

4. The studies generally credited with establishing this advance in peri-odization are: Li Xueqin 李學勤, "Xiaotun nandi jiagu yu jiagu fenqi" 屯南地甲骨與甲骨分期, *Wenwu* 1981, no. 5: 27–33; Qiu Xigui 裘錫圭, "Lun Lizu buci de shidai" 論歷組卜辭的時代, *Guwenzi yanjiu* 古文字研究 6 (1981): 262–320, and Lin Yun 林澐, "Xiaotun nandi fajue yu Yinxu jiagu duandai" 小屯南地發掘與殷虛甲骨斷代, *Guwenzi yan-jiu* 9 (1984): 111–54; for an English-language resume of these studies, see Edward L. Shaughnessy, "Recent Approaches to Oracle-Bone Periodization: A Review," *Early China* 8 (1982–1983): 1–13. For a more recent and more devel-oped study, see Huang Tianshu 黃天樹, "Yinxu wang buci de fenlei yu duandai" 殷虛王卜辭的分類與斷代 (Ph.D. diss.: Peking University, 1988; rpt. Taibei: Wenjin chubanshe, 1991).

5. I should hasten to point out that in developing this methodology of micro-periodization I am very much indebted to the work of Dong Zuobin 董作賓, especially as represented in his monumental work *Yinli pu* 殷曆譜 (Nanqi, Sichuan: Guoli Zhongyang yanjiuyuan Lishi yuyan yan-jiusuo zhuankan, 1945). My refinements lie mainly in systematizing his method of analysis and integrating it with the more recent advances in oracle-bone periodization mentioned in note 4.

6. The analysis of example #1 in the text seems to provide conclusive evi-dence that the Shang month did in fact alternate between "long" and "short" months. However, the average length of a lunation is actually 29.53 days, ren-dering this alternation somewhat irregular over longer periods of time. This irregularity was controlled in all later times for which there is documentation by allowing for two consecutive "long" months about every fifteen months, and I assume that this must have been roughly the practice during the Shang period as well. In the analyses presented in the present paper, however, since the intervals involved will not exceed fifteen months I will not attempt to account for possible consecutive "long" months.

7. References to publications of oracle-bone inscriptions are given as in David N. Keightley, *Sources of Shang History: The Oracle-Bone Inscriptions of Bronze Age China* (Berkeley: University of California Press, 1978), 229–31: bibliogra-phy A, except that they are uniformly rendered in *pinyin* romanization. In addition to the publications listed in Keightley's bibliography, I will also refer to three subsequently published works: *Oracle Bones from the White and Other Collections,* ed. Hsu Chin-hsiung (Toronto: Royal Ontario Museum, 1979), which I will refer to as *White; Jiaguwen heji* 甲骨文合集, 13 vols., ed. Guo Moruo 郭沫若 (n.p.: Zhonghua shuju, 1982), which I abbreviate as *Heji;* and *Yingguo suocang jiagu ji* 英國所藏甲骨集 (*Oracle Bone Collections in Great Britain*), 2 parts, ed. Li Xueqin 李學勤, Qi Wenxin 齊文心, and Ai

Lan 艾蘭 (Sarah Allan) (Beijing: Zhonghua shuju, 1985), which I abbreviate as *Yingcang*. In this paper, I provide whenever possible cross references between an inscription's original place of publication and its location in *Heji*, which is now becoming the standard source of reference in Chinese oracle-bone studies. When reference is made only to *Heji*, it is the only formal publication of the piece of which I am aware.

I might note as well that I provide two-part notations indicating the period and typology of all inscriptions translated in this paper, the first part (a Roman numeral) indicating the period within Dong Zuobin's five-period division, and the second part indicating the diviner group. Most of these notations should be unobjectionable, though that given here for *Heji* 11485 requires some comment. While most inscriptions of the Bin group belong to Dong's Period I, those on this piece display the group's latest calligraphy, which Qiu Xigui has demonstrated probably spills over into Period II; "Lun Lizu buci de shidai," 304–16. For this reason, I denote it as II.Bin.

8. David N. Keightley has argued that the record "it was heard" appended at the end of this eclipse record suggests that the eclipse was not actually visible at Anyang and that the record may therefore be mistaken; see David N. Keightley, "Shang China is Coming of Age—A Review Article," *Journal of Asian Studies* 41, no. 3 (1982): 551. While this argument may be correct (though the eclipse of 25 November 1181 B.C. is a reasonable candidate for it, as both Homer Dubs and Fan Yuzhou 范毓周 have suggested; see Homer H. Dubs, "The Date of the Shang Period," *T'oung Pao* 40 [1951]: 332; Fan Yuzhou, "Jiaguwen yueshi jishi keci kaobian" 甲骨文月食記事刻辭考辯, *Jiaguwen yu Yin-Shang shi* 甲骨文與殷商史 2 [1986]: 323; see, too, note 11 below), I do not think it negates the value of the record. Even if there were no eclipse, I expect that the Shang scribes would not have considered the possibility at any time other than the full moon.

9. There are two generally consistent almanacs available for the Shang period: Dong Zuobin, *Zhongguo nianli zongpu* 中國年曆總譜, 2 vols. (Hong Kong: Hong Kong University Press, 1960), and Zhang Peiyu 張培瑜, *Zhongguo xian-Qin shi libiao* 中國先秦史曆表 (Jinan: Qi-Lu shushe, 1987). Despite the general consistency of these two almanacs, since they both represent idealized calendars some allowance must be made in using them to account, for instance, for different schedules of intercalation or "long" and "short" months. By allowing for a margin of error of one day and/or one lunation, I believe that these almanacs can be used with considerable confidence.

10. As mentioned above, most if not all of the Bin-group inscriptions

derive from the reign of King Wu Ding. Wu Ding is credited in most historical sources with a reign of fifty-nine years (whether or not he actually reigned that long is a question beyond the scope of this paper). There are at present two types of evidence that provide broad parameters for this reign: extrapolations based on average lengths of generations beginning with the date of the Zhou conquest of Shang, and identifications of four other Bin-group lunar eclipse records (*Heji* 11483a [=*Bingbian* 59], *Heji* 11484a [=*Bingbian* 57], *Yingcang* 886b [=*Kufang* 1595b], and *Heji* 11482b [=*Fuyin* "Tian" 2]. Both of these types of evidence deserve—and have received—more detailed discussion than it is possible to give in this paper, and both suggest that Wu Ding's reign may have come to an end in the decade or so after 1200 B.C. The date of the Zhou conquest is of course one of the most studied questions in all of early Chinese history. For reasons why I believe it took place in 1045 B.C., see Edward L. Shaughnessy, *Sources of Western Zhou History: Inscribed Bronze Vessels* [Berkeley: University of California Press, 1991], 217–87). If the six generations of Shang kings after Wu Ding had average reigns of about twenty-five years (consistent with average regnal generations in later dynasties, as demonstrated by Lei Haizong 雷海宗 ["Yin Zhou niandai kao" 殷周年代考, *Wuhan daxue wenzhe jikan* 武漢大學文哲集刊 2, no. 1 (1931): 1–14]), then such a date for the Zhou conquest suggests that Wu Ding's reign might have ended about 1195 B.C. There have also been many studies of the Bin-group lunar eclipse records, including especially the three studies mentioned in note 8 above. These three studies are generally consistent and show, I believe, that the records correspond to eclipses that occurred in 1201, 1198, 1192, and 1189 B.C. The record of the 1189 eclipse (i.e., *Heji* 11482b) displays calligraphy similar to that of 1 above (i.e., *Heji* 11485), which, as noted above (note 7), is the latest type of Bin-group calligraphy; it must date either to the very end of Wu Ding's reign or perhaps even into the reign of his son Zu Geng.

11. As noted briefly above (note 8), the identification of the eclipse record in *Heji* 11485 with the lunar eclipse of 1181 is not unproblematic. The eclipse of 1181 occurred on 25 November, seemingly too late in the year for the eighth month notation of the inscription. While there may be ways to reconcile this discrepancy (and it bears noting that there are no other lunar eclipses that provide a better match), I prefer for the present just to suggest a possible identification.

12. *Xiaotun Dierben: Yinxu wenzi bingbian*, 3 vols., 6 parts, ed. Zhang Bingquan 張秉權 (Nangang: Academia Sinica, 1957–1972). *Bingbian* has now been superseded by *Jiaguwen heji* (see above, note 7), but it remains valuable for Zhang's transcriptions and commentaries.

13. Zhang Bingquan transcribes the graph 𠀬 as *zhou* 胄 (*Yinxu wenzi bingbian* "Kaoshi" 考釋, 1, 3) and is followed in this by David Keightley (*Sources of Shang History*, 43) and by Kenichi Takashima ("Negatives in the King Wu Ting Bone Inscriptions" [Ph.D. diss.: University of Washington, 1973], 110), among others. However, the graph for *zhou* in other paleographic sources, 㒸 (see, e.g., Gao Ming 高明, *Guwenzi leibian* 古文字類編. [Beijing: Zhonghua shuju, 1980], 143), clearly differs from this graph. I prefer to give a literal transcription of the two components of the graph, and to take the pronunciation from the bottom component 甘, i.e., *xi* 西.

14. Inscriptions concerning this attack sometimes refer to the enemy as Jifang (e.g., *Heji* 6570, 6573), sometimes as Jifang Fou (e.g., *Heji* 6572, 13514a), sometimes as either Jifang or Jifang Fou on the same shell (e.g., *Heji* 6571a), and sometimes as Fou (e.g., *Heji* 6834a, 6860). That Fou is the name of an individual and not the name of another state (as suggested by, for instance, Chen Mengjia 陳夢家, *Yinxu buci zongshu* 殷虛卜辭綜述 [Beijing: Kexue chubanshe, 1956], 288) seems clear from inscriptions about his coming to see the king (*Heji* 1027a), his hunting (*Heji* 10241), and especially his dying (*Heji* 17100).

15. For these divination sets, see Keightley, *Sources of Shang History*, 37–40.

16. It is unclear whether the month notation refers to the day of the divination, *renzi* (day 49), or to the day of the attack, *jiazi* (day 1). However, since month notations often accompany inscriptions that contain only the preface and divination charge (i.e., not a verification), I will assume in the micro-periodization analysis below that the month refers to the day of the divination. While a micro-periodization analysis based on an assumption that the month notation refers to the date of the verification would potentially give a different result, I do not believe that such a difference would affect the analysis of the inscriptions pertaining to the campaign studied here.

17. Qiu Xigui, "Lun Lizu buci de shidai," especially 277–80.

18. Li Xueqin 李學勤, *Yindai dili jianlun* 殷代地理簡論 (Beijing: Kexue chubanshe, 1959), 87–88, had previously regarded these two graphs (as well as yet a third graph, 猶) as representing the same state, there being one Li-group inscription (*Heji* 20530 = *Shiduo* 2.170) written almost identically to the Bin-group graph (viz. 𠀬). Of course, at the time that he was writing, Li still believed that Li-group inscriptions dated to the reign of King Wen Ding, and thus did not identify this state with that found in the Bin-group inscriptions.

19. The mention of Lin here is further evidence for the contemporaneity of these Li-group inscriptions with the Bin-group inscriptions from this general campaign. Compare, for instance, his mention together with Que (men-

tioned also in inscription #2c above) in the following Bin-group inscription proposing an attack on Jifang.

壬寅卜殼貞：共雀雳卣隻基方.

Crack-making on *renyin* (day 27), Ke divining: "Levy Que, and let it be Lin to capture Jifang."

(*Heji* 6571a; I.Bin)

20. Nivison, "The Dates of Western Chou," 484.

21. There may be yet another fully dated Li-group inscription pertaining to an attack on Xi. Li Xuequin *Yindai dili jianlun,* transcribes *Houbian* 2.43.9 as:

甲〔辰〕...王...伐...才鼍. 一月. 八日辛亥允戋伐.
二千六百五十六人，隊貓.

Jia-[chen] (day 41) . . . the king . . . attacks . . . at Guo. First month. The eighth day xinhai (day 48), (we) really did conquer, decapitating two-thousand six-hundred and fifty-six men. Xi fell.

If this transcription is accurate, and if Xi (here written 貓) refers to the state of Xi elsewhere written 㠱 or 栖, then the inscription would provide even more information than that in inscription #2a translated above. Unfortunately, however, the rubbing in *Houbian* is virtually illegible, and I can distinguish no more than half of the graphs Li does.

22. Hsu Chin-hsiung, "The Chinese Text," in *Oracle Bones from the White and Other Collections,* 93.

23. See Nivison, "The Dates of Western Chou," 524–35.

24. Personal communication from James Hsu, 23 November 1992.

25. Nivison, "The Dates of Western Chou," 494.

26. There are a couple of Li-group examples that include a final "*zai* Place-name," but these place-names could also be read within the syntax of the charge, as in the following inscription:

癸亥貞：旬亡田. 才彎.

Divining on *guihai* (day 60): "In the next ten-day week there will be no misfortune, at Pei."

(*Heji* 33145; I.Li)

27. The term "page design" is that of David Keightley. He notes that the design of this type of Li-group inscription is "as if the engraver were less sure about their position or its relation to a larger design" (*Sources of Shang History,* 108).

28. I would like to be deliberately cautious in suggesting this date, knowing all too well the propensity of readers of chronological studies to focus on dates at the expense of methodology. As mentioned above (p. 62 and note

10), the portion of King Wu Ding's reign during which these divinations were produced was probably within the fifty-year period from 1225–1175 B.C. As I further explained in note 10, four lunar eclipse records correspond to eclipses in the years 1201, 1198, 1192, and 1189 B.C. Of these records, the two corresponding to the years 1201 (*Heji* 11483a [=*Bingbian* 59]) and 1198 (*Heji* 11484a [=*Bingbian* 57]) both come from pit YH127, the same pit that produced many of the inscriptions concerning the Shang attack against the Xi, Bu, and Fou. The calligraphy and formal characteristics of these campaign inscriptions seem to be somewhat earlier than those of the two eclipse records (being of the type referred to by Lin Yun, Qiu Xigui, and Huang Tianshu [see note 4] as the Shi-Bin Transitional Group [Shi-Bin *jianzu* 師賓間組]). This certainly argues for the earlier possible years, either 1215 or 1210; and since I assume inscriptions from pit YH127 were produced during only a relatively circumscribed span of time, I thus choose the nearer of these two dates to 1201: i.e., 1210 B.C.

Figure 1
Rubbing of inscription #1a–1e; *Heji* 11485

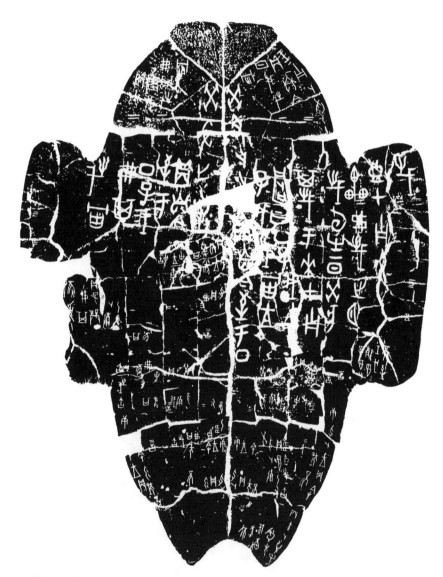

Figure 2
Rubbing of inscription #2a–2d; *Heji* 6834a

Figure 3
Rubbing of inscription #3; *Heji* 6830

Figures 4a–4c
a: Rubbing of inscription #10; *Heji* 33083 (top right)
b: Rubbing of inscription #11a–11c; *Heji* 33082 (left)
c: Rubbing of inscription #12a–12b; *White* 1640 (bottom right)

The Mean in Original Confucianism

Kanaya Osamu

The objective of this study is to attempt to clarify, in as logical a fashion as possible, the nature of the Mean in original Confucianism and to link it to our own practice in the present age.[1]

It has already become generally accepted in academic circles that in its present form the book known as *The Mean* (*Zhongyong* 中庸) cannot be regarded, as tradition would have it, as the work of Confucius' grandson Zisi 子思. Moreover, the division of the text into two parts, as proposed by Takeuchi Yoshio 武內義雄 and Feng Youlan 馮友蘭 (with the first part corresponding to the section beginning with chapter two and going to the first half of chapter twenty in Zhu Xi's 朱熹 pagination and the latter part consisting of chapter one and the section from the second half of chapter twenty to chapter thirty-three) is probably correct. The latter part expounds the philosophy of "sincerity" (*cheng* 誠), constituting a supplement to the Mean propounded in the first part, and it represents an expression of the transformation of Confucianism into a monistic philosophy in response to political circumstances reflected in the establishment of the Qin and Han empires.[2] Thus, when examining the Mean in original Confucianism, we must exclude this latter part from our considerations.

The word "Mean" (*zhong yong*) appears for the first time in *The Analects* (*Lunyu* 論語), but only once, and though its virtues are extolled, no explanation is given of the meaning of this term.[3] *The Analects* also records the exhortation to "hold to the middle" (*zhong* 中) among the traditions of the ancient sage-kings.[4] From ancient times, this "middle" had been interpreted as signifying the Mean. Nevertheless, its meaning is also not clear. It becomes clearer in the phrase *zhong xing* 中行: although it is ideal to associate with men described as *zhong xing*, if this should not be possible, then a *kuang zhe* 狂者 or *juan zhe* 狷者 will do, the former being defined as active and enterprising and the latter as passive and cautious.[5] *Zhong xing* denotes the "middle road." In other words, neither being active nor being passive is the best course of action; the ideal lies in between these two extremes.

The Mean contains a very similar passage, which serves as an explanation of the Mean. "Why is it that the correct path is not practiced? The reason is that the wise act in excess and go beyond it, while the foolish are wanting in ability and do not come up to it."[6] This means that the ideal lies in between going too far and falling short. The well-known passage in *The Analects* to the effect that "overshooting the mark is the same as falling short" gives expression to the same philosophy.[7]

The first answer to our question concerning the nature of the Mean has now been obtained. The Mean refers to the middle ground lying between the two opposite states of going too far and falling short. This corresponds to Zhu Xi's interpretation according to which the *zhong* of *zhong yong* means "a state that is not one-sided and neither goes beyond nor falls short." If going beyond and falling short are regarded as two extremes, then the Mean corresponds to the state midway between these two extremes. In point of fact, an old form of the character *zhong* 中 took the form of a single straight line with a circle in the middle, and there was also another form with marks of streamers added to both ends of the straight line, thus indicating that *zhong* does indeed denote the point midway between two extremes. The first meaning of the Mean is, therefore, "the middle between two extremes, inclining neither to the left nor to the right".

Another passage in *The Mean* related to this meaning is, "If one divulges secrets and behaves strangely, one will attract attention. I myself do not approve of this. . . . The gentleman follows the Mean. Avoiding public attention and living in obscurity without any regrets, only a sage is capable of this."[8] Here too the man of action and the contemplative recluse are posited as two extremes and the Mean is defined as lying midway between them. But in this case it is also possible to educe, in addition to this, a slightly different meaning. Since the two extremes in this instance are both quite out of the ordinary, the Mean may, by way of contrast, be conceived of as that which is commonplace and ordinary.

In this sense, the Mean is not something startlingly unusual or special, but the moderate middle of ordinary existence. Zhu Xi is correct in stating in his commentary that "the *yong* of *zhong yong* means normality." *Zhong* and *yong* are, however, rhyming words with the same vowel formation, and when these are combined in a single compound, they assume a similar meaning. Therefore, the emphasis in *zhong yong* is after all on *zhong,* and it may be considered to mean that the state midway between two extremes is by nature endowed with the placidness of everyday normality.

If one pays attention to this aspect of everyday moderation, it becomes clear that the middle between two extremes is not a single fixed and constricted point, rather, it corresponds to the mean as described by Aristotle when he writes that the mean is not necessarily the number six, midway between two and ten, but may vary.[9] In the *Mencius* this elasticity or adaptability is referred to as *quan* 權 and the need for it is stressed: "Even if one holds to the middle, a middle without *quan* is no good."[10] The middle between two extremes is not fixed at a single central point but is an approximate middle that moves while maintaining a balance between two extremes.

The reason for the difficulty of practising the Mean would appear to lie here. A single point at the center would be more explicit and would enable one to establish an unmoving goal for one's practice. The reason that the realization of "sincerity" was emphasized in the latter half of *The Mean* was probably in order to establish a single point and thereby stabilize the goal of practice. An approximate middle is on the contrary, difficult to identify, and there also emerges a tendency to lapse into a spineless opportunism or mugwumpery that is swayed by surrounding circumstances, in which case it is difficult to understand why Confucius should have extolled it. *The Mean* also contains these rather severe words, "The temptations of position and wealth may be declined, even a naked blade may be trod upon, but it is difficult to practise the Mean."[11]

To sum up, the middle between two extremes, inclining neither to the left nor to the right, implies avoiding any proclivity toward either of these two extremes and adhering to the approximate middle. This requires a flexible adaptability. An "approximate middle" is, however, rather vague and lacks concrete attributes. For this reason, there is a great danger that the practice of the Mean will degenerate into fence-straddling compromise and a lack of self-reliance. In order to avoid this pitfall, it is necessary to consider the import of the Mean in greater detail.

A lead for a fresh examination of the Mean is provided by a passage in *The Mean* that describes the government of the sage-king Shun: "Shun loved to question others, and he carefully considered what was said within his hearing. He praised what he thought to be good and concealed what he thought to be bad and grasping these two extremes employed the middle in his government of the people."[12] Special note should be taken of the final words: "grasping (*zhi* 執) these two extremes" means that instead of rejecting them he took firm hold of them. Although it is the middle that is actually adopted in government, it may be assumed that the two extremes are assimilated by and put to good use in this middle. In other words, the middle between two extremes, inclining neither to the left nor to the right, is in fact endowed with the capacity to encompass both the left and the right.

It is with some interest in this regard that one calls to mind the expressions relating to Confucius' personality, to be found in various early texts, as well as other expressions describing the ideal state in which two extremes are integrated into a single whole. On the subject of Confucius' personality, the *Mencius* says, "Confucius did not do anything extreme."[13] This suggests that he was someone who had attained the Mean. Of particular importance in the present context is the statement in *The Analects* that says, "The Master was mild yet stern, majestic yet not fierce, respectful yet at ease."[14] These three phrases consist of pairs of contrary and usually incompatible terms linked by means of the conjunction *er* 而, and they indicate that Confucius' personality was not simple and one-dimensional but united within it mutually conflicting aspects. That he was "mild (*wen* 溫) yet (*er* 而) stern (*li* 厲)" means that Confucius' personality existed on an integrated plane that was neither simply mild nor simply stern but encompassed both aspects. This may be described as the standpoint of the middle that takes into account the two extremes of mildness and sternness, and it facilitates our understanding of the all-encompassing nature of the Mean.

Similar characterizations of Confucius may be found in other works too, but I shall omit these here. Of greater import are the following words from *The Analects*, "Only when refinement (*wen* 文) and simplicity (*zhi* 質) are equally blended does one have a gentleman."[15] This well-known statement attributed to Confucius is preceded by words advising against both inclining toward refinement and inclining toward simplicity. This means that the state of gentlemanliness is one in which the two opposing states of refinement and simplicity are suitably blended to create a well-balanced state of integration. This also tallies with the description of Confucius' personality and clearly accords with the all-encompassing "grasping of two extremes."

When the all-encompassing nature of the Mean is revealed in this manner, it is to be surmised that this middle is not so much a middle lying on a straight line and distinguished from the two extremes of left and right, but is rather a structural middle in which the two extremes of left and right have moved an equal distance toward the center, undergoing a synthetically qualitative rise in the process or creating a vertex as it were.

Let us consider this in terms of a cone. If we link two opposite points on the circumference of its base by means of a straight line passing through the center, we have two extremes and a middle. Any point on the circumference represents one extreme, with its corresponding extreme on the opposite side. By moving toward one another, these two opposites shorten the distance between them and undergo a corresponding qualitative rise, and by rising ever higher they eventually assume the form of a cone-shaped hat. The top of this cone-shaped hat or the vertex of the cone, corresponds to the middle and the opposition that existed at the base has been not rejected but rather assimilated within this middle. Since the base is, moreover, continually moving in accordance with the circumferences, in its capacity as an approximate middle, the middle at the vertex of the cone is also moving flexibly while maintaining the balance of the whole. The all-encompassing nature of the Mean can, I believe, be more readily understood by considering it in terms of a conical structure such as this.

Here I also wish to touch on the nature of special oppositional relationships such as have found general currency in China. Space does not permit me to deal in detail with this subject, but an example may be seen in the *yin* 陰 and *yang* 陽 of *The Book of Changes*. It is true that *yin* and *yang* stand in an oppositional relationship to one another and that they do at times resist and contend with one another. But theirs is basically a relationship in which the existence of one is sustained by the existence of the other, and it is essentially a cooperative relationship. Reference may also be made, in this connection, to the exposition of the relativity of all things described in the second chapter of the *Laozi*: "Something and Nothing produce each other; the difficult and the easy complement each other; the long and the short reveal each other . . ." Generally speaking, contrasts tend to be conceived of not in terms of ultimately contradictory relationships, but rather as things that can basically be reconciled. The idea that through the opposition existing between two opposites a worthwhile result may be attained (*xiang fan xiang cheng* 相反相成) is also related to this way of thinking. Needless to say, the thought of the Mean, encompassing and integrating two extremes, was also born of the same milieu.

Focusing on the all-encompassing and integrative nature of the Mean raises the issue of the relationship between the Mean and the concept of harmony. In China, the middle and harmony have in fact been traditionally conceived of as being closely related to each other. Although considerably postdating the period of original Confucianism, a variant recension of the early dictionary *Shuowen jiezi* (說文解字) dating from the Later Han Period, records the notion that "middle" is "harmony". Examples of similar ideas and commentaries expressing related notions from still later times are also by no means few in number. But why should the "middle" signify "harmony"? In order to understand the subtleties of this logic, it is necessary to examine the theories relating to rites and music that are thought to have developed in the school of Xunzi (荀子) toward the end of the Warring States Period. Rites are explained in connection with the middle, while music is expounded in relation to harmony, and the two are said to cooperate and interrelate to create a single ideal world. These ideas are found expressed in the *Xunzi* and the *Book of Rites* (*Liji* 禮記) and may be considered to date from around the end of the Warring States Period.

"Rites are for establishing the middle."[16] "The sage-kings of ancient times acted in accordance with the middle and this middle corresponded to the rites."[17] This implies that the form assumed by rites is created in accordance with the Mean which inclines to no extreme. Therefore, an active person cannot go beyond the stipulations of the rites, while a passive person cannot but follow them. This corresponds to the "middle" of the rites.[18] The statement in *The Analects* that "As a function of rites harmony is to be prized" also becomes easier to understand if considered in this manner, through the medium of the Mean.[19]

As a function of rites, however, order and differentiation are also emphasized in contrast to the consonance of music: "Music is the harmony of heaven and earth and the rites are the order of heaven and earth. Because of harmony all things follow it, and because of order all things are differentiated . . . Music implements harmony, while rites implement differentiation. Because of harmony people associate with one another, and because of differentiation people respect one another. It is the task of rites and music to adorn the inner spirit and the outer form."[20]

In this division of roles between rites and music, what exactly is meant when rites are identified with differentiation? Unlike the definition of rites as that which "establishes the middle," differentiation would appear to be far removed from the concept of harmony. But this is not in fact the case, for here there is a form of logic according to which division conversely leads to union and harmony is obtained by means of differentiation.

Xunzi expresses this quite clearly, "If distinctions of class are established on the basis of social justice, then the harmony of the whole is achieved, and it is only when harmony is achieved that there is unity and the superior abilities of man are exercised over all things."[21] The original reads literally, "If divided, they harmonize, and if they harmonize, they become one." Xunzi's explanation of this is rather interesting, for he maintains that by establishing distinctions ranging from the Son of Heaven above to the gatekeeper below, each preserves his own lot and manifests his *raison d'être,* and by this means the harmony and development of the whole are achieved. The Son of Heaven cannot monopolize everything just because of his position, and even a gatekeeper enjoys a certain security. If we consider this form of differentiation not as a class system but rather in terms of specific duties or a division of labor, its logic becomes more readily comprehensible to us today. Harmony is achieved through differentiation, and if this is understood then one should have no trouble in understanding what is meant when it is said that rites establish the middle and aim at harmony while exhibiting the function of differentiation.

Let us now consider this in conjunction with the all-encompassing and integrative nature of the Mean examined earlier. By assimilating in the middle, between two opposite extremes, an integrative Mean encompassing both left and right was attained. This may be described as a form of harmony dependent upon differentiation, and it is in fact this conception of harmony that accords with the true meaning of harmony. Let us now consider this in a little more detail.

First we may note the following passage in *The Analects,* "The Gentleman harmonizes with others but does not echo them; the common man echoes others but does not harmonize with them."[22] Harmonizing or agreeing (*he* 和) with others is not the same as echoing (*tong* 同) them, and while harmonizing is admirable, echoing is to be avoided. When people echo one another, they become a homogeneous whole adhering to a single opinion, and although harmony resembles this insofar as everyone is integrated as a single whole, it is in fact suffused with a diversity of opinions. Although the forms assumed by these two types of unity are similar, there is a considerable qualitative difference between them. That which is as one from the outset does not represent harmony; it is only through the commingling of many diverse elements that harmony is produced.

Similar expositions of harmony that are in fact fairly well known may also be found in both the *Zuozhuan* (*Zuo's Commentary on the Spring and Autumn Annals*) and the *Guoyu* (*Conversations of the States*). The passage above is attributed to Yanzi (晏子) of the state of Qi (齊), one of Confucius' senior contemporaries. Having noted that there is a difference between harmonizing and echoing, he describes their relationship in the following manner, "Harmony is similar to soup (*geng* 羹). Soup is made by adding various kinds of seasoning to water and then cooking fish and meat in it. One mixes them all together and adjusts the flavor by adding whatever is deficient and reducing whatever is in excess. It is only by mixing together ingredients of different flavors that one is able to produce a balanced, harmonious taste. One cannot make anything tasty with just water or just salt."[23] He then moves on to the subject of music and states that it is only when various musical instruments producing different sounds intermix and cooperate that the harmony of music is produced. In the *Conversations of the States* there is a noteworthy passage attributed to Shibo (史伯) of the state of Zhou (周): "Harmony produces something new, while echoing does not produce anything new."[24] It is indeed true that if everyone simply echoes the views of a single person, nothing new will come about; it is also only by debating the merits of various divergent viewpoints that new developments are made possible.

True harmony is thus of miscellaneous content, and this must be reflected in the whole. Usually harmony is immediately associated with mutual concession, and it is not uncommon for individual opinions to be silenced for the sake of overall harmony. But this is simply echoing the views of others and might well be described as false harmony. In true harmony, a spirit of concession that gives thought to others and takes the whole into consideration is of course important. At the same time, it is also necessary for a miscellany of entities to exercise their potential in their relations with others, by putting forward their own views and by pitting themselves against and vying with one another. Otherwise, it is impossible to produce a really tasty soup. While making efforts to understand the other party and conceding what must be conceded, one remains true to oneself, and thereby contributes to the harmony of the whole.

It is precisely this kind of harmony that may be said to correspond to the harmony of the Mean. In the context of the Mean, the middle was a middle that existed only on account of the existence of the two mutually opposing extremes. Instead of being rejected, these two extremes were put to good use and assimilated in an all-encompassing manner into the approximate middle, thereby creating a Mean marked by a harmonious structure. The creation of this Mean represents the creation of true harmony. The difficulty of practising the Mean may still remain, but when compared to the difficulties involved in the vagueness and elusiveness of simply choosing the approximate middle, the ideal of overall harmony provides us with a clear objective.

Today we are surrounded by various conflicting questions, and it frequently happens that practical solutions are demanded of us on a daily basis. As a mode of thought for use in resolving these questions, is it not perhaps conceivable that the thought of the Mean in original

Confucianism, which we have considered here, may prove to be of some value? It is true that the thought of the Mean is rather ambiguous in regard to ethical issues. A further weakness, which I have been unable to discuss here, lies in the fact that it represents a worldly and aesthetic ethic (*weltliche, aesthetische Ethik*). But if one abstracts this thought and regards it as a mode of thinking, I believe it has the potential to take on an important role as a practical ethic for the present age.

A mode of being in which opposing parties vie with one another without losing their sense of rivalry and yet recognize the other party and concede what the occasion demands; the stance of remaining true to oneself while pursuing the ideal of overall harmony; the attitude of seeking a stable medium in continually changing circumstances by gathering a wide range of information—in such a composite mode of being is where the essence of the Mean lies. In my view, here is where its great significance for the present day is to be found.

NOTES

1. It gives me great pleasure to dedicate this essay to Professor David S. Nivison in recognition of his numerous achievements in the field of the study of Chinese philosophy.

2. See my *Shin-Kan shisōshi kenkyū* 秦漢思想史研究. (*A Study of the History of Qin-Han Thought*). Tokyo: Nippon Gakujutsu Shinkokai, 1960.

3. *Lunyu* 論語 (*The Analects*) 6.29. *Harvard-Yenching Institute Sinological Index Series* (hereafter *HY*). Supplement no. 16. Reprint. Taiwan: Taipei, 1966.

4. *Lunyu* 20.1.

5. *Lunyu* 13.21.

6. *Zhongyong* 中庸 (*The Doctrine of the Mean*) chap. 4. Cf. James Legge, tr., *The Doctrine of the Mean*. In *The Chinese Classics*. vol. 1. Reprint. Hong Kong: Hong Kong University Press, 1970: 387.

7. *Lunyu* 11.16.

8. *Zhongyong*, chap. 11.

9. See *Nicomachean Ethics* 2.5, 1106a26–1106b8. Terence Irwin tr., Cambridge: Hackett Publishing company, 1985: 42–43.

10. *Mengzi* 孟子 (*The Mencius*) 7A26. *HY*. Supplement no. 17. Reprint. Taiwan: Taipei, 1966.

11. *Zhongyong,* chap. 9.

12. *Zhongyong,* chap. 6.

13. *Mengzi* 4B10.

14. *Lunyu* 7.38.

15. *Lunyu* 6.18.

16. *Liji* 禮記 (*The Book of Rites*), chap. 28, Cf. James Legge, tr., *Li Chi: Book of Rites.* vol. 2. Reprint. New York: University Books 1967: 271.

17. *Xunzi* 荀子 (*The Xunzi*), chap. 8. *HY.* Supplement no. 22. Reprint. Taiwan: Taipei, 1966.

18. For these ideas see *Xunzi,* chap. 19 and *Liji,* chap. 38.

19. *Lunyu* 1.12.

20. *Liji,* chap. 19.

21. *Xunzi,* chap. 9.

22. *Lunyu* 13.23.

23. *Zuozhuan* 左傳 (*The Zuo Commentary*). Book 10; Duke Zhao, 20th year. Cf. *The Ch'un Ts'ew with the Tso Chuen.* James Legge, tr. In *The Chinese Classics,* vol. 5. Reprint. Hong Kong: Hong Kong University Press, 1970: 684.

24. *Guoyu* 國語 (*Conversations of the States*), chap. 16. Shanghai: Guji Publishing Company, 1978.

Women in the Life and Thought of Zhang Xuecheng

Susan Mann

This essay examines the role of women in what I call Zhang Xuecheng's moral imagination. "Moral imagination" refers here to the mental images that came to Zhang's mind when he wrote about women's virtue. Zhang's writing about women was unusually animated, and debates about women's roles inspired him to blistering attacks on contemporaries with whom he disagreed.[1] The animus in Zhang's discussions of "ritual propriety" (*li*), "chastity" (*jie*), or "moral will" (*zhi*) was fed by physical images of women's bodies and women's words and deeds in his moral imagination—images revealed to us in Zhang's own works. Ironically, although Zhang often quoted the classical injunction that "women's words should not pass beyond the inner chambers" (*nei yan buchu men wai*), he wrote intimate accounts of women outside his own household. Every scholar who has written about Zhang has called attention to women who may have shaped his ethical and moral values. But no one has tried to make sense of Zhang's relationships with women as integral parts of his intellectual and emotional life.[2]

Women's compelling hold over men's imagination in Chinese culture has been the subject of numerous scholarly studies.[3] Women were central to the construction of men's emotions, we know, partly because of the close ties between sons and mothers in the Chinese family system. Among the upper classes of the late empire, the structure of the family system combined with intense competition for success in the civil service examinations to intensify the mother-son bond. In elite families, the mother was often her son's earliest teacher, and the impoverished widow would support her son's education with earnings from spinning and weaving. Debts to mother's sacrifice are weighty themes in the biographies of successful Chinese men.[4]

In Zhang Xuecheng's personal experience, women figured in three spheres. Women in his immediate family, especially his mother, were responsible for his earliest scholarly training. Since Zhang was an only son surrounded by sisters, he also enjoyed more sisterly influence in early childhood than was typical in upper-class Chinese families. More important than his immediate female relatives were the women who acted as Zhang's surrogate mothers and sisters, befriending him when he left home to work or study. These women may have found Zhang easy to approach precisely because he was reared among so many sisters. Finally, we have evidence that women played a distinctive symbolic role in the local culture where Zhang grew up, and with which he strongly identified himself.

Female Relatives: Mother and Sisters

David Nivison's intellectual biography of Zhang calls our attention to several women in Zhang's life, all relatives: his mother, his sisters, a paternal aunt, his wife, and his concubines.[5]

Zhang had one elder sister—six years his senior—and (according to Hu Shi) "too many younger sisters to describe in detail." Of these siblings virtually nothing is known. Zhang's paternal aunt, mentioned in the following characteristically brief reference from Nivison's biography, suffered in middle age from a degrading mental illness[6] and does not seem to have played an important role in his life:

> He had no uncles on his father's side and only one aunt, who had married into a family of the Du surname in Kuaiji. The aunt died when he was eleven, but before that time she had occasionally returned to the household to help his mother with the family accounts. In his second or third year, he recalls, when he was learning to talk, his elder sister would carry him around in her arms all day and would amuse him by inducing him to speak.[7]

When Zhang was five *sui*, in 1742, his father Biao won the *jinshi* degree, then spent the next ten years teaching at home in Shaoxing. With his father busy teaching to support the family, Zhang's own earliest instruction was in the hands of his mother, who taught him to read using the rhymed book *One Hundred Family Names* (*Baijia xing*).[8]

Zhang's mother's life was chronicled after her death by Zhang's mentor Zhu Yun (1729–1781) in his "Funeral Ode for the Mother (née Shi) of Zhang Xuecheng."[9] Lady Shi's given name is unknown. She was the ninth child—some sources say the ninth daughter—of Shi Yizun, a scholar-official who once served as prefect of Yingzhou, Anhui. The Shis, like the Zhangs, resided in Kuaiji. For centuries, since Song times, Shis and Zhangs had intermarried, and the union of a gifted youngest daughter with a promising young scion (already a licentiate at the time of wedding) produced clucks of gratification from local wags. So begins Zhu Yun's story.

Stylized though it is, Zhu Yun's funeral ode provides us with some individual detail. Lady Shi was a gifted child, whose reputation in her large lineage (the Shi clan was prominent in Beijing, as well as in their local ambit) caused a younger male relative to exclaim in delight when at last, in the capital, he met his famous "auntie." Her talent as a poet while still a young girl was likened to that of the famous women poets in Xie An's clan, well known for upstaging their male relatives in poetry contests. Despite her talent, however, Zhang's mother professed from an early age only the homely wish to serve. She preferred simple, shortsleeved gowns, the better to tend to household chores and to wait upon her mother-in-law, tasks she was to perform with singleminded devotion.

The best-known story about Zhang's mother concerns the years during Zhang's father's tenure as magistrate of Yingcheng, Hubei, a post from which he was dismissed in 1756, when Zhang was nineteen *sui*:

> He [Zhang Biao] never imprisoned people unjustly, and he never called for troops needlessly. His wife accompanied him to his post, and her words of counsel were always apt. Yet she was modest and never spoke outside the home. Each valued the other as jade, grave and dignified. Every day she saved something from her household accounts. At home she kept a safe box, and the extra cash she would hide there, saying "I am looking out for our future happiness." In 1756 her husband was dismissed from office, and when the official replacing him charged him with embezzlement, she produced a thousand taels to pay off the debt. She was a woman of foresight. She said to him: 'Your humble servant knows you; you would not wish us to be in debt to others.'[10]

Thus Zhang's mother counseled her husband during his term in office, stood by him at the nadir of his career, and—thanks to her frugal investment of the household budget surplus—spared him further public humiliation when he lost his post.

Such images—the wife who sustains the family by skillfully investing meager resources, the wife who offers sage advice to her beleaguered husband—recur in Zhang's own records of women's lives. (Probably, in fact, it was he who told the story about his mother to Zhu Yun.) In Zhang's mother's biography we hear the first sounding of the twin capacities that, in Zhang's view, mark the virtuous woman: practical managerial skills, and moral knowledge.

Zhang's marriage in 1751 was to a young girl who, like the other women in Zhang's family, is known only by her surname, Yu.[11] (We shall explore the significance of this fact later.) At the time of the wedding, both bride and groom were unusually young, Zhang being only fourteen *sui*. His wife's first child, a son named Yixuan, was not born until nine years later, in 1760; a second son, Huafu, arrived five years after that, in 1765. Three years later, in 1768, Zhang had a third son by a concubine née Cai. It is not clear why he took a concubine, although his wife's long birth intervals suggest infrequent sexual intercourse or difficulty conceiving. In any case, the third son, named Huashou, was given in adoption to Zhang's elder paternal cousin Yuanye, whose own wife played a crucial role in Zhang's moral imagination, as we shall see.[12] Yixuan, the eldest son, studied with Zhang's friend Shao Jinhan (1743–1796) and was groomed for the examinations,[13] while Huafu trained to become a legal secretary with Wang Huizu (1731–1807).[14] A second concubine, née Zeng, bore two more sons, Hualian and Huaji.[15]

A single anecdote survives to describe Zhang's wife. At the time of his early marriage, Zhang, a slow learner, had not yet completed his studies of the *Four Books*. Following the wedding he immediately departed to accompany his father to his new official post, where he continued his studies. In his father's yamen, growing restless when he ran out of books to read, Zhang secretly begged from his wife one of her dowry hairpins and some earrings, which he exchanged for brushes and paper. These he gave to the clerks in the yamen, whom he commissioned to spend day and night copying for him the *Spring and Autumn Annals* and its various commentaries, along with the philosophical works and the histories of the late Zhou and Warring States periods.[16]

Like the epitaph for Zhang's mother, this story about Zhang's wife anticipates plots in Zhang's writing about other women in his life. In this case, the common theme is women who sell or pawn their dowry items to provide for a spouse or in-laws. Surviving portraits of these women in Zhang's immediate family are sketchy, nonetheless. Even the flattering memories preserved in Zhu Yun's biography of Zhang's mother pale when compared to Zhang's vivid, often wrenching accounts of other women in his life.

Surrogate Mothers and Sisters

Among women outside his family whom Zhang knew personally, four stand out. Two were older women who became surrogate mothers: the wife of his elder paternal cousin Yuanye, née Xun; and the mother of his friend Shao Jinhan, née Yuan. The other two were younger women whom he treated like sisters: the two daughters—only children—of his elder cousin and Lady Xun.

Zhang wrote long, moving accounts of the two older women's lives. In memory of Lady Xun, he composed a "Factual Record (*xing shi*) of the Deeds of Goodwife Xun."[17] For Lady Yuan, at Shao Jinhan's request, he wrote an epitaph (*muzhiming*).[18] Zhang's two young female cousins are sketched briefly in their mother's biography, but Zhang also compiled a "little biography" for both,[19] and later penned a sad, short funeral ode for his favorite, the younger.[20] These records, drawn from Zhang's memories and from interviews with family members, illustrate womanly virtue with dramatic crises, tart vignettes, even dreams. Peppered with direct quotations and tragic expletives, they also serve as a forum for Zhang's own judgments, by turn worshipful (of his heroines) and scathing (of the men who ruined their lives).

Lady Xun, twenty-three years Zhang's senior, married Zhang's elder cousin on his father's side, Yuanye. In her natal family, she was the youngest and brightest of seven children, reared in luxury as her indulgent parents' favorite. Her husband, alas, proved incapable of managing money and irresponsible about providing for his family's security. In fact, in Zhang's account Lady Xun's conduct serves as a critique of her husband's negligence. Zhang gave one of his own sons in adoption to Yuanye and his wife, to fulfill a wish of Lady Xun's after her death,[21] and to supply the family with an heir since no male off-spring survived.[22]

Residing as they did in Beijing, Lady Xun and her husband regularly hosted the four generations of sojourning Zhang clansmen who were seeking examination degrees or government jobs at the time. As a result, not only did Lady Xun have to cope with demanding parents-in-law, a task at which, we are told, she was unfailingly successful ("they were never displeased"). In addition, she had to stretch her meager household budget to feed and house scores of unpredictable visitors, who sometimes required additional loans to tide them over their stay.

Under these trying circumstances, Zhang Yuanye left the household accounts to his wife. During the worst of the family's travails, it was Lady Xun who figured out how to keep the household afloat. Zhang's admiration for her fortitude, her ingenuity, and her dedication to the Zhang family suffuses his careful record of her role as head of her household. He and his cousins, who spent months of their young and anxious lives relying on her for comfort, wept freely when they shared stories of her memory. As Zhang wrote after she died:

> My visits at her home spanned the course of more than thirty years, from the time my father obtained his *jinshi* degree until I myself became an academy student. The years passed so quickly they seem like a single day. That is how I came to know her so well.[23]

Lady Xun, we are told, was not classically educated. Zhang in fact acknowledges that she was "not terribly at home with books." But she loved popular novels and heroic opera tales, especially stories of faithful widows and loyal ministers who stood fast in the face of great adversity. When she read these books or saw these plays, he recalled, she appeared transported to the scene herself, carried away by their example.

As her husband's fortunes waned, Lady Xun found ways to protect her parents-in-law from the privations the rest of the family had to suffer. When her credit account with the butcher ran out, she pawned jewelry from her dowry so that she could continue to serve them pork with their meals. Zhang found this devotion to her in-laws especially moving. He recalled that as Lady Xun's mother-in-law neared death, she developed an illness that left her unable to open her mouth and chew her food. For six months, Lady Xun rose early to prepare special dishes that would be easily swallowed and digested, and spent hours feeding her mother-in-law bite by bite, carefully opening her mouth and tilting each spoonful between her lips.[24]

As if these trials and tribulations were not enough, Lady Xun's father-in-law had acquired a concubine who took to drinking heavily and cursing as she aged. Lady Xun, Zhang tells us, not only endured this with quiet respect, but later, when the concubine as well grew ill and incontinent, cleaned her body of waste and saw that she was kept comfortable.

At this juncture in his woeful story, Zhang records an amusing aside. The concubine had been a devout Buddhist, but as she lapsed into alcoholism, she abjured her vegetarian vows and began to consume great quantities of meat. Lady Xun's response was to provide the concubine with the meat she craved—and then to abstain from meat herself. "I do this," she said, "to make amends for her profligate behavior." Stressing the magnitude of the gulf separating these two women, Zhang could not resist adding: "She herself [Lady Xun] would have nothing to do with Buddhist teachings. Even when the family was too poor to eat meat, she refused to call herself a vegetarian."[25]

In 1751, when Lady Xun's two girls were tiny (the elder still a toddler, the younger only five months old), her husband Yuanye left her alone with six dependents while he accompanied Zhang's father on a long trip. As her spouse departed with a guilty conscience, he entrusted to her his collection of rare books, with the understanding that if worse came to worst, she could sell them to support the six or seven persons who relied on her for support. In a telling vignette, Zhang describes his cousin's return years later. Yuanye inquired at once about his books. His wife looked him in the eye and said, "I sold them all for food." Rushing out to ask his kinsmen what had happened, Yuanye was mortified to discover that his wife was being ironic. The entire collection was complete and untouched.[26]

Such revealing tales were partly culled from Zhang's own conversations with Lady Xun. "She loved to talk with me," he remembered. She even told Zhang about her dreams. She also found her own dramatic ways to convey her side of the family's story: once she took him aside and wordlessly showed him her old account books.[27] Zhang supplemented these recollections with stories told to him by his cousin Yuanye, who shared his guilty memories with Zhang. The younger daughter also wrote out for him a long and detailed account of her mother's words and deeds.[28] Perusing Zhang's narrative, observing the superior virtues of this noble wife and the moral frailty of her inferior spouse, the reader can only nod grimly when the heroine dies, as her husband weeps bitterly: "How I failed you! How I failed you!"[29]

Zhang also wrote about the unhappy lot of Lady Xun's daughters, revealing that even the wisest mother cannot protect a daughter from an unhappy marriage. Just as Lady Xun's wealthy parents married her into a household where she suffered unexpected privation, so Lady Xun and her husband betrothed their own unfortunate daughters to families who in various ways failed them (in Zhang's words, "they did not get what they deserved" [bude suo yu]).[30]

His account of their lives makes it clear that the girls did not suffer for lack of proper training—indeed, they were "just like their mother" (you mufeng). They were so circumspect in their conduct, in fact, that one relative complained to Zhang that their home reminded him of a monastery. Even Zhang allowed that the girls' upbringing had perhaps been too strict.[31] He first met them in Beijing in 1760, when the elder was about 14 years old, and the younger just over ten. At the time he noticed that "although they were reared in the women's quarters, they act just like students in a classroom."[32]

When Zhang returned to Beijing five years later, the elder was already married to a widower named Hu as a "successor wife" [jishi]. Her husband was from a wealthy family engaged in the salt trade. The young bride had to rear a daughter from Hu's first marriage as well as supervise a concubine kept by her husband, while caring for his aging parents. She was so devoted and so scrupulous in her conduct that her in-laws found her comical, and said so.

Miserable in her new life, and separated from her parents by some distance when her husband moved, she was resolutely cheerful on her annual visits home. No one guessed at her unhappiness until after her death in childbirth when she was just past twenty years of age, when her personal maid visited her natal family with tales of her dedication as a daughter-in-law and her silent suffering as an isolated wife.[33] The maid told her parents, for example, that when her in-laws laughed at her mistress for her exaggerated devotion to proper conduct, her young mistress would reply: "I am far from my parents. If I dare to be disrespectful, it will cause them grief." After she died the Hus, a contentious lot, may have had second thoughts, for Zhang records that they finally agreed on one thing: the virtues of their late daughter-in-law.[34]

In 1768 Lady Xun died grieving for her elder daughter,[35] and a year later the younger daughter was hurriedly married, at the age of twelve, to a young man surnamed Zhao. Zhang's initial appraisal of this match was positive, he tells us. The Zhao family had been farmers for generations, and the prospective groom was the first in the family to obtain an education, having already won a licentiate degree. When Zhang met the young man before the marriage, he congratulated Lady Xun and her husband on finding such a good match for their daughter. "He seemed so educable," Zhang recalled.[36]

The groom, Zhao Guotai, entered the Zhang household following Lady Xun's death as a resident son-in-law, which allowed his young wife to continue supervising her father's household in her late mother's place.[37] Just at that time, Zhang Xuecheng brought his own mother with him to Beijing. He was delighted to watch the young bride treat his mother like her own grandmother, waiting on her hand and foot and "anticipating her every wish."[38]

Not long afterward, the Zhao family came upon hard times and called their son and his wife home, after which the younger daughter's life grew increasingly miserable. The Zhaos took charge of her dowry, selling it off quickly in an effort to salvage their declining fortunes. Eventually the Zhaos' situation grew so desperate that the girl could no longer return home to take care of her father, so she arranged the purchase of a concubine who could tend to his needs. On her rare visits to see him, her father noted her shabby dress with concern, but when questioned she refused to complain.

Zhang happened to spend three days with the Zhaos during a trip north in 1775. By then his young cousin's health had failed, and she could be heard coughing day and night, though even illness could not dull her joy upon seeing him. At that point, Zhang remembered, it had been two years since she had been able to visit her own father. During a subsequent visit, as her health deteriorated, she confided to

Zhang that her husband had abandoned his scholarly career, though she was hopeful that her father's admonitions might once again put him on the right path, which would enable her at least to die in peace. Within a few months, she was dead.

In his biography of the Zhang girls, Zhang remarked caustically that the Zhaos, who had often visited the Zhangs with requests for help during his young cousin's lifetime, never bothered to notify Zhang kinsmen of her death. "They were that inhuman, that benighted!" he exclaimed.[39] Contemptuously Zhang recalled that when his young cousin tried to establish an ancestral shrine in the Zhao household in order to conduct spring and autumn sacrifices before the ancestral tablets, her husband's relatives—incredibly—laughed at her: "They did not even know their ancestors!" Repulsed by her husband's vulgarity, and ridiculed for her beliefs, Zhang's young cousin died isolated and alone. The final insult was yet to come, however, when after her death her husband was heard making crude remarks about her to outsiders.[40]

Not all of Zhang's ideal women were hapless mates of unworthy men. One of the four, Shao Jinhan's mother, née Yuan, is the case in point. A learned person, she was married to a man who shared her interests and matched her talent. Zhang came to know her well because the Zhangs and the Shaos had longstanding personal ties, and as a close friend of Shao Jinhan, he visited frequently at her home ("which is why," said Jinhan, "I am asking you to write about my mother; you know my family so well").[41]

Lady Yuan was descended on her mother's side from the Lüs of Yuyao county, east of Shaoxing. Her ancestor Lü Zhangcheng had served at the exiled Ming court in Kuaiji, fraternizing as a young man with illustrious Ming loyalists including Gu Yanwu. Her own father, Yuan Susheng, had compiled Lü Zhangcheng's collected works. So when the young Yuan daughter was married into the learned Shao family, both sides exulted that once again "marriage bonds served to deepen scholarly ties."[42]

Lady Yuan's husband, Shao Jiayun, was a licentiate from Ciqi county in Ningbo prefecture, adjacent to Yuyao.[43] The young bride's father-in-law had been reared from the age of seven by his mother, a faithful widow, who died before the wedding could take place. After the mourning period was completed and the wedding ceremony could be held, her father-in-law wept that his mother had not lived to see the entry of such an illustrious young woman into his son's home: "This new wife will surely make our family greater," he said through his tears.[44]

The most remarkable thing about the family into which Lady Yuan married was this unusual pairing of scholarly pedigrees. In a verbal family portrait, Zhang paints the Shao children gathered at their mother's knees while she kept her husband company reading late into the night.[45] Although Lady Yuan professed not to understand the great books, deferring to her spouse as the children's teacher, after a drink or two she could rise to the intellectual occasion, retelling tales of Ming history she had learned sitting at her own mother's feet.[46] Zhang comments, in a pointed reference to Lü Zhangcheng, "Although her stories were 'family tales' (*jia yu*), all had a basis in fact; they were far from hearsay."[47]

Lady Yuan reared her children strictly. To teach them discipline, she would hang out a basket filled with fruits and buns and beat the child who ate more than his or her share. She told them: "Spoiled children who eat whatever they like grow up to be untrustworthy."[48] But her sharp advice was not reserved for her children alone. Like the other women Zhang admired, Lady Yuan had keen foresight, and her clear vision and common sense saved her husband from more than one crucial political misstep.[49] She had other talents too: she brought a dowry of ten *mu* to her marriage and increased it tenfold by the time she died.[50] She was the perfect combination: mistress of household management, transmitter of historical knowledge—truly, Zhang wrote, a woman in the tradition of Liu Xiang and Ban Zhao.[51]

Together the stories of these four women give us a clear sense of what Zhang meant when, throughout his long essay on women's learning (*Fu xue*), he stressed that the most important thing for a woman to learn was ritual propriety (*li*), not poetry.[52] To fully realize their moral capacities as women, all of these women had to understand and undertake the full complement of Confucian family roles, from daughter to wife to mother and daughter-in-law. In those roles women, not men, became the persons responsible for the welfare, survival, and prosperity of the descent line. Erudition was not essential to play such a role well; poetry was beside the point. Such women made their impact on the public realm through their management of the inner domestic sphere. At best, anything more "public" would have been superfluous; at worst, a woman distracted from her domestic responsibilities by "public" pursuits compromised the welfare of those most dependent on her care and advice: spouse, children, and in-laws.

Local Culture and Women's Roles

There is some evidence that Zhang derived his ideal women's roles from norms touted in the local culture where he grew up. The Shao family, including Shao Jinhan's mother, Lady Yuan, was heir to Zhang's own intellectual culture: the tradition associated with the region Zhang called "Eastern Zhejiang," or Zhedong.[53]

By "Zhedong" he meant the area south and east of the Qiantang River. Its major center was the town of Shaoxing, but the region extended through the counties of Shanyin, Kuaiji (Zhang's own birthplace), Yuyao, and Ciqi, to the hinterland of Ningbo, home of Quan Zuwang and other leaders of what Zhang called the "Zhedong school." To the north and west of the Qiantang lay Zhexi ("West of the Zhe"), reaching from Hangzhou into towns and cities of the Yangzi delta, including Jiaxing and crossing into Jiangsu province through Suzhou and Changzhou.

The difference between Zhedong and Zhexi culture was once summed up by the late Qing scholar Li Ciming (1830–1894), like Zhang a native of Kuaiji:

> Our Zhe area is divided into two regions, east and west. The mountains and rivers in each are not the same, and the climates also differ. Thus the literary culture nourished in west and east differs as well, along similar lines.

Citing an earlier work, Li characterized the scholars of Zhexi as *xiu er wen*—"refined and cultivated"—and the scholars of Zhedong as *shun er pu*—"pure and simple."[54]

In an essay written in 1800 on which Li's comments were undoubtedly based,[55] Zhang pointedly contrasted the intellectual heritage of the two regions. Zhexi was heir to the legacy of Gu Yanwu, Zhedong to that of Huang Zongxi. In Zhexi the emphasis was on "breadth and elegance" (*bo ya*), while Zhedong scholars valued specialized studies (*zhuan men*). The Zhexi school derived its premises from the teachings

of Zhu Xi; the Zhedong school honored Lu Jiuyuan and Wang Yang-
ming. In Zhexi, scholars preferred to conduct research on philology
and textual verification; in Zhedong, the focus of scholarship was history and "statecraft" (*jingshi*).

Although no specific codes for women's conduct can be attributed
to "simple" Zhedong culture, Zhang's observations about women
reveal strong objections to the high "public" visibility of women in the
literary culture of the Zhexi region.[56] Quite possibly flagrant differences in local norms governing women's conduct lay at the heart of
Zhang's conviction that Zhedong was "simple" when compared to
Zhexi.

It would be unwise to press these distinctions too far, however.
David Nivison has suggested that Zhang's intellectual temper fit more
squarely with the literary values of the Tongcheng writers than with the
philosophical values of the so-called Zhedong school, if such a thing
actually existed. Affinities with Tongcheng thinkers are apparent in
Zhang's views on women, many of which would certainly have been
shared by the Tongcheng leader Fang Bao. Perhaps it would be more
accurate to say that a combination of native-place identity, intellectual
affinity, and personal networks shaped Zhang's views on women and
the arguments he picked about them.[57]

In any case, his views on women were compatible with Tongcheng
scholarly teachings, and sharply antagonistic to the Zhexi style.
Zhang's ideal woman exemplified the simplicity and purity he associated with Zhedong culture: she remained cloistered within the inner
apartments, devoted to classical ritual obligations, and untainted by
the pursuit of public fame that pervaded the Zhexi region.[58] In Zhedong, educated women were perhaps no less common than they were
in Zhexi, but they were less often known outside their families and
their virtues, as Zhang would approvingly note, were confined to the
home.[59]

A dramatic emblem of the importance of cloistering women within
the "inner apartments," which may have been the preferred custom in
the area he called Zhedong, appears in women's naming practices in
Zhang's own descent line. In striking contrast to the practice common
in Zhexi, especially among Yuan Mei's circle, the given names of
Zhang's female relatives are all unknown. Every source recording the
history of Zhang's family, including the most intimate eulogies, refers

to these women only by surname, using the honorific *shi,* "of the XX lineage," translated in this essay as "Lady."

These naming practices send important signals for two reasons, as Rubie Watson has pointed out. First, a given name, and especially a literary and an intimate name, is a particular mark of social identity in Chinese culture. A name was used to mark transitions in the life cycle; to convey social meaning (assigning the bearer to a generation in the lineage, for example); to confer magical power, when selected to compensate for some deficiency in a child's horoscope, for instance; and to express a literary persona. Thus, to be nameless in Chinese society was to be deprived of social or "public" identity.[60] For Zhang, women's names had precisely this significance, and naming became a symbolic arena for debating the issues of women's public identity and domestic roles.

Debates with Wang Zhong and Yuan Mei

Zhang's personal experiences with women in his life help to explain some of the more puzzling aspects of his antagonistic relationship with two of his contemporaries, Wang Zhong and Yuan Mei. Zhang's debates with the latter have drawn the most attention, with Yuan Mei commonly seen as the liberated patron of women's letters, Zhang as the straight-laced moralist bent on returning women to their homely duties.[61] But as Nivison recognized, Zhang's views about women were considerably more complicated than that. If we wish to understand where Zhang stood with respect to women's roles, we must keep returning to his moral imagination, asking how we can make intellectual and emotional sense of his views. To illustrate, let us examine two small and less well known arguments that appear in Zhang's attacks on Wang Zhong and Yuan Mei.[62] In each, Zhang's personal experience with women makes his stance more intelligible.

One of Zhang's major sorties in his attack on Yuan Mei was an essay criticizing Yuan's *Poetry Talks* (*Shi hua*). In this essay, in a seeming nonsequitur, Zhang departs from his discussion of literary genres and attacks Yuan for "giving names" to women poets. He reviles Yuan for bandying those names about publicly, as if a name were an identity so revealing that in respectable families, it should not be known abroad. On first reading, this appears to be merely an extreme extension of

Zhang's insistence that women's speech should not pass beyond the women's quarters:

> What women say within the home should not pass beyond the inner apartments. Yet in his poetry notes, Yuan Mei gives these women names of his own making, noising them about with great fanfare, but whether what he says is fact or fiction, I have no way of knowing.[63] [A note here adds: "How can a poetry commentary obtain this kind of detailed information about women? Really, it borders on the perverse!"]

Zhang then continues:

> "A man's name is broadcast like arrows all over the country; how can one keep a secret of a name written out in the poetry notes!" (*Zhangfu xingzi, gushi si fang; shi hua suo ming, qi neng zhong mi!*)

Placing this confusing passage in the larger context of Zhang's personal experience, however, recalls the importance of naming women in Zhedong culture, and in Zhang's own family. The argument about naming speaks to Zhang's moral imagination, flagging other concerns: his concern about women who travel beyond the home to consort with men instead of serving the families who need them, for instance; or his conviction that women can be good advisors because they are protected from the corruption of the public world. In order to make sense of Zhang's intellectual criticism here, in other words, we must look to his moral imagination.[64]

If we turn to Zhang's other *bête noir*, Wang Zhong, we find again that key arguments between Zhang and Wang concerning women's roles make better sense in light of Zhang's personal experience with the women in his life. Zhang attacked Wang's essay titled "A Critical Opinion on Female Suicide Following the Death of a Fiancé and on Widow Chastity" (Nüzi xu jia er xu si congsi ji shouzhi yi),[65] in which Wang criticized the principle of wifely fidelity (*jie*), a womanly virtue that had become a veritable state cult in Zhang's day. The tightly argued essay charged that blind obedience to the chastity norm encouraged by the state and honored in contemporary society was in fact based on a distorted understanding of the original meaning of classical texts. By a careful investigation of the *Book of Rites*, Wang demonstrated that a wife's lifelong obligation to her husband did not begin until the marriage ceremony, and that betrothal was not to be regarded as a lifelong commitment if other circumstances intervened.

The essay singles out for criticism women who are taught from childhood that once betrothed to a man, they must never break the commitment:

> Marriage rites are completed with the ceremony of *qinying*, during which the bride is received by her new husband's parents. In later times people have not understood this, and so they have stressed instead the importance of the ceremony *shoupin*, during which the bride's family receives betrothal gifts. I have in mind certain cases, such as the case of Yuan Mei's younger sister, who was betrothed as a child to a man named Gao, and the maid of Zheng Huwen, who was betrothed as a girl to a man named Guo. In both cases the young men to whom they were engaged fell into bad company and did not become good sons, such that after ten years had passed the parents of both sides agreed to call off the engagement and make other plans. In each case, however, the young girls themselves resolved to remain faithful to their original marital agreement and could not be persuaded to change their minds. For years Yuan Mei's sister was brutally beaten by her husband, who finally sold her. Only after her elder brother brought a law suit was she returned to her natal family, where she died. The Zheng maid's husband insulted her so grievously (*jiong*) that she swallowed poison and died. In the *Analects* it says: "To love benevolence without loving learning is liable to lead to foolishness (*qi bi ye yu*)."[66] We may call such women as these foolish. They knew nothing of the rites yet they believed themselves to be preserving the rites, to the point where they lost their lives (*yun qi sheng*)—how pitiful! Tradition teaches that "A woman who is wife to one person should take no other for the rest of her life." This is not the same as saying once you have received betrothal gifts you may take no others for the rest of your life. Tradition also holds that "A virtuous woman does not serve two husbands." But this is not to say that one cannot receive betrothal gifts from two persons.[67]

Zhang's response to this, as Hu Shi once observed, seems absurdly out of proportion to Wang's own restrained tone. Zhang raged that Wang was either mad (*sang xin*), shameless, or crazy. Conceding "it is true that we cannot find injunctions in the classics charging a betrothed young woman whose affianced spouse dies to 'preserve her chastity' or 'follow him in death,'" and acknowledging that "the practice of suicide by bereaved fiancées may even have been criticized by early Confucians as not in accordance with the rites," Zhang went on:

> But we cannot claim that the injunctions that inspire these suicides subvert proper human relationships . . . When Wang Zhong invokes the rites to discredit this practice and slander it, he is not only deluded, but shameless; his behavior is comparable to madness, as if he had said to himself that he would preserve the teachings of this world without realizing that he was doing violence to their true meaning and significance. . . . Even if a young woman who remains faithful to someone without ever being married to him is not following the true Way, the meaning of what she is doing is very close to it. Why should Wang attack it so bitterly?

Here again, as in his attack on Yuan Mei, Zhang appears to fly off on an emotional tangent. But his views gain coherence if we recall the women in Zhang's life, especially his ill-fated young cousins. Remembering their stories, we can understand Zhang's scorn for Wang's scholarly and literal reading of classical injunctions. Zhang's moral imagination saw *li* as a code embodied by living women who interpreted it in the broadest sense possible within the circumstances of their lives. What he admired in women was their intuitive ability to sense what they ought to do in every demanding situation, and to act on it with alacrity, competence, and consummate grace. The demands were overwhelming, the toll was enormous, yet their capacity to meet the demands and absorb the toll appeared to him to be infinite. A mere text could hardly specify the range of deeds that women who truly understood the rites would be called upon to perform, or the virtues they might unexpectedly display.

Practical considerations derived from Zhang's personal experience with women may also figure in his reading of classical texts on women's roles. Zhang was aware that few women escaped suffering in marriage. Even what promised to be a good marriage might turn sour if fate intervened, and no one could set it right. Zhang may also have reasoned that a young woman once betrothed would be unlikely to find an optimal marriage partner should she seek a second betrothal. Like his young cousin who married into the Hu family, such a woman might become a successor wife forced to live in loneliness.

Women in the Historical Record

Having reviewed Zhang's arguments about women in the new light of his moral imagination, let us briefly turn to his views on women in the historical record, views that were also deeply influenced by his personal experiences with the women in his life. As Nivison has pointed out, in compiling the local history of Yongqing county, Hebei (between 1778–1779), Zhang paid special attention to biographies of living women:

> Those who were selected for the honor of inclusion in his history he interviewed personally, often sending carriages to bring them to the yamen to tell their life stories. In this way he sought—he felt successfully—to introduce variety and human interest into these more or less obligatory accounts of feminine virtue.[68]

There can be no doubt that Zhang's fascination with the stories women told, and his skill at drawing their stories out, stem from his formative years of conversation and intimacy with the women in his life. But much more was involved than storytelling. Given his intimate knowledge of the inner side of women's lives, Zhang had no use for the narrowly stereotyped ideals of womanhood honored in imperial commendations and reproduced in standard histories and local gazetteers. So, for instance, in his preface to a eulogy for one extraordinary woman, he complained that whereas unusual women's actual lives display an enormous range of virtue, the biographies that chronicle those lives rarely celebrate anything but chastity:

> What of the clever spouse who is companion to her husband? Or the wise mother who teaches her son? Or the far-sighted wife who sustains the family? Women like these are praised to the skies in surviving memoirs, but history books relegate them all to the same short section. How are we to unearth their hidden virtues and display their obscure deeds to influence those who will come later?[69]

Zhang's own treatment of exemplary women, not surprisingly, portrays women in diverse roles. He took care that women of talent found a place in the panoply of women's biographies, telling their stories with the same admiration he reserved for Lady Yuan, especially their ability to provide intellectual companionship for a spouse.[70] Most notably, Zhang took women seriously as historians in their own right. As we see in his memoir for Lady Yuan, the "family tales" (*jia yu*) to which women were privy often made them the primary transmitters of historical records when men died or were incapacitated. Zhang celebrated such women in his essay on women's learning, when he praised Ban Zhao and others who conveyed what they had learned in the inner apartments to the public realm where learning had been extinguished. Recalling that for Zhang, the historian was the scholar whose "words are everyone's" (*yan gong*),[71] we can now see that from Zhang's point of view, a woman was as capable as a man of speaking "public" language. The inner quarters were the sanctuary where women in the family sustained the pure Dao, free from the corruption that overwhelmed upright men.

In the concluding paragraph of his biography of Zhang Xuecheng, David Nivison reflects on the challenge of intellectual biography, musing that while some of his conclusions might anger Zhang, one thing would have pleased him: "I have tried to understand him as a man." Zhang would also be pleased, I think, with the proposition that we can understand him even better if we pay attention to the women in his life.

NOTES

1. See Nivison 1966, 262–67; Mann 1992.

2. In a recent book, Patricia Ebrey (1991) has demonstrated the close connections between personal emotional experience and the writing of ritual texts.

3. Some studies have emphasized men's morbid fascination with women's suffering. In a profusely documented monograph, T'ien Ju-k'ang (1988) has argued that in Fujian during Ming and Qing times, men displaced the anxiety caused by pressures to pass the exams and the frustration resulting from repeated failures by displacing their feelings onto the bodies of suffering

women, especially widow suicides. In a somewhat different vein, Kang-i Sun Chang (1991), among others, has dramatized the link between men's commitment to loyalism and women's sacrifice in the late Ming. See also Elvin (1984); Wakeman (1985, II:943, 1118, 1123); Mann (1987).

4. This argument has been made for both elite and peasant families. In Hsiung Ping-chen's studies of childrearing in the late imperial upper class, mothers are self-sacrificing teachers and moral exemplars who pass on to their young sons powerful debts of gratitude and heavy burdens of responsibility. (See Hsiung, 1994.) Literati memoirs often protest that whatever a man may have achieved in his lifetime is all due to his mother's sacrifice, labor, and encouragement—a self-conscious evocation of the story of the young Mencius and his mother. Margery Wolf, using data from a Taiwan village study, revealed the mother's perspective on this intense bond, citing the vulnerability and isolation of young brides in the marital family, and their need to secure their future power and emotional sustenance by bearing and bonding with sons (Wolf 1972).

5. Hiromu Momose's biography of Zhang in *ECCP* mentions no women at all, but most accounts of Zhang's life refer to several women. Hu Shi's classic biography, annotated by Yao Mingda, alludes to women in Zhang's family and to writings by Zhang about women he knew. Paul Demiéville's sketch of Zhang's life recounts an incident involving his very young wife that I discuss below.

6. *Yishu* 28/16b–17a.

7. Nivison 1966, 22.

8. Hu/Yao 1931, 5.

9. Zhu Yun 1936, 327–28.

10. Quoted in Hu/Yao 1931, 8; see Zhu Yun 1936, 327.

11. Nivison 1966, 23; Hu/Yao 1931, 6.

12. Nivison 1966, 27.

13. Nivison 1966, 86.

14. Nivison 1966, 251.

15. Nivison 1966, 102 n. "el."

16. Hu/Yao 1931, 6–7. This story is recounted in English in Demiéville 1961, 171.

17. *Yishu* 20/28a–33a.

18. *Yishu* 16/68b–72a.

19. *Yishu* 20/16a–18b.

20. *Yishu* 23/44a–45b.

21. *Yishu* 20/32a.

22. Lady Xun herself bore seven children, but the first, a son, died in infancy, and none of the next four, all girls, survived. Only the last-born, the two girls Zhang came to cherish, grew to adulthood. See *Yishu* 20/32a.

23. *Yishu* 20/28b.

24. *Yishu* 20/29a.

25. *Yishu* 20/29a–b. Zhang appears here to dramatize the fact that Lady Xun was a strict Confucian moved only by her benevolence to aid the superstitious concubine. Of course, whether Lady Xun would have given the incident the same reading is another question.

26. *Yishu* 20/29b, 30b.

27. *Yishu* 20/30a.

28. *Yishu* 20/32b, 31b.

29. *Yishu* 20/31b.

30. *Yishu* 20/16a.

31. *Yishu* 20/31b.

32. *Yishu* 20/16a.

33. *Yishu* 20/16b.

34. *Yishu* 20/31b.

35. *Yishu* 20/17a.

36. *Yishu* 20/17a.

37. This fact increased the odds that the unfortunate Zhang girl would have a less desirable mate, uxorilocal marriage being the preserve of upwardly mobile young men from families of lower status.

38. *Yishu* 20/17a.

39. *Yishu* 20/17b–18a.

40. Zhang termed this "nauseating" (*Yishu* 20/18a).

41. *Yishu* 16/68b–69a.

42. *Yishu* 16/68a.

43. *Yishu* 16/69a.

44. *Yishu* 16/69b.

45. *Yishu* 16/70a–b.

46. *Yishu* 16/70b.

47. *Yishu* 16/70b.

48. *Yishu* 16/70b.

49. *Yishu* 16/71a.

50. *Ibid.*

51. *Yishu* 16/71a–b.

52. Mann 1991.

53. Nivison 1966, 278–79.

54. Li Ciming, *Yueman tang wenji* 2/12b. On Li Ciming, see *ECCP,* 493.

55. "Zhedong xueshu" (The scholarship of Eastern Zhejiang), in *Wen shi tongyi* 1964, 51–53.

56. Intellectual historians Yu Yingshi and Qian Mu have noted that Zhang himself at times appeared reluctant to contrast the intellectual heritage of the two regions too starkly, and that the dichotomies he drew are difficult to defend when closely analyzed. See the literature reviewed in He 1991. A description in English of the Zhe schools appears in Elman 1981; see also Demiéville 1961, 169–70. In her detailed study of leading Zhedong scholars, including Quan Zuwang, Lynn Struve has singled out the following traits of the region's intellectual culture: "(1) philosophical independence, (2) a related tendency to find middle ground between Cheng-Zhu and Lu-Wang positions on learning, (3) erudition and scholarly achievement, and (4) resistance to political cooptation, especially during turmoil and alien conquest" (Struve 1988, 116). The last is a particularly important element in Zhedong thought that seems related to at least some of Zhang Xuecheng's own fascination with women's moral conviction. Struve suggests that we might read the Zhedong cultural heritage as one that valorizes women's devotion to virtue in the face of corrupt politics. Certainly this is one important theme in Zhang's writing about women. At the same time, Nivison has noted that whereas emotionally or intuitively Zhang may have identified with Wang Yangming, intellectually and philosophically he preferred the teachings of Zhu Xi (Nivison 1966, 276), in part because he was, in Nivison's words, a "moral conservative."

57. Nivison 1966, 277. Tongcheng was home to a particular school of Zhu Xi Confucianism whose major spokesman was Fang Bao. Fang Bao's views on women are not well known, but he drew criticism in the eighteenth century from Wang Zhong for an essay arguing that women's tablets should not be installed in ancestral shrines. Wang Zhong, a native of Jiangdu in Yangzhou prefecture, and a disciple of Gu Yanwu's thought, was one of Zhang's two most bitter opponents in his debates over women's roles. (See Chow 1986).

58. It must be noted that however "conservative" the Shaoxing area was with respect to women and their conduct, its claim to "simple values" was belied by its fame as a homeland for the empire's most flagrant pettifoggers. Shaoxing as early as the seventeenth century was known for its "shyster" legal experts, and in the late eighteenth century a Jesuit resident in China called Shaoxing natives "the greatest adepts in chicanery of any in China" (quoted in Cole 1986, 10). Hu Shi and Yao Mingda even play with this association by at one point referring to Zhang's tone in his essay on women's learning as the "twisted talk of a Shaoxing shyster" (*Shaoxing shiye*) (Hu/Yao 1931, 130). (See Cole 1986, 9 *et passim* for a discussion of the term and its connotations.) Perhaps one could argue that the complex interplay between Huang Zongxi's

elite intellectual legacy and Shaoxing commoners' legal chicanery fueled the strongly moralistic flavor of Shaoxing's public culture.

59. An analysis of Hu Wenkai's list of women writers shows nine counties in Qing times that surpassed all others in claiming women writers as native daughters. All are Zhexi counties. Figures show the total number of writers from each county and then estimate that number as a percentage of the total number of Qing women writers whose place of birth can be identified. The tenth county on the list, falling far short of Zhexi standards but still demonstrating high levels of female erudition, is Shaoxing, with 72 women writers, or 2.3 percent of the total 3184 women writers for whom native place is known.

TABLE 1

County	No. writers	% of total
Qiantang	276	8.6
Changzhou	213	6.7
Wu xian	148	4.7
Jiaxing	132	4.1
Changshu	106	3.3
Haining	96	3.0
Wuxing	94	3.0
Wujiang	91	2.9
Songjiang	86	2.7

60. Rubie Watson's analysis of naming practices in a Hong Kong village (Watson 1986) focuses on gender hierarchies, but I would argue that in the eighteenth century, naming practices were more likely to reflect regional differences or local custom, within the circle of highly educated upper-class women. In Zhexi households like that of Zhang Qi, for example, a common character (*ying* 英) was used in the name of each of the four daughters, following a custom generally reserved for boys in Watson's study (see *ECCP*, 26). Each daughter also had her own "marriage name" or *zi*, which she retained and used after marriage, unlike the peasant women in Watson's study who, if they had a name at all, ceased to use it upon marriage (Watson 1986, 627). Watson associates naming with other ceremonial markers of the life cycle, and notes that women have few rites of passage (Watson 1986, 627–28).

61. See especially Chen (1977, 270) *et passim*. Nivison (1966, 264–66) takes a more complex view.

62. On Zhang's debates with Yuan Mei, see Hu/Yao 1931, 129–31, and works cited therein.

63. For the passage in question, see *Wen shi tongyi* 1964, 159: *Funü neiyan buchu kun wai, shi hua wei zhi si li mingzi, piaopang shengqi, wei xu wei shi, wu bu de er zhi ye.*

64. Not all women writers had given names. Of the total 3,557 Qing women writers listed in Hu Wenkai's survey, nearly ten percent (351) are identified only by surname, as XX *shi.* In fact the number of "nameless" women writers was higher than ten percent, since this figure excludes those whose given name is a sobriquet such as "virtuous daughter" (*zhennü*) and not a proper name at all. In many cases, an otherwise nameless woman may be identified as a particular man's wife or daughter.

65. Wang Zhong (1960), *neibian* 1/14a–15b.

66. *Analects* 17/8. I have followed the translation by D. C. Lau (1979, 144). My thanks to Philip J. Ivanhoe for reminding me of this allusion.

67. Wang Zhong (1960), *nei bian* 1/15b. Quoted in Hu/Yao 1931, 117; see also Chow 1986, 307. Waley (1956, 36–38) discusses this essay, since one of the cases Wang cites involves the tragic misalliance of Yuan's younger sister; c.f. Nivison 1966, 262, n. j.

68. See Nivison 1966, 83. The *lienü* section of the Yongqing gazetteer begins on 12/12b of Zhang's "outer writings" (*waibian*) in his collected works. See *Yishu waibian* 12/12b–93b. Zhang's biographers all recount his eagerness to conduct investigations on the spot when preparing local gazetteers, especially when this required that he go to call personally on widows and virtuous women whose biographies were to be included. See Demiéville (1961, 175), citing Hu/Yao (1931, 43, 76).

69. *Yishu* 16/74b.

70. Zhang's biographies of talented women appear in *Yishu* 30/108b–111b. Zhang wrote a preface for the collected poems of the wife of his friend Cai Xun (1729–1788), which Nivison says reveals "a rather conservative view of the place of women in a man's world" (Nivison 1966:86–87). But once we understand how Zhang saw a learned woman's place in a man's world, it is more difficult to call his view "conservative." For Cai Xun's wife, see *Yishu* 23/33a;29/9–10.

71. Nivison 1966, 127–33.

REFERENCES

Beattie, Hilary J. 1979. *Land and Lineage in China: A Study of T'ung-Ch'eng County, Anhwei, in the Ming and Ch'ing Dynasties.* Cambridge: Cambridge University Press.

Chang, Kang-i Sun. 1991. *The Late-Ming Poet Ch'en Tzu-lung: Crises of Love and Loyalism*. New Haven: Yale University Press.

Chen, Dongyuan 陳東原 1977. *Zhongguo funü shenghuo shi* 中國婦女生活史 (History of the lives of Chinese women). Orig. ed. 1928. Reprinted Taibei: Shangwu yinshu guan.

Chow, Kai-wing. 1986. "Scholar and Society: The Textual Scholarship and Social Concerns of Wang Chung (1745–1794)." *Hanxue yanjiu* 4, no. 1 (1986): 297–312.

Cole, James H. 1986. *Shaohsing: Competition and Cooperation in Nineteenth-Century China*. Tucson: University of Arizona Press.

Demiéville, Paul. 1961. "Chang Hsüeh-ch'eng and His Historiography." In W. G. Beasley and E. G. Pulleyblank, eds., *Historians of China and Japan*, 167–85. London: Oxford University Press, 1961.

Ebrey, Patricia Buckley. 1991. *Confucianism and Family Rituals in Imperial China: A Social History of Writing about Rites*. Princeton: Princeton University Press.

ECCP see Hummel

Elman, Benjamin. 1981. "Ch'ing Dynasty 'Schools' of Scholarship," *Ch'ing-shih wen-t'i* 4, no. 6 (1981):1–44.

Elman, Benjamin A. 1990. *Classicism, Politics, and Kinship: The Ch'ang-Chou School of New Text Confucianism in Late Imperial China*. Berkeley: University of California Press.

Elvin, Mark. 1984. "Female Virtue and the State in China." *Past and Present* 104:111–52.

He, Guanbiao 何冠彪. 1991. "Qingdai 'Zhedong xuepai' wenti pingyi" 清代「浙東學派」問題評議 (A critical assessment of the controversy surrounding the Zhedong school of scholarship). In *Mingmo Qingchu xueshu sixiang yanjiu* 明末清初學術思想研究 (Studies of scholarship and thought in the late Ming and early Qing period). Taibei: Taiwan xuesheng shuju.

Hsiung, Ping-chen. 1994. "Constructed Emotions: The Bond Between Mothers and Sons in Late Imperial China," *Late Imperial China* 15.1: 87–117.

Hu, Shi 胡適. 1931. *Zhang Shizhai xiansheng nianpu* 章實齋先生年譜 (Yearly chronicle of the life of Zhang Shizhai [Xuecheng]). Expanded and amplified by Yao Mingda. Shanghai: Shangwu yinshu guan.

Hu, Wenkai 胡文楷. 1985. *Lidai funü zhuzuo kao* 歷代婦女著作考 (A survey of women writers through the ages). Shanghai: Shanghai guji chuban she.

Hu/Yao 1931. See Hu Shi.

Hummel, Arthur W., ed. 1943. *Eminent Chinese of the Ch'ing Period.* 2 vols. Washington, D.C.: United States Government Printing Office.

Lau, D.C. 1979 [1982]. *Confucius: The Analects.* New York: Penguin Books.

Li, Ciming 李慈銘. 1975. *Yuemantang wenji* 越縵堂文集 (Collected works from the Yueman Hall). Preface dated 1930. Reprinted in series Jindai Zhongguo shiliao congkan xubian no. 17. Taibei: Wenhai chuban she.

Mann, Susan. 1992. "Classical revival and the gender question: China's first *querelle des femmes.*" In *Family Process and Political Process in Modern Chinese History.* Taibei: Institute of Modern History, Academia Sinica, I:377–412.

Mann, Susan. 1991. "'Fuxue' (Women's Learning) by Zhang Xuecheng (1738–1801): China's First History of Women's Culture." *Late Imperial China* 13, no. 1:40–63.

Mann, Susan. 1987. "Widows in the Kinship, Class, and Community Structures of Qing Dynasty China." *Journal of Asian Studies* 46, no. 1:37–56.

Nivison, David S. 1966. *The Life and Thought of Chang Hsüeh-ch'eng, 1738–1809.* Stanford: Stanford University Press.

Struve, Lynn A. 1988. "The Early Ch'ing Legacy of Huang Tsung-hsi: A Reexamination." *Asia Major,* 3d ser., 1, no. 1: 83–122.

T'ien, Ju-k'ang. 1988. *Male Anxiety and Female Chastity: A Comparative Study of Chinese Ethical Values in Ming-Ch'ing Times.* Leiden: E.J. Brill.

Wakeman, Frederic. 1985. *The Great Enterprise.* 2 vols. Berkeley: University of California Press.

Waley, Arthur. 1956. *Yuan Mei: Eighteenth Century Chinese Poet* New York: Grove Press.

Wang, Zhong 汪中. 1960. *Shu xue* 述學 (An account of learning). Preface dated 1815. Reprinted Taibei: Guangwen shuju.

Watson, Rubie S. 1986. "The Names and the Nameless: Gender and Person in Chinese Society." *American Ethnologist* 13:619–31.

Wen shi tongyi. See Zhang Xuecheng 1964.

Wolf, Margery. 1972. *Women and the Family in Rural Taiwan.* Stanford: Stanford University Press.

Yishu. See Zhang Xuecheng 1922.

Zhang, Xuecheng 章學誠. 1964. *Wen shi tongyi* 文史通義 (General Principles of Literary Art and History). Edition of 1832. Reprinted Hong Kong: Taiping shuju.

Zhang, Xuecheng 章學誠. 1922. *Zhangshi yishu* 章氏遺書 (Bequeathed writings of Master Zhang). Ed. Liu Chenggan 劉承幹. Jiayetang edition.

Zhu, Yun 朱筠 1936. *Sihe wenji* 筍河文集 (Collected works of [Zhu] Sihe [Yun]). Preface dated 1815. Congshu jicheng edition. Reprinted Shanghai: Shangwu yinshu guan.

Zhang Xuecheng Versus Dai Zhen:

A Study in Intellectual Challenge and Response in Eighteenth-Century China

Yü Ying-shih

In the learned judgment of modern intellectual historians, Dai Zhen 戴震 (1724–1777) and Zhang Xuecheng 章學誠 (1738–1801) are the two towering scholars in eighteenth-century China.[1] Perhaps nothing would strike the contemporaries of Dai and Zhang, including their common friends, such as Zhu Yun 朱筠 (1729–1781) and Shao Jinhan 邵晉涵 (1743–1796), as more absurd than this modern judgment. In their own times Dai was widely acknowledged as the foremost leader of the new philological movement in Confucian classical studies whereas Zhang, though well respected as a serious theorist of history and literature in a small coterie of learned friends, was practically unknown to the general intellectual world. With *kaozheng* 考證 ("philology") firmly established as the sole criterion of Confucian scholarship in the eighteenth century, the academic standing of Zhang was nowhere near that of Dai. Even as late as the last decade of the nineteenth century when Zhang's work was gradually gaining recognition, he was still rated far below Dai as a scholar. For example, the young Zhejiang scholar Sun Baoxuan 孫寶瑄 (1874–1924), in his diary of 1894, expressed only a limited appreciation of Zhang's original ideas and criticized the *Wenshi Tongyi* 文史通義 as a whole as narrow in conception and interpretation. By contrast he showed unbounded admiration for Dai when he devoted a whole week in 1898 to a close reading of Dai's collected essays.[2]

With the turn of the century, however, a new criterion of scholarly excellence gradually emerged. It was the scholar's ability to rise above philology in order to search for the hidden meanings in a classical text that was prized above all other qualities. Here we detect a subtle shift in emphasis in late Qing intellectual history from *kaozheng* to *yili* 義理 or, in David S. Nivison's neat translation, from "philology" to "philosophy." As a result, since the beginning of the twentieth century Dai's philosophy has become the focus of intellectual attention while his philology has been praised rather than studied.[3] It is also the rise of this modern criterion that has elevated Zhang to the niche in the mid-Qing world of Confucian learning which he truly deserves.

In this study I propose to examine the intellectual relationship between Dai and Zhang which, hopefully, may also throw some light on the inner complexities as well as tensions in the academic community of eighteenth-century China. It has been well established since Hu Shi 胡適 (1891–1962) that Dai exerted a considerable influence on Zhang's early view of Confucian scholarship. It is also common knowledge now, as Nivison has rightly pointed out, that "Zhang both admired and denounced Dai."[4] As a matter of fact, Zhang referred to Dai explicitly as well as implicitly in many dozens of his essays and letters, the last one being the essay "Intellectual Tradition of Eastern Zhejiang" ("Zhedong xueshu") 浙東學術 written in 1800. Moreover, he not only denounced Dai vehemently but also defended him with equal intensity and vigor. Such strong feelings on Zhang's part suggest that Dai's influence on him must have been much more profound and enduring than has been heretofore recognized by scholars. This under-recognition has arisen, however, not so much from misreading and misunderstanding on the part of his modern interpreters as from the fact that some of Zhang's writings, discovered relatively late in the 40s and 50s, have not been sufficiently studied. It is these new materials, now conveniently collected together in the 1985 edition of the *Remaining Writings of Zhang Xuecheng*, that compel us to re-examine Zhang's intellectual development in the light of his lifetime struggles with Dai's philology as well as philosophy.

The First Encounter

To begin with, we must first clarify the obscurities around Zhang's first meeting with Dai. Nivison tells the story as follows:

One older scholar to whom Zhu [Yun] may have introduced his pupil (i.e. Zhang) was Dai Zhen, a leading philologist and a man who, unlike most advocates of "solid learning," was seriously interested in philosophy. It is likely that Zhang first met Dai Zhen in 1766 when Dai was in the capital to lecture and to attempt the *jinshi* 進士 examination.[5]

This is a close and learned guess summing up all the modern findings on the event of singular importance in Zhang's intellectual life. Fortunately, among the above-mentioned new materials, we find a letter in which Zhang gives his own account of his first meeting with Dai. In "A Letter in Reply to Shao Jinhan," he recalled:

Sometime between spring and summer of 1766, at the suggestion of Zheng Chengzhai 鄭誠齋 (i.e. Zheng Huwen 虎文, 1714–1784), the Hanlin Compiler, I went to see Mr. Dai at the hostelry of Xiuning 休寧. I asked him about his learning and Dai outlined it for me in a general way. A suspicion was immediately aroused in my mind that what Compiler Zheng had told me about Dai might be an understatement. I was then staying with our teacher Zhu [Yun] and had the good fortune of making acquaintances with all the accomplished scholars of the time, which needless to say had greatly widened my intellectual horizon. However it was only in Mr. Dai that I found someone who could almost be said to have grasped the essentials of ancient sages and penetrated far into the realm of universal truth. At that time, it may be remembered, both Mr. Zhu [Yun] of Daxing and Mr. Qian [Daxin] 錢大昕 of Jiading were the two towering figures of highest academic reputation among scholar-officials in the capital. They both admired Dai but only to the extent of Dai's penetrating and refined studies in textual criticism, philology, etymology and mathematics. When it came to Dai's [philosophical] treatises, such as the *Yuan Shan* 原善, they regretted to see [Dai] applying his good self to a field of futility. At that time I argued forcefully in front of Master Zhu contending that [Dai's philosophical] theories were indeed the most rewarding part of his textual investigations. Unfortunately my position was humble and my words carried little weight. None of the esteemed scholars was listening to me. During that period you yourself were also in the company of Jiading 嘉定 (Qian) and Daxing 大興 (Zhu). But I didn't hear you take my side by saying a word to convince both

[Qian and Zhu] that [Dai] was actually the number one scholar of the Qianlong period.[6]

This letter reveals a number of important facts about the first encounter. First, it confirms not only the modern conjecture about the year of the meeting as 1766 but also gives the more precise time as between spring and summer. Second, contrary to the earlier speculation, it was Zheng Huwen, not Zhu Yun, who introduced Zhang to Dai. Zheng had known Dai at a much earlier date when he was the Director of Ziyang 紫陽 Academy in Xinan 新安, Dai's native city.[7] Third, modern scholars are in general agreement that, in the first encounter, Zhang was utterly shattered by the powerful logic of Dai's philological point of view. Now, in the light of this letter, we know that Zhang was also deeply impressed by Dai's philosophical project. This is a very important point to which I shall return later. Fourth, in his "Postscript to Zhu 朱 and Lu 陸," Zhang deplored that while scholars of the day admired Dai's philological accomplishments they nevertheless failed to grasp the central significance of Dai's contribution to Confucian philosophy. However, he stopped short of identifying these "scholars of the day." From this letter it is clear that when he made this statement he had specifically in mind his teacher Zhu Yun and the eminent scholar Qian Daxin, both of whom he highly respected. Thus the letter provides us with a most important clue to Dai's inner tension arising from his choice between philosophy and philology.[8]

Shortly after his first meeting with Dai in 1766, Zhang reported part of their conversation to Zhang Runan 章汝楠 as follows:

Formerly in reading books I set out to get the general meaning, and being young and enthusiastic I applied myself merely to wide reading in all branches of literature, without having any end in view. I was fond of advancing theories that were lofty rather than acute, and attacked textual scholarship, soaring about in emptiness. I was always pleasantly satisfied, supposing that I understood things. But I was astonished when I heard Dai Dongyuan 戴東原 of Xiuning shake his fist and shout, "Present-day scholars, no matter what they deal with, are primarily guilty of never having learned to read correctly!" Startled, I asked him what he meant; he said, "If I were unable to comprehend the ideas of 'before heaven' and 'after heaven' or the subtle wealth of meaning in the books from the He and the Luo, I would not pretend to have read the *Classic of Changes;* if I were unable to understand the courses of the stars, the variations in the heavens from year to year, the constellations, and the patterns of earth, I would not pretend to have read the astronomy sections of the *History.*" . . . We were indeed perfect examples of what he was saying, for we actually never opened a volume of a single Classic of the Four Books. How shameful! How shameful![9]

Based on this letter alone, it is only natural to assume, as scholars actually did in the past, that the conversation between Zhang and Dai in their first meeting was confined to philology. However, the above-quoted letter to Shao Jinhan shows beyond doubt that their conversation must have also turned to Confucian philosophy. I can give two reasons to support this point: First, in preparing Zhang for the first meeting Zheng Huwen must have, like everybody else, praised Dai's philology in the highest possible terms. Then why did Zhang find Zheng's description an "understatement"? This can only mean that during the conversation Zhang discovered, much to his surprise and delight, that Dai was not only a classical philologist but also a Confucian philosopher. Second, after the meeting Zhang began to defend Dai's philosophical work, especially the *Yuan Shan (On Goodness)*, against the attacks of Zhu Yun and Qian Daxin. This strongly suggests that the *Yuan Shan* must have been mentioned and perhaps even discussed in their conversation. It happened that in early 1766 Dai had just completed the revised and expanded version of his *Yuan Shan*. He was so excited about this new accomplishment in Confucian philosophy that it was the first thing he told his disciple Duan Yucai 段玉裁 (1735–1815) when the latter arrived in Peking.[10] Almost surely when Dai outlined his own scholarly work to Zhang he would have mentioned the *Yuan Shan*.

At this juncture a further question must be asked, namely, why did Zhang take the trouble to honor Dai with a formal visit? Given our knowledge of Zhang's introverted personality sometimes even bordering on eccentricity, it was indeed a matter of unusual seriousness for him to initiate such a well-prepared visit to a perfect stranger. It is unlikely that he was primarily motivated by a simple curiosity, let alone vanity, to meet and interview a famous scholar. I am inclined to think that at this point Zhang was experiencing some kind of self-doubt with regard to his pursuit of learning. Nivison has neatly summarized a general distinction Zhang made between two types of scholars as follows:

> Intellectual tempers differ. There are, in the broadest terms, those who tend to grasp intuitively the significance of things, to see things in large wholes, and there are others who are naturally interested in detailed matters of fact.[11]

This is almost exactly a Chinese version of Isaiah Berlin's distinction between the hedgehog and the fox. According to his self-analysis, Zhang was a person of the first type or, in Berlins' term, a hedgehog. From childhood he had developed a keen interest in grasping the general significance of things as well as a distaste for textual details. As he reminisced with his sons in 1791,

> When I studied the writers of old, I had more insight than patience. Therefore I often neglected minute philological and textual matters. However, my intuitive understanding guided me at times to see things often overlooked by previous scholars.[12]

But this hedgehog's point of view was seriously challenged when he came to seek instruction from Zhu Yun in Peking in 1765. As he reported in his 1766 letter to Zhang Runan,

> Recently I have come to study under Mr. Zhu. He also says that he disapproves very much of those shallow but bright young scholars who, lacking sufficient knowledge, like to indulge in empty talk of philosophy. Therefore when he gives instruction to his students he wants them to begin with investigating hard facts, only after which they are allowed to develop general views of their own.[13]

Peking in mid-eighteenth century was the center of what may be called the movement of philologism, and philologists were by definition foxes due to either intellectual temper or pressures generated by the movement. By "philologism" I refer to a widely held belief among radical advocates of philology in Zhang's time that a philological approach alone can lead to the discovery of the *Dao* long buried in the pre-Confucian as well as Confucian texts. After Zhang joined the academic circle of Zhu Yun in 1765, he was directly exposed to the dominant influence of philologism. Surrounded by philological foxes he was probably somewhat less sure than before about going his own way as a hedgehog. I would venture to suggest that it was most likely this self-doubt that prompted him to pay Dai a formal visit.

Having thus reconstructed the states of mind of both Dai and Zhang on the eve of their first meeting, it should occasion no surprise if the range of their conversation included both philology and philosophy. There remains one more question about their first meeting, namely, what did the meeting mean to Zhang? I am inclined to believe that it had a double meaning for Zhang in a critical moment in his intellectual life. It gave him a challenge as well as a reassurance. The challenge, as has been well established, was a philological one whereas the reassurance was philosophical in nature. But the two are interconnected. It probably did not take long for Zhang to discover that Dai never meant to pursue philology for its own sake. On the contrary, Dai had been all along typical of a hedgehog, seeking to "know one big thing"—the Confucian *Dao*—and placed philology squarely in the service of philosophy. To put it in a different way, Dai, like Zhang, was a person who also sought to grasp the significance of things and, above all, relate everything to a single central vision. To Zhang, who was now in his late twenties but still in quest of intellectual self-definition, this discovery must have been a great revelation. Dai alone was able to make him see the inner connectedness between philology and philosophy. In the age of Confucian intellectualism a true philosophical vision worthy of pursuit could only be built on solid philological grounds. This perhaps explains why Zhang was, at least for a while, thoroughly convinced of the importance of philology. But he was also reassured by the encouraging example of Dai that he had been after all steering his course of study in the right direction. His immediate task, however, was how to meet the philological challenge to which we now turn.

The Search for an Intellectual Base

In order to understand the nature of the "philological challenge" faced by Zhang Xuecheng, we need to know something about the general intellectual mode of the Qing period as distinguished from the preceding age. As keenly observed by the Confucian thinker Gong Zizhen 龔自珍 (1792–1841),

The Confucian *Dao* 道 consists of two main strands, namely, "honoring the moral nature" (*zun dexing* 尊德性) and "following the path of inquiry and study" (*dao wenxue* 道問學). In the beginning, these two strands do not contradict but lend support to each other; they are expected to end in unity. In the past, however, only a few in a generation or even one in several generations may be regarded as having successfully combined the two strands in such a way. The majority merely followed whichever trend happened to dominate their own times. Since the beginning of our dynasty, the scope of Confucian studies has been greatly broadened. Nevertheless ours is an age dominated by *dao wenxue*.[14]

For want of a better English term, I choose to call *dao wenxue* "Confucian intellectualism." I have interpreted Chinese intellectual history during the Ming-Qing transition in terms of the rise of Confucian intellectualism primarily because, as Gong Zizhen and other Qing scholars clearly recognized, the transition was from *zun dexing* to *dao wenxue*.[15] Under the dominant mode of *zun dexing*, Confucians of both the Cheng-Zhu 程朱 and the Lu-Wang 陸王 schools tried to enunciate the moral principles of ancient sages mainly through metaphysical speculation. Philological explication of classic texts was considered at best peripheral and at worst obstructive to the pursuit of the *Dao*. However, metaphysical disputes between the Cheng-Zhu and the Lu-Wang schools eventually led both sides to textual studies in the sixteenth century. Wang Yangming's 王陽明 (1472–1529) effort to restore the so-called "old text of the *Great Learning*" initiated a series of philological exercises on this classical text in the seventeenth century. On the Cheng-Zhu side, Luo Qinshun 羅欽順 (1465–1547) also advocated "return to the sources" as the way to settle philosophical disputes. Defending the Cheng-Zhu theory of "the nature is principle" against Lu Xiangshan's 陸象山 "the mind is principle," for example, Luo quoted several passages from the *Book of Changes* and the *Mencius* to make his point. He concluded his argument by saying, "Thus if one carries on his studies *without seeking evidence in the classics* and is utterly arbitrary and opinionated, it is inevitable that he will be misled."[16] It was this deeply felt need on the part of some late Ming Confucians to "seek evidence in the classics" in support of their philosophical views that step by step pushed Confucianism from within to a new direction.

It resulted in a fundamental shift in the frame of mind from *zun dexing* to *dao wenxue* in the middle of the seventeenth century. Gu Yanwu 顧炎武 (1613–1682), as has been generally held since the eighteenth century, was more responsible than anyone else for the establishment of the new paradigm in Confucian classical learning. His best-known statement, "the proper study of principles is the study of the Classics" (*jingxue ji lixue* 經學即理學) was one of the fundamental assumptions of Confucianism throughout the entire Qing period. Once the focus shifted to classical texts, philology, including especially, etymology, phonology, paleography, and textual criticism, began to assume a role of central importance in Confucian learning. Almost without exception, Qing classicists believed that philology alone can provide us with the key to the world of ideas and institutions supposedly created by the ancient sages. As Dai Zhen argued forcefully,

> It is precisely because free speculation cannot lead one to the philosophical ideas of the sages of antiquity that one has to seek them from the ancient Classics. Since messages contained in the surviving records have gradually fallen into oblivion due to the expanse of time between the past and the present, one therefore has to seek them through philological studies [of the Classics]. Thus only if philology is clear, can the ancient Classics be understood; and only if the Classics are understood, can then the sages' philosophical ideas be grasped.[17]

Since Zhang also shared the intellectualistic assumptions of Qing Confucianism, his initial response to Dai's philological challenge was not rejection but shock and shame, as clearly shown in his 1766 letter to Zhang Runan quoted earlier. However, seven years later, in 1773, when Zhang met Dai again, he not only appeared to be completely recovered from his initial shock but also, as Nivison rightly observes, began to "crystallize his own distinctive point of view toward history and letters."[18] In that year, the two scholars ran into each other twice, first in Ningbo and then in Hangzhou. A brief review of the two encounters will throw considerable light on the extent to which Zhang had reached his self-definition in Confucian learning with regained confidence since he first met Dai in 1766.

According to Zhang, he had a heated debate with Dai in Ningbo

寧波 on the subject of local historiography. As Dai saw it, the main
concern of local history is to give a detailed, accurate account of the
geographical, especially territorial, changes of the locality as an administrative unit (i.e., county, prefecture, or province). His emphasis on
historical geography led him to such an extreme view that he denied
biographical status to Buddhist monks and instead treated them as
mere appendages to monasteries or temples in two of his recently
completed local histories. On his own part, however, Zhang took it to
be the true function of local history to preserve what he called "the
unpublished documents and the memories of the living elders" (wenx-
ian 文獻) of a locality which are of contemporary relevance and practical usefulness. Citing Sima Qian's Shi Ji 史記 as authority, he
argued that it is in the nature of history to give greater attention to the
recent past than the remote past. Historical geography, in Zhang's
view, is important only for the study of the antiquity of a locality. It was
on these grounds that Zhang came to the conclusion that Dai, with all
his erudition and profundity in classical learning, did not understand
history at all.[19] Thus the dispute on local history reveals unmistakably
the differences between Dai as a philologically oriented classicist and
Zhang as a present-minded historian. In the case of Dai, it can be readily seen that he was applying the same kind of philological techniques
in his study of the classic of historical geography—the Shuijing Zhu
(Commentary on the Classic of Waterways)—to the compilations of
local histories.[20] It is also important to note that by saying that Dai, a
great classicist, did not understand history, Zhang was not only advocating the autonomy of history but also elevating history to a status
comparable to that of classical scholarship. I shall return to this point
later.

In Hangzhou, Zhang overheard Dai's severe criticism of Zheng
Qiao's 鄭樵 (1104–1160) Tong Zhi 通志 (General History). From a
strictly philological point of view Dai found the Tong Zhi full of errors,
especially in the section on astronomy. Zhang disagreed profoundly,
though he kept silent at the time. Later he wrote a series of essays in
defense of Zheng Qiao. In his view, the Tong Zhi as a historical synthesis is a truly outstanding work in terms of its "broad conception" (hong-
gang 弘綱) as well as its grasp of the "meanings" (yi 義) of the history of Chinese learning. To denounce this monumental work

philologically is to miss its main purpose wholly.[21] Here we encounter
the problem of what is known in the West as the hermeneutic circle. As
methodological individualists Dai and other Qing philologists seem to
have held that, in the process of understanding and interpretation,
one must understand the parts before one can begin to grasp the
whole. On the other hand, as a methodological holist Zhang tended to
place his emphasis on comprehension of the whole as a precondition
for understanding the parts. This turned out to be one of Zhang's fundamental disagreements with Dai which he developed further in later
writings.[22]

Thus the two meetings in 1773 show unmistakably that Zhang's
intellectual struggle with Dai's radical philology finally came to
fruition. Unlike during the first conversation Zhang was no longer a
passive listener. On the contrary, he was able to refute Dai's views point
by point from his own intellectual base—history. Let us turn to see
how he established and developed this intellectual base of his own.

Zhang was a holistically oriented theorist in the age of Confucian
intellectualism. Like classicists of the day he was equally committed to
the intellectualist ideal of scholarship as a Confucian calling. However,
he was by intellectual temper disposed to history rather than classics.
By his own admission, he showed a natural aptitude for history since
childhood, but had little talent for classical philology.[23] His first long
discussion with Dai in 1766 helped shape his academic career in two
important ways. First, he became keenly aware that one could not possibly make one's mark in whatever one's specialization in Confucian
learning without first meeting the basic intellectualist requirement of
grounding it in empirical, especially textual, scholarship. In Zhang's
case, needless to say, it was historical scholarship. Second, greatly
encouraged by Dai's example of making philology subservient to philosophy, he began to develop his theories of history and literature by
working extensively in a great variety of texts. The results were the two
projected books, *Wenshi Tongyi* and the *Jiaochou Tongyi*, 校讎通義
the origins of both of which can be traced to 1772.[24] Here a word
about the relationship between these two works is in order.

As Nivison rightly points out, the term *wenshi* has both a literal
meaning ("literary art and historical writing") as well as a specific
meaning ("literary and historical criticism") as traditionally used by

bibliographers. On the other hand, *jiaochou*, for Zhang, "was a free-ranging historical study of books and traditions of writing and learning to which they belong, a study that was to be somehow at the same time both explanatory and critical."[25] Moreover, Nivison also describes the *Jiaochou Tongyi* as follows:

> It is a theoretical work, ostensibly on the uncompromising subject of bibliography; in other words, it is a book about books—how to analyze and catalog them, after comparing texts to determine questions of authenticity, authorship, and completeness. Certainly it is this, but it is also in tight and systematic form a presentation of Zhang's most fundamental theses on the philosophy of history and the criticism of literature and scholarship. It is a basic statement of his philosophical position as far as it had developed at this time.[26]

This is certainly an accurate description of the book. Here, however, an interesting puzzle emerges: Thus described, where are we to draw the line between Zhang's *jiaochou* and *wenshi*? In the process of considering this puzzle, I have stumbled on a startling discovery. Since the whole matter is too complicated to be adequately treated here, I can only give a brief report of my findings.

It has been a generally accepted view that Zhang began writing his *Wenshi Tongyi* in 1772. As this view is firmly established from Zhang's letters to friends written in 1772 and 1773, there seems no reason to question it. Let me begin by citing some of these letters. He first mentioned the *Wenshi Tongyi* in his 1772 letter to Zhu Fenyuan 朱棻元 (1727–1782) in which he reported:

> Since leaving the capital (i.e. in 1771), I have busied myself much with writing: I have worked over the entire field of letters and have written a *Wenshi Tongyi;* and although the work is not complete I have shown the general drift in three essays from the first part (i.e. *neipian* 內篇) of it, which I copied into a letter to Qian Daxin.[27]

Then in his 1773 letter to Yan Dongyu 嚴冬友, he said:

> I thought I would cull out the essence of my reflections and make up a study of bibliography [*jiaochou*]; so I studied the writings of Ban Gu 班固, Liu Xiang 劉向, and Liu Xin 劉歆, reasoning back from them to Zhou 周 institutions, and I examined the *Wenxin Diaolong* 文心雕龍 and the *Shi Tong* 史通; I have analyzed and distin-

guished between assertions and facts, and have classified and evaluat-
ed divergent traditions, and have written a *Wenshi Tongyi*.[28]

Obviously these two letters talk about the same thing, only with more
details in the second one. If we trust his own words, then what he
referred to as the *Wenshi Tongyi* at this early date bears little resemblance to what we now have under the same title. Rather it fits perfectly the description of the *Jiaochou Tongyi*, or, as Nivison says, "it is a book
about books." So a reasonable explanation would be that what Zhang
had written up to this time under the title of *Wenshi Tongyi* was later to
become part of his *Jiaochou Tongyi*, a title that he did not actually have
until, perhaps, 1779. This observation is further confirmed in his preface to the *Hezhou Zhi Yu* (和州志隅 *A Synopsis of the History of
Hezhou*) written in 1774 in which he said:

> I have shown my [*Wenshi*] *Tongyi* to others, and they still have hesitated
> to read it with confidence, presumably thinking it is mere theory
> [*kongyan* 空言, "empty words"] without any demonstration in reality.
> My *Synopsis* in twenty sections will have a hint as to how it may be
> applied, and by inference one may see that the *Wenshi Tongyi* is not
> vague and impractical theory.[29]

In this particular case, it is quite obvious that his reference to the *Wenshi Tongyi* would not make sense at all if it were to be identified with
the *Wenshi Tongyi* as it exists today. What theories or principles can we
possibly find in the present *Wenshi Tongyi* that may be "applied" to the
bibliographical section in the *History of Hezhou*? Clearly, Zhang's statement makes sense only if we substitute the *Jiaochou Tongyi* for the *Wenshi Tongyi*. As a matter of fact, the *Jiaochou Tongyi*, in structure as well as
in substance, resembles the bibliographical treatise ("Yiwen Zhi"
藝文志) of the *Hezhou Zhi* so much that Nivison even suggests that it
was a development of the latter.[30] As far as I can judge, what really happened may be surmised to have been as follows: In 1772, he had
already developed some central ideas about what he called *wenshi jiaochou* in a number of essays. These essays, as the above-quoted letter of
1773 to Yan Dongyu clearly indicates, turned out to be about the theory of bibliography (*jiaochou*) rather than that of literary and historical
writing (*wenshi*). In other words, they were the first drafts of essays that
later went to form the first part (*neipian*) of the *Jiaochou Tongyi*. Howev-

er, since at this time the title of *Jiaochou Tongyi* was nonexistent, he therefore referred to "the three essays" he had shown friends (including Qian Daxin) as "from the first part of the *Wenshi Tongyi*." This confusion has been further aggravated by the fact both the *Wenshi Tongyi* and the *Jiaochou Tongyi* are divided into "first part" (*neipian* "Inner Chapters") and "second part" (*waipian* 外篇 "Outer Chapters"), which makes the detection doubly difficult. For decades scholars have tried to identify the "three essays" in the present *Wenshi Tongyi* without getting anywhere. Now at least we are more or less sure that they must be among the eighteen essays in the first part of the *Jiaochou Tongyi*, especially those in chapter one dealing with general principles.

Nivison makes a sensitive comment on this problem. He says,

> In these letters Zhang mentions for the first time the name of the volume of essays which is now his best-known piece of writing. But we can only guess what this early *Wenshi Tongyi* must have been. Most of the work now in existence was written later. Moreover, there is an indication that Zhang at one time intended to use this title as a collective title for all his writings, or at least for all that he proposed to save.[31]

Two points in this comment particularly deserve attention. First, it has been well established that practically all the important theoretical essays in the present *Wenshi Tongyi* were written much later between 1783 and 1792.[32] So the early *Wenshi Tongyi* is more likely to have been the predecessor of the present *Jiaochou Tongyi*. Second, it is also well grounded to say that Zhang had originally intended to use the *Wenshi Tongyi* "as a collective title for all his writings." As Nivison further explains, "Zhang may, however, have modified this intention after changing the title of his *Jiaochou Lue* 校讎略 to *Jiaochou Tongyi* (which could not very logically be included in another *tongyi*.)"[33] This certainly makes sense, but there is also another possibility. By the time he wrote the *Jiaochou Tongyi* in 1779, new ideas may well have grown in his mind to the extent that he decided to reserve the *Wenshi Tongyi* as the title for a more ambitious project. Moreover, we can easily see the vast differences between the early *Wenshi Tongyi* and the later one from his entirely different attitudes toward them. In 1772–1774, he was very anxious to show his essays of the early *Wenshi Tongyi* to his friends in the hope of being appreciated. However, in the case of the later one, he made a special point to keep his most original ideas concealed from the reading public during his lifetime. As his letter to Wang Huizu 王輝祖 of 1796 makes abundantly clear, he was afraid that these ideas "might startle the world, horrify common folks, and be severely criticized by people."[34] It seems safe to conclude that the essays for the *Wenshi Tongyi* he referred to between 1772 and 1774 were the first drafts of what became the *Jiaochou Tongyi*.

The discovery of the simple fact that the early *Wenshi Tongyi* was in reality the first version of the *Jiaochou Tongyi* throws a good deal of new light on the development of Zhang's thought in response to Dai's philological challenge. In the first place, contrary to the previous speculation, in the early 1770s Zhang did not write on topics of a highly philosophical nature as those in the present *Wenshi Tongyi*. His essays during this period were largely distillations of bibliographical studies (*jiaochou*), close to the textual base he had specifically chosen to develop. This shows that he had indeed taken Dai's words of 1766 to heart: One must not theorize without the support of some work of substance.

In the second place, in his letter to Qian Daxin, originally written in 1772 but probably revised in 1798,[35] Zhang described what he was doing as *wenshi jiaochou* 文史校讎. What did he refer to by this term? Now we know that in 1772 he could not have possibly referred to the two famous books later published under the names of *jiaochou* and *wenshi* respectively. At this juncture we must return to the question raised earlier: Where to draw the line between the *wenshi* and the *jiaochou*? The fact that he grouped the two parts together indicates that he had conceived of the two parts as inseparable from each other. However, as his work progressed he gradually came to the realization that there were problems unique to the methodology of *jiaochou* which needed to be treated separately. Hence the *Jiaochou Tongyi* of 1779. From beginning to end Zhang promoted *jiaochou* as a legitimate field of study in Confucian learning, the function of which was not indiscriminate collection and cataloguing of texts but clarification of the different traditions of thought and scholarship through systematic classification of texts.[36] Important as it was, Zhang nevertheless did not regard *jiaochou* as an end in itself. Rather it was to serve the higher purpose of his literary and historical studies (*wenshi*) which reveal the truth about *Dao*. Thus it may not be too far-fetched to suggest that his deliberate choice of the expression *wenshi jiaochou* was intended to challenge the hegemony of Dai's classical scholarship built on philology (*jingxue xungu* 經學訓詁). However, from 1772 to 1783 he devoted himself wholly to the building of his own intellectual base through studies in historical bibliography (*jiaochou*). A newly-discovered manuscript confirms my observation here. In a letter to Qian Dian 錢坫 (*Zi* Xianzhi 獻之, 1744–1806), a relative of Qian Daxin, dated 1778, Zhang began by praising Qian's profound knowledge of classical philology (*xungu wenzi* 訓詁文字). Then he went on to reflect on his own work as a contrast, saying,

> As for myself, I can only understand the general meanings [of the Classics] but I am unable to engage in philological studies. Following my own inclination, I would much prefer to discuss the historical work of Ban [Gu], Liu [Xiang] and Liu [Xin]. I set for myself the central task of delineating the origins as well as the traditions of all the writings. However, I am not sure if I have really grasped the ideas of the ancients.[37]

This new evidence helps establish two important facts about his early thinking: First, as late as 1778 he still characterized himself primarily as a historical bibliographer. There is no hint whatsoever of his discovery of the philosophical ideas concerning history and literary writing which are found in the present *Wenshi Tongyi*. Second, the contrast between Qian's "philology" and his own "bibliography" reveals that he was consciously developing his intellectual base in *jiaochou* as a counter-challenge to *xungu* of the classicists of his day including, especially, Dai. As a matter of fact, later in this letter he specifically mentioned Dai's excellence in "philology" (*xungu*) while at the same time criticizing his excessive competitiveness to the extent of "pretending to know what he did not really understand."[38] In making this criticism he must have had in mind his remark of 1773 that "Dai the classicist did not understand history." There can be little doubt that the methodological tool of Zhang's bibliographic studies was as central to his critical understanding of literature and history as Dai's tool of philological researches was to his interpretations of the Confucian classics.

In the third place, we can now distinguish two stages in Zhang's intellectual development since his first meeting with Dai in 1766. The first stage stretched approximately from 1771 when he began writing on a projected book, to 1783, when he produced his first essays of what became the *Wenshi Tongyi*. During this period he was more emphatically concerned with establishing and solidifying his intellectual base by way of *jiaochou* than developing his philosophical views on history and writing. His *Jiaochou Tongyi* of 1779 may be taken as the representative product of this stage. The second stage covered the period from 1783 to his death in 1801. During these two decades his main effort was to work out in a systematic fashion the central ideas of his *Wenshi Tongyi* which, unfortunately, remained more or less incomplete. The most productive years in this stage turned out to be 1788 to 1790 when a breakthrough took place in his theoretical thinking. Previously, due to the confusion arising out of the title of *Wenshi Tongyi*, we generally assumed that he had been working on *wenshi* and *jiaochou* simultaneously since 1771. Now, with this confusion removed, we can discern more clearly than ever before a sensible pattern in his intellectual growth from the textual base to the theoretical superstructure. Here Dai's influence is unmistakable. As Zhang emphatically pointed out, Dai's lifetime work in philology (*xungu*) was but a preparation for the reconstruction of Confucian philosophy.[39]

Needless to say, the two stages of Zhang's intellectual development must be understood in relative terms. His emphasis in the first stage was placed on *jiaochou* and the second stage on *wenshi* but in neither case was it a matter of total exclusion of the other. However, true to the intellectualist spirit of his age, in both stages he demonstrated a remarkable consistency in testing the validity of his ideas by applying them to empirical research projects. It often resulted in a symbiotic growth of theory and practice in Zhang's work. We have already seen how closely his *Jiaochou Tongyi* and *Hezhou Zhi* were related to each other. Now let us briefly examine how his other major project, the *Shiji Kao* 史籍考 (*Critique of Historical Writings*), helped the writing of his *Wenshi Tongyi*. He first proposed this ambitious project to Bi Yuan 畢沅 (1730–1793), Governor of Henan, in 1787 and then from 1788 on he worked on it, with interruptions, until the end of his life.[40] As Nivison rightly observes, "The enormous labor required by such a work was not expended for nothing, for it must have been a major stimulus to Zhang's thinking during the years when he was writing the most interesting of those essays expressing his historiographical theories."[41] I wish to cite Zhang himself to substantiate this observation. In

1788, he wrote two letters to Sun Xingyan 孫星衍 (1753–1818) which bear importantly on our discussion here. The first letter, written in mid-spring, says,

> Recently I have been working on the *Shiji Kao* project together with Hong [Liangji 洪亮吉, 1746–1809] and Ling [Tingkan 凌廷堪, 1747–1809] on behalf of His Excellency [Bi Yuan]. Having read a great variety of books, I have made some progress [in my own learning]. Probably I would be able also to take this opportunity to complete the writing of my *Wenshi Tongyi*.[42]

The second letter, written a few months later, further states,

> After I complete this project for His Excellency [Bi Yuan], I would like to use all the findings made in the course of it to establish my own theories. However, I would do this only for my own enjoyment. I would not dare to publish them at the moment. But nor would I dare to conceal them from a few friends who really understand me.[43]

The letters speak for themselves. However, it must be noted that it was in the second letter that Zhang first articulated what proved to be the most celebrated of his theories, "the six classics are all history." His attempt at a new classification of historiographical bibliography led to the discovery of this idea which, in turn, also served as a guiding principle in his compilation of the *Shiji Kao*.[44] Not coincidentally early in 1789, after having worked on the project slightly over a year, he was able to produce no less than twenty-three core essays of the *Wenshi Tongyi* within a period of two months. Such a sudden enlightenment even surprised Zhang himself who later said, "In my whole life I have never produced things at a speed as fast as this."[45]

"The Six Classics are all History"

Zhang's central thesis in the *Wenshi Tongyi*, "the Six Classics are all history," is one of the most thoroughly discussed topics in modern historical scholarship of China.[46] In this study no attempt will be made at a comprehensive review of this thesis and its full implications in Qing intellectual history. Rather it will be examined strictly from the point of view of intellectual challenge and response between Zhang and Dai.

The late Professor Qian Mu 錢穆 (1895–1990) was the first among modern scholars to suggest that Zhang's thesis was intended to challenge the dominant paradigm of classical philologism of his day by questioning its fundamental assumptions.[47] Let us take this paradigm as our point of departure. By the second half of the eighteenth century, Gu Yanwu's apt catch phrase, *Jingxue ji lixue* ("the proper study of principles is the study of the Classics"), quoted earlier, had become something of a self-evident truth. It was such a widespread notion that Zhang also copied the phrase into one of his notebooks.[48] As the leading philosophical spokesman of Qing classical philologism, Dai elaborated on the implications of that notion in many of his letters and occasional writings. The following succinct statement in Dai's letter to his leading disciple Duan Yucai (1735–1815), written a few months before his death, may be taken as an example:

> Since I was seventeen years old, I have set the quest of *Dao* as my life goal. I was convinced that *Dao* can be found only in the Six Classics and the works of Confucius and Mencius. But unless we study the meanings of the words, institutions, and terminologies [in the classical texts] we will not be able to understand the language of the texts. Song Confucians ridiculed philology and ignored language. Thus they may well be compared to people who wish to cross rivers without boats or climb high without ladders.[49]

This statement may very well be understood as a commentarial unpacking of Gu Yanwu's original idea. It makes clear not only Gu's deep distrust of metaphysical speculation but also his advocacy of the philological approach to the Classics as the only way to repossess the *Dao*. Implicit in this statement are three important assumptions: First, the *Dao* had already been discovered by the sages in classical antiquity, especially Confucius and Mencius; second, this *Dao* is recorded in the texts of the Six Classics; third, only philology can explicate the original meanings of these ancient texts. It was specifically against Dai's arguments like these, as we shall see, that Zhang developed his thesis "the Six Classics are all history."

As noted earlier, 1789 was the most fruitful year of Zhang's intellectual life as far as the writing of his *Wenshi Tongyi* was concerned. In that year he wrote a preface to a group of theoretical essays which reveals unmistakably that the crystallization of his central vision of Confucian learning resulted as much from a genuine lifetime quest of the *Dao* as from a decade-long inner struggle with Dai's challenge. As late as 1789, twelve years after Dai's death, the specter of his greatest intellectual rival continued to haunt him. Thus he wrote,

> I am only qualified to discuss literature and history (*wenshi*), and cannot claim that I know the *Dao*. However, if I exclude literature and history from the *Dao* in my discussion, then literature and history would not be worthy of their names. I therefore examined the origin of *Dao* and wrote these thirteen essays. I wish to show how literature and history actually began as well as how Confucian learning eventually evolved into literature and history. Those Confucian scholars are mistaken when they say that the *Dao* resides in a realm outside literature and history.[50]

In writing the last sentence of the above quote Zhang particularly had Dai in mind. This point is fully borne out by his "Letter to Zhang Zhengfu 章正甫 on Writing Again," written in 1789 or 1790, where he said,

> The historical writings of Sima [Qian, c.145–85 B.C.] and Ban [Gu, c.32–92] and the literary works of Han [Yu 韓愈, 768–824] and Liu [Zongyuan 柳宗元, 773–819] are related to *Dao* much in the same way as are the philological studies of Ma [Rong 馬融, 76–166] and Zheng [Xuan 鄭玄, 127–200] and the classical commentaries of Jia [Kui 賈逵, 30–101] and Kong [Yingda 孔穎達, 574–648]. But Dai [Zhen] says that these [historical and literary writings] are only "art" (yi), not *Dao*. This is quite comparable to a person who happens to come to the capital by boat denying that there is also a land-route to Peking.[51]

In the light of this letter, it is clear that Zhang's preface of 1789 was but a subtle criticism of Dai without mentioning his name. He meant that his *wenshi* ("literature and history") was no less immediate to *Dao* than Dai's *jingxue* ("classical scholarship"). Here we must also point out that Zhang's criticism was directed specifically against Dai's "Letter to Fang Xiyuan [Ju] 方希原（矩）", dated 1755. It was in this letter that Dai explicitly stated, on the one hand, that the writings of Sima Qian, Ban Gu, Han Yu, and Liu Zongyuan could only be regarded as "art" (yi) rather than *Dao* and, on the other hand, that "the *Dao* of the Sages is all contained in the Six Classics."[52]

Zhang rejected all the three assumptions of Qing philologism as repeatedly elaborated by Dai. To begin with, he did not share Dai's unlimited faith in philology. He showed considerable respect for the technically sophisticated philology of Dai and other contemporary classicists. However, technical competence in philology was far from being decisive in the interpretation of the meanings of a classical text. "In the past several thousand years," he said, "Confucian scholars have failed to reach agreements" on such technical matters as the Six Graphic Principles (*liu shu* 六書) or ancient system of phonetics. As a methodological holist, he believed that it was possible to grasp the general meanings of classical texts without the technical assistance of philology.[53]

Zhang also seriously questioned the validity of the other two assumptions of Qing philologism, namely, all important truths about *Dao* had already been discovered by ancient sages and they are all preserved in the Six Classics (an assumption which, it may be noted, had been generally accepted in the Confucian tradition since the Han dynasty). He was able to challenge such a long-established tradition because he had developed a wholly new conception of *Dao*. As modern students of Zhang generally agree, Zhang's *Dao* is thoroughly historicized.[54] As lucidly summarized by Nivison,

> Indeed, the Classics by themselves, Zhang thinks, are not sufficient to reveal the *Dao* fully. For what they do reveal, they reveal by showing what has been and what has happened in the past. Ultimately it is history itself, the course of events, that reveals the *Dao,* and obviously the Classics cover only a part of this.[55]

What concerns us here, however, is not his now well-publicized view of *Dao* as such but how he used it to formulate his central thesis, "the Six Classics are all history," as a response to Dai's radical philology. We have seen that in his preface of 1789 he argued vigorously that his *wenshi* has as legitimate a claim to manifesting the *Dao* as Dai's *jingxue*. This is a view that he held to the end of his life. In 1796 he wrote to Zhu Gui 朱珪 (1731–1807) and presented him a copy of the first printed edition of the *Wenshi Tongyi*. In this letter he returned to his favorite theme, this time, however, speaking exclusively of classics and history. He said:

> In antiquity people never drew a distinction between classics and history, or took either one as more important than the other. In my unconventional view, without a clear understanding of history, even great masters of the Confucian classicists like Fu Sheng 伏勝 [3rd and 2nd centuries B.C.] and Kong Anguo 孔安國 [c. 156–74 B.C.], Jia Kui and Zheng Xuan, could at most attain half of the *Dao*. What I try to present in my [*Wenshi] Tongyi* is an attempt at a holistic grasp of the essentials of the ancients.[56]

What is particularly revealing about this statement is that it was again a criticism of Dai. A few lines back he practically repeated his view about Dai in their 1773 debate on local history that with all his profundity in philology Dai nevertheless did not know anything about history. Against this background we are almost certain that the following passage from part three of his essay "On the *Dao*" is a contrast between Dai and himself:

> For that part of the *Dao* which is complete in the Six Classics and of which the meanings and implications are hidden in the past, it is sufficient for textual and philological studies to bring it to light. However, as to events and changes that occurred in later times, the Six Classics cannot possibly say anything about them. It is therefore important [for people in later times] to produce writings from time to time according to principles abstracted from the Six Classics in order to illustrate the *Dao*.[57]

According to this view, Dai, like great Confucian masters of the Han dynasty, grasped no more than half of the *Dao*.

At this juncture, we must pause and ask. Would Zhang admit that since he did not study the Classics by way of philology his understanding of the *Dao* was therefore also partial? The answer must be a resounding no. As the last sentence of his letter to Zhu Gui, quoted above, indicates, he was confident that he had arrived at a holistic understanding of the *Dao* in its essentials, though not the details. As a holistically oriented historian, he discovered a truth of singular importance: "the Six Classics are all history." But the reverse is not true; historical writings must not be taken as classics. As a matter of fact, he considered the term "classic" (*jing*) to be a misnomer or a historical error. In his essay "Jing Jie" 經解 ("An Explanation of [the Term] Classic") he tried to show that etymologically *jing* meant no more than outlines. It was commonly used in Mohist and Legalist rather than Confucian texts. Only long after Confucius' death was the term *jing* sacralized and applied to texts of the Confucian school. "In the beginning," he emphatically pointed out, "the Six Classics were not necessarily venerable titles."[58] The Classics are sacred not because they are Classics, but because they are originally historical in nature. As he expressed it unequivocally elsewhere, "Men of later ages venerated the Classics because they are the history of the Three Dynasties (i.e. Xia, 夏, Shang 商, and Zhou 周)."[59]

With the thesis "the Six Classics are all history," Zhang not only demolished Dai's monopolistic claim to the *Dao* but also sacralized history at the expense of classical scholarship of his day. Like all students of Zhang, I fully recognize the profundity and richness of this thesis in its philosophical as well as historical implications. It is far from my intention to simplify it by way of psychological reduction. Under no circumstances can intellectual history be reduced to personal psychology. All I am suggesting here is that had it not been for Dai's challenge, almost surely Zhang would not have formulated and argued his thesis in the way he actually does in the *Wenshi Tongyi*.

Zhu and Lu: Two Intellectual Genealogies

Finally, Zhang's life-long intellectual tension with Dai culminated in his historical reconstruction of the two rival Neo-Confucian genealogies of Zhu Xi 朱熹 (1130–1200) and Lu Xiangshan (1139–1192). Dai's death in 1777 provided Zhang with an opportunity to reflect on the strengths as well the weaknesses of his rival's scholarship. This he did in an essay entitled "Zhu and Lu."[60] Then, in 1800, a year before his own death he wrote another essay under the title "Intellectual Tradition of Eastern Zhejiang" ("Zhedong xueshu") in which he traced his own intellectual ancestry all the way back to Lu Xiangshan. Though a quarter century apart, the two essays nevertheless complement each other in meaning and therefore constitute a single unit. What is left unsaid in the earlier essay ("Zhu and Lu") is said in the later one ("Intellectual Tradition of Eastern Zhejiang") at least by implication if not by design.[61]

In these two pieces of writing he reconstructed two intellectual genealogies beginning with Zhu Xi and Lu Xiangshan respectively. Before we comment on their substance, let us first look at the two genealogies. In "Zhu and Lu," the Zhu genealogy runs as follows:

> First generation: Huang Gan 黃榦 (1152–1221) and Cai Chen 蔡沈 (1167–1230); second generation: Zhen Dexiu 眞德秀 (1178–1235), Wei Liaoweng 魏了翁 (1178–1237), Huang Zhen 黃震 (1213–1280), and Wang Yinglin 王應麟 (1223–1296); third generation: Jin Luxiang 金履祥 (1232–1303) and Xu Qian 許謙 (1270–1337); fourth generation: Song Lian 宋濂 (1310–1381) and Wang Wei 王褘 (1323–1374); fifth generation: Gu Yanwu 顧炎武 and Yan Ruoju 閻若璩 (1636–1704).

It must be pointed out that the idea of "generation" in this essay is used very loosely, but it does not affect our discussion here. Then, in "Intellectual Tradition of Eastern Zhejiang" the following lineage from Lu Xiangshan is established:

> Yuan Xie 袁燮 (1144–1224), Yuan Su 袁肅 (jinshi, 1199) and Yuan Fu 袁甫 (jinshi, 1214)—Wang Yangming (1472–1529)—Liu Zongzhou 劉宗周 (1578–1645)—Huang Zongxi 黃宗羲 (1610–1695)—Mao Qiling 毛奇齡 (1623–1716), Wan Sida 萬斯大 (1633–1683) and Wan Sitong 萬斯同 (1638–1702)—Quan Zuwang 全祖望 (1705–1755).

With regard to the two genealogies themselves, I wish to make the following observations: First, they are lists of "Confucian scholars" rather than "Neo-Confucian philosophers." In both essays Zhang explicitly stated that his criteria of selection are "mastery of the Classics and respect for tradition" (tongjing fugu 通經服古) as well as avoidance of "empty talk on moral nature" (kongyan dexing 空言德性). Nowhere is his Confucian intellectualism more clearly revealed than in these two genealogies. Second, according to his "Postscript to Zhu and Lu,"[62] he wrote the earlier essay as a criticism of Dai. He traced Dai's intellectual lineage from Gu Yanwu all the way back to Zhu Xi in order to show that Dai, in attacking Zhu Xi, "failed to understand his own historical position."[63] Third, in the essay "Zhu and Lu" of 1777, what is conspicuously missing is the genealogy of the Lu school. It is in the "Intellectual Tradition of Eastern Zhejiang" (1800) that this missing genealogy is provided. However, a closer scrutiny reveals that this genealogy does not cover the Lu school as a whole but is restricted to Lu's followers in Eastern Zhejiang. There can be no question that Zhang's genealogical reconstruction in 1800 was intended primarily to place himself in the Lu tradition vis-a-vis Dai in the Zhu tradition. This point is fully borne out by the fact that Yang Jian 楊簡 (1140–1226), the leading disciple of Lu Xiangshan, and Qian Dehong 錢德洪 (1497–1574) and Wang Ji 王畿 (1498–1583), the two most outstanding philosophical heirs of Wang Yangming, are omitted from Zhang's genealogy even though all were natives of Eastern Zhejiang. In other words, this genealogy was tailored to the precise specifications of his own intellectual identity.

Zhang's reconstruction of the two Neo-Confucian genealogies throws a new light not only on his intellectual relationship with Dai but also his own stature as a philosophical spokesman of Qing Confucian intellectualism. However, due to space, only a brief account of these two related aspects can be given below.[64]

According to Nivison, Zhang discovered Huang Zongxi rather late, probably as late as 1795, after his own work had been basically accomplished. Only then did he begin to fully realize the importance of Eastern Zhejiang historical scholarship. On this basis, therefore, Nivison dismisses the notion that Zhang was a "member" of the "Eastern Zhejiang School":

> To talk of an "Eastern Zhejiang School" as including Zhang Xuecheng is to fall into Zhang's own historical-essentialist manner of speaking. Influence there may be, but Zhang's self-identification with a special Zhejiang tradition was a lifetime's afterthought.[65]

To call Zhang's self-identification with the "Eastern Zhejiang Intellectual Tradition" "a lifetime's afterthought" is a true insight. But this insight needs to be developed so that the very nature of Zhang's "afterthought" may be brought to light. To begin with, we must first ask this question, Why in his "Zhu and Lu" of 1777 is only the intellectual genealogy of Zhu Xi given, but not that of Lu Xiangshan? Was this due to the fact, as Nivison has shown, that Zhang was unfamiliar with Huang Zongxi's work until as late as 1795? This is certainly an important part of the answer, but not the whole story. The other part, I would suggest, lies in the fact that Zhang was yet to reach the full maturity of his thought and scholarship. Now we know that in 1777 Zhang's work was largely concentrated on the bibliographical and methodological (*jiaochou*) studies. His theoretical breakthroughs, such as "the Six Classics are all history," were still a decade away and the *Wenshi Tongyi* did not really exist except as a title. He could not justifiably conceive the intellectual rivalry between Dai and himself in terms of Zhu Xi versus Lu Xiangshan in the Southern Song or Gu Yanwu versus Huang Zongxi in the early Qing as he actually did in "Intellectual Tradition of Eastern Zhejiang." Our next question is, When did he identify himself with the Qing tradition of historical scholarship in Eastern Zhejiang beginning with Huang Zongxi? It is true that the death of his friend Shao Jinhan in 1796 provided him with the occasion to review this tradition. He particularly praised Huang Zongxi, Shao Tingcai 邵廷采 (1648–1711), and Quan Zuwang for their contributions to the study of history.[66] But it is not clear whether he also considered himself a latter-day heir to this tradition. Moreover, there is evidence to the contrary. In 1797 he wrote a letter to Zhu Xigeng 朱錫庚 in which he summed up his characterization of Dai in "Zhu and Lu" with basically the same genealogy. However, the Qing part of the genealogy reads as follows:

> Down to the beginning of our dynasty Gu Yanwu, Huang Zongxi and Yan Ruoju all followed this [Zhu] tradition even more closely than in the genealogy of Confucian classicists of the Han dynasty. Dai's classical scholarship actually took the works of these scholars as its point of departure. And yet he was harshly critical of the learning of Zhu Xi. This is indeed like a person who drinks the water but forgets its origins.[67]

It is most surprising that even as late as 1797 Zhang not only placed Huang Zongxi in the Zhu Xi tradition but also regarded him as one of Dai's intellectual ancestors. Even if we consider this to have been a mere "slip" on Zhang's part, the very "slip" itself is not without some deep psychological significance. At least it reveals that at this time his self-identification with the East Zhejiang tradition of historical scholarship was not yet final. This simple fact also explains why he was unable to establish a genealogy for the Lu school in his 1777 essay on "Zhu and Lu." In this sense, then, his "Intellectual Tradition of Eastern Zhejiang" of 1800 was indeed "a lifetime's afterthought."

In 1800 his eyes were failing and his health in general deteriorated rapidly. He was no longer able to write without assistance. Already he knew that his days were numbered. Nevertheless he found it necessary to give a finishing touch to his *magnum opus*. "Intellectual Tradition of Eastern Zhejiang" was the last theoretical essay to go into the core chapters of the *Wenshi Tongyi*. There cannot be the slightest doubt that it must have meant a great deal to him. What, then, were some of the compelling reasons that prompted Zhang to write this last essay? We can only make a few guesses. First, as he was about to turn over the drafts of his *Wenshi Tongyi* to a friend for final editing, he must have discovered that the 1777 essay on "Zhu and Lu" was grossly unbalanced in content: It traced Dai's intellectual genealogy all the way back to Zhu Xi but said nothing about how his own work could be linked to the tradition of Lu Xiangshan. This is exactly the gap that the essay "Intellectual Tradition of Eastern Zhejiang" was intended to close.[68] Second, with his own system of Confucian learning basically completed, he now probably felt justified to take Dai and himself as each representing a main line of approach to the *Dao* in the Confucian tradition, namely, Dai's classical as opposed to his historical studies. In order to find a definite place for himself in the history of Confucian learning, he also needed an intellectual genealogy of his own and nothing could serve this purpose better than the Eastern Zhejiang tradition of historical scholarship. It was obviously for this reason that he had to assign the pivotal role in this tradition to none other than Huang Zongxi whom, it may be recalled, he had generously offered to Zhu Xi's school three years earlier. As he said in "Intellectual Tradition of Eastern Zhejiang":

> It is generally acknowledged today that Gu Yanwu was the founder of Confucian learning of our dynasty. Gu, however, actually belonged to the intellectual tradition of Western Zhejiang. It is less well-known that there was also a contemporary scholar Huang Zongxi from Eastern Zhejiang who stood shoulder to shoulder with Gu as the two towering

figures. Intellectually he not only followed in the wake of Wang Yang-
ming and Liu Zongzhou but also broke new ground for Wan Sida and
Wan Sitong. Thus, compared to Gu, we must say that his intellectual
lineage was much longer. Gu was a follower of Zhu Xi and Huang that
of Lu Xiangshan . . . but they respected each other and never
exchanged derogatory remarks . . . Therefore the Eastern Zhejiang
and the Western Zhejiang have been two parallel rather than conflicting traditions. The emphasis of Eastern Zhejiang tradition is placed on
zhuanjia 專家 ("specialization") whereas that of Western Zhejiang
tradition on boya 博雅 ("erudition"), each following its own established practice.[69]

Here Zhang exaggerated the historical importance of Huang Zongxi
to the point of contradicting his own account of Gu Yanwu as given in
the long genealogy of the Zhu school in the essay "Zhu and Lu." He
presented Gu Yanwu as an isolated scholar by confining him geographically to the Western Zhejiang (Zhexi) region even though he knew
very well that Gu's influence had been nationwide all along.[70] However, this exaggeration is perfectly understandable once we realize that
he was in fact comparing himself with Dai by indirection.

Last but not least, Zhang's last essay must be understood in the
light of his central idea in the *Wenshi Tongyi*, "The Six Classics are all
history." An important passage of "Intellectual Tradition of Eastern
Zhejiang" reads, in part, as follows:

Learning in the period of the Three Dynasties (i.e. Xia, Shang, and
Zhou) consisted only of history, not classics . . . Men of later ages venerated the Classics because they are the history of the Three Dynasties
. . . In the Eastern Zhejiang intellectual tradition, scholars interested
in such philosophical topics like "nature" and "destiny" have invariably
turned to study history. This is precisely why it is so excellent.[71]

Modern interpreters generally believe that by this statement Zhang
referred only to the Eastern Zhejiang tradition during the Qing period
because it is obviously untenable if extended earlier than the seventeenth century.[72] However, this turns out not to be the case. In his
"Biography of Shao Jinhan," also written in 1800, he said explicitly:

Since the Southern Song, Confucian philosophers in Eastern Zhejiang
by and large devoted themselves to historical scholarship as a way to

study such topics as "nature" and "destiny." This tradition passed from generation to generation.[73]

It is beside the point to say that Zhang exaggerated his case incredibly which he indeed did. The real question is why he did it. As far as I can discern, he was probably suggesting two points. First, since according to the theory of "the Six Classics are all history," the *Dao* is fully revealed only in history, the long tradition from which he comes has been on the right track all along. Eastern Zhejiang philosophers never engage in "empty talk"; they do philosophy by way of history. Second, the dominant paradigm in Confucian learning from Gu Yanwu to Dai Zhen must now be radically modified. Instead of "the proper study of principles is the study of Classics" (*jingxue ji lixue*), he would propose to say "the proper study of principles is the study of history" (*shixue jhi lixue* 史學即理學). This seems implicit in his exaggerated statement about the Eastern Zhejiang tradition since the Southern Song. Thus, the two justly famous theses in his *Wenshi Tongyi* turn out to reinforce each other and jointly form a powerful argument against Dai's classical philologism. With this last essay Zhang concluded his long intellectual struggle with Dai at the very end of his life.

The significance of Zhang's two Neo-Confucian genealogies, however, far transcends the personal dimension of his intellectual development. With all their imperfections the two genealogies nevertheless reveal Zhang's profundity and incisiveness as an intellectual historian who alone among his contemporaries penetrated beneath the surface of textual studies to discover the deeper meanings of the apparently thoughtless activities of mid-Qing philologists. This is not to suggest, of course, that he made this discovery wholly unaided. As shown above, his final views on both Neo-Confucian traditions in the Qing period evolved over decades as his response to the challenge of Dai's classical philologism gradually deepened. As he followed Dai's work closely, at some point it must have dawned on him that behind much of Dai's anti-Zhu Xi talk on philological grounds there was a hidden philosophical project which was nevertheless continuous from Zhu Xi.

Philologists in eighteenth-century China including Dai, almost without exception, counterposed their own philologically orientated Han Learning to the metaphysical speculation of Song Learning. This Han-Song opposition implies that a complete rupture occurred between Song-Ming Neo-Confucianism and Qing classical scholarship in mid-seventeenth century. Zhang, as far as I am aware, never took part in this type of discourse; we have yet to discover in his writings that he took the Han Learning–Song Learning distinction as meaningful. From his point of view, both Neo-Confucian traditions continued well into the Qing period. What did change was the frame of mind with *zun dexing* giving way to *dao wenxue*. He was aware, perhaps more fully than most contemporary scholars, that his was an age of *dao wenxue* and, what is more, he accepted it wholeheartedly. In this sense, he not only shared Dai's intellectualist outlook but also, like Dai, assumed the responsibility as a philosophical spokesman for Qing Confucian intellectualism. However, there is this difference: While Dai may be construed as a spokesman from the Zhu Xi tradition,[74] Zhang's apologia for Confucian intellectualism was clearly made from the Lu-Wang position.

It was relatively easy and straightforward for Zhang to demonstrate that Dai was in fact a latter-day heir to Zhu Xi. After all, *dao wenxue* has been traditionally accepted as a built-in feature of the Zhu Xi tradition. On the other hand, his effort to bring the Lu-Wang tradition into accord with Qing intellectualism was a heroic one. His arguments are complex, circuitous, and, at times, even tortuous. One or two examples may be given here. He often emphasized that in learning one must first see the "large whole" (*dati* 大體) rather than getting lost in details. This is, needless to say, a reference to the Mencian idea of "establishing the nobler part of one's nature" as particularly emphasized by Lu Xiangshan. In Mencius and Lu Xiangshan, this "large whole" could only mean a person's "moral nature." But for Zhang, it turned out to be an intellectual ability to grasp holistically the central significance of things. Sometimes he also referred to it as *zhuanjia*, which literally means "specialist" or "specialization." But we must not confuse it with the term "specialist" in the modern sense. What his *zhuanjia* "specializes" in is none other than the hedgehog's "one big thing." Take another example. In some of his essays he made references to Wang Yangming's *zhi liangzhi* 致良知 ("extending good-knowing") which again is moral in nature. In Zhang's hands, however, *liangzhi* 良知 also took an intellectualistic turn. What he meant by that term is but a scholar's intuitive inclination toward a particular type of intellectual work.[75] In this way, he intellectualized the Lu-Wang tradition to suit the needs of his Eastern Zhejiang historical scholarship. With the *Dao* historicized on the one hand and the Lu-Wang tradition intellectualized on the other, he succeeded in raising Confucian intellectualism to a new height in eighteenth-century China.

NOTES

I wish to thank Frederick W. Mote and Willard J. Peterson for reading the first draft of this essay and making suggestions for improvement.

1. Zhang Binglin 章炳麟 (1869–1935), Liang Qichao 梁啓超 (1873–1929), Hu Shi 胡適 (1891–1962) and Ch'ien Mu 錢穆 (1895–1990) have been mainly responsible for promoting, each in his own way, this modern view. In Japan a similar evaluation may be found in Shimada Kenji 島田虔次, "Shô Gakusei no ichi" 章學誠の位置 *Tôhô Gakuho* 東方學報 *(March, 1970): 519–530.*

2. Sun Baoxuan 孫寶瑄, *Wangshan Lu Riji* 忘山盧日記 (Shanghai: Shanghai Guji Chuban She 上海古籍出版社, 1983), 24, 207–10.

3. The only notable exception is Dai's collated text of the *Shuijing Zhu* 水經注. See Hu Shi, *Hu Shi shougao* 胡適手稿, series 1–6 (Taibei: Hu Shi jinian guan 胡適紀念館, 1966–69).

4. David S. Nivison, *The Life and Thought of Chang Hsüeh-ch'eng, (1738–1801)* (Stanford University Press, 1966), 142.

5. Ibid., 32–33.

6. *Zhang Xuecheng Yishu* 章學誠遺書 (hereafter "*Yishu*") (Peking: Wenwu Chuban She 文物出版社, 1985), 645.

7. See *Qingshi liezhuan* 清史列傳, punctuated by Wang Zhonghan 王鍾翰 (Peking: Zhonghua Shuju 中華書局, 1987), 8: 5888–89.

8. Yü Ying-shih, "Tai Chen's Choice between Philosophy and Philology," *Asia Major*, 3d. ser., 2, pt. 1 (1989): 79–108.

9. *Yishu*, 224; English translation in Nivison, *op.cit.*, 33.

10. Duan Yucai 段玉裁, *Dai Dongyuan xiansheng nianpu* 戴東原先生年譜, included in *Dai Zhen Wenji* 戴震文集 punctuated by Zhao Yuxin (Hong Kong: Zhonghua Shuju, 1974), 228; Qian Mu, *Zhonguo jin sanbai nian xueshu shi* 中國近三百年學術史, (Shanghai, Commercial Press, 1937), 1: 326–27.

11. Nivison, op.cit., 156.

12. *Yishu*, 92 ("Family Letter, no. 3").

13. *Yishu*, 224.

14. *Gong zizhen quanji* 龔自珍全集, collated by Wang Peizheng 王佩諍, (Shanghai: Zhonghua Shuju, 1961), 1: 193.

15. Yü Ying-shih, "Some Preliminary Observations on the Rise of Ch'ing Confucian Intellectualism," *Tsing Hua Journal of Chinese Studies*, n.s., 11, nos. 1–2 (December, 1975): 105–44.

16. Lo Qinshun 羅欽順, *Kunzhi ji* 困知記, Congshu jicheng 叢書集成 edition, 13. English translation by Irene Bloom, *Knowledge Painfully Acquired* (New York: Columbia University Press, 1987), 144–45. However, I have changed Bloom's "without reference to the classics" to "without seeking evidence in the classics" because it is closer to the literal meaning of *qucheng yu jingshu* 取證於經書. Italics are also mine.

17. *Dai Zhen wenji*, 168.

18. Nivison, op.cit., 47.

19. *Yishu*, 128.

20. See Dai's "Rules of Compilation" for the *Fenzhou Fu Zhi* 汾州府志, now included in *Dai Zhen Quanji* 戴震全集 (Peking: Qing Hua University Press, 1991), 1: 489.

21. *Yishu*, 37.

22. *Yishu*, 337–38; Nivison, op.cit., 188.

23. *Yishu*, 93 ("Family Letter, No. 6").

24. Nivison, op.cit., 41.

25. Ibid., 41–43.

26. Ibid., 56.

27. *Yishu*, 225; English translation in Nivison, op.cit., 41.

28. *Yishu*, 333; English translation in Nivison, op.cit., 42.

29. *Yishu*, 552; English translation in Nivison, op.cit., 46.

30. Nivison, op.cit., 57–60.

31. Ibid., 41.

32. Qian Mu, op.cit., 420–24.

33. Nivison, op.cit., 174.

34. *Yishu*, 82; Nivison, op.cit., 253.

35. I believe the original letter to Qian Daxin was probably written in 1772 because part of its content agrees with his letter to Zhu Fenyuan, cited above. However, the letter as it now stands may have been expanded and revised as late as 1798 in order to be included in his collected work. This was a common practice among Chinese writers in the past. See Qian Mu, op.cit., 418; Paul Demiéville, "Chang Hsüeh-ch'eng and His Historiography," in W. G.

Beasley and E. G. Pulleyblank, eds., *Historians of China and Japan* (London: Oxford University Press, 1961), 172n.; Nivison, op.cit., 183n.

36. Nivison, op.cit., 196.

37. *Yishu*, 694.

38. *Yishu*, 696.

39. *Yishu*, 16.

40. Luo Bingmian 羅炳綿, *Qingdai xueshu lunji* 清代學術論集 (Taipei: Shihuo Chuban She 食貨出版社, 1978), 1-115.

41. Nivison, op.cit., 205-6.

42. *Yishu*, 335.

43. *Yishu*, 86.

44. See "Shikao shi li" 史考釋例 in *Yishu*, 615-18 and "Shikao zhelu 史考摘錄" in *Yishu*, 648-56.

45. *Yishu*, 325.

46. For some of the important modern discussions on this thesis, see works cited in Yü Yingshi 余英時, *Lun Dai Zhen yu Zhang Xuecheng* 論戴震與章學誠, (hereafter, *Dai and Zhang*) (Hong Kong: Longmen Shudian 龍門書店, 1976), 76n.

47. Qian Mu, op.cit., 380-86.

48. *Yishu*, 381.

49. *Dai Zhen quanji*, 1: 213. Similar but more detailed arguments may be found in *Dai Zhen wenji*, 44, 140, 145-46, 164-65, 168.

50. *Yishu*, 325.

51. *Yishu*, 338.

52. *Dai Zhen wenji*, 143-44.

53. *Yishu*, 73-74.

54. Qian Mu, op.cit., 382-84; Demièville, op.cit., 178-80; Nivison, op.cit., 140-62.

55. Nivison, op.cit., 151.

56. *Yishu*, 315. See also "Notes of 1795," in *Yishu*, 387-88.

57. *Yishu*, 12.

58. *Yishu*, 8-9.

59. *Yishu*, 15.

60. In my opinion, Zhang most likely wrote "Zhu and Lu" in 1777 when he heard about Dai's death. For different views, however, see Hu Shi, *Zhang Shizhai xiansheng nianpu* 章實寶齋先生 revised by Yao Mingda 姚名達 (Taibei: Yuanliu Chuban Gongsi 遠流出版公司, 1986), 73-77; Qian Mu, op.cit., 419; and Nivison, op.cit., 105.

61. *Yishu*, 14-16.

62. *Yishu*, 16-17.

63. Nivison, op.cit., 162.

64. For a fuller documentation and analysis, see Yü Ying-shih, *Dai and Zhang,* 53–75.

65. Nivison, op.cit., 279. See also pp. 249–50.

66. *Yishu,* 117–18. On this Eastern Zhejiang tradition of historical scholarship, see Lynn Struve, "The Early Ch'ing Legacy of Huang Tsung-hsi: A Reexamination," *Asia Major,* 3d ser., 1, pt. 1 (1988): 83–122.

67. *Yishu,* 611.

68. Wang Zongyan 王宗炎 (1755–1826), to whom Zhang entrusted his *Wenshi Tongyi* for editing, suggested, in 1801, some editorial changes for the first paragraph of the last essay. See *Yishu,* appendix, 624.

69. *Yishu,* 15.

70. Demiéville considered it a mistake on Zhang's part to identify Gu Yanwu geographically with Zhexi ("West of the Zhe River"), op.cit., 171n. However, Zhang's identification was based on the new study of Quan Zuwang 全祖望. See *Jiqi Tingji* 鮚埼亭集, *Sibu congkan suoben* 四部叢刊縮本 edition, *waibian* 外編, *juan* 卷, 49: 1057–58.

71. *Yishu,* 15.

72. Jin Yufu 金毓黻, *Zhongguo shixue shi* 中國史學史 (Shanghai: Commercial Press, 1957), 252.

73. *Yishu,* 177.

74. See Yü Ying-shih, "Tai Chen and the Chu Hsi Tradition," in *Essays in Commemoration of the Golden Jubilee of the Fung Ping Shan Library,* ed.: Chan Ping-leung (Hong Kong University Press, 1982), 376–92.

75. Yü Ying-shih, *Dai and Zhang,* 63–65, 73–75.

Beyond Post-Modernism[1]

Henry Rosemont, Jr.

Once upon a time, when students used to respond to a difficult philosophical question in class with statements like "It's all a matter of opinion," or "It's a question of semantics," or "It's all relative," I used to scold them gently. I can no longer do that, for the more knowledgeable among them can now easily cite many of the more prominent practitioners of the craft of philosophy in support of such statements. And they can cite as well no small number of anthropologists, historians, psychologists, sociologists, and literary theorists in the same vein.[2] All, it seems, is indeed relative.

I take this relativism to be a central characteristic of what is called the post-modern condition. Actually, I shouldn't say "central" because of course there are no genuine centers now; any claimed center would have to be seen as arbitrary and discourse about it could only be construed as masking power relations between oppressors and oppressed. Our conceptions of truth, beauty, justice, and the good are all of them altogether dependent on our time, place, language, and culture, and in the extreme, equally dependent on our age, gender, race, and/or class within a given culture. Babel has been rebuilt. At best, we're all natives now; at worst, the other, any other, is wholly other, and here am I, alone and afraid in a world I never made.

This is a rather frightful state of affairs, not least because if this relativistic thrust of post-modernism is at all correct, then, rather than celebrating the manifold scholarly achievements of the person to whom this volume is dedicated, we should instead lament the waste of such a gifted intellect in the futile attempt to penetrate the inherently impenetrable. On this account, a thorough deconstruction of the writings of David Shepherd Nivison would reveal that, appearances to the contrary notwithstanding, we have not learned much of the life, times, or thought of, for example, Mencius, Zhang Xuecheng, or He Shen;[3]

the most we might learn is bits and pieces of the life, times, and thought of David Shepherd Nivison.

If there is a hint of a *reductio ad absurdum* argument here, it is intentional, and parallels one Nivison himself sketched over a quarter of a century ago:[4]

> I have occasionally said frankly what I think of Zhang (Xuecheng's) ideas. Some may think this is a mistake. They may hold that Zhang's problems were his and not mine, and that his conceptions must therefore be outside the range of my criticisms, good or ill. I differ with this view. For it seems to me that if it were right, I could not have understood Zhang at all.

Clearly, however, no relativistic skeptic worth his or her philosophical salt will be persuaded by either Nivison's or my own attempted *reductio*. They would simply accept the consequent, and so much the worse for Nivison (and myself) in particular, and for the field(s) of comparative studies more generally. It therefore seems important to me to confront head-on this relativistic feature of post-modernism. In doing so, however, I am not merely attempting to save the professional skins of comparativists. Rather do I want to mix together some epistemological, logical, political, and moral concerns to suggest that certain features of relativism have been, and can be, intellectually and morally liberating, progressive, and humane, but that the fundamental thrust of it has been, and can be, fairly close-minded; cognitively, politically, and morally.

I want to begin by considering two different claims falling under the heading of relativism. The first I have already sketched: our basic beliefs about the world, our value structures, our tastes, standards of rationality and evidence, and much else, are dependent upon the time, place, and culture in which we live, and on the language we learn to articulate those beliefs, values, and standards. Let us call this the culture dependency claim.[5]

The second claim has been stated in various ways, including (a) disclosure invariably conceals more than it reveals and interpretations of discourse invariably tell us more about the interpreter than about the discourse itself; (b) there are impassable barriers to breaching the historical ruptures separating the several Western pasts from its present, and the pasts of other culture from their presents as well; (c) there are incommensurable conceptual frameworks that create uncrossable boundaries separating linguistically and culturally diverse peoples; and (d), in the extreme case, that these barriers and boundaries can and do even isolate contemporaries sharing the same language and culture. I will refer to this second claim as the impassable barriers claim.[6]

If I have stated these claims accurately, we can learn much from their juxtaposition. First, they are logically independent; neither entails the other. Going quickly from the second claim to the first, one culture might be dependent for its beliefs on the way the world really is, in which case the impassable barriers claim could be true, and the culture dependency claim false. This is extraordinarily improbable, but not logically impossible.

The more interesting point, however, comes by looking from the other side. From the premise of culture dependency, the impassable barriers claim cannot be inferred as conclusion. Culturally dependent I may well be, but between my culture and any or all others, there may be no barriers at all, or some barriers, or very formidable barriers, or indeed impassable barriers. All of these are equally possible states of affairs. There are, to be sure, significant entailments of the culture dependency claim, but impassable barriers is not among them, from which it follows that we can accept the former claim while rejecting the latter, and it follows in turn that if we wish to advance the second claim, independent reasons will have to be proffered for doing so.

What might those reasons be? We can note here in passing that if we accept culture dependency this question gains special force, because clearly the impassable barriers claim can't then be seen as a statement on the way the world really is. On the contrary, the barriers must be seen as a conceptual construct within the contemporary Western intellectual tradition, and consequently the intellectuals who built the barriers must be responsible for the result, which to me resembles nothing so much as a philosophical dungeon. Again, then: what reasons can be given for advancing the impassable barriers claim?

Clearly, it cannot be construed as an empirical statement. Even after fully relativizing the concept of fact to our cultural tradition, and allowing that facts are theory-laden, it is obvious that the facts of our everyday life overwhelmingly suggest the negation of the impassable barriers claim. There is general agreement that we are coming to see ourselves as part of a global village. Millions of dollars of goods are bought, sold, and traded cross-culturally every day. Summit meetings and international conferences are held regularly, treaties are signed. People travel to the corners of the world, and attend schools in different countries. There are millions of bilingual people. In short, cultural barriers are crossed countless times every day, and to suggest that in some important factual way these barriers aren't really being crossed is at best special pleading, at worst, ludicrous. No, the impassable barriers claim can't be construed as a factual statement.

It can't be taken as an inductive generalization either, for if it is, it resembles the equally widely proclaimed domino theory of the 1960s in that they are both inductive arguments based on zero instances, hence worthless as anything more than propaganda.[7] There could not be any specific instances of the impassable barriers claim, of course, because they would be self-defeating. That is to say, I could only argue that someone had given a bad interpretation and/or translation of a text or cultural practice—evidence, that is, that the barriers had not been surmounted—on the basis of a good, or at least better one; and I could only do that on the assumption that the barriers had indeed been overcome.

Now if the impassable barriers claim can't be credited either as a direct empirical statement or as an inductive generalization, then perhaps it should be construed as an *a priori* statement, the statement, in other words, of a corollary or implication of some other theoretical considerations for which arguments have been, or can be, put forth. But for myself at least, this won't do either. Elsewhere I have argued at some length that a great many relativistic claims, especially the impassable barriers claim, reduce significantly to one, the claim of linguistic relativity.[8] I do not have space to rehearse those arguments here, but can briefly state their conclusion: the plausibility of many relativistic claims hinges crucially on one's views of what it is to be a natural language, and the linguistic views adopted by relativists as different as Quine and Derrida—from stimulus meanings to the primacy of script—are highly implausible, and at great variance with those views of language current in the field of generative linguistics, which I personally endorse.[9]

I conclude from these brief reflections that the impassable barriers claim is not an entailment of the culture dependency claim, and that it is neither empirical, nor an inductive generalization, nor an a priori statement; or, if it is any of these latter three, it is mistaken, because good reasons can be given for affirming its negation. Many other arguments against the claim could also be advanced, not least among them being that it is worse than worthless as a methodological assumption for cross-cultural research, for it nullifies in advance any intellectual value that might result from that research.[10]

In sum, there are fundamental logical, empirical, epistemological, linguistic, and methodological difficulties attendant on the impassable barriers claim, many of which are well known, straightforward and obvious. If this be granted, we are immediately confronted with another question: why is the impassable barriers claim so widely held, or at least given great credence, among so many Western scholars and intellectuals today? (To the best of my knowledge, it is not widely held in any other culture).[11] Or put another way: why would anyone want to maintain that the other was in principle wholly other?

An adequate answer to this question would oblige us to delve much deeper into Western intellectual and political history—especially of the late nineteenth and twentieth centuries—than there is space for herein. All I can do is sketch the outline of an answer, which, highly encapsulated, is as follows: we are inclined to take the impassable barriers claim seriously less for empirical or conceptual reasons—because these are fairly weak—and more for political and moral reasons, which can be quite strong. As I read it, the claim is best understood, despite its grammatical camouflage, as a normative judgment; a number of "oughts" lie just below the surface structure. The culture dependency claim also has strong normative overtones, but whereas I see these as on the whole liberating, humane, and progressive, I find those attendant on the impassable barriers claim much less so. The blanket term "relativism" obscures crucial differences between the two claims, which I will now take up briefly, in turn.

As its name suggests, relativism in its modern form grew in response to absolutism, a catch-all term not just encompassing Hegelianism, but standing duty for Western philosophy generally within the Cartesian tradition. Truth with a capital T, the quest for certainty, universal moral values, objectivity, and the scientific method were (and are) part of what came under the heading of absolutism. By themselves, of course these beliefs are one thing; but when coupled with related, more personal beliefs, they contributed significantly to some of the most mischievous chapters in the history of Western civilization. These other beliefs were held by absolutists, and included the following: we know a number of these truths, and know universal moral values. We know as well the cultures of the savages of this world, and know they do not have these truths, nor values. It seemed to follow, then, that the benighted of the world had to be brought under the tutelage of the West. Thus the "White man's burden," heavy though it was, could be borne, because it was not merely an excuse for greed, adventurism, exploitation, rapacity, and much else; rather was it borne for the welfare of the yellow, red, black, and brown peoples who were receiving the teaching. The fact that these peoples had not requested the instruction, or that their tuition included death in the millions, the destructions of their lands and their cultural traditions, was of little moment; destiny was destiny, it was manifest, and it would usher in a glorious tomorrow—at least for those who survived.

Against this unrelievedly sordid background of jingoistic imperialism any questioning of absolutist values had to be seen as salutary, and relativism was indeed just that. To argue that differing belief systems could form coherent wholes, that values were deeply embedded in culture, that so-called "primitive" peoples regularly exhibited highly sophisticated qualities—all of this made the task of justifying the attitudes and behaviors of merchants, missionaries, and colonial overseers increasingly difficult. Once it began to become clear that there was no culturally independent stance one could assume in order to judge the merits of other cultures, the moral imperative implicit in relativism also became clearer: we should see these peoples as different from ourselves. Not barbaric, primitive, simple, or what have you, just different; and consequently, unless they request our presence, on their terms, we should leave them alone.

Some related relativistic "oughts" were generated as raw imperialism gave way to the Cold War. To take just one (very personal) example: Even before the People's Republic of China was proclaimed on 1 October 1949, the "Who lost China?" question began infecting the U.S. body politic, and the virus continued to spread long after the richly deserved disgrace of Senator Joseph McCarthy five years later. Chiang K'ai-shek and the Kuomintang were good; they were preserving and enhancing the best of traditional Chinese culture, especially proto-democratic Confucianism. Mao Tse-tung and the Communists were evil; they were destroying traditional Chinese culture *in toto*, especially Confucianism, and were replacing it with Marxist totalitarianism.[12]

To be sure, there were a few written works that painted the Chinese Civil War and its aftermath less starkly; Edgar Snow's *Red Star Over China* and Theodore White's and Annalee Jacoby's *Thunder Out of China* come immediately to mind. But these people could be dismissed as mere journalists—and pinko ones at that. The scholarly voices were very quiet. An exception was David Shepherd Nivison. In 1956, he had the audacity to suggest that while there were unmistakable and profound differences between China's (largely) Confucian past and her Communist present, the similarities and continuities were equally deserving of consideration and attention. And he argued well—cogently, and with much textual evidence—that although neither Confucianism nor Maoist communism were democratic in anything resembling the Western sense of the term, they nevertheless advanced similar moral principles which, when contextualized, were deserving of everyone's moral reflection.

Again, then, we can discern another "ought:" Threaten less, don't call names so much; endeavor to understand. (It is for this reason that while I have enjoyed and profited from all of Nivison's work over the years, "Communist Ethics and Chinese Tradition" has, and always will have, a special place in my mind—and heart.)[13]

Another highly salutary effect of the culture dependency claim of relativism is in the area of scholarship, and stems from the claim itself. After our attention is directed closely, it becomes fairly easy to see how and why members of other cultures are more or less products of their environment. The West seemed, and claimed, however, to be the exception. This was the result simply of the extreme difficulty of laying bare the presuppositions of one's own conceptual framework, but more important, of the modern West, alone among the world's cultures past and present, having at the center of its cultural tradition the intellectual stance of being acultural and antitraditional. Who cares in which language Descartes wrote the *Meditations*? Or that he was very

probably traumatized, as were so many others, by the assassination of
Henry of Navarre? Or that he was a close observer-participant in the
Thirty Years War? All that matters is *cogito ergo sum;* then, now, forever-
more; anywhere.[14] Value-free objectivity, eternal sentences, disinterest-
ed study of the world and its peoples. The Enlightenment. Universal
laws, of science, of politics, of morals. Always the new, not the old.
Tomorrow. These, of course, are the defining features of modernism.

The culture dependency claim provided the basis for the revisionist
work—by radicals, feminists, post-colonial critics, and others—that has
laid bare the sexism, racism, arrogance, elitism, and much else in modernism. It has shown how certain forms of discourse privilege one view
of the world over others, thereby shrinking intellectual horizons, and
entrenching in power those who advance the privileged view. All of
this, I submit, is for the good. It has given us a better sense of who we
are, how we got to be the way we are, and why the future of Western
culture has to make some sharp breaks with its modern past.

These, then, are a few of the reasons—and there are others—why
intellectually open, internationally minded, politically progressive people of good will might well give credence, if not their allegiance, to this
relativist orientation of post-modernism. Tolerance is a good thing,
and it is also good to subject the presuppositional beliefs of one's culture to critical examination, especially when it brings to light their
unsavory elements. Note, however, that in order to bring about these
results, the most we may need from relativism is the culture dependency claim. When we turn to the second claim, of impassable barriers, a
less intellectual, international, progressive, and morally praiseworthy
thrust can be seen. Or so it appears to me at least.

Let us first consider seriously that the other must be seen as wholly
other. The key term here of course is the modifier: *wholly* other. Once
we leave the technical and abstract vocabulary of speculative written
texts we can ask a down-to-earth but still philosophical question: what
would it be like to experience another human being as *wholly* other? In
answering this question I do not wish to invoke, although I would
endorse, the Schiller/Beethoven dream of "Alle Menschen Werden
Brüder." Even my blood relatives—parents, children, grandchildren—
are distinct from me. Very close they are, but nevertheless other. And
the same must be said for my friends, neighbors, students, co-workers,

colleagues, and so forth. They are other; more or less close, some of them, yet other.

And there are others who appear to me as radically other. But radically other still implies some points of contact, some similarities that form the basis for exploring differences, and for generating responses to them. These responses can range from curiosity to puzzlement, from respect and/or admiration to dislike or loathing, and much more. As Slavic inheritors of the Great Russian tradition and living before my time, I must see Peter Kropotkin and Josef Stalin as alike in many respects, but both of them radically other with respect to myself. Nevertheless, naively perhaps but no less sincerely I admire the former and loathe the latter. And with regard to the living, I would say pretty much the same thing about the Dalai Lama and Pol Pot respectively.

Let me give a less personal but more poignant example of this point. It is fair to say, I believe, that the average American is radically other than the average Iraqi, and each sees the other this way. Language, religion, history, government, and physical environment are each and all of them very different between the two. And many of the American peoples cheered the attacks and advances of the U.S. troops in the monstrous invasion of Iraq. For myself, however, I believe the following: if, instead of so regularly displaying Nintendo-type fireworks raining over Baghdad the U.S. media had shown Iraqi grandmothers crying over the dead bodies of their grandchildren, who were victims of Tomahawk missiles, there would have been far less flag-waving on behalf of Desert Storm in the U.S. Perhaps, without at all negating the significance of pluralism and differences, it can nevertheless be said that if you can relate to one dear grandmother you can relate to them all.[15]

But it seems to me if I were to see some other as wholly other, then I do not know how I could respond either sympathetically or with hostility, with affection or dislike, admiration or loathing. If there are *no* points of contact between us that I can discern, if I cannot, in other words, even begin to imagine what it might be like to inhabit the other's world, then, it seems to me, the only attitude I could assume toward this other would be indifference. Stated alternatively, so long as I can identify with you at all, it must be as a fellow human being, an acting subject, with beliefs, life projects, hopes, fears, joys, and sorrows.

But if I cannot identify with you at all, if you are wholly other, then you must be merely an object, about whose future I can be as indifferent as I am about the fate of a grain of sand in the desert.

Now for those of you who can sympathize with these meditations it should be clear that obeying the imperative to see the other as wholly other can all too easily result, *ceteris paribus,* in a dehumanization of the other, and an attendant dehumanization of myself. But important as this point is, it is not the one I want to emphasize here. Keep in mind that the impassable barriers claim is a modern Western conceit. Keep equally in mind that the members of the Western capitalist industrial democracies comprise only twenty percent of the world's peoples, but own and control almost eighty percent of the world's wealth. If the eighty percent of the world's peoples who live in cultures distinct from our own are seen as other, or very other, or even as radically other, then they must nevertheless be seen as human beings, towards which we can have more or less sympathetic, hostile, respectful, or many other responses, all of which, however, will equally force the moral question of how a minority of human beings can justify living in excess while the great majority of their fellows live in want. But if that eighty percent of the world's peoples aren't really people, if they are wholly other and indifference becomes the Western stance taken toward them, then the moral question almost surely will not, cannot be confronted.[16]

Thus, just as the cultural dependency claim can open our vistas with respect to our culturally diverse fellows, the impassable barriers claim can close them. I wish to keep the parallelism of the arguments, and maintain that just as the culture dependency claim extends our intellectual horizons, the impassable barriers claim shrinks them. Our regnant metaphor I believe apt. Within the Western conceptual framework of post-modernism on which I am focusing herein, impassable barriers have been constructed around all other cultures. But such barriers must equally serve as barricades around our own, and it must therefore be asked whether or not it is a good thing to keep ourselves in, and others out.

To ask this question, obviously, is simultaneously to answer it: no. Leaning very heavily on the Western tradition of which I am a part, I insist that I can only flourish when I can leave my house freely, and when others can equally freely enter it.

A related way in which the impassable barriers claim can be seen as profoundly conservative is that it reduces significantly the possibility of a thoroughgoing critique of the Western tradition of modernism that would go beyond the post-modern critiques. To see how and why this is so, let us consider how a person committed to modernism—and when modernism includes the Enlightenment project we are considering a great many persons—might respond to the polemic against both modernism and post-modernism I have been developing thus far.

First, to the culture dependency claim, the response might be simply, So what? So what if these views of value-free objectivity in science, constitutional government, democracy, individual rights, rule by law, and so forth grew up only in the modern West, and can be shown to be culturally dependent for their development on other factors? What is wrong with such views? This person, in other words, would undoubtedly invoke the logic of discovery/logic of justification distinction that has been important in Western philosophy, especially philosophy of science, since the heyday of the Vienna Circle. How all of these views associated with the Enlightenment came about is one thing—and relatively unimportant—while arguing for their universal applicability is something else; whatever its origin, shouldn't, for example, the concept of human rights be cross-culturally applicable? Shouldn't it be seen, that is, as a universal concept despite its birthplace?[17]

A second and related response to my own and other critiques of modernism would be to admit that all of the horrors attendant on its rise and development in the West are indeed horrors: slavery, imperialism, the destruction of entire cultures, the subjugation of others, environmental devastation, racism, sexism, elitism. All of these are certainly sorry chapters in the history of the modern West, but they go no way toward challenging the views and the values of modernism. All that has been shown is that we have not well practiced what we have preached, which is certainly regrettable, but as an argument against modernism, it is nevertheless paradigmatically *ad hominem*.

Still a third response to critiques of modernism might run as follows: anti-foundationalist, deconstructive, feminist, post-colonial and other recent writings show that Western universalist views of rationality, science, politics, and morality have indeed been more culturally linked than was heretofore believed. But these views were self-consciously developed in an attempt to be culturally independent, and that attempt, along with the openness that has flowed from it, has been, or can be, salutary for everyone, both because of what those modernist ideas have already developed, and because the conceptual resources of modernism, seemingly alone, provide the intellectual openness to cope with change, and to be self-correcting. Those ideas have, in the first instance, been salutary for all those who would be dead except for modern Western medicine; starving if not for modern Western agricultural techniques of growing and transporting more food; or rotting in prisons were it not for the universalist views of groups like Amnesty International. And when we look today at the belief systems of other cultures, we find that they do not appear to have the conceptual resources either to do these things, or to cope with the changes necessary for the human race to survive the twenty-first century. The widespread fundamentalist movements in both Hinduism and Islam are backward rather than forward looking; Confucianism, Daoism, and Chinese Buddhism were and are not rich enough conceptually to meet the challenges even of the twentieth century, and are no longer taken seriously even in their country of origin. And in ethnic enclaves ranging from Serbia to South Africa, from Indonesia to Armenia, virulent nationalisms are coming to the fore, nationalisms which are irrational, regressive, and intolerant, and incompatible with modernist views of rationality, of politics, and of morality. If not modernism, then, this response might well conclude, what are the alternatives?

I have put these responses to post-modern critiques of modernism as strongly as I could, both because I believe they are indeed strong responses, and to show as well that so long as post-modern challenges are developed solely within the Western intellectual tradition, modernism will almost surely be able to meet them, which suggests that in some crucial respects, post-modernism is not all that different from modernism. More is going to be needed if the modern Western intellectual tradition is going to be challenged at its foundations, as I believe it must be.

First, and most obviously, the impassable claim guarantees that there will be very few, and perhaps no answers to the question just asked, what are the alternatives? If, some way or somehow, it is impossible for us to inhabit any of the conceptual worlds of eighty percent of the human race, then it seems that except perhaps for some aesthetic concerns, we will remain largely indifferent to those belief systems, except to be sharply critical of any behaviors based on those beliefs that conflict with our universalist beliefs. If your belief system does not include beliefs about scientific objectivity, rule by law, or inviolable human rights, then so much the worse for you, your beliefs, and your culture. Here, then, is another reason for seeing the conceptually constructed barriers really as barricades. We can continue, like the Seventh Cavalry, to hold the fort, or draw the wagons in a circle, and/or, if need be, either give the Indians a few blankets or break out our Gatling guns and charge.[18] We need not, in sum, ever take them seriously by their own lights, but only as they may threaten our existence.

Second, if anyone wishes to claim that only the modern West seems to have the conceptual resources to deal adequately with change, and with conflict within the tradition, it can be replied that at best, this is a case not proven, and is more probably false. There is surely much evidence that Hinduism, Confucianism, Islam, Daoism, and other non-Western belief systems did not and have not adequately met the challenges of the twentieth century brought about by the West. But this observation leaves open the question of whether or not those belief systems contain the conceptual resources to respond to the problems and paradoxes of their traditions in the context of change. The imperialist physical occupation of the lands wherein those cultures flourished made it all but impossible for those belief systems to be carefully reexamined, stretched, reaffirmed, modified. It is, to put the matter starkly, hard to philosophize with a gun at one's head.

We may note in this regard that two of the relatively few non-Western countries that have been successfully coming to terms with modernizing change while yet keeping many of their distinctive cultural traditions are Thailand and Japan. They are also two of the very few non-Western countries that were not physically occupied by the Western imperialist powers. If this is a coincidence, it is surely an incredible one. And I daresay that if the Islamic world had physically overrun and occupied European Christendom in the mid-fifteenth century, as it seems to have had the capacity to do, then very probably the Western Christian philosophical heritage, as an integral component of a conquered culture, would not have endured, nor been renewed.

If these belief systems, and the other diverse cultural traditions which they produced, are really dead now, then perhaps the cause of their demise has less to do with their own inherent weaknesses and limitations, and much more to do with the conquering modern West, which may consequently be equally to blame for the several desperate attempts by the conquered to salvage those belief systems and traditions by stridently appealing to their most chauvinistic and regressive elements. These are extremely painful possibilities for the West to contemplate, and one way to avoid their contemplation is to believe there are impassable barriers to truly understanding those traditions.

For myself, the non-Western intellectual traditions are not dead, nor should they be seen merely as being in their reactionary last throes. Of course I have been saddened by the extent to which those traditions have been weakened and/or regressively subverted in their homelands, and largely ignored in the West. But I am encouraged greatly by the fact that they have endured at all given the economic, political, military, and intellectual onslaught their adherents have endured for the past century and a half.[19]

Those traditions form a significant part of the legacy of humankind, and hence their loss can only lead to a diminution of cultural diversity, and to a consequent diminution of the richness of all human lives. They deserve our care and our attention, because in reconstructing these traditions we will simultaneously be reconstructing the modern Western intellectual tradition as well, and thereby take it beyond the narrow parochialism of post-modernism.

Postscript

The most succinct statement I know of one of the themes of post-modernism considered in this essay is the following:[20]

> If you examine systematically a man's writings, and then set down the things that occurred during his life, and show how he himself was involved in them, you will understand why he wrote what he did; in his way . . . you can know a man by appraising his world.

These lines imply that the present essay must say something about me and my world, just as the writings of David Shepherd Nivison must say something about him and his world. They must equally, then, also say something about their author and his world, even though they were composed two hundred years ago, in Chinese. Nivison knows this author well, and has introduced him to many more of us through his great skill in crossing cultural barriers.

NOTES

1. Prefatory remarks: 1) Portions of this paper were first read at the plenary panel of the Twenty-Fifth Anniversary Conference of the Society for Asian and Comparative Philosophy 25 July 1993 (which is partly responsible for its conversational style); I am grateful to the participants for their comments and encouragement. 2) My use of "we" and "our" herein refers to everyone, regardless of race, class, gender, age, or ethnicity, who is more or less a product of the modern Western intellectual tradition, particularly the philosophical tradition. 3) Finally, I am grateful to Philip Ivanhoe for conceiving this volume in the first place, for inviting me to contribute to it, and for his editorial skills in working through the results of his invitation.

2. To round up all of the usual philosophical suspects would be to compose a bibliography longer than this essay. I cite a few of them in "Against Relativism," in Gerald Larson and Eliot Deutsch, eds., *Interpreting Across Boundaries* (Princeton University Press, 1988). (And see note 18). For the rest, readers of post-modernist works who draw different implications from them than I do— who see those works, that is, as uniformly progressive—need not bother reading beyond this note. Of course I am lumping together a number of different thinkers who deserve to be distinguished, but for my present purposes, the two scholars associated with post-modern relativism that I exempt from my challenges herein are Clifford Geertz—who is responsible for my "we're all natives now" line in the text—and Paul Feyerabend; both of whom, I think, would endorse at least the spirit, if not the letter, of what is said in this paper.

3. Specifically and respectively: "Mencius and Motivation," in Henry Rosemont, Jr. and Benjamin I. Schwartz, eds., *Studies in Classical Chinese Thought* (Scholars Press, JAAR Thematic Studies Series, 1979); *The Life and Thought of Chang Hsüeh-ch'eng* (Stanford University Press, 1966); "Ho Shen and His Accusers: Ideology and Political Behavior in the Eighteenth Century," in David S. Nivison and Arthur F. Wright, eds., *Confucianism in Action* (Stanford University Press, 1966).

4. *The Life and Thought of Chang Hsüeh-ch'eng*, op. cit., ix.

5. Either "cultural influence" or "cultural determinism" might have seemed better terms, as both are common. But for the question about post-

modernism I want to address, to have used the former would have begged the question in my favor, and the latter would have done the same for the other side. By "dependency" I do *not* wish to imply that culturally (or linguistically) dependent beliefs or practices can have no applicability or relevance outside the culture (language) of origin.

6. See note 2. To take only one recent example:

One cannot advocate the Hindu case for vegetarianism without accepting the axioms of Hindu theology.

The issue is not only moral relativism . . . A cultural relativist may be led to believe that we cannot understand other cultures. The ethnographer may travel hopefully, but never leaves his mental homeland. There is no escape from cultural apartheid. This is, indeed, the dispiriting conclusion that has been reached by some contemporary American anthropologists, such as George Marcus, Renato Rosaldo, Vincent Crapanzano and Michael Taussig. Adam Kuper, "Adaptable Man," *Times Literary Supplement,* 16 July 1993.

7. My later arguments should make clear why I chose this particular analogy.

8. "Against Relativism," op. cit.

9. Ibid. The most recent work I have in mind is Noam Chomsky, "A Minimalist Program for Linguistic Theory," MIT Working Papers, no. 1, 1992. The *locus classicus* for Quine is his *Word and Object* (MIT Press, 1960), esp chap. 2. For Derrida, *Of Grammatology* (John Hopkins University Press, 1976).

10. It is now a commonplace that after the deconstructive work has been done, the work itself must then be deconstructed in turn, which probably, in the end, will leave only the trace of a Cheshire grin. The logic is impeccable, but it should not go unnoticed that such logic provides a splendid excuse for deconstructors and other post-modernists to avoid intellectual, moral, and/or political responsibility and commitment if they wish to do so.

11. Indeed, post-colonial critics usually claim to know the West all too well; and from my reading of them, they are correct. See, for example, Ziauddin Sardar, ed., *The Revenge of Athena: Science, Exploitation, and the Third World* (London: Mansell Publishing Ltd., 1988).

12. Worries that my phrasing here may be exaggerated can be dispelled by reading almost at random the *Congressional Record* from roughly 1948 through 1962, and not only the reports of the House Un-American Activities Committee. The documentary film "Point of Order" also serves well to recreate the stultifying intellectual atmosphere of those years.

13. In the *Journal of Asian Studies* 16, no. 1 (1956–1957): 51–74.

14. On Descartes' cultural milieu, I have profited from Stephen Toulmin, *Cosmopolis: The Hidden Agenda of Modernity* (New York: Free Press, 1990).

15. This point and some of its implications are developed further in my *A Chinese Mirror: Moral Reflections on Political Economy and Society* (La Salle, Ill.: Open Court Publishing Co., 1991).

16. Ibid.

17. I have begun to reply to these modernist challenges in "Rights vs. Rituals," in Mary I. Bockover, ed., *Rules, Rituals and Responsibility: Essays Dedicated to Herbert Fingarette* (La Salle, Ill.: Open Court Publishing Co., 1992).

18. In a recent article, Richard Rorty has said:

> The real work of building a multicultural global utopia, I suspect, will be done by people who, in the course of the next few centuries, unravel each culture into a multiplicity of fine component threads, and then weave those threads together with equally fine threads from other cultures . . .

"A Pragmatist View of Rationality and Cultural Difference," *Philosophy East and West* 42, no. 4 (October 1992): 593, omitting subscripts. Despite my concurrence with these views, I still see Rorty as the contemporary intellectual equivalent of Colonel George Armstrong Custer, given how consistently he continues to focus on the American Liberal tradition, while altogether ignoring any others East of Paris. Yet Rorty is now seen as somehow on the Left—I suspect he would demur—while someone like Alasdair MacIntyre is seen as sharply conservative. Perhaps he is, but unlike virtually all other contemporary American philosophers of note, MacIntyre takes non-Western moral traditions seriously. See, for example, his "Incommensurability, Truth, and the Conversation Between Confucians and Aristotelians about the Virtues," in Eliot Deutsch, ed., *Culture and Modernity* (University of Hawaii Press, 1991). It is even more instructive, I think, to compare this paper to Rorty's in the same volume. In fairness to Rorty, and to make my own interest in the matter explicit, it must be said that his rejection of comparative philosophy as an intellectual enterprise is linked to the different ways it is currently being practiced, and one of those practices he dismisses curtly is my own. See his review of *Interpreting Across Boundaries* in *Philosophy East and West* 39, no. 3 (July, 1989): 332–37. Related perspectives on this matter are well treated by Bryan W. Van Norden in his own contribution to this volume (and I am grateful to him and the editor for sharing it with me before it went to press); see especially his note 61.

19. I have of course also been encouraged by learning just how rich, diverse, and complex those systems are, thanks in large measure to the work

of scholars like Nivison. A splendid example, dealing with tensions in the state examination system, is his "Protest Against Conventions and Conventions of Protest," in Arthur F. Wright, ed., *The Confucian Persuasion* (Stanford University Press, 1960).

    20. *The Life and Thought of Chang Hsüeh-ch'eng,* op. cit., 1.

Duty and Virtue

Chad Hansen

8

The last decade has seen a surge of interest in *virtue ethics*. Virtue theorists contrast their focus on moral character with the dominant trend in Western ethics, which they characterize as *duty* ethics. The paradigms of duty ethics are utilitarianism and Kantian deontology. Both are universalistic theories about the moral duties every person owes every other person. The logic of moral duty (*"ought* implies *can"*) requires that every moral agent can see and execute her duty. These duties follow from one's status as a rational being. Duty ethics thus concentrates excessively on the lowest common denominator in moral behavior—the minimum required of any responsible moral agent.

Virtue theorists prefer to attend to character cultivation. Preoccupation with one's duty, they argue, leads to a shallow and juvenile conception of moral behavior. An agent who focuses only on her duty becomes the embodiment of a formula—obeying an instruction rather than reacting as a complete person. She has no essential moral personality beyond entertaining and interpreting duty formulae. Something beyond that bare minimum should interest a mature agent. She should seek a dynamic and rich structure of ethical relations.

Virtue theorists see advantages in traditional ethical theorists—particularly Aristotle. They value the complex structure of traditionally evolved *thick* ethical terms such as 'loyal', 'courageous', 'compassionate', and 'charitable' which they contrast with the 'thin' focus of duty ethics on 'right' and 'wrong'.[1]

Defenders of *duty* ethics, however, worry that this focus on virtue leaves important questions of ethics unanswered—or worse, favors unreflective acceptance of status quo answers. Since Socrates raised the issue, we have seen our status as moral agents bound up with being able to wonder if traditional virtues are really virtuous. If it does not lead reliably to correct action, why should we value a character trait or action disposition?

We can easily add theories of moral education and psychology to a properly reflective duty-based moral system. Still, deciding *how* to teach presupposes knowing *what* to teach. We must reflect on which actions are correct before we try to implant virtues. We do not want to successfully foster dispositions to perform immoral actions.

Partisans of each position read the history of Western ethics differently. One sees in the dialectic leading from Aristotle to Kant a growing depersonalization and separation of morality from human nature. The growth of duty ethics represents a loss of genuine moral sensibility. The other sees a gradual maturing of a conception of moral behavior from primitive tribalism and familism to one consistent with a world in which all humans are interconnected. Celebration of virtue ethics looks like a frontal attack on the possibility of moral reform and progress in moral attitudes.

The Chinese Conceptual Scheme: *Dao* and *De*

I shall leave the debate at this elementary point. I did not intend to advance or sharpen the issues. My hope is that I have captured enough of the *tone* of the dispute to help us recognize its close cousin in classical Chinese thought. I shall argue that a central dispute in ancient China did trace parts of this Western dialectic. As usual, however, the differences are more interesting than the parallels. The differences are these:

1. Technically, Classical China had no duty ethics. I do not know the counterpart's name, but I shall call it *dao*-ethics.[2] *Dao* 道 differs from duty ethics in not having sentential form. It also lacks the axiomatic or theoretical structure of Western systems. *Dao* guides discourse in general. *Dao* 道 is like duty, however, in referring both to the intended performance and the quasi-linguistic prescription that dictates it.

2. *De*^{virtue} 德 does not simply consist in favorable attitudes, feelings, or motivations. It is a hypothetical structure of dispositions essential to the proper performance of any *dao* 道 . It is the ability to recognize, interpret, and perform a *dao*. I will usually gloss it as *de*^{virtuosity} to signal this distinguishing feature.

3. This unfamiliar conceptual structure with its background assumptions generates a fresh dynamic. The dominant position, I will argue, is that any plausible ethical stance requires both *dao* 道 and *de*[virtue] 德. The reasons, however, are not the familiar Western points that we must do moral actions "for the right reason" or "with the right attitude." We require *de*[virtuosity] 德 to vouch safe correct performance of a *dao*[way] 道.

Despite this recognition of the importance of *de*[virtuosity] 德, I shall argue, the Chinese dialectic favors the view that *dao* is more basic to ethics. At least, I shall argue, this is the Daoist position. Thus, virtue ethics does not *theoretically* dominate Chinese philosophy. It dominates it in the *historical* sense. Mencius is an excellent paradigm of the Chinese version of the virtue position. Neo-Confucianism, which adopts Mencius' position, dominates the medieval and early modern period. Mencius adopted, however, one extreme end rather than the central classical ethical position.

The Chinese compound that most frequently translates *ethics* is *dao-de*[way-virtue] 道德.[3] Classical thinkers used the component terms separately through most of the period. They occur together most famously in the Daoist *Canon of Dao De* and in later writings—the *Zhuangzi* and the *Xunzi*. My hypothesis is that the compounding accompanies the emergence of a dominant position. Any complete ethical stance requires both *dao* and *de*[virtuosity]. I will focus on this development from the *dao* side. My explanation will trace developments in theory of *dao* 道 and analyze the role that development *creates*. In that development, a more specialized virtue, *ren*[humanity] 仁, figures centrally. Its intimate association with specifically Confucian ethics and its specific content, I assume, led non-Confucian philosophers to focus on the genera of which *ren*[humanity] 仁 is a species—*de*[virtuosity] 德. The role of *ren*[humanity] in Confucian systems shaped the theoretical space which *de*[virtuosity] came to fill.

I intend my analysis to draw Daoism back into the ethical dialogue. My claim is that the famous Daoist classic is, as its title suggests, a theory of ethics (actually metaethics).[4] I treat it as a critique of ethics in general, including Mencius' virtue-centered position. The point of Laozi's text is both that *de* 德 is parasitic on *dao* 道 and yet *dao* 道 is indeterminate without *de* 德. No ethical doctrines, by themselves, give neutral, constant, and reliable guidance. Yet our moral desires and attitudes that shape our interpretation of *dao* are themselves variable products of training in a *dao*.

The late Classical Chinese formula that my analysis draws on for this explanation is "*De*virtuosity 德 is *dao*way 道 within" and "*de*virtuosity 德 is *de*obtained 得." I will illustrate this relation with a group of models, some familiar and some new. One newer model is computer languages and programming. *Dao* 道 is a program, an instruction set. *De* 德 is the transformed physical state of the computer when we read the program into memory. *De* causes the output, the performance. *De*virtue 德 is a translation of a *dao* 道 into physical form, the physical realization of a disposition to execute those instructions in "real time."[5] (See figure 1.)

A related way of modeling the process is the more familiar skill model. It includes gaining skill at conventions.[6] A third, perhaps the most venerable, model is aesthetic. I will give it a new twist by focusing on the model of aesthetic interpretation.

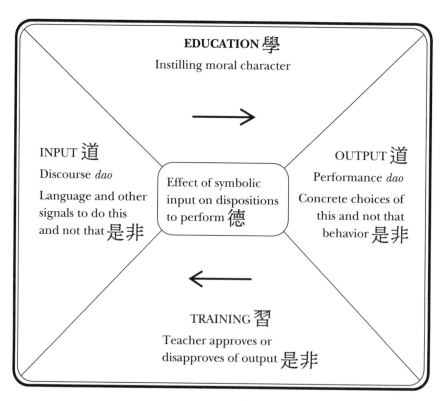

EDUCATION 學
Instilling moral character

INPUT 道
Discourse *dao*
Language and other signals to do this and not that 是非

Effect of symbolic input on dispositions to perform 德

OUTPUT 道
Performance *dao*
Concrete choices of this and not that behavior 是非

TRAINING 習
Teacher approves or disapproves of output 是非

I abandon, however, the usual moral drawn with these models. The role of this counterpart of *virtue* in the Chinese dispute is not to motivate a morality or to accompany it with the right feeling. *De*[virtuosity] 德 rectifies performance interpretation. All the models illustrate one key point. For a *dao* 道 to work (to produce the intended performance) we must translate it into an internal, physical potential.[7] My hypothesis is that theorists join *de*[virtue] 德 to *dao* 道 partly because they treat it as a genus of character traits that fill the practical interpretation role. Any *dao*-based ethic would thus be incomplete without assuming some *de*.

My gloss of the pair *dao-de* 道德 identifies them roughly as *guiding discourse* and *virtuosity* (specifically in performing or executing guiding discourse). Moral discourse is the instructions, slogans, sayings, examples, and so forth, intended to influence our behavior. I take the "and so forth" seriously. Consider one example from the skill group—the *dao* of kipping on a high bar. You use the pendulum swing of your body to flip your center of gravity above the bar. The "muscle-up" by contrast relies more on sheer strength. My teacher says things to guide my learning, uses examples, gives me feedback on my early attempts, "spots" or physically helps me. All of that input I treat as *discourse dao*.

If the training takes, then, on cue, my body traces a specific path through the air under the bar and I end up above the bar with my arms locked. That path or course that my body traces through spacetime is the *performance dao*. Once I learn to do it—like riding a bicycle or walking—I always can. Despite the difficulty of learning, once we have mastered these skills, they become effortless. Learning physically changes us. The training, the discourse *dao* 道, is now *in* our bodies. It becomes part of our spontaneous repertoire of basic actions. That is the *de*[virtuosity] 德.

My models explain why translators sometimes see connotations of power in *de*[virtuosity] 德. It is a practical ability to put a *dao* into effect in the real world and get the intended results. Furthermore, the ability is transferable. Once I "get it," I can also kip up on parallel bars or from the floor. *De* makes performance look and feel effortless.

As I have argued elsewhere,[8] one striking feature of ancient Chinese moral discourse is the absence of thin, categorical, verbs of duty—*ought* and *should*. I treat the absence of explicit prescriptive connectives as a reflection of two general features of Chinese theory of language. First, we attribute to Chinese theorists an assumption that language guides behavior. To do that, we know to identify the objects, ranks, and actions referred to in guiding discourse.

Second, Western rules, *oughts, shoulds,* obligations, etc. are sentence-sized bits of prescriptively marked language. Chinese language theorists found no compelling reason in general to individuate language strings at sentence length. I have argued that Chinese thinkers never developed a clear concept of the sentence.[9]

The Historical Development

The Chinese philosophical curtain opens with Confucius making the assumption that history and historical figures (the sage kings) have bequeathed a *dao* 道 to us. It comes to us in the form of traditional literature—centered on etiquette (the *li*[ritual] 禮). Western analysts see *rules* of etiquette, but *li*[ritual] 禮 lacks any explicit structural individuation into rules or into the thin (purely evaluative) concepts of "ought" and "ought not." Books of *li*[ritual] are "strings" of "thick" world-guided terms. They look as if they are simply describing correct behavior. They become prescriptions only with the addition of the above assumption. The role of literature is guiding behavior.

Confucius added history and poetry to the *li*[ritual] 禮 to round out his curriculum. The traditional attitude toward both also is prescriptive. The use of history suggests that the recorded behavior of historical figures make up part of a *dao* 道. Confucians write history, that is, not intending to record facts but to guide our evaluations.[10] The use of poetry underlines the wide sense of 'guidance' I am using. It also highlights the important emotive function of language. Poetic language, Confucius argues, stimulates correct behavior.[11]

Philosophical debate in China starts with the questioning of the traditional basis of Confucius' *dao* 道. Mozi argued that *our present* concept of *yi*[morality] 義 and *ren*[humane] 仁 are such that we can recognize that traditions, customs, established practices, and guidance may not be *yi*[moral] 義 or *ren*[humane] 仁.[12] What guiding discourse content, then, should we instill in our teaching, in public, conventional discourse, in our laws and institutions? This question, for Mozi, is another way of asking, "What prescriptive language should we use?" "What distinctions should the terms of guiding language make?" "How should we program people?" "What should they recite as the internal dialogue directing their acts?"

Mozi and Confucius share the assumption that civilizing, socializing, and internalizing a linguistic *dao* 道 does guide action. The implicit Chinese psychology comes in a theory of the *xin*[heart-mind] 心 which combines cognitive and affective functions. It executes the instructions in the *dao*. Society programs those instructions by "reading them" into the heart (in the form of public discourse and the content of childhood education). Conventions, thus, instill and shape the heart's dispositions to behavior.

Both Mozi and Confucius regard education (the internalization of some *dao* 道) as natural—the specifically human form of character cultivation. Such training explains people's behavior patterns. Our learning discourse *dao* shapes our dispositional potential for action. To change language is to change the way we *shi*[this:right] 是 and *fei*[not-this:wrong] 非 in guiding action choices.

The skepticism of tradition was not his only argument against Confucianism. Mozi also argued that particularistic moralities, like Confucianism, are, as Derek Parfit put the matter, self-defeating.[13] General adherence to Confucianism would be less likely to result in achieving its implicit moral goal (the well-being of my family) than would general adherence to universal altruism.

Mozi, then, argues for the connection between *yi*[morality] 義, *ren*[humanity] 仁 and utilitarian altruism—*li*[benefit] 利. He treats it as instinctively obvious that our *dao* 道 should maximize *li*[benefit] 利 for all. So, although we have not yet introduced the contrast of duty and virtue, we find one theme of the duty-virtue dialectic. Ethical *reflection* prompts philosophers to abandon traditional, conventional, *partial* moralities for a more comprehensive moral vision. What worries normative theorists about the revival of virtue ethics, the dangers of traditional ethnic particularity and rivalry, is a version of the claim that traditional ethical systems are self-defeating. We can make this point using the notion of *dao*[guiding discourse] 道 as easily as we can using either *duty* or *right*.

What of the balancing concerns of the virtue ethicist? Is Mozi concerned with character cultivation, with the type of person we ought to
be as well as what we ought to do? As we would expect of a conscious
dao reformer, Mozi does not focus on such matters. Ability to apply the
correct *dao* should not require the tedious training and cultivation of a
Confucian gentleman. Ordinary people who simply use their "eyes and
ears" should be able to follow the discourse. The appropriate psychology will come with learning the selected *dao*. The initial character needed to learn it is simply the natural social inclination to conform to
one's superior and to absorb training. Mozi also assumes a natural
inclination to promote *li*^{benefit}.

Mozi did argue for instilling an attitude of universal love. The utilitarian *dao* justifies promoting this character trait. It is the translation of
his proposed reformed *dao* into dispositions. Mozi acknowledges that
the proposed attitude differs from existing moral intuitions and
impulses. He recognizes that his opponents would insist that familial
particularism is natural.[14]

So, Mozi does not ignore character cultivation but he regards it as a
natural result of setting out the correct *dao*. He parallels his argument
that traditional *dao* 道 might be wrong with the implicit consequence
that traditionally instilled impulses or natural, pre-reflective impulses
could also be improved. Dispositions of character are shaped by our
collective discourse. The argument against traditions translates perfectly against status quo instincts as long as a *dao* can affect them. The
fact that an attitude is instinctive does not make it right—especially
when it is inconsistent with more reflective, well thought-out moral
daos.

Mozi's concern with using language to cultivate character
reemerges in his political theory. There he argues that the way to get a
unified (presumably utilitarian) morality *into* the population relies on
the natural inclination to conform to the behavior and speech of perceived social superiors. The form this takes is conformity in *shi*^{this: right}
是 and *fei*^{not-this:wrong} 非 reactions and responses to things. Classifying
items in a group and responding to them in similar action guiding
ways are linked phenomena. *Shi-fei*^{this:right-not this:wrong} thus combine thin
descriptive and thin *prescriptive* functions.

That analysis informs the classic Daoist statement of the disagreement between Mohists and Confucians. Mohists *shi* 是 what Confucians *fei* 非 and *fei* 非 what Confucians *shi* 是. Both claim to be yi^{moral} 義 but, as Mozi construes it, they differ in what they call yi^{moral} 義 and bu-$yi^{not\ moral}$ 不義. (Actually, Mozi, less detached than the Daoists, says Confucians *don't know how to make* the distinction between yi^{moral} 義 and bu-$yi^{not\ moral}$ 不義.)[15]

Thus, Mozi would carry off his moral reform by reforming linguistic dispositions. The linguistic disposition underlies any *dao* 道 programming and, together with *dao* programming, leads us to concrete behaviors in specific circumstances. The process of deriving a discourse *dao* 道 from these assumptions and the goal of general utility does not yield a unique solution. The result of programming people with a guiding discourse depends on their existing interpretive dispositions.

Mozi's problem points to a gap between what I have called the *discourse dao* 道 and the *performance dao* 道. It is not, however, the first[16] such development in classical thought. Confucius' doctrine of $zheng^{recti\text{-}fying}$ $ming^{names}$ 正名 signals a related concern with the interpretation of a code. Between the instruction set (the guiding discourse) and the course of action lies a practical, interpretive step. Confucius suggests a strategy like Mozi's for achieving conformity in performance interpretation—modeling of proper language use by superiors.[17]

We will wonder how the superiors know which use is proper. Confucius implicitly relies on the mysterious concept of $ren^{humanity}$ 仁 to provide the performance intuition required to escape the implicit circularity of his proposal. Its vaguely stated but crucial role is interpreting the li^{ritual} 禮 into the correct action.[18] Mozi's own proposal similarly requires (as we saw above) a natural human disposition to prefer $li^{benefit}$. We conclude that Confucius, as much as Mozi, treats correct *performance* as the crucial ethical goal.

Confucian doctrine produces a dynamic tension[19] between treating the traditional form of discourse and traditional traits of character as the central moral element. The implicit early resolution of the tension analyzes $ren^{humanity}$ as the crucial notion. The question is whether it is an internalization of the code or an independent standard of behavior. Either that internalization or that intuition produces the desired performance.

Here the third venerable model helps us explain the internalizing virtue. The long tradition of viewing Chinese thought (Confucian thought) as aesthetically inspired makes most sense in this interpretive context. What ties all the models together is the notion of practical interpretation of a form into action in "real time."[20] Practice with the artistic form produces virtuosity—practical skill in interpretative performance. Good internalization results in inspired performances in the real world.[21]

This model implicitly recognizes a distinction between a virtuoso performance and a bad one of the same score (here thought of as the li^{ritual} 禮). So we can see a further problem with saying that virtuosity comes from learning the code. The whole point of talking about virtuosity is the recognition that one score can be performed in many ways. We find here a reason for the Confucian stress on historical models of performance and on the importance of the teacher as a model, not merely as a source of cognitive information.

Formally, however, the same problem arises with models that arises with the code itself. We can know the actions of a historical model only through descriptions in literature. These raise exactly the same problem of interpretation that the literature of the code raised in the first place. (It was formally descriptive as well.) Rectifying names also could be used to address the interpretive problem as applied to models. One version of the problem is, "Who should we treat as models of *father, minister, ruler,* and *son?*" If the problem is translating a discourse *dao* 道 into a performance *dao* 道, using models still presupposes that we can rectify names.

A live model, on the other hand, is not straightforwardly a bit of literature. Interpretation is, however, still involved. We have to extrapolate from the rich detail of her performance the parts we want to copy and to discard in the altered context of the next performance. Virtuosi, notoriously, seldom perform the same way twice.

Notice that the aesthetic model of pragmatic interpretation admits of multiple structures. We go from a linguistic structure (the score) to a performance of it. We can think of the whole score (whether divided into section, measures, individual notes etc.) as guiding our performance. We do not imagine the virtuosi to be processing definitions of notes or abstract assignment to sounds. Most artists insist that they do not have time to "think" during their performance. They emphatically do not process a belief and a desire to play each note in a definable way.

In using the music and skill models, I am most anxious to make a point that the computer model also highlights. The notion of de^{virtuosity} 德 that I am after is not a matter of feelings or motives. Western expression traditionally includes locutions that suggest that aesthetic performance results from some psychological attitude—feeling, spirit, energy, vibrancy, and creativity. We characterize the resulting performance in the same terms. Virtuosi, we say, play *with* these feelings and those feelings produce good to excellent performances.

As an internal state, a feeling may indeed *accompany de* 德. There is a "what it's like" to do a kip just as there is a "what it's like" to play the concerto just that way and a "what it's like" to ski smoothly. Romantic analyses, however, get the explanatory direction of feelings and *de* 德 backwards. An instructor may tell you to "stop thinking and let your feelings take over." That may indeed describe what it feels like to perform when one has successfully internalized *de* 德, but it is not helpful at the instruction stage nor is it an explanation of the skill. The feeling is an epiphenomenon that inertly accompanies the skilled performance.

We might, as I noted above, think of conventional performances as skillful or artistic. Since most humans can perform the common rituals that dominate our attention, we seldom describe the matter in aesthetic or skill terms. Still, there are external conditions of adequate performance even of these, and successful use of conventions does require timing and responsiveness to the situation. We do go through a learning phase and take pride in getting it right.

The weak parallel, however, introduces the same issue in explaining Chinese philosophy. One familiar line is that proper performance of conventional acts requires proper feeling. This should produce correct performances, and, more, performances that meet an aesthetic criteria. Without the proper feeling a conventional performance may be wooden or uninspired.

As we have argued, however, smooth, inspired performance of conventions does not require the feeling per se but the internalized, interpretive *de* whose operation *may be accompanied* by a feeling. The inner feeling is causally and conceptually irrelevant. The criteria of a correct performance are all external. One simply must be in the correct circumstances, with the proper authority and use the words and gestures properly—as determined by those public criteria. An insincere promise is still a promise—unless you cross your fingers.

The dynamic of the Chinese posture, thus, does not highlight beliefs, feelings, or other contentful conscious states. What ties discourse and virtuosity together is the psycho-physical state the educational experience produces. It is a physical realization of the pertinent *dao*. It is the capacity to interpret the discourse *dao* into the performance *dao*.

We can understand the key difference between the two early schools, then, as lying in what they are willing to vary to produce the desired performance *dao*. Confucians take the discourse *dao* 道 to be given. Performance depends on cultivating the appropriate interpretive character. For Mozi, the utility standard determines correct performance like a plum bob determines what is below a point. The only attention to character comes via the programming discourse, which he advocates changing as necessary to get the desired outcome given existing dispositions. He simultaneously envisions the existing dispositions being changed by the changed programming.

Thus, Chinese theory ties *dao*^{guiding discourse} and *de*^{virtuosity} more tightly together than Western theory does *duty* and *virtue*. We cannot dispense with the interpretive step. Conventional discourse may have more "thick" (world-guided) concepts, but they are never thick enough to avoid gaps in practical interpretation. That a duty ethic is a "minimal" account of morality does not worry Chinese thinkers. They worry that *any* prescriptive discourse will be theoretically *thin*. All require an additional interpretive tendency. Which performance any discourse will engender depends on the virtuosity that guides its practical interpretation.

The *dao* 道 advocate would flatly agree with his duty cousin on a key point. We cannot specify what is a good disposition to action without addressing what is good action. They also would agree that we cannot *a priori* rule out moral reform. *Dao-de* analysis of moral reform, however, could proceed by changing moral discourse *or* the interpretive dispositional virtue or both. This is how I propose to understand Mencius' twin charges that Mozi's theory has "two roots" and that one should not "$de^{get\ it}$ 得 from $yan^{language}$ 言."

Mencius, I argue, bites the virtue theorist's bullet. He makes a "one root" moral choice and abolishes the "creative tension" in Confucius' Confucianism. He gives the inner behavioral disposition theoretical priority. As a necessary corollary, he downgrades the textual li^{ritual} 禮. The cost of this turn to *virtue* is status quo ethics. We cannot contemplate reflective moral reform. Morality simply means following the existing dispositions.

Mencius, still, implicitly agrees with the background descriptive moral psychology and linguistic assumptions of Confucius and Mozi.[22] Language does influence behavior. This explains Mencius' worry that the "$yan^{language}$ 言 of Yang and Mo fill the empire!" His concern, like theirs, still lies in practical guidance. His fourth heart, the knowledge of what to do, grows out of the heart's inner inclination to $shi^{this:right}$ 是 and $fei^{not\text{-}this:wrong}$ 非.

Mencius, however, is more definitive and clear about what proper cultivation is *not* than about what it *is*. It is *not* language guided. Yet, even this point generates problems for Mencius. Mencius assumes that the language of Confucian tradition will dovetail with and reinforce the natural direction of the growth of practical intuitions. Otherwise, his position would be hard to distinguish from primitivist Daoism. Obviously, he can offer no proof of this assumption of compatibility. His position discourages his giving any *theoretical* account of what counts as correct development. Yet only the assumption of compatibility allows him to view his position as a defense and vindication of Confucianism against Mohism.

In sum, although Mencius manages to work the traditional discourse in, it is no longer pivotal to identifying the performance *dao* 道. $Ren^{benevolence}$ 仁 is not here a mysterious interpretive concept for use with li^{ritual} 禮, it does all the work alone. It now not only has content, but has become the wholly independent source of moral reactions and proper action. Accordingly, on pain of "two-root" tension, it must be the only source. It has taken over the entire weight of morality. Mencius translates even $yi^{morality}$ 義 and li^{ritual} 禮 into dispositional structures in our psyche. The content of knowledge is the set of particular $shi\text{-}fei^{this\text{-}not\ this:right\text{-}wrong}$ 是非 verdicts delivered by the $xin^{heart\text{-}mind}$ 心 in real circumstances of practical choice.

The Daoist Analysis

I distance myself here from two traditions of interpretation of Daoism. One treats it as a *less moralistic* copy of Mencius' position—intuitive nativism. The other alleges that Daoists change the meaning and grammar of *dao*way 道. It becomes a singular metaphysical term. We have so far used a paired concept of *dao* 道—*discourse* and *performance*. In our analysis, we would talk of multiple *dao* of both types. Many rival moral discourses each generate many possible performance interpretations. *Dao* 道 is a doubly general practical, prescriptive concept.

One reason for the metaphysical interpretation lies in the Daoists' having a different kind of ethical interest. They focus mainly on metaethics. They do not propose a straightforward, alternative normative *dao* 道. The conditions of knowledge and the constancy (reliability) of any *dao* is what preoccupies Daoists. Theirs is a skeptical take on ethics. They raise questions about all the Chinese ethical positions we have so far discussed. Can we give any perspective-free moral-reform of the type offered by Mozi? They also accept, however, Mozi's point that traditions or conventions are not obviously right.

An explanation for the temptation to understand Daoism as intuition arises from their concentration on the interpretive gap separating a discourse *dao* and its performance *daos*. The Laozi opens with the general claim that no discourse *dao* (one that can be put into guiding discourse) will be constant—will unambiguously pick out a single performance *dao*. Discourse *daos* consist of *ming*names 名 and names do not unambiguously name. The convention/skill of marking distinctions with names differs with different *dao*-perspectives. Assuming Daoism offers a solution to this linguistic difficulty tempts one to the "unspeakable intuition" interpretation. The alternative, which I have championed, is the skeptical interpretation.

Logically, the practical and political sections of the *Canon of Dao-de* 道德經 should play a role in this skeptical, metaethical project. They are not statements of Laozi's contribution to normative ethics. His is the metaethical project of showing that linguistic guidance is never constant. The text details a *dao* of reversal—one that gives advice diametrically opposed to both Confucianism and Mohism. The advice makes sense and is plausibly realistic. The text probably draws much of this content from popular political maxims, practical aphorisms, and other familiar wise sayings. It advises valuing submissiveness, passivity, non-deliberation, having no learning, and non-being—valuing the terms which most conventional systems disvalue.

If, per hypothesis, this advice includes the slogans that guided famous, successful, practical statesmen, then it too is the product of virtuosi—of *de* 德.[23] Plainly, there are many *des* as there are many *daos*. We can state them using the same *words* used in stating Confucianism and Mohism. This shows we can change the pattern of preference or desire associated with each word. There is no fixed way that words incline us to act. Add that any way we find to select among the different *daos* is itself as controversial as the *dao* itself. The plain conclusion is that we have little prospect of identifying a single constant discourse *or* performance *dao* 道.

So what? What follows from this skepticism—aside from a puncturing of confidence in conventional moral views? I do not want to debate the possible lines of interpretation of Laozi's Daoist views in detail here. Mainly, I want to challenge the common interpretation of Laozi that treats him as a theoretical twin of Mencius.[24] I do grant a common anti-language thrust. Still, I think Laozi's analysis undermines Mencius' position.

Laozi offers a deeper explanation of the assumption with which we began—language guides behavior. The challenge to Mencius flows out of that more complete explanatory theory. Laozi's poetry repeatedly ties *ming*[names] 名 to *yu*[desires] 欲 and *wei*[action] 爲—opposing all three. On Laozi's analysis, desires do not signal a natural disposition. They do not give us a neutral basis for a normative theory. Learning names is learning to have certain desires. We learn language by following sincere and urgent instructions. Parents and others correct our performance of these daily practical instructions not as school exercises, but out of regard for our safety and welfare. Thus, we learn not only to make distinctions as our social group does, but also to have a pattern of desires that our community normally associates with those distinctions. That we desire to bury our parents does not give us a neutral moral argument for doing so. That disposition could be a product of the very tradition that is under discussion.

Implicitly, then, the point is that Mencius' appeal to existing moral desires to justify his moral stance begs the question. Our ordinary language training may have instilled those desires. Without language and names, Laozi suggests, we might be free from all but the most basic urges. Our moral desires are not natural, but, extending Mozi's argument, are the product of convention. They are thus subject to doubt and revision; they are not constant.

Now we can still understand Laozi's position as closely related to Mencius'. The difference would be that Laozi recognizes *few* natural desires. Mencius, by contrast, envisions an entire moral road map imprinted in each of us. Graham calls Laozi's the primitivist version of Daoism. It denies Mencius' assumption about what dispositions to action would survive the absence of language. Primitive—enough only to sustain isolated "natural" village life or enough to unify all under heaven?

The Laozi thus also makes the general point about *dao*[discourse] 道 and *de*[virtuosity] 德. *De*[virtuosity] is not natural but is instilled in the process of learning a *dao*. And the *de* we instill depends on how we learn the words, what models the community exhibits, and what pushes and shoves it gives us as we practice it. What then appears the right and obvious interpretation to one person will look as obviously wrong to another. Thus no *dao*-guide can be constant. The idea, implicit in Mencius, that a form of virtue is innate in human nature apart from language (from a *dao*) is a fantasy. As Zhuangzi puts it, you cannot have a *shi-fei*[right-wrong] 是非 in the heart without having a *cheng*[completed:prejudiced] 成 heart. There are no non-linguistic *shi-fei*[this-not this] 是非 judgments. Any virtuosity ethic presupposes some *dao* ethic.

So we do find a counterpart of the duty-virtue divide in classical China. It recalls some features of the modern Western debate, but differs in many others. It shares part of the traditional versus moral reform dynamic and part of the conflict about universality versus more limited moral concern.[25] The issue is whether to focus on linguistic formulation or on cultivating and shaping moral character. Still, no Chinese theorist individuates the formulae into rules, duties, obligations, or rights. More important, the Chinese conceptual dynamic really has three elements—discourse, (interpretive) virtuosity, and actual *course*. They understood the counterparts of Western virtues as mediating between the discourse and the performance *dao* 道. Among those who focus on *dao* 道,[26] the key virtue is interpretive virtuosity.

The role of virtue here is not merely to motivate behavior or to have the feeling, but actually to interpret it correctly into action. So, Mencius aside, it is implausible to propose an ethics based on only one element. The motivating role of character, further, is less prominent because of the initial assumption that language does guide behavior. Motivation emerges only in the context of directing practical interpretation. Virtue is virtuosity, hence *power*.

Although my analysis does justify denying that classical Chinese ethics is duty ethics, it does not justify the converse. We may not say that Chinese thought is predominantly virtue-ethics. The only school that makes moral psychology the sole source of ethics is the Mencius wing of Confucianism. Chinese ethics is *Dao-de* 道德 ethics. In the *dao-de* pair, the emphasis in the classical period is on *dao* 道. The Daoists are Daoists because they theorize about *dao* 道. They are, however, moral skeptics, not romantic mystics.

NOTES

1. This distinction comes from Bernard Williams, 1985.

2. Cadence borrowed from the *Daode Jing*, chap. 25

3. The other is *lunli*principles of human relations 倫理. I shall not address this translation.

4. In taking this posture, I do not intend to contradict the received view that the title came from the first character of the two "books" that make up the traditional canon. I also do not intend to prejudge or settle the syntax of the compound term in later texts such as the *Zhuangzi* and the *Xunzi*. They may be using the compound either as a term compound (a sum) or as an adjective-noun pair (contrasted in both with *tian-de*natural-virtuosity 天德). If anything, I am more attracted to the latter view.

5. I develop this model in more detail in my 1992. I will not elaborate it in further detail here.

6. Angus Graham has emphasized this model most among recent commentators. I believe it is also implicit in and compatible with Fingarette's conventional, performative analysis.

7. In this formulation, I assume without argument that Chinese theorists are not mind-body dualists. I have argued this point elsewhere—most recently in my 1992—and will not dwell on it here.

8. See my 1972 and 1985a.

9. See my 1985 and 1992, 42–46. Graham argued that the Later Mohists did make this *discovery*—though it was the "last and most difficult of their discoveries" (Graham 1978, 25). In any case, it was not a discovery that carried over to other philosophers who were otherwise aware of and influenced by Later Mohist linguistic theory—Zhuangzi and Xunzi.

10. This would include the behavior of labeling historical figures with thick evaluative terms or ranks. It identifies the models of good and bad behavior and thus guides later generations.

11. *Lunyu* 論語 ("The Analects") 8.8. Harvard-Yenching *Institute Sinological Index Series* (hereafter *HS*) Supplement no. 16. Reprint. Taiwan: Taipei, 1966.

12. *Mozi* 墨子 ("The Mozi") 39/25/75–78. *HS* Supplement no. 21. Reprint. Taiwan: Taipei, 1974.

13. See Hansen, 1992, chap. 3.

14. See Mozi 26/16/35–41.

15. Mozi 29/17/14.

16. The dating of the corresponding doctrine in *The Analects* is controversial. In this comment, I assume the traditional view that it is earlier than Mozi, but dating is not crucial to the interpretive argument.

17. I argue that this is the basic mechanism by which Confucius envisions the process of rectifying names in my 1992, 63–71. Names are rectified, essentially, by example—the usage and model of social and political superiors.

18. This explains passages in which Confucius treats ren[humanity] as crucial to any value derived from li[ritual]. Other accounts of this relation are the more familiar "proper feeling" account (Graham 1989 and Fingarette 1972) and an explanation by Shun (1993) that formally parallels my own but focuses on the relation of conceptual content rather than practical interpretation.

19. This phrase comes from Tu Wei Ming (1968).

20. Some philosophical discussions of this relation treat the performance as a token of the play or piece which is its type.

21. Many interpreters, including Graham (1985 and 1989), Hall and Ames (1987), Fingarette (1972), and Eno (1990) have noted and stressed this feature of Confucian theory.

22. Mencius' moral psychology is famous and highly regarded. On its most plausible interpretation, however, his four hearts state no substantial disagreement with what is presupposed in both Confucius and Mozi. See the discussion in my 1992.

23. This feature of the text makes it especially liable to be appropriated as a handbook by statesmen—the legalists and Huang-Lao school. But it requires

ignoring the metaethical point and treating the sometimes cruel and manipulative advice as a straightforward normative theory advocated by Laozi.

24. I do think there are strong parallels, some of which I have developed more fully in my 1992, 196–232.

25. I say only part because Mencius is arguably as universalist as Mozi, theoretically. Inadverdently, it seems, he actually provides the missing natural psychological base for Utilitarianism—a pan-human impulse ($ren^{benevolence}$) to help others solely in view of their needing it. Mencius' description of the sage, apart from the internal motivation difference, is of the perfect utilitarian: one who, while doing what seems intuitively right in particular circumstances, in fact cares for and succors all within the four-seas.

26. Even for Mencius, this assumption may hold. The mature intuition of the sage determines the correct interpretation of the Confucian traditional code. But for Mencius, this comfortable outcome is less comforting, since it essentially determines by determining the correct action directly. Thus, it could as well count as the correct interpretation of utilitarianism, Christianity, or Kant. *The Mencius* pointedly lacks any discussion of rectifying names.

REFERENCES

Eno, Robert. 1990. *The Confucian Creation of Heaven.* Buffalo: SUNY Series in Chinese Philosophy and Culture.

Fingarette, Herbert. 1972. *Confucius—The Secular as Sacred.* New York: Harper and Row.

Graham, Angus. 1978. *Later Mohist Logic, Ethics and Science.* Hong Kong and London: Chinese University Press.

———. 1985. *Reason and Spontaneity.* London: Curzon Press.

———. 1989. *Disputers of the Tao: Philosophical Argument in Ancient China.* La Salle, Ill.: Open Court.

Hall, David, and Roger Ames. 1987. *Thinking Through Confucius.* Albany: State University of New York Press.

Hansen, Chad. 1972. "Freedom and Moral Responsibility in Confucian Ethics." *Philosophy East and West* 22, no. 2

———. 1983. *Language and Logic in Ancient China.* Ann Arbor: University of Michigan Press.

———. 1985. "Chinese Language, Chinese Philosophy, and 'Truth'." *Journal of Asian Studies* 44, no. 3.

———. 1985a. "Punishment and Dignity in China." In Munro, ed., *Individualism and Holism: Studies in Confucian and Taoist Values.* Ann Arbor: University of Michigan Press, 359–82.

————. 1992. *A Daoist Theory of Chinese Thought.* New York: Oxford University Press.

Ivanhoe, P. J. 1990. "Reweaving the 'One Thread' of *The Analects.*" *Philosophy East and West* 40, no. 1 (January): 17–33.

Nivison, David. 1979. "Mencius and Motivation." *Studies in Classical Chinese Thought Journal of the American Academy of Religion, Thematic Issue* 47, no. 3: 417–32.

Northrup, Filmer S. C. 1946. *The Meeting of East and West.* New York: Macmillan.

Parfit, Derek. 1984. *Reasons and Persons.* New York: Oxford University Press.

Shun, Kwong Loi. 1993. "Jen and Li in the Analects." *Philosophy East and West* 63, no. 3 (July): 457–79.

Tu, Wei-Ming. 1968. "The Creative Tension between Jen and Li." *Philosophy East and West* 18 (Jan.–Apr.): 24–40.

Waley, Arthur, trans. 1934. *The Way and its Power: A Study of the Tao Te Ching and Its Place in Chinese Thought.* London: Allen & Unwin.

Williams, Bernard. 1985. *Ethics and the Limits of Philosophy.* Cambridge: Harvard University Press.

A Villain in the *Xunzi*

Donald J. Munro

9

"But Xunzi's Confucianism really is something new; it is a Confucian vision that no philosopher could have conceived until after Zhuangzi's Daoism had happened."[1] With this example, David Nivison shows us how much greater our understanding of one thinker becomes when we grasp his links to others. Nivison's interest here is in Xunzi's view of the mind, in his ability to accommodate a mind exhibiting both an engaged and a detached mode. So Xunzi owes Zhuangzi a debt for a positive contribution.

Xunzi had his philosophical enemies as well as those to whom he owed a positive debt. This essay is about such an enemy, namely the teachings of Mozi. Rather than dealing with the inner life, the essay focuses on some of Xunzi's ideas about the outer world. A knowledge of the reaction of Xunzi to those teachings of Mozi reveals where his concerns in the world of things lies and how he proposes to deal with those concerns.

Based on the frequency with which he engages the topic of social chaos (and associated evils such as universal poverty), his diagnosis of their cause (inadequate socialization of human desires according to rank), and his institutional solution to them (teaching the ritual rules as a precise standard for socialization), I argue that Xunzi's main interest is not in the topic for which he is famous. It is not in providing a thorough analysis of the nature of humans or of their inner life. This does not mean that these psychological matters are trivial. Rather that they are secondary to and derive their significance from the issues of chaos and poverty, and their causes and institutional remedies. This is the explanation for the relative prominence that he gives to Mozi, as compared with Zhuangzi. Mozi does not receive this space because he has a wrongheaded theory of the mind. He warrants it because his teachings about music, expenditures, and blurred role-duties generate chaos and poverty.

In speaking of the relative prominence that Xunzi gives to Mozi, as compared with Zhuangzi, I am speaking about explicit comments. Of course, Nivison argues for the implicit rather than explicitly acknowledged impact of Zhuangzi on Xunzi. It is difficult to demonstrate the magnitude of this debt quantitatively, though Nivison argues his case well.

Xunzi notes the same commonplace that his predecessor Mozi had observed, namely that there is a disparity between the almost unlimited quantity of human desires, on the one hand, and the dearth of goods to satisfy them, on the other. Mozi's solutions included asceticism, namely the elimination of music and the recreational activities, and the advocacy of frugality. In addition, this approach of Mozi included the potential submission of any proposed choice of an act, belief, or policy to a utility test, where utility was often defined in the severely limited terms of maximizing agricultural and population growth, fostering defense against enemies, and securing social order. With these measures in place, Mozi said, sufficient goods would be available to enable the population to meet survival needs. Mozi also advocated a strict chain of command, from Heaven down to the king at the top, and on down the ladder from officials to people. These policies, he believed, would cause the chaos that comes with the struggle for the means of existence to disappear. But Xunzi will have none of Mozi's ascetism as a way to avoid anarchy and dearth of goods. He asks directly of Mozi's doctrines: If we follow these proposals, "How can there be enough to satisfy [desires]?"[2] His own alternative solution forms the core of the text that bears his name.

It is no wonder that until 1990, many English-reading students of the Hundred Schools missed the centrality of this issue and of Mozi's role in it. This is because the translator of the standard English edition of the *Xunzi* issued in 1928, in his translation of chapter ten ("A Rich Country") never even bothered to render into English the long attack on Mohist doctrine.[3] John Knoblock corrected the gap in the second volume of his *Xunzi: A Translation and Study of the Complete Works.*[4]

Xunzi has two main arguments against Mozi's proposed path to social order and to ensuring that people have something to eat. One is that his ascetism allows no incentives for those who exert effort, no reward that elevates their privileges above those of the lazy and incompetent. Productive work diminishes. The other is that the world is denied the services of the best and brightest. A meritocracy evaporates.

As the population decreases and hardship becomes widespread, everyone is reduced to scrounging at the same tasks, to satisfy survival needs. Not only is the world left without the administration by those most skilled at it, but also the people will revert to anarchy, having no regard for authority. He is assuming that people will only be orderly if they revere a ruler. For that reverence to occur, the ruler and his officials must have the trappings of power and privilege that come with unequal financial remuneration.

A corollary to this second argument assumes Xunzi's metaphysical position, namely that hierarchy is built into nature and that things have their natural places, which are hierarchically related. In spite of his affirmation of the need for a chain of command, Mozi appeared to Xunzi to be an advocate of some kind of limited status-equality. This derived in part from his advocacy of universal love, which seemed to promote treating people the same in terms of the affect of love. Xunzi says, "Mozi identified something in treating people equally, but he neglected that in which they differ."[5] In addition, Mozi's partial status-equality comes from the shared poverty to which Mozi's policies inevitably will lead. Such status-equality undercuts the ability of humans to model on the hierarchical trait of nature. In that lies the immorality and the doom of such a condition. Rather than "all things losing their appropriate [position]" (*wan wu shi i*), as they do with Mozi's policies, Xunzi insists that "all things should gain their appropriate [position]" (*wan wu de i*).[6]

To say that Xunzi's primary concern lay with avoiding the chaos and disunity that stem from the imbalance between unlimited human desires and limited material goods, is to confirm an insight of Kanaya Osamu.[7] It is also to invite a challenge. That challenge is that tradition holds that Xunzi's concern, rather, was on proving the evil of human nature. Long ago I argued against the position that this thesis, developed in the chapter "On Human Nature as Evil," is something that permeates any of the other chapters of the work.[8] I will not repeat those arguments here. Instead, my aim now is to provide the evidence to back up the claim about what I regard as the alternative candidate for his main concern. I do so by offering textual evidence for the alternative and by showing how the topic of human nature is derivative from it.

The evidence lies in the frequency with which the theme of the imbalance of goods and desires appears in various chapters. In contrast, the statement that human nature is evil does not appear in any chapter except for the one so entitled. Here are some of Xunzi's words on the former topic:

> But if all men gave free rein to their desires, the result would be impossible to endure, and the material goods of the whole world would be inadequate to satisfy them. Accordingly, the Ancient Kings acted to control them with regulations, ritual, and moral principles, in order thereby to divide society into classes, creating therewith differences in status between the noble and base . . . This indeed is the way to make the whole populace live together in harmony and unity.[9]
>
> When power and position are equally distributed and likes and dislikes are identical, and material goods are inadequate to satisfy all, there is certain to be contention. Such contention is bound to produce civil disorder, and this disorder will result in poverty. The Ancient Kings abhorred such disorder. Thus, they instituted regulations, ritual practices, and moral principles in order to create proper social class divisions. . . . A *Document* says: "There is equality only insofar as they are not equal."[10]
>
> All people desire and dislike the same things, but since desires are many and the things that satisfy them relatively few, this scarcity will necessarily lead to conflict.[11]
>
> Moderate the use of goods by means of ritual principles . . .[12]
>
> The way to make the entire world self-sufficient lies in making clear social-class divisions.[13]

In contrast to Mozi's purported advocacy of limited status-equality, Xunzi called for rank or social role (*fen*) differences and parallel differences in privilege. The broadest set of roles (*ta fen*) consisted of farmers, merchants, artisans, officers, and son-of-heaven,[14] though Xunzi says that the roles are also listed in the *Book of Odes, Book of Documents, Record of Rites,* and the *Music.*[15] Xunzi has another list with eight social roles and corresponding duties: lord, minister, father, son, elder brother, younger brother, husband, and wife.[16] Through socialization with the ritual rules (*li*), people will learn to desire only those goods that are consistent with their rank. For example, the son-of-heaven enjoys status, wealth, and power on behalf of everyone.[17] Others are conditioned to be satisfied with lesser shares of the existing goods.

Through use of his innate moral sense (*i*) which discriminates rank difference and the learned ritual rules that enforce them, humans have the solution to the chaos and shortage of goods that were his chief concern.

The textual evidence is unmistakable. Xunzi explicitly takes the themes of ending chaos and poverty, along with the theme of the imbalance of desires and goods, and ties them into the theme of role differentiating rules, in his chapter "A Discussion of Rites." The rites or ritual rules are the means of socializing differential desiring of limited goods based on rank or role.

> From wrangling comes disorder and from disorder comes exhaustion. The ancient kings hated such disorder, and therefore they established ritual principles in order to curb it, to train men's desires and to provide for their satisfaction. They saw to it that desires did not overextend the means for their satisfaction, and material goods did not fall short of what was desired. Thus both desires and goods were looked after and satisfied. This is the origin of rites.[18]

Rejecting Mozi's equally shared survival tasks and equally apportioned love, Xunzi here provides his alternative answer to chaos.

Not only does hierarchically varied desiring work practically in solving the problem of limited goods, but it is also morally correct. This is because it is consistent with the patterns in nature, from which the sage kings derived the model for moral codes in use. Almost as frequently ignored as Xunzi's animosity to the doctrines of Mozi has been Xunzi's metaphysics. He did believe that there is a pattern in nature, partially non-empirical, that serves as the legitimation for human moral rules. He says, "We all know how things [such as rain and wind] come to completion, but we do not know the formless agent [causing the process]."[19] The pattern of nature includes hierarchy, immediately accessible to humans in the relation of heaven and earth: "Just as there are Heaven and Earth, so too there exists the distinction between superior and inferior."[20] And,

> The relationships between lord and minister, father and son, older and younger brother, husband and wife, begin as they end and end as they begin, share with Heaven and Earth the same organizing principle [*yu tiandi tong li*], and endure in their same form through all eternity.[21]

Thus according to Xunzi, "To follow the dictates of the innate moral sense [*i*] is to follow the natural patterns [*li*]."[22] If the natural patterns include hierarchy, so too must human society and individual action in order to be considered good.

Having shown what Xunzi's primary concern was and having argued that it was not in developing a well-fashioned theory of human nature, I have a remaining task. That is to explain how the topic of human nature derives from the primary focus. This will underscore that it is secondary to the topic of the imbalance of goods and desires, which is curable through socializing differential desiring according to rank.

Had developing a theory of human nature been his interest, I doubt that Xunzi would have left it in such a mess. There are, of course, the famous chapter "On Human Nature as Evil" and remarks about the lowly character of humans. But then, in contrast, there are also the endless passages that refer to or assume innately positive traits in humans. The most important of these is the one that says that people are born with an innate moral sense (*yi*).[23] However, there are the other passages too: people carry the sentiment in favor of rules that bring social order;[24] they love the virtues of ritual propriety, duty, loyalty, trustworthiness and so forth, and they possess the endowment or natural pattern that enables them to practice these;[25] of all creatures, they have the greatest amount of the knowledge (*zhi*) that is involved in love of kin.[26] A very confusing, mixed bag of claims, when it comes to condemning or lauding human nature.

There is a contrasting consistency, however, on one particular point about the nature of humans: "Accordingly, the essential nature of one thousand or ten thousand men is in that of a single man."[27] The content of their natures consists of the sentiments (*qing*) that manifest as desires (*yu*). These desires are all the same. And every single person desires the most and the best, meat from domesticated grain-fed animals, fancy cloth for their clothing, and chariots when they travel:[28]

> It is the natural desire common to the essential nature of mankind to want the eminence of the Son of Heaven, the wealth of one who possesses the world, and the fame of the sage-kings, and to regulate all mankind but to be regulated by no man. . . . It is also the natural desire common to the essential nature of all men to want to wear what-

ever colors he values, taste foods with whatever flavors he prefers, and
regulate whatever commodities and goods he attaches importance to,
to join the world together and have dominion over it, to want food
and drink that are rich and plentiful . . .[29]

The fact that everyone desires the same top of the line list of goods
explains why there are too many desires for the limited number of
goods that exist, let alone top of the line goods. So, though the topic
of human nature enters the picture, it does so because it explains part
of the problem, namely the surfeit of desires. But the imbalance, and
its cure through ritually enforced, rank-ordered desiring, remains the
core issue.

The cure itself also works best if the human sentiments (*qing*, the
essence of human nature) are common to all persons. In other words,
the theses about human nature also serve to bolster Xunzi's specific
proposals for curing chaos and poverty. These proposals are for the
teaching of ritual rules that have the universality of the tools used by a
carpenter. Duties and expectations are differentiated according to
social role relations, but the fundamental roles or *da fen* exist everywhere. So do the abstract principles behind them, such as hierarchy,
natural place or role (*fen*), and proper relationships, because the
social roles "have the same principle as heaven and earth" (*yu tiandi
tong li*).[30] Xunzi uses about five different carpentry tools regularly as
examples of standards that are universally applicable with an impartial
precision not subject to individual whim. These include the plumb
line, the carpenter's square, and the compass.

In referring to the metaphorical use of these tools, we encounter
one of the matters on which Xunzi and Mozi do agree. This is that
there are universally valid standards. Mozi refers to such tools in
describing the applicability of the "will of Heaven."

If the basic patterns in nature are Dao or *li*, and if they manifest in
human society as *fa* (standards), the ritual rules are one form that such
counterparts of nature's patterns takes (others being the activities of
the sage kings and of the superior man). Xunzi claims that these social
rules, when they reflect the fundamental principles of nature, have the
same universal applicability as the carpenter's tools. Such a position
can only work if there is the parallel thesis that humans are pretty
much the same everywhere. This requirement is met by the discussions

of human nature or of *qing.*

Mozi's writings helped motivate Xunzi to explore both the primary and the derivative issues because Mozi's doctrines lead people astray. They obscure the cause and the solution of social chaos with their themes of equally shared poverty and equal love. But to repeat the point made earlier, to say that human nature is a derivative theme is not to say it is trivial. It is to place it in context.

NOTES

All references to passages in the *Xunzi* text contain in parentheses a reference to the same passage in the *Sibu congkan* (Comprehensive Collection of the Four Categories) (Shanghai: Commercial Press, 1929), abbreviated as *SBCK.*

1. David S. Nivison, "Hsun Tzu and Chuang Tzu," in Henry Rosemont ed., *Chinese Texts and Philosophical Contexts* (La Salle, Ill.: Open Court, 1991), 137.

2. *Xunzi,* Fu guo (*SBCK* 6.11b).

3. Homer H. Dubs, *The Works of Hsuntze* (London: Arthur Probsthain, 1928), 151–54.

4. John Knoblock, *Xunzi: A Translation and Study of the Complete Works,* vol. 2 (Stanford: Stanford University Press, 1988).

5. *Xunzi,* Qiang guo (*SBCK* 11.25a).

6. Ibid., Fu guo (*SBCK* 6.12b).

7. Kanaya Osamu, "'Junshi' no bunkengaku teki kenkyū" (A Textual Study of Xunzi's Work), *Nihon gakkushiin kiyō* (Bulletin of the Japanese Academy) 9, no. 1 (March 1951).

8. Donald J. Munro, *The Concept of Man in Early China* (Stanford: Stanford University Press, 1969), 77–81.

9. Knoblock I, 195, from *Xunzi,* Jung ju (*SBCK* 2.22a–b).

10. Ibid., II, 96, from *Xunzi,* Wang Zhi (*SBCK* 5.3b–4a).

11. Ibid., II, 121, from *Xunzi,* Fu guo (*SBCK* 6.1a–2b).

12. Ibid. (*SBCK* 6.3a).

13. Ibid., II, 127, from ibid. (*SBCK* 6.8b).

14. *Xunzi,* Wang ba (*SBCK* 7.12a).

15. Ibid., Rong ru (*SBCK* 2.21b).

16. Ibid., Zhun dao (*SBCK* 8.3a–b).

17. Ibid., Wang ba (*SBCK* 7.14b–15a).

18. Burton Watson, trans., *Hsün Tzu Basic Writings* (New York: Columbia University Press, 1963), 89. From *Xunzi*, Li lun (*SBCK* 13.1a–b).

19. *Xunzi*, Tian lun (*SBCK* 11.17a).

20. Knoblock II, 96, from *Xunzi*, Wang zhi (*SBCK* 5.3b).

21. Ibid., II, 103, from ibid. (*SBCK* 5.12a–b).

22. *Xunzi*, Yi ping (*SBCK* 10.13a).

23. Ibid., Wang zhi (*SBCK* 5.12b–13a).

24. Ibid., Wang ba (*SBCK* 7.14b).

25. Ibid., Chiang guo (*SBCK* 11.7b) and Xing e (*SBCK* 17.10b).

26. Ibid., Li lun (*SBCK* 13.21a) and Jie bi (*SBCK* 15.16a).

27. Knoblock I, 179, from *Xunzi*, Bu gou (*SBCK* 2.7b). See also *Xunzi*, Xing e (*SBCK* 17.9a–b).

28. Knoblock I, 180, from *Xunzi*, Bu gou (*SBCK* 2.9b). See also *Xunzi*, Fu guo (*SBCK* 6.1b). Reference to the fact that everyone desires top of the line food, clothing, and so forth can be found in *Xunzi*, Rong ru (*SBCK* 2.20a).

29. Knoblock II, 160, from *Xunzi*, Wang ba (*SBCK* 7.14b–15a).

30. *Xunzi*, Wang zhi (*SBCK* 12a–b).

Xunzi on Moral Motivation

10

David B. Wong

> *"Virtue" is valuable to have, and praiseworthy to have; and so one is moved to seek it, even to compete for it. Yet it is gained through self-denial—and, it must seem, squandered by self-seeking.*
>
> —David Nivison[1]

One of the most distinctive contributions of David Nivison is his focus on issues of moral psychology in thinkers such as Mencius and Xunzi. His treatment of these issues manages to be impeccable in scholarly terms and at the same time to show how Chinese concerns, problems and solutions are and should be relevant to us. This essay attempts to make a contribution to the tradition Nivison has established. I want to start with Xunzi's moral psychology and show that he has serious problems explaining how we achieve virtue when we start from a "self-seeking" nature. These problems lead me to suggest a reconstruction of his theory that places it closer to Mencius. The result is a theory of moral motivation that is naturalistic in the way Xunzi intended but that is clearer than he was about the way we achieve virtue.

From a modern, secular and naturalistic perspective, Xunzi is of great interest. He denies Mencius's view that somehow rightness is revealed in certain shared emotional reactions of the heart-mind (*xin* 心),[2] a view that will seem mysterious on a naturalistic perspective, especially if the moral reactions are given by a Heaven (*tian* 天) that is somehow sympathetic to the human ideals of morality. For Xunzi, morality is a system of rules devised by human beings, and Heaven is indifferent to the fulfillment of these rules. Therefore, we must not expect Heaven to have given us a nature that would dispose us toward morality.

There is nothing in our nature that Xunzi thinks can be called good. He defines human nature, (*renxing* 人性), as that which is inborn and not acquired through human effort, and clearly, he argues, moral goodness is an achievement. What is inborn is the motive for gain (*haoli* 好利), a self-seeking tendency to satisfy desires (*yu* 欲) of the ear and eye and liking (*hao* 好) of sound and beauty. These desires are responses to feelings such as pleasure, joy, anger, and sorrow, and they have no natural limit. This makes for chaos when combined with scarcity of resources:

> Man is born with desires. If his desires are not satisfied for him, he cannot but seek some means to satisfy them himself. If there are no limits and degrees to his seeking, then he will inevitably fall to wrangling with other men. From wrangling comes disorder and from disorder comes exhaustion. The ancient kings hated such disorder, and therefore they established ritual in order to curb it, to train men's desires and to provide for their satisfaction. They saw to it that desires did not overextend the means for their satisfaction, and material goods did not fall short of what was desired. Thus both desires and goods were looked after and satisfied. This is the origin of rites.[3]

Many have observed that this story of the origin of ritual (*li* 禮) anticipates Hobbes' story of why human beings need to escape from the state of nature. One way in which Xunzi's story differs, however, is that after recognizing the need to restrain their search for satisfaction of desire, human beings see the need not only to restrain their behavior but to transform their very characters through ritual, music, and righteousness (*yi* 義).[4] They see that it is in their interests to love these things, and not merely to be curbed by them. As Nivison has observed, Xunzi's conception of the requirements of enlightened self-interest includes not merely the belief that the Way is best for everyone concerned, but also the cultivation of behavior and a love of what one believes in.[5]

By contrast, Hobbes never expected the self-interested motivation of human beings to change in the transition from the state of nature to civil society.[6] His egoistic psychology allows the internalization of no standards other than that of direct concern with individual preservation and contentment. This psychology creates a problem for his theory that only the state can solve. The rules that curb the pursuit of desire are mutually beneficial to all, but individuals can benefit even more if they can cheat on them while others generally comply. Since everyone knows this fact, no one will have confidence that others will comply, and therefore no one will have a self-interested reason to comply. The solution to this problem is the state as the enforcer of the rules. It must create a risk of punishment that makes it irrational for any individual to try to cheat. Only with the state does it become perfectly rational for the egoist to obey the rules.

By comparison, Xunzi recognized force as a necessary means, but not the primary means: "One who truly understands how to use force does not rely upon force."[7] While he may have been skeptical of most people's willingness and ability to become truly moral, he saw the need for a ruling elite to transform themselves so that they come to love and delight in virtue and morality. This elite, with supreme benevolence, righteousness, and authority would attract the people and inspire them with respect. In this, Xunzi seems to affirm the Confucian belief in the ability of a ruler with *de* (德) to win the hearts and minds of the people.

Hobbes's solution to the egoism of human beings has some serious disadvantages. As David Gauthier has observed, his use of the state to make it irrational for individuals to cheat is a political solution to the problem, not a moral one.[8] A morality that gives one reason to obey only by virtue of the threat of punishment is not a genuine morality. A moral reason to obey should be one that is more internal to the motivations of individuals. This is not to deny that compulsion may have some role to play. Ideally, we need enough enforcement of the moral rules so that we would not be fools to obey the rules. We would be fools if we obeyed while others did not. Xunzi assigns enforcement the role of creating enough security so that we feel safe enough to embark on the project of transforming our characters: "Encourage [men of perverse words and deeds] with rewards, discipline them with punishments, and if they settle down to their work, then look after them as subjects; but if not, cast them out."[9] But also crucial to that security is the character of the ruling elite. It is because they have transformed their characters that they can be trusted. They love benevolence (*ren* 仁), are benevolent to the people, and so are trusted by the people. Their moral influence and not just their capacity to punish affects the characters of others so that a general climate of security is created.

Xunzi, then, has in this respect offered a better solution to the problem of the self-interested behavior of human beings. His solution is a moral solution because it envisions an internal change in human beings that makes a reliance on force unnecessary. Moreover, in locating the greatest transformation in a ruling elite, Xunzi offers a solution to another problem Hobbes has. It has often been pointed out that Hobbes did not adequately address the problem of corruption of the state. His solution to the state of nature requires the assumption that the state will be an impartial enforcer of the rules. But given that the state is run by human beings with the same egoistic nature as their subjects, Hobbes seems not entitled to this assumption. By contrast, Xunzi avoids this problem by requiring a moral transformation of those who run the state. Therefore Hobbes's solution to the dangerous nature of human beings is unstable without an envisioned change in their motivations.

So both Hobbes and Xunzi begin with similar premises about human nature and its propensities to seek the satisfaction of desires that if unchecked would lead to chaos. But they end with very different visions of what people can become. For Hobbes, self-interested human beings accepted the authority and power of the state on the basis of their long-term interests. While the same is true for Xunzi, he also holds that one's long-term interests dictate a radical transformation in one's character. As we have seen, his vision can claim certain advantages over Hobbes's. But Xunzi's vision has its own problems in explaining how moral transformation is effected. The question is how one becomes a person who loves rites, benevolence, and righteousness when one starts with a repertoire of "very unlovely" emotions that cause a man to neglect his parents once he acquires a wife and children, or to neglect his friends once he has satisfied his cravings and desires, or to cease to serve a sovereign with a loyal heart once he has attained high position and a good stipend.[10]

There is another way to put the problem for Xunzi. In a beautiful and illuminating essay on Xunzi and Zhuangzi, Nivison finds a Daoist theme in Xunzi's recognition of moral rules as conventional, as the result of cool calculation on how to maximize the satisfactions of one's desires.[11] The Daoist theme furthermore includes an acceptance of one's basic social, political, and psychic commitments as inevitable. Where Xunzi goes beyond the Daoist Zhuangzi, however, is in recognizing the human world of institutions, ideals, and norms as the flowering of what is most fundamental in nature. Even though they are conventional, these human forms are an inevitable part of nature precisely because they are the best answer to the chaos that threatens all human beings.

On this interpretation, Xunzi goes one step beyond Daoism in accepting not just the nonconventional part of nature but that more inclusive whole that contains human forms. Such an interpretation of Xunzi, offers Nivison, would explain the two contrasting Xunzi's: the cool detached observer who sees morality as a set of conventions designed to maximize self-interest; and the one who bursts out in "paeans of praise" of rites and the gentleman as having a place in the cosmic order. At the end of his essay, Nivison addresses a question similar to the one I posed above: how could the sage-kings have created morality unless morality were already a part of their nature? They created it not only out of a recognition that it is required by self-interest, but also out of an awareness of human nature and the inescapable human situation. They recognized their moral order "as having the same sort of ordering authority over all human life as do the rising and setting of the sun." And through their "superior creative intelligence," they moralized themselves.[12]

This interpretation explains the exalted place that Xunzi gives to rites and to the human beings who devised them. Even though rites were created, they are discovered in another sense as the single best way to order society and therefore having supreme authority over human beings who must live in and through society. And Nivison is undoubtedly right in saying that for Xunzi the sage-kings must have moralized themselves through a heroic use of their superior creative intelligence. But just *how* did they use that intelligence to transform themselves? The question seems difficult to answer precisely because Xunzi shares with Hobbes a pessimistic (from the moral viewpoint) conception of human nature. How did they, with their "unlovely emotions" and self-regarding desires, turn themselves into beings who loved and delighted in morality? To accept rites and morality as not only necessary to self-interest but as part of the natural order is not yet to love and delight in them. It is not yet to make oneself willing to die for them, as Xunzi thinks the sage-kings were. Nivison identifies precisely this unresolved problem in a later unpublished essay on Xunzi.[13]

A clearer view of how moral transformation could take place seems to require a clarification of the mind's power over innate desire and emotion. Bryan Van Norden draws an interesting contrast between Mencius's and Xunzi's views of agency. According to Van Norden, Mencius held that what we do is determined by what we most desire. In order for us to be capable of acting out of unselfish motivation, we must have incipient virtuous inclinations that can be cultivated to be our strongest motivations. By contrast, Xunzi believes that we can override our desires through what we approve of. The beginner in moral cultivation can make herself do what she does not yet desire to do through approving of an action. Such action would include submission to rites and the dictates of righteousness, and would if practiced rigorously and consistently, result in the transformation of the desires themselves. Ultimately, the mind's power over desire results not just in overriding them but in retraining them.[14]

Van Norden's interpretation of Xunzi receives some *prima facie* support from the following passage from "Rectifying Names":

> There is nothing a man desires more than life and nothing he hates more than death. And yet he may turn his back on life and choose death, not because he desires death and does not desire life, but because he cannot see his way clear to live, but only to die. Therefore, although a man's desires are excessive, his actions need not be so, because the mind will stop them short. If the dictates of the mind are in accord with just principles, then, although the desires are manifold, what harm will this be to good government? Conversely, even though there is a deficiency of desire, one's actions can still come up to the proper standard because the mind directs them. But if the dictates of the mind violate just principles, then, although the desires are few, the result will be far worse than merely bad government. Therefore, good or bad government depends upon the dictates of the mind, not upon the desires of the emotional nature.[15]

Van Norden is clearly onto something in Xunzi when he emphasizes that the mind's approval can override desire. Nevertheless, I think his interpretation cannot help us with the problem of explaining how we can make the transition from self-interest to truly moral behavior. The power of the mind to override desire might seem to provide such an explanation, but I shall argue that it does not.

To begin to see why not, let us distinguish between a weak and a strong sense in which the mind's approval can override desire. In the weak sense, the mind's approval can cause an agent to act contrary to what the agent desires most immediately, but what the mind approves is ultimately based on what it will take to best satisfy over the long term the total set of the agent's desires. On this view, the mind's function is to determine what desires are possible to satisfy given the world as it is, and whether actions dictated by our immediate desires might be self-defeating in the end. The weak sense is closer to a means-ends view of the role of practical reason. Reason is a Humean "slave of the passions," but it can manage the passions for the sake of their long-term optimal satisfaction. The more sophisticated versions of the means-ends view need not limit reason to a purely instrumental determination of what actions will have the greatest likelihood of satisfying an agent's desires. It also allows an adjudicative function of selecting among desires to be satisfied when there is conflict between them. But the basis of this decision will have to be something like the comparative intensity of conflicting desires, or which of the conflicting desires are tied to the greater number of other desires.

In the strong sense, approval can override desire even when it has no relation at all to what will satisfy over the long term the agent's total set of desires. The western analogue to this interpretation would be the Kantian view of the efficacy of pure practical reason, or the different view that moral qualities can be perceived and that such perception is intrinsically motivating. Notice, however, that if approval overrides desire in this strong sense, there must be some basis for approving of an action other than its relation to the satisfaction of desire. Kant, of course, held that pure practical reason yielded the categorical imperative, which applies to all rational agents regardless of the content of their particular desires and emotions. On the moral perception view, it is simply the apprehension of moral qualities that is the basis of approval.

If the possibilities of interpretation are divided in this way, then it would seem that only a weak sense of the mind's overriding desire can emerge from Xunzi's philosophy. The only basis for approval of an action given in his philosophy is desire—that the action is best, given the agent's long-term interests, even if it is not dictated by her immediate desires. Even if the mind can override emotions and desires, it does so in their interests, so to speak:

[As for the king's officials] let them understand clearly that to advance in the face of death and to value honor is the way to satisfy their desire for life; to spend and to supply what goods are needed is the way to satisfy their desire for wealth; to conduct themselves with respect and humility is the way to satisfy their desire for safety; and to obey ritual principles and good order in all things is the way to satisfy their emotions. He who seeks only to preserve his life at all cost will surely suffer death. He who strives only for profit at all cost will surely suffer loss. He who thinks that safety lies in indolence and idleness alone will surely face danger. He who thinks that happiness lies only in gratifying the emotions will surely face destruction.[16]

This quote certainly rules out the Kantian option of holding that the mind can act on the dictates of pure practical reason. Nor can Xunzi hold that the mind can act on an approval based on perception of irreducible moral properties, because he does not think there are such properties. In short, Xunzi cannot allow any sense in which approval can override desire except the weak sense. And if Xunzi had in mind only the weak sense, then there cannot be as dramatic a contrast between Xunzi's and Mencius's views of agency as Van Norden claims there is.

On both views, the ultimate motive force of the mind's judgments would derive from desire. In both theories, the mind makes decisions as to which desires to act on. In Xunzi's case, it is a choice between one's immediate sensual desires on the one hand, and the desires arising out of reflection on one's long-term interests. In Mencius's case, the mind must make a choice between one's moral desires and sensual desires that come into conflict with them. Consider Mencius's explanation of why some people become greater than others even though they are equally human: "He who is guided by the interests of the parts of his person that are of greater importance is a great man; he who is guided by the interests of the parts of his person that are of smaller importance is a small man" (*Mengzi*, 6A:15).[17] Mencius goes on to say that the difference comes down to the heart-mind performing its function of thinking. If this interpretation is right, then we need not interpret Mencius as believing that we act simply on the strongest desire of the moment.[18] Rather, he allows for the mind's approval to have an effect on what we desire.

What is the relevance of this discussion to the problem of explaining the moral transformation from self-interest to love and delight in morality? If for Xunzi approval can override desire only in the weak sense, any path to self-transformation must start from the self-interested nature of human beings, and not from a capacity for an approval that can motivate independently of self-interest. Changing oneself on the basis of approval would be changing oneself on a more sophisticated and long-term view of what is in one's self-interest, but it would be self-interest after all that.

We still have the problem of explaining how approval based on self-interest can lead to a transformation of one's selfish desires. How does one become a person who sacrifices himself for morality when the raw material for such a transformation is a self-interested nature? We can see the self-interested grounds for transforming our characters, but what remains unclear is how the transformation takes place given the nature of what we have to start with. Of course, Xunzi is not trying to convince his audience to undertake the transformation from self-interest to morality. The audience, after all, has already been transformed to at least some extent. His account is a retrospective explanation of how we came to be the way we are. But the question is how to fill in the explanation.

Even if we attribute to Xunzi a belief in the strong sense of the mind's overriding power, we still have essentially the same problem of explanation. If the mind has a non-self-interested motivation that is separate from selfish desires, there is still a need to explain how the mind can actually *reshape* selfish desires and create new ones for morality. How are desires to be transformed or created, instead of merely being overridden by the mind's approval? We cannot attribute to Xunzi a belief in a magical ability to transform desire, for that would make no sense of his emphasis on the *training* of desire through rites and music. But when we take this emphasis into account, we still have a problem of explanation. If we continually submit ourselves to rites and to righteousness, we may form a habit of practicing them, but how do we come to delight in them and be willing to die for them?

P. J. Ivanhoe has noted that Xunzi thinks of human nature as highly plastic, like hot wax that can be shaped by something external.[19] At the same time, Ivanhoe notes that on Xunzi's account we encounter new sources of satisfaction by adopting morality. The question is how we can *take* satisfaction from such new sources given our nature. For example, Ivanhoe has written illuminatingly of Xunzi's conception of rites as "bringing human needs and Nature's bounty into a harmonious balance by achieving a *happy* symmetry."[20] Xunzi's gentleman clearly takes this kind of delight in ritual, and it is important to note that the delight is not simply based on the fact that rites provide for the satisfaction of human needs. The delight is in the balance, the symmetry itself between human need and what Nature provides. But how does the gentleman acquire the capacity to take this delight in symmetry? The capacity clearly goes beyond the mundane and self-seeking drives highlighted by Xunzi when he is trying to persuade us that human nature is evil. The theme of the plasticity of human nature seems to obscure the question. It is mysterious how a motivationally efficacious delight in symmetry can be imprinted upon the heart-mind like the impression of a seal on hot wax. How can a completely new motivation be imparted to the heart-mind?

Xunzi carried the theme of the plasticity of human nature too far, creating for himself the problem of explaining moral transformation. He may have been grappling with this problem in "Human Nature is Evil." There he directly opposes Mencius in denying that goodness is part of the innate endowment of human beings. He turns to the question of the origin of goodness if it is not in human nature already. The answer he gives is quite curious:

> Every man who desires to do good does so precisely because his nature is evil. A man whose accomplishments are meager longs for greatness; an ugly man longs for beauty; a man in cramped quarters longs for spaciousness; a poor man longs for wealth; a humble man longs for eminence. Whatever a man lacks in himself he will seek outside. But if a man is already rich, he will not long for wealth, and if he is already eminent, he will not long for greater power. What a man already possesses in himself he will not bother to look for outside. From this we can see that men desire to do good precisely because their nature is evil.[21]

One interesting feature of this passage is the mention of the *desire* to do good, indicating that the difference between agency by desire and agency by approval cannot be so stark for Xunzi, and further supporting the interpretation that he must have had the weak sense in mind when he said that the mind can override desire. But the other way in which this passage is interesting is its very oddness. We have trouble figuring what Xunzi is up to here. He seems to be saying that human nature is evil because we desire goodness. What sense can we make of this?

Antonio Cua suggests that the truth in the above passage is a conceptual point about desire. Desire, by its very nature, is premised on a perception that one is lacking what one desires. Therefore, if one desires goodness, one lacks it, and human nature is evil or at least morally neutral. Cua observes that such an argument does not prove that human nature is not good. One could desire more of something that one already has, as long as one is not satisfied with the degree to which one has it.[22] But I suspect that Xunzi was not just trying to prove that human nature is evil in the above passage. This passage occurs after the question is raised about the origin of goodness, and in particular, the question of how human beings can become good if they do not already have some goodness in them. Xunzi is attempting to show how human beings could transform themselves into moral beings when their original nature is to seek the immoral. The basis of transition is precisely this seeking after what they lack. So perhaps the point of the passage is not so much a proof that human nature is evil, but to show, *contra* those who think that goodness must come from goodness, that goodness can come from evil.

And this would be an answer to the question of transformation we have been raising. If besides the motive for gain, we have a desire to be good, that would explain how we can begin transforming ourselves into moral beings. But at this point, a fair question to raise is whether Xunzi has obliterated any difference between himself and Mencius. Mencius did not, as Xunzi often implies, believe that we are born with full-blown goodness. Mencius only believed that we have the beginnings of goodness, in the four sprouts (*duan* 端) of morality. A. C. Graham in fact holds that Xunzi attributed moral desires to human nature and that the difference between him and Mencius is not clear. Graham's interpretation is rooted in the above passages and others in which Xunzi mentions a "love of right"[23] and a "sense of duty."[24] According to his interpretation, Xunzi thinks that human nature is bad, not because it lacks any good impulses, but because it is an anarchic mix of selfish and moral desires.

Graham's solution would make it clear how the sage-kings could have transformed their characters so as to love virtue and delight in ritual. Their motivations to transform themselves would not only be pure self-interest, but a sense of duty and a desire to do good. And in transforming themselves, they could make use of the raw material of good inclinations they already had. Training in ritual and the rules of morality could reinforce those inclinations and their superiority over selfish desires. But Graham's interpretation has the disadvantage of rendering Xunzi completely mistaken about his disagreement with Mencius. If Graham is right, then Xunzi actually agrees with Mencius in believing that there are sprouts of goodness in human nature. Both agree that the good inclinations would go undeveloped without training and education. Furthermore, Mencius certainly granted that there were tendencies in human nature that could lead us astray.

Now it is true that Xunzi misconstrued in an important respect his relation to Mencius. He argues against Mencius as if they both had the same definition of 'nature' (*xing*), but in fact Mencius does not define nature as that which is inborn and which need not be acquired through effort. When he says that human nature is good, he cannot mean that we are inborn with a full-blown goodness that requires no effort. And if this is true, then Xunzi misses the mark when he tries to refute Mencius by pointing to the fact that we must work for goodness.

There is one clear difference between Mencius and Xunzi, however, which Graham's interpretation does not capture. The difference comes from Xunzi's naturalistic account of morality. If morality is born of the need to create a social order that will benefit all, then it seems to make no sense to do as Mencius does and posit an original desire to do good or a sense of duty in human nature. Goodness and right are determined by the rules created by the sages. They cannot be prior to the sages in the sense required by their having innate desires for these things. This must true even if, as Nivison emphasizes, it was inevitable that the sages create such rules.

Because of this problem with Graham's interpretation, we must consider an alternative interpretation: that for Xunzi the desire to do good and the sense of duty are not original to human nature but derived from calculation on what is in our self interest. We come to have these things when we see in terms of our own long-term self-interest that we should have a certain character that we now lack. This certainly would fit with Xunzi's story of why morality is necessary. Feng Youlan gives such an interpretation:

> So-called goodness, says Xunzi, is a combination of social ceremonies, institutions, culture, and moral qualities such as human-heartedness and righteousness, together with just laws. These things are not originally desired by man, but he is left no alternative but to desire them.[25]

This interpretation is consistent with Xunzi's naturalistic account of morality. But if we are to interpret the desire to do good and the sense of duty as derived from a desire to do what is in one's long-term interests, we still have no explanation of how self-interest turns into love of and delight in morality. How does one start with the attitude that "one has no alternative but to desire" morality and create within oneself a genuine love for and a delight in it?

In view of the problems with either interpretation and in view of the fact that Xunzi gives no clear signal about the status of the desire to do good, it may well be that he was confused or ambivalent about the status of the desire. And if this is true, there will be no determinate answers from Xunzi about the nature of moral transformation. What we can do, however, is to construct an explanation of moral transformation that is compatible with his theory. I will consider two possible explanations.

One explanation is suggested by J. S. Mill's answer to the question of why moral virtue came to be valued for its own sake. The question is a problem for Mill because he thinks people desire only various kinds of pleasure and the absence of pain. At first glance, it seems that he could only allow virtue to be a means to pleasure and the absence of pain, just as it may seem that Xunzi could only allow moral virtue to be a means to the optimal long-term satisfaction of desire. But Mill, like Xunzi, does not want this result. Mill's answer is an analogy: just as money is originally only a means to pleasure, so virtue is originally only a means; but the constant association of money with pleasure, and virtue with pleasure, results in money and virtue being in themselves sources of pleasure. In other words, we are *conditioned* to take pleasure in virtue.[26]

In order for this idea to help Xunzi, however, there must be an explanation of how the sage-kings could have created the connection between virtue and pleasure in the first place. On Xunzi's account, morality can be a means to satisfying desire over the long-term only when the sage-kings have internalized it and gained the following of the people. Only then will they be able to create the secure social order that benefits all, including themselves. But if that is the story, then the sage-kings cannot *first* condition themselves by associating pleasure with virtue. The constant connection between pleasure and virtue only comes after they have succeeded in transforming themselves and creating a social order that *makes* virtue pleasurable. The problem is a general one. Theories that explain the presence of genuine moral virtue on the basis of transformation of a recalcitrant human nature have difficulty explaining how the conditions favorable to such a transformation are ever effected. The temptation is to illicitly presuppose the presence of those conditions.

We can get a clue to a better interpretation of moral transformation by looking at Nivison's interpretation of those passages in which Xunzi seems to attribute to the heart-mind an original desire to do good and a sense of duty. Nivison rejects Feng's interpretation of the origin of these things in self-interest for the reasons I have given above. His own conclusion is that Xunzi must assume that human beings just have a sense of duty.[27] This sense of duty, for Nivison, amounts to a capability of performing moral duty for its own sake and not for self-interested reasons. So far this interpretation sounds like Graham's, but it is intriguing in the way that it is different from Graham's. Nivison observes that the sense of duty as an original feature of human nature need not have any particular *content*. Thus qualified, Nivison's interpretation of the sense of duty may be compatible with Xunzi's naturalism in a way that Graham's interpretation is not.

As noted above, the heart-mind can have no original capability to discern any particular content to the ideas of right and wrong because the content is invented (or discovered as the best way to promote the interests of all). Even if the human heart-mind has an original capability to perform moral duty for its own sake, the content of morality cannot be there in the capability from the beginning. Now, without implying that Nivison would approve the way I use his interpretation, let me suggest that we must look for capabilities that satisfy three requirements: when attributed to human nature, they must be consistent with

Xunzi's claim that human nature is evil; they must not have moral content; but they must provide some motivational efficacy to beliefs about duty when duty is invented/discovered.

We find such capabilities in those chapters where Xunzi describes the transforming effect of ritual and music. Consider the chapter on rites and in particular the discussion of the rationale for the three-year mourning period for the death of a parent. Why this particular period? Xunzi explains that this is the time when the pain of grief is most intense. But why is grief the emotion felt upon the death of a parent? Xunzi explains that nothing that possesses consciousness fails to love its own kind and that "Among creatures of blood and breath, none has greater understanding than man; therefore man ought to love his parents until the day he dies."[28] On the subject of sacrificial rites, Xunzi says that they "originate in the emotions of remembrance and longing for the dead," which come to those who lose loved ones. Rites are needed to give expression to these emotions, which otherwise will be "frustrated and unfulfilled." Rites "express the highest degree of loyalty, love, and reverence."[29]

In the chapter on music, Xunzi says that when performed in an ancestral temple it produces harmonious reverence. When performed in the household, it produces harmonious kinship. When in the community, harmonious obedience. Music, says Xunzi, is a necessary requirement of human emotion. When it enters deeply into men, it transforms them deeply. When it is stern and majestic, the people become well behaved and shun disorder. If seductive and depraved, the people become abandoned and fall into disorder. "If people have emotions of love and hatred, but no ways in which to express their joy or anger, they will become disordered."[30]

In the chapters on rites where Xunzi is as specific as he ever is on the way that the human heart is transformed, he *presupposes* human emotions that are quite different from the ones he cites in arguing for the evilness of human nature. There is love for and grief and remembrance of lost parents. There is the suggestion that love of one's own kind is natural to all creatures, and greatest among human beings. In the chapter on music, Xunzi sometimes speaks as if music writes noble emotions on the slate of the mind, which if not blank, is at any rate not good. But at other times, he writes as if music expresses emotions that are latent within the heart. The middle and most plausible path between these extremes is the view that in one respect music does express latent emotion, but that it serves to stimulate and connect its expression to various situations defined by the rites.[31] The capacity to be inspired by a musical expression of harmony, for Xunzi, may be closely related to the capacities to be inspired by harmony between human beings and by the happy symmetry between human needs and Nature's bounty.[32]

Given the loves and feelings Xunzi describes in the chapters on rites and music, there is a way to see how the sage-kings could have transformed themselves. Rites and music work on some raw material in human nature that is amenable to being shaped toward a love of virtue and a delight in ritual. Human beings may have a desire for harmony and coherent wholes and may therefore delight in the harmony between each other and between the human world and nature that is established by rites. The virtue of filial piety (*xiao* 孝) strengthens, refines, and directs the primitive impulse of love of one's parents and the primitive impulse to reciprocate for the greatest of benefits—one's life and nurturance. The three-year mourning period and sacrificial rites strengthen, refine, and direct the natural feelings of grief and remembrance. We can come to love morality because it allows full expression of natural and deep human emotion.

Scholars have often observed that Mencius de-emphasizes the role of ritual in the shaping of character, while Xunzi gives it a very strong role. One reason for this difference is that Mencius believes the innate moral feelings provide a kind of direction for action and attitudes while Xunzi obviously cannot rely on any innate direction toward the moral. If the interpretation offered here is right, there is another reason for Xunzi's emphasis on ritual: his insight that rituals are especially effective in shaping and channeling human feeling because they regulate and partially define occasions on which human beings have strong feelings of the sort that can become moral feelings.

So far I have addressed the requirement that capabilities attributed to human nature provide beliefs about right and wrong and some motivational efficacy once these beliefs are acquired. But what about the requirement that the capabilities have no original moral content? The natural feelings that rites and music work upon are not yet moral in content. They are primitive responses not yet refined and regulated by moral rules. One originally delights in harmony and in wholeness of various sorts, with no thought that it is somehow morally right. One mourns for a parent simply, with no thought of its rightness or of the forms it should take. By contrast, Mencius holds that our natural feelings of mourning are feelings that reveal the rightness of mourning and that identify certain sorts of actions that ought to be taken. Consider *Meng Tzu* 3A:5, in which the story is told of people who did not bury their deceased parents. Not only do they eventually bury the bodies, not being able to bear looking at the bodies thrown into a ditch, but Mencius describes the covering of them as right. So on the proposed reconstruction of Xunzi's theory of moral transformation, he still denies the Mencian claim that innate, shared reactions reveal rightness to us. The proposed reconstruction is consistent with Xunzi's claim that morality is constructed out of self interest. But he now has a picture of human nature that allows him to explain the transformation from self interest to a love and delight in morality. On this view, we love it because it expresses, channels, and strengthens some of our natural human feelings.

And it is quite plausible that we do have some natural feelings that are congenial to morality even if they aren't moral feelings. For example, David Nivison has observed that the feeling of a debt of gratitude for a kindness or a gift is something we all know, and that in Chinese society that feeling is greatly magnified.[33] Such a feeling, as an innate impulse, need not be interpreted as a moral feeling, but simply a strong impulse to return good for good.[34] It becomes a moral feeling after the rules of morality are devised. The rules come to govern and even be embedded in the intentionality of the feeling (feeling that it is one's duty to return good for good). Further, there is good reason to think that the rules of morality would require reciprocity as well as define its acceptable forms. As Xunzi argued, human beings cannot get along without helping each other. And it seems plausible, as Lawrence Becker has observed, that helping behavior would be extinguished if it were systematically unreciprocated.[35]

But what about the requirement that capabilities attributed to human nature be consistent with Xunzi's claim that human nature is evil? Even if the feelings of love of parents and grief and remembrance when they die are not yet moral feelings, how could human nature be evil if it contains them? How could it be evil if it contains feelings that are congenial to morality? The answer, I think, lies in construing his claim that human nature is evil to be more sophisticated. Human nature is not evil because it contains nothing but selfish desire and feeling. It is evil because these kinds of desire and feeling *dominate* in conditions of insecurity and lack of order. It is evil in precisely the sense that Xunzi says it is: without the transforming effect of rites, music, and righteousness, human beings would act for themselves. So interpreted, Xunzi's claim has a great deal of plausibility to it. It also should be noted that love and grief may be expressed in a wide range of ways, only some of which are compatible with morality. These feelings must be moralized in order for them to result in moral behavior.

To conclude, let me make a case for the idea that we have not only found a plausible way for Xunzi to explain the path to moral transformation, but that the path found is of general significance for moral psychology. An exploration of Freud's moral psychology by Richard Wollheim results in some of the same conclusions reached here. Much of Freud's explanation of the growth of the moral sense, Wollheim observes, paints a rather unhappy picture of our relation to morality. Human beings are first bullied into internalizing morality. The child first experiences anxiety and terror at a parent or someone upon whom he is utterly dependent. He perceives that figure as obstructing or threatening the satisfaction of his sensual desires. The child internalizes the demands of the external figure as a way of dealing with his terror:

> We are frightened in childhood, we interiorize the fear by substituting an internal for an external object, we placate the internal representative of fear by the sacrifice of instinctual gratification, the gain in tranquillity outweighs the crippling loss in satisfaction, but the sacrifice has nothing independently to recommend it . . . A happier interpretation of morality would be deserved if it could be shown that there are some needs, some desires, other than the avoidance of fear, and not shallow ones, that the establishment of the superego satisfies.[36]

The basis for a happier interpretation that Wollheim derives from Freudian and neo-Freudian theories is a postulated need to control aggression toward a loved person. Wollheim's conclusion parallels the conclusion we have reached about Xunzi. Human nature is for him still evil in a very substantial sense. But there are elements in that nature that make it possible for human beings to be fulfilled by morality. And by "fulfilled," I do not mean simply have one's narrow self-interest satisfied. Morality serves to express certain latent emotions such as love and the desire to reciprocate for benefits received. Further, righteousness, ritual, and music not only allow expression of these emotions but channel and shape them so that originally narrow self-interest becomes much broader and more firmly connected to the interests of others. Morality does not eliminate nonmoral sensual desires but limits them in such a way that they are more compatible with moralized emotions and desires. Morality can provide a coherence to our characters that was not there before. It seems to me that only such a view of human nature could make possible what many of us, not only Xunzi, envision: the possibility of genuine love and delight in morality.[37]

NOTES

1. David Nivison, Feature Book Review of *The World of Thought in Ancient China* by Benjamin Schwartz, *Philosophy East & West* 38 (1988): 415.

2. For such an interpretation of Mencius, see David Nivison, "Two Roots or One," Presidential Address delivered before the Fifty-Fourth Annual Pacific Meeting of the American Philosophical Association, 28 March 1980, in *Proceedings and Addresses of the American Philosophical Association* 53 (1980): 739–61; Nivison, "Philosophical Voluntarism in Fourth Century China," delivered before the Twenty-fifth Annual Meeting of the Association for Asian Studies, 1973; Kwong-loi Shun, "Mencius' Criticism of Mohism: An Analysis of *Meng Tzu* 3A:5," *Philosophy East & West* 41 (1991): 203–14; and Shun, "Mencius and the Mind-Inherence of Morality: Mencius' Rejection of Kao Tzu's Maxim in *Meng Tzu* 2A:2," *Journal of Chinese Philosophy* 18 (1991): 141–69.

3. Burton Watson, trans., *Hsün Tzu: Basic Writings* (New York: Columbia University Press, 1963), 89.

4. This comparative point has been made by Bryan Van Norden, "Mengzi and Xunzi: Two Views of Human Agency," *International Philosophical Quarterly* 32 (1992): 178.

5. Nivison, Review of *The World of Thought in Ancient China*, 416.

6. He did believe, however, that our self-interest can become more expansive in civil society. Part of his account in *Leviathan* of the growth of civility and civilization hinges on an explanation of how we can come to appreciate the arts and sciences as answering to an expanded sense of self-interest.

7. Burton Watson, trans., "Regulations of a King," in *Hsün Tzu: Basic Writings* (New York: Columbia University Press, 1963), 40.

8. David Gauthier, *Morals By Agreement* (Oxford: Clarendon Press, 1986), 162–63.

9. Watson, "Regulations of a King," 34.

10. See Burton Watson, trans., "Human Nature is Evil," in *Hsün Tzu: Basic Writings* (New York: Columbia University Press, 1963), 168.

11. David Nivison, "Hsün Tzu and Chuang Tzu," in *Chinese Texts and Philosophical Contexts: Essays dedicated to Angus C. Graham*, ed. Henry Rosemont (La Salle, Ill.: Open Court, 1991): 129–42.

12. *Ibid.*, 142.

13. David S. Nivison, "Hsün Tzu on 'Human Nature'." In Bryan W. Van Norden, ed., *The Ways of Confucianism: Investigations in Chinese Philosophy* (Chicago Land La Salle, Ill.: Open Court, forthcoming 1996–1997).

14. Bryan Van Norden, "Mengzi and Xunzi: Two Views of Human Agency," 161–84.

15. Burton Watson, trans., "Rectifying Names," in *Hsün Tzu: Basic Writings* (New York: Columbia University Press, 1963), 150–51.

16. Burton Watson, trans., "A Discussion of Rites," in *Hsün Tzu: Basic Writings* (New York: Columbia University Press, 1963), 90–91.

17. D.C. Lau, trans., *Mencius* (Harmondsworth: Penguin, 1970), 168.

18. This seems to be Van Norden's interpretation of Mencius. See "Mengzi and Xunzi: Two Views of Human Agency," 106–7. Van Norden here draws our attention to *Mengzi* 6A:10, where the beggar, in refusing food, desires rightness more than life. Van Norden interprets this to mean that the beggar is moved by a stronger desire for rightness. However, as Kwong-loi Shun has pointed out to me in personal communication, this passage might be read in a different way: it is not that the beggar has a desire for life that is overridden by a stronger desire for rightness; rather, the beggar has a desire for rightness over life which might be a consequence of the approving activity of the mind. Shun notes, however, that the passage probably does not provide enough material for a conclusive reading of Mencius's view of human agency.

19. Philip J. Ivanhoe, "Human Nature and Moral Understanding in Xunzi," *International Philosophical Quarterly* 34, no. 2 (June 1994): 167–75.

20. Philip J. Ivanhoe, "A Happy Symmetry: Xunzi's Ethical Thought," *Journal of the American Academy of Religion* 59: 315.

21. Watson, "Human Nature is Evil," 161–62.

22. See Antonio Cua, "The Quasi-Empirical Aspect of Hsün Tzu's Philosophy of Human Nature," *Philosophy East and West* 28 (1978): 3–19.

23. A. C. Graham, trans., *Xunzi* (荀子) HY, 27/65–67, in *Disputers of the Tao: Philosophical Argumentation in Ancient China* (La Salle, Ill.: Open Court, 1989), 248.

24. Watson, "Regulations of a King," 45–46.

25. Derk Bodde, trans., *A History of Chinese Philosophy* (Princeton: Princeton University Press, 1952), 1: 294.

26. John Stuart Mill, *Utilitarianism*, chap. 4, in *Utilitarianism, On Liberty, Essay on Bentham* (New York: World Publishing, 1962), 290–91. There is a basis in Mill for a less reductive explanation of the pleasures of virtue, even though this is not the explanation he gives in *Utilitarianism*. Mill does not have an egoistic psychology, so he can acknowledge the existence of sympathetic emotions that are not based on any calculations of self-interest. The pleasures of virtue may on this view be derived from the satisfaction of our concerns for others. Below, I shall suggest a similar move for Xunzi.

27. Nivison, "Hsün Tzu on 'Human Nature.'"

28. Watson, "A Discussion of Rites," 106.

29. Ibid., 109–10.

30. Burton Watson, trans., "A Discussion of Music," in *Hsün Tzu: Basic Writings* (New York: Columbia University Press, 1963), 115.

31. There is a tradition in Western aesthetics that focuses on the relation between music, emotion, and the way that music can transform emotion. See, for example, H. R. Haweis, *Music and Morals* (New York: Harper, 1871), 1–54. Haweis holds that music stimulates certain "indefinite" feelings, i.e., feelings without definite objects or accompanying thoughts. When music is mixed with words, he says, the stimulated feelings may be wedded with definite ideas. His description of the effects of "patriotic, or languishing, or comic," "sublime or degraded" music is similar to Xunzi's.

32. The work of Claude Levi-Strauss draws our attention to a human striving for coherent wholes, in music, myth, kinship structures, and science. See *The Savage Mind (La Pensée Sauvage)* (London: Weidenfeld and Nicolson, 1962); *Structural Anthropology*, trans. C. Jacobson and B. G. Schoepf (New York: Basic Books, 1963); *Totemism*, trans. R. Needham (Boston: Beacon Press, 1963); *The Raw and the Cooked*, trans. J. & D. Weightman (London: Jonathan Cape, 1969); and *The Elementary Structures of Kinship*, trans. J. H. Bell, J. R. von Sturmer, & R. Needham (ed.) (Boston: Beacon Press, 1969).

33. David Nivison, "'Virtue' in Bone and Bronze," Walter Y. Evans-Wentz Lectures, February 1980.

34. This does not mean that the good that is returned must be of the same kind as the good received. A child cannot return the same kind of good that is received from parents, but can return a good nevertheless.

35. See Lawrence Becker, *Reciprocity* (London: Routledge & Kegan Paul, 1986), 90–91. Also see pp. 347–59 for an excellent bibliography of anthropological, sociological, and psychological works on the appearance of reciprocity in various cultures. He also gives references for theories of reciprocal altruism arising from evolutionary biology.

36. Richard Wollheim, *The Thread of Life* (Cambridge, Mass.: Harvard University Press, 1984), 205.

37. I have greatly benefitted from comments on an earlier version from Kwong-loi Shun and Amélie Rorty.

What Should Western Philosophy Learn from Chinese Philosophy?

Bryan W. Van Norden

> *For I go about, doing nothing else besides persuading you all, both young and old, to be concerned not about your body or your possessions, but rather that your soul shall be the best.*
>
> —Socrates

> *I, too, desire to rectify people's hearts.*
>
> —Mengzi

David S. Nivison's works on Chinese philosophy have all the characteristics of true classics: they are deep, they are widely admired, and they are seldom actually read. Consider two outstanding recent histories of ancient Chinese philosophy—Benjamin Schwartz's *The World of Thought in Ancient China*[1] and A. C. Graham's *Disputers of the Tao*.[2] Of the two papers by Nivison that Schwartz cites, neither is on philosophy.[3] Graham, on the other hand, cites three articles by Nivison, only one of which is philosophical.[4]

What is distinctive about Nivison's (neglected) contribution to the study of Chinese philosophy? I hope to provide a partial answer to this question by addressing a larger one: What should Western philosophy learn from Chinese philosophy? Although Nivison has, to my knowledge, never directly answered this larger question, my aim is to show that his work helps lay a solid foundation for one kind of answer to it.

I do not plan to provide, in the space of this brief article, a definitive answer to the larger question I raise. Instead, I want to suggest some of the issues that arise when one attempts to answer it. In particular, two issues have an important bearing on the kind of answer one might give. The first is how different Western and Chinese philosophy really are. The second is how one understands and evaluates the Western philosophic tradition as a whole.

1. Two Issues

1.1 How different?

In addressing the first of these issues, one temptation to avoid is identifying "Western philosophy" with some trend or fad within Western philosophy. There is, after all, great variety within Western philosophy itself. Plato, Thomas Aquinas, Descartes, Kant, and Bertrand Russell emphasize different issues, have different methodologies, and arrive at very different conclusions from one another, but they are all paradigmatic Western philosophers. We must also be prepared to discover that the difference between Western and Chinese philosophy is a matter of degree and not kind. Two people can agree that the two are significantly different, yet disagree about the extent and significance of that difference. Furthermore, if what we tentatively identify as Chinese philosophy turns out to be sufficiently different from Western philosophy, we may have to recognize that it is simply not philosophy at all.[5] Of course, since *philosophy* is a concept with fuzzy edges, it could also turn out to be a borderline case, in which whether we recognize the Chinese discipline as philosophy is guided not only by the facts, but also by our *decision* to count this newcomer to our conversation as philosophy (or not). But at least some things are clearly inside, and some others clearly outside, even a fuzzy boundary.

To decide that Chinese thought is too different to be called "philosophy" would not be to disparage it; it would simply be to recognize that there has to be enough similarity between Western philosophy and any non-Western candidate for us to recognize (or sensibly decide) that they are engaged in the same activity. Some may complain that this is assuming a Western definition of "philosophy." It is. But what else can we do? "Philosophy" is a Western word, coming to English from Cicero's Latin, and before that from Plato's Greek. It is just as ethnocentric to assume that every other culture must be engaged in what we call "philosophy" as it is to assume that no other culture could do philosophy. Before we assume either one of these things a priori, we should look at what other cultures in fact do. So, with these qualifications in mind, how different are Chinese and Western philosophy? I shall focus on two areas in which Chinese philosophy is frequently thought to differ from Western philosophy: content and methodology.

1.1.1 Content

There are certain concepts in traditional Chinese thought that have no exact equivalents in Western philosophy; there are, likewise, certain concepts from Western philosophy that have no equivalents in Chinese thought. The differences in conceptual content may turn out to be so great that we cannot sensibly recognize Chinese thought as philosophy. I am not inclined to think that this is the case. However, even if the conceptual content of Chinese thought is recognizably philosophic, we still must decide whether adopting those concepts, that is, learning to see the world in those terms, is a real option, or a merely notional option.

The terminology of "real" and "notional" options was developed by Bernard Williams. He writes that a system of beliefs

> is a real option for a group if either it is their [system of beliefs] or it is possible for them to go over to [it]; where going over to [it] involves, first, that it is possible for them to live within, or hold, [that system] and retain their hold on reality, and, second, to the extent that rational comparison between [that system] and their present outlook is possible, they could acknowledge their transition to [the new system] in the light of such comparison.[6]

Adopting a system of beliefs is a notional option if it is not a real option. Williams also remarks that many systems of beliefs

> which have been held are not real options now. The life of a Greek Bronze Age chief, or a mediaeval Samurai, and the outlooks that go with those, are not real options for us: there is no way of living them. This is not to say that reflection on those value-systems may not provide inspiration for thoughts about elements missing from modern life. . . .[7]

If one decides that adopting a concept from Chinese philosophy is a real option, then the next question to ask is, How much change will be required in Western philosophy to incorporate these new concepts? Minor adjustments or wholesale revolution? If one decides that adopting the concepts in question is a notional option, the next question to be asked is, How central are these concepts to Chinese philosophy? More specifically, can Chinese philosophy be done without them? If it turns out that we cannot seriously entertain the possibility of adopting certain concepts, and if it also turns out that Chinese philosophy cannot be done without these concepts, then we cannot seriously entertain the possibility of adopting Chinese philosophy.

Let's look at some concrete examples. There is nothing in Western philosophy corresponding to either *li* 禮 or *qi* 氣. *Li*, usually translated (inadequately) as "ritual" or "rites," is a central concept in Confucianism. It is central, in a different way, for other Chinese schools, such as Daoism and Mohism, insofar as they define themselves in terms of their rejection of the importance of *li*. *Li* refers to things that are covered by several different terms in contemporary English: religious ceremonies, etiquette, conventions, rituals, and certain parts of ethics. Now, some philosophers (most notably Herbert Fingarette) have suggested, first, that we can learn a great deal from Chinese philosophy by recognizing the important similarities among the activities grouped together under the notion of *li*, and, second, that *li* is a very human and humanizing sort of activity that has been neglected in Western philosophic discussions.[8]

Qi is translated in a variety of ways, reflecting the difficulty translators have in finding anything like an equivalent, including "ether," "psychophysical energy," and "passion-nature." Originally, *qi* was the term for the mist that arose from heated sacrificial offerings, and it soon came to refer to mist generally (fog, clouds). Eventually, though, for thinkers like Mengzi 孟子 (Mencius) and Zhuangzi 莊子, *qi* became a technical medical notion, referring to a fluid, present in the atmosphere and the human body, that was responsible for the intensity of one's emotional states. Finally, beginning at the end of the classical period, *qi* began to be thought of as the primal stuff out of which everything else in the universe condenses. The medieval Neo-Confucians emphasized *qi* in this last sense.[9] *Qi*, like *li*, does not have any exact equivalent in Western thought. Is adopting *qi* a real option for us? Here, I think it is important to distinguish between earlier and later uses of *qi*. I want to suggest that adopting *qi* in the sense it was used by the Neo-Confucians is a purely notional option, for the following reasons.

What is the book you are holding made of? I think that it is made mostly of paper, which I think is made of atoms. A Neo-Confucian like Zhu Xi 朱熹 will agree that this book is mostly paper, but he will also say that the paper is (ultimately) condensed *qi*.[10] Say we want to believe (or at least entertain believing) that it is true both that this book is made of atoms and also that this book is made of condensed *qi*. Now, it is of course possible for different descriptions of the same object to be true. I think it is true both that this book is mostly paper and also that this book is made of atoms, because I think paper is made of atoms. But in order for me to believe both that this book is made of atoms *and* that it is condensed *qi*, I need some kind of account, some sort of story, about how these two different descriptions of the same object relate to one another.[11]

One tempting move is to identify *qi* with the physicist's mass-energy. Then we could hold both that this book is made of atoms and that this book is made of *qi*, because the atoms would be made out of *qi* (i.e., mass-energy). However, this move will not work. If the sentence, "Atoms are made out of *qi*," means precisely the same thing as "Atoms are made out of mass-energy," then we have not succeeded in adopting any distinctively Chinese concepts into our conceptual scheme. All we have done is to introduce a new word, "*qi*," that means precisely the same thing as "mass-energy." Alternatively, if "*qi*" in the sentence "Atoms are made out of *qi*" is being used in the way the Neo-Confucians used it, then the sentence is simply false. *Qi* does not, in the Neo-Confucian scheme, make up atoms. *Qi* does not, in the Neo-Confucian scheme, manifest itself sometimes as mass and sometimes as energy. *Qi does*, in the Neo-Confucian scheme, help to account for the moral development of particular individuals. If an individual's *qi* is "turbid," this will retard her moral development; if an individual's *qi* is "limpid," this will assist her moral development. However, in the language of contemporary physics, it does not make any sense to say that mass-energy is either turbid or limpid, nor does it make any sense to say that the quality of one's mass-energy affects one's moral development. So we are faced with a dilemma. The statement "Atoms are made out of *qi*" is either just another way of saying "Atoms are made out of mass-energy," in which case adopting this new term should do nothing to change our conceptual scheme, or it is patently false.

At this point, some might object that I have fabricated a problem by assuming that we have to *choose* between viewing this book as composed of atoms and viewing it as composed of *qi*. Why can't we view it *both* ways? To begin with, I am not sure what it would be like for a reflective person to *not* make a choice. It seems a little fatuous to say that we are going to view the world as made out of *qi* Monday, Wednesday, and Friday, but out of atoms Tuesday, Thursday, and Saturday (leaving Sunday for agnosticism). Moreover, it seems to me that there are two reasons why one would care about the issues I'm discussing in this paper. First, one might care what the truth is. If one does care about the truth, then it is clear why we cannot hold both that the world is, and is not, composed of atoms. These things simply cannot *both* be true, for the reasons I gave above. However, some thinkers are suspicious of the notion of "truth" in general. For such thinkers, it seems to me, world views (whether Western or non-Western) are interesting only because of the practical consequences of accepting them.[12] A difference in world views can, sometimes at least, make a difference in how one acts, feels, etc. For the pragmatically minded truth skeptic, there is a reason to be interested in the question of whether the world is composed of atoms or *qi* only if looking at the world one way as opposed to the other has practical consequences. But then there is a practical contradiction in holding both views simultaneously. If we are trying to decide what to do, and two ways of looking at the world have different practical consequences, we *have* to decide between them.

So adopting *qi* is a notional option. This does not bode well for Neo-Confucianism, because a metaphysics employing *qi* is central to Neo-Confucian thought. To say that adopting *qi* is a notional option is to say that adopting Neo-Confucianism is a notional option. However, not all Chinese thought is Neo-Confucian. Although Mengzi and Zhuangzi, for example, employ the notion of *qi*, they use the term in a different sense, which corresponds loosely to the roles played by several different concepts in Western thought. For example, where Mengzi talks of *qi*, we could instead talk about adrenalin, or blind emotions, or morale (in 2A2), or the effects of rest and a calming environment (in 6A8), and still have a philosophy that was recognizably Mengzian.

So some concepts found in Chinese philosophy will be absent from Western philosophy. Adopting some of these concepts will be a real option, while other concepts will be such that our adopting them is a notional option, and then we will need to ask to what extent these concepts are essential to Chinese philosophy. We shall also find, of course, that certain Western philosophic concepts will be absent from Chinese philosophy. For example, Chad Hansen has claimed (notoriously) that

the early Chinese philosophic tradition does not employ concepts corresponding to truth, belief, or reason.[13] Obviously, both kinds of content differences will affect whether we judge that there is such a thing
as Chinese philosophy, and what we expect to learn from it.

1.1.2 Methodology

Chinese and Western philosophy are also thought to differ in their
methodologies, especially in the extent to which the two employ rational argumentation. This point has been stressed by Donald Munro:

> Western readers, especially those with some philosophical training . . .
> look first for the "argument," or demonstration that the position being
> advocated in the Chinese work is true; when they find no systematic,
> step-by-step argument, there is often a feeling of frustration.[14]

This admission that the Chinese tradition is deficient in argumentation is often combined with an advertisement of compensating virtues.
Munro remarks that

> The Chinese thinker's regrettable lack of attention to the logical valid-
> ity of a philosophical tenet is balanced by his great concern with prob-
> lems important to human life. There are times when Western philoso-
> phy has been characterized by the reverse situation—an enormous
> interest in epistemological and logical problems and a seeming uncon-
> cern with the bearing of its mental labors on the well-being of man.[15]

The tendency to emphasize the differences between Chinese and Western philosophy is also evident in Munro's students. Robert Eno, for
example, has claimed that Confucianism "was not philosophical in the
Western analytic sense," or "was not nonphilosophical, but was rather a
nonanalytic species of philosophy."[16] Furthermore, one of the principal themes of Chad Hansen's recent *A Daoist Theory of Chinese
Thought*,[17] seems to be how inept Confucians (allegedly) are at rational
argumentation. My own view is that Munro is justified in praising Chinese philosophy for its emphasis upon "problems important to human
life," but that he (and his students) have underestimated the amount
of rational argumentation present in early Chinese texts.[18] But I shall
say more about this below.

1.2 The Western Tradition

Let us turn to the question of how one understands and evaluates the Western philosophic tradition as a whole. Within the Anglo-American philosophic community (at least), there is sharp disagreement on this issue. Some critics charge that the Western philosophic tradition (or some significant trend within that tradition) is in a kind of crisis, and has reached a dead-end, in the sense that it has encountered problems that cannot be solved within the prevailing framework for how philosophy has been done.[19] Among the leading figures who agree that Western philosophy is in a sort of crisis are Jacques Derrida, Richard Rorty, and Alasdair MacIntyre.[20] However, while these thinkers agree that there is some serious crisis, they disagree about many other important issues, including the issue of what major problems the Western tradition faces, and where philosophy should go from here. Derrida, for example, looks back to Nietzsche and Heidegger for inspiration, Rorty looks to those two thinkers as well as the American Pragmatists, while MacIntyre calls for a return to Aristotle.[21] Finally, many philosophers at major research institutions reject completely the suggestion that there *is* any crisis in Western philosophy at all. Hector-Neri Castañeda spoke for many when he said, ". . . philosophy has never before been in as great a shape as it is today. . . . I am most optimistic about the future of philosophy."[22] Obviously, where one stands on these issues will greatly influence *whether* one feels a need to look for salvation from non-Western philosophy, and *what* one hopes to find there.

The two issues that we have isolated, the degree of difference and our evaluation of the Western philosophic tradition, interact to affect how worthwhile we will find the study of Chinese thought. In order to discuss how they interact, I am going to take the liberty of greatly simplifying the various positions one might take on each of these issues. Along the spectrum of views one can take about the degree of difference between Western and Chinese philosophy, I shall isolate three positions: radical difference, moderate difference, and little difference. In addition, I shall isolate only three positions regarding the successfulness of the Western tradition: the tradition is triumphant, it is moderately successful, and it is a failure.[23] One holds that the Western philosophic tradition is "triumphant" if one believes all of the following: it is not in a state of crisis, it is not deadlocked on problems that seem insoluble from within the tradition, it has not become irrelevant to the larger culture of which the academic community is a part, and there are not significant problems recognizable as philosophic that the tradition has ignored. One would regard the tradition as moderately successful if one thought that the tradition had at least some important insights, concepts, or methodologies, but also thought that the tradition had some problems that seemed hard to solve from within the tradition, or that the tradition had become irrelevant to the larger culture of which the academic community was a part, or had ignored or underemphasized certain problems recognizable as philosophic. Finally, one regards the tradition as a failure if one thinks it is in some state of crisis that seems insoluble with the resources provided by the mainstream of the tradition.

If one regards the Western philosophic tradition as triumphant in the sense I have defined, then it is hard to see what the Western tradition has to learn from the Chinese tradition, regardless of how similar or dissimilar one regards the Western and Chinese traditions. If the Chinese tradition turns out to be very similar to the Western tradition, then there is little to learn: Why study Mozi 墨子 if he turns out to be just a pale imitation of Mill? Why study Xunzi 荀子 if he turns out to be just a second-rate Hobbes? Furthermore, if one regards the Western tradition as triumphant, the more dissimilar the Western and Chinese traditions are, the more this will seem to amount to a failure on the part of the Chinese tradition to live up to the Western paradigm.

If one regards the Western philosophic tradition as moderately successful, then Chinese philosophy will seem most worthy of study if it is moderately different from Western philosophy. If it is close to being the same as Western philosophy, it will prove uninteresting for the reasons I offer above. If it is too radically different from Western philosophy, it will seem difficult if not impossible to assimilate it to the insights acknowledged to have been gained by the Western tradition.

Finally, if one regards the Western tradition as an almost complete failure, the more different the Chinese tradition is, the more interesting an object of study it will seem, because it will offer an alternative to our failed, or dead-ended tradition. Of course, this is only true up to the point at which Chinese thought is still recognizable as philosophy (see my comments in § 1.1).[24]

So far, I have been treating Western and Chinese philosophy as if each were a monolithic entity. In reality, though, the two-dimensional matrix I have described will need to be employed for every distinct "subtopic" within philosophy.[25] Consider formal logic. The Western tradition seems triumphant in this area, so there is little if anything to learn from the Chinese tradition on this topic. On the other hand, one might think that, when it comes to theories of ethical self-cultivation, the Western tradition has been only moderately successful, and has much to learn from the different, but recognizably philosophic, Chinese views on this topic.[26]

In summary, Chinese philosophy will seem *most* worthy of study if you have one of two sets of beliefs. It will seem worth learning from (a) if you regard the Western philosophic tradition as neither hopelessly dead-ended, nor as completely triumphant, and (b) if you think that Chinese thought is similar enough to Western thought to be recognizable as dealing with some of the same problems, but not so similar as to have nothing new to offer to the Western tradition. I shall refer to this as the Moderate View. Chinese philosophy will also seem worth learning from (a) if you think the Western philosophic tradition *has* dead-ended, but (b) also think that Chinese philosophy offers a new alternative because it is radically different from most of the Western tradition. I shall refer to this as the Radical View.[27]

TABLE 1

	Little Difference	Moderate Difference	Radical Difference
Triumphant			
Moderately Successful		Moderate View	
Failure			Radical View

2. Two Views

2.1 The Radical View

The most explicit and articulate defenders of a version of the Radical
View are David L. Hall and Roger T. Ames. The differences between
the Chinese and Western traditions are such, they note, that it "is quite
likely that the majority of Western philosophers would refuse Confucius a membership in the offical canon of Anglo-European philosophy,
since he did not consider the 'real philosophic problems.' "[28] Moreover, they insist that Western philosophy is in a crisis, resulting from
what they say is the Western tendency to emphasize metaphysics of
transcendence, and to sharply distinguish theory from practice and
fact from value. They further suggest that the efforts of recent Western
philosophers to overcome these problems "have not been entirely successful, even considered in terms of their own criteria of success. . . ."
Why not?

> The reason for this is obvious to anyone who rehearses the history of
> Western philosophy: the dichotomy of theory and practice has so long
> been presupposed in our tradition that the philosophical categories
> that form the inventory of our speculative notions are themselves con-
> structed with reference to this dichotomy.[29]

They go on to suggest that ". . . it is doubtful whether the resources
available within our own cultural tradition are adequate to resolve successfully the crucial dilemmas associated with attempting to think
one's way through to a sufficiently novel understanding of thinking."[30]
Consequently, Western thinkers should look to Chinese thought for
"an alternative model of the activity of thinking."[31] Hall and Ames
describe their methodology in some detail:

> . . . turning away from the apparently impoverished sources for specu-
> lation in our philosophic present, the philosopher moves to the more
> esoteric elements of his cultural milieu, in order to find novel evi-
> dence. But if he is to find such novelty, he needs to discover a place
> from which to view it. The dominant modes of his cultural present
> offer no such vantage point, since these are seen to be consequences
> of the historical past as construed from that dominant present. For
> this reason, it becomes necessary to seek out other cultures as well.

What from our perspective might appear radically novel may be found within an alternative cultural mainstream.[32]

Hall and Ames deserve kudos for presenting an articulate and coherent vision of the Western and Chinese intellectual traditions that makes clear the relevance and importance of comparative research. However, the ultimate value of their work depends upon whether the controversial claims they make (about both Chinese and Western philosophy) can be substantiated.[33]

2.2 The Moderate View

Arthur Waley famously says of Mengzi that, "As a controversialist he is nugatory," and claims that, "he would have been utterly routed [in debate], had not his enemies been as feeble in argument as he was."[34] As we have seen, Waley is not alone in perceiving a lack of able argumentation in Mengzi and other early Chinese thinkers. However, as anyone who has been through an introductory philosophy class knows, recognizing and reconstructing an argument in a piece of text is a far from straightforward matter. One of the reasons for this is that most arguments in ordinary language are enthymemic. That is, the conclusion, or some of the premises, are not stated explicitly. It may have been superfluous to state the implied conclusion or premises for the original audience, to whom they would have been obvious. But to an audience separated from the original author by gulfs of culture and time, the loss of background knowledge of key premises may make even the most powerful argument seem a tangle of sophistries and non-sequiturs. In my opinion, much of the best work in comparative thought in the last few decades has been done in explaining the argumentation underlying passages that seem incomprehensible at first glance.

One of the reasons I regard Nivison's work as especially important and irreplaceable is that I think he, along with A. C. Graham, D. C. Lau, and others, has produced careful philological and philosophical work that helps us understand that Chinese thinkers are doing something that, both in terms of content and methodology, is not as radically different from Western philosophy as it might, at first, seem.[35]

Nivison's two most important published papers, "Mencius and Motivation"[36] and "Two Roots or One?"[37] are typical of his contributions.[38] In each paper, he takes a passage from the *Mengzi* that has not been the focus of critical discussion, and that might seem an example of some special "Oriental logic," and shows how the passage, when properly understood, is both comprehensible and philosophically challenging. Instead of a muddled controversialist, Mengzi appears as a philosopher with original insights on weakness of the will, self-cultivation, and moral argumentation. Of course, interpretation of any thinker should be "holistic," in the sense that we interpret particular passages in the light of a thinker's complete work, and in the sense that we locate a thinker within the complex of ideas and debates in her era. Nivison's extensive work (including his unpublished writings) provides an interpretation that is holistic in both these senses. We learn how the problem of weakness of the will is treated in Chinese thought from Kongzi to Mozi through Mengzi and on to Wang Yangming 王陽明 and Dai Zhen 戴震. We learn how Mengzi's debate with Gaozi 告子 in book 6A relates to his comments in 2A2, which tie in to issues dealt with by both Mozi and Yi Zhi 夷之 (in 3A5). We also see how parts of the *Zhuangzi* are a response to *Mengzi* 2A2, and how Xunzi develops a Confucian response to Zhuangzi's challenge.[39]

So Nivison has made a significant contribution to what I have described as the Moderate View by showing us that ancient Chinese thinkers *were* engaged in comprehensible argumentation, and that they were arguing about recognizable philosophic issues. This is not all that is needed to establish the Moderate View, however. We need a motivation for turning to Chinese thought. Nivison's colleague, Lee H. Yearley, has made a contribution to the Moderate View by showing the relevance of Chinese philosophy, especially Confucianism, to the virtue ethics movement in recent Western philosophy.[40] The virtue ethics movement has diverse strands, and resists any brief summary. Some of the more radical virtue ethicists take inspiration from G. E. M. Anscombe's claim that Western ethics is in a crisis, and needs to return to a study of the virtues in order to put itself back on a firm footing.[41] This view received powerful, but very controversial, development in Alasdair MacIntyre's *After Virtue*.[42] Radical virtue ethics has many critics.[43] However, many contemporary ethicists agree that (at the least) there is much fertile but neglected ground for philosophical discussion around the virtues.[44] Furthermore, even some of the most enthusiastic proponents of Western virtue ethics agree that this tradition is far from "triumphant," in that many outstanding problems remain to be solved. So far, the paradigms dominating discussions of the virtues have been the theories of Aristotle and Thomas Aquinas. Yearley's work suggests, however, that Confucians provide new, and challengingly different, paradigms for virtue ethics.[45]

Among the issues for further research suggested by this approach are the following. How does the conception of the ideal life (or "human flourishing") in Confucianism compare to the political and contemplative lives advocated by Western virtue ethicists? Is there anything in Confucian moral psychology corresponding to the rational part of the soul? If not, how does this affect the conceptions of the virtues in the two traditions? Does the role of *li* simply correspond to the role of convention in Western ethics, or (as Fingarette has argued) does it suggest new possibilities for human cultivation?[46] Is there anything in the Confucian tradition corresponding to the Socratic doctrine of the unity of the virtues? Why do the lists of "cardinal virtues" from the Confucian and Western traditions differ?[47] What can Confucians teach us about the role of texts, teachers, and one's innate moral judgment in the process of moral cultivation?[48] How do the differences within the Confucian movement reflect different strategies of self-cultivation?[49]

My focus on Confucianism should not be taken to imply that other Chinese intellectual movements are not worthy of study. Mohism, as a form of universalistic consequentialism, is perhaps the Chinese philosophy most recognizable to those trained in contemporary Western normative ethics. Reading the debate between Confucians and Mohists in the light of the contemporary Western debate between utilitarians and their critics[50] may both improve our understanding of early Chinese thought and inform current philosophic discussion.[51]

At this stage in our understanding of Chinese thought, the various strands of Daoism are harder to classify. For example, Chad Hansen has interpreted Zhuangzi as a moral anti-realist and relativist, who would feel at home with twentieth-century analytic ethicists like Gilbert Harman or J. L. Mackie.[52] A. C. Graham seemed to understand

Zhuangzi as having what we in the West would describe as an "ideal observer theory" of ethics (although Graham did not use that phrase himself).[53] Benjamin Schwartz and Lee Yearley both interpret Zhuangzi as a mystic, though in very different ways. Schwartz sees Zhuangzi as very similar to Christian, Jewish, and Islamic mystics in advocating mystical union with a higher reality.[54] Yearley, in contrast, sees Zhuangzi as an "intra-worldly" mystic, who advocates detached contemplation of each moment of experience as it arises.[55] Most recently, Paul Kjellberg has stressed the similarities between Zhuangzi and Hellenistic Skeptics.[56] My own view, for what it is worth, is that Zhuangzi and the Confucians each present us with an ideal for human life. In addition, they agree that an important part of their respective ideals is acting in an *wu wei* 無為 fashion.[57] However, they disagree over the content of the ideal life (the life of a sage-king like Shun vs. the skill of a craftsperson like Cook Ding of *Zhuangzi,* chapter 3), and over how to achieve this ideal state (active self-cultivation vs. the "fasting of the heart" advocated in *Zhuangzi,* chapter 4).[58] Whatever interpretation one agrees with, though, it seems clear that much valuable work remains to be done in interpreting and assessing the challenge that thinkers like Zhuangzi present to Confucianism and to Western ethics.

3. Concluding Dogmata

One point that may have been especially misleading about my presentation so far is that it suggests that the questions I have discussed are related so that we could answer them in a linear fashion. I have made it seem as if we could just determine how different Western and Chinese philosophy are, and where the Western tradition lies on the spectrum from triumph to failure, and then proceed to find out what we can learn from Chinese philosophy. In fact, I think that our understanding of the three questions will be improved (gradually, by many scholars, over many years) by asking all three questions at once.[59] We will come to understand better the nature of Western philosophy, and (in so doing) transform that philosophy, while (and through) coming to understand the nature of Chinese philosophy. As the Greek poet George Seferis said, "And the soul, if it is to know itself, into a soul must look. The stranger and the enemy, we saw him in the mirror."[60] Of course, we must be guided in this process by tentative hypotheses about what we expect to find. There is nothing wrong with such (unavoidable) biases so long as we, and the intellectual communities of which we are a part, strive to provide evidence and arguments for our beliefs, and remain open to changing our minds through ongoing discussion. The reader can no doubt guess many of my own biases from what I have said already. But allow me to conclude with a manifesto to suggest more directly one orientation for approaching these questions.

In my opinion, the report of the death of the Western philosophic tradition is an exaggeration. Interesting and worthwhile work is currently being done in many areas of contemporary philosophy. Nonetheless, I do *not* think that the Western tradition is "triumphant." At the same time, I think that many of the most noted critics of the tradition have misdiagnosed its problems. I almost wish it were true that the problem with the tradition was something like "logocentrism" (Derrida), or "the correspondence theory of Truth" (Rorty), to pick two trendy catch phrases.[61] If the problem were something fundamental and systematic like that, it would be easier (in some ways) to recognize and address it. The problem, though, is considerably more subtle.

Of the students who come into a philosophy course for some purpose other than merely satisfying a distribution requirement, many come with the expectation that the course will teach them something about how to live better lives. This, it seems to me, is an entirely reasonable expectation. It is also an expectation that is too often dashed. We frequently confront introductory students with paradoxes about the Morning Star and the Evening Star, or brains in vats, or improbable scenarios about the engineers of runaway trains. I do not want to say either that smart people cannot reasonably find some of these problems interesting, or that they have no place in a philosophic curriculum. But one of the defining interests of Western philosophy at least as far back as Heraclitus and Pythagoras, and of Chinese philosophy since its inception, has been, How should one live?[62] I think that contemporary philosophy has, to a great extent, abdicated answering this question.[63] If there is a "crisis" in contemporary philosophy, it lies here.[64] The role of philosophy in helping people to see how to live has been taken up, to some extent, by pop-psychology, pop-philosophy, and pop-religion. Not everything that is popular is bad, of course. But I submit that, as Nivison has helped us to see, Western and Chinese philosophy can speak to each other and to us about how to live well—if only we would make the effort to listen.

NOTES

I am indebted to Charles Guignon, P. J. Ivanhoe, Arthur Kuflik, and S. Rebecca Thomas for insightful comments on earlier drafts of this paper.

1. Benjamin Schwartz, *The World of Thought in Ancient China* (Cambridge, Mass.: Belknap Press, 1985).

2. A. C. Graham, *Disputers of the Tao* (La Salle, Ill.: Open Court Press, 1989).

3. David Nivison, "The Dates of Western Zhou," *Harvard Journal of Asiatic Studies* 43, no. 2 (December 1983): 481–580; and "Royal 'Virtue' in Shang Oracle Inscriptions," *Early China* 4 (1978–1979): 52–55.

4. David Nivison, "Mencius and Motivation," *Journal of the American Academy of Religion* 47, no. 3, Thematic Issue S (September 1980): 417–32. (Note that "Thematic Issue S" is a special supplementary volume of this journal, distinct from the regular volume 47, no. 3.) The other two works Graham cites are "The Dates of Western Chou," loc. cit., and "1040 as the Date of the Chou Conquest," *Early China* 8 (1982–1983): 76–78.

5. For one discussion of whether early Chinese thought is philosophical, see Russell Hatton, "Chinese Philosophy or 'Philosophy'?" *Journal of Chinese Philosophy* (hereafter *JCP*) 14, no. 4 (December 1987): 445–73, and the earlier articles referred to in Hatton's notes 2 and 3 (p. 467). The particular discussion of which Hatton was a part is perhaps obsolete, since it assumed (as Hatton recognized) a very narrow conception of what Western philosophy is, which most philosophers today would reject.

6. Bernard Williams, "The Truth in Relativism," *Moral Luck* (New York: Cambridge University Press, 1981), 139. Precisely speaking, Williams is discussing systems of belief, while I am discussing concepts, but I take it that the extension of his terminology to my topic is straightforward.

7. Williams, 140.

8. See Herbert Fingarette, *Confucius: The Secular as Sacred* (New York: Harper Torchbooks, 1972). For an insightful critique of Fingarette, see Schwartz, 67–85. Another important philosophic analysis of *li* is Kwong-loi

Shun, *"Jen* and *Li* in the *Analects," Philosophy East and West* 43, no. 3 (July 1993): 457–79.

9. I am using the term "Neo-Confucian" to cover only the Cheng-Zhu 程朱 and Lu-Wang 陸王 schools. One work that serves as a helpful introduction to the thought of Cheng Yi 程頤 and Cheng Hao 程顥, and to Neo-Confucianism in general, is A. C. Graham's, *Two Chinese Philosophers* (La Salle, Ill.: Open Court, 1992; op. 1958).

10. More precisely, he will say it is a composite of condensed *qi* and *li* 理 (principle). See Graham, *Two Chinese Philosophers,* op. cit.

11. Note that I am not assuming physicalism here. Physicalism is the view that the only things that exist are the things that can be understood by physics. As a matter of fact, I think physicalism is false. But even if we think there are things that physics (or even all of natural science) knows not of, we have to be able to coherently explain the relationships among the various accounts of the things that exist.

12. Of course, someone who finds the notion of truth intellectually respectable can *also* find world views interesting because of the practical effects of accepting them.

13. "Clearly, Chinese thought has a conceptual content drastically different from that of Western thought." (Chad Hansen, *A Daoist Theory of Chinese Thought* [New York: Oxford University Press, 1992], 26.) See also idem, *Language and Logic in Ancient China* (Ann Arbor: University of Michigan Press, 1983); idem, "Chinese Language, Chinese Philosophy, and 'Truth,'" *Journal of Asian Studies* 44, no. 3 (May 1985): 491–519; idem, "Should the Ancient Masters Value Reason?" in Henry Rosemont, ed., *Chinese Texts and Philosophical Contexts* (La Salle, IL: Open Court, 1991), 179–207. For criticisms (which I find decisive) of many of Hansen's claims, see the reviews of *Language and Logic* by P. J. Ivanhoe, *Chinese Literature, Essays, Articles and Reviews* 9 (1987): 115–23; and A. C. Graham, *Harvard Journal of Asiatic Studies* 45, no. 2 (1985): 692–703; as well as Graham's response to Hansen's claims about reason in Rosemont, 291–97; Christoph Harbsmeier's criticisms of Hansen's claims about truth in "Marginalia Sino-logica," in Robert Allinson, ed., *Understanding the Chinese Mind* (New York: Oxford University Press, 1989), 125–66; and my review of *A Daoist Theory of Chinese Thought*, in *Ethics* 105.2 (January 1995): 433–35.

14. Donald Munro, *The Concept of Man in Early China* (Stanford: Stanford University Press, 1969), ix.

15. Munro, loc. cit.

16. Robert Eno, *The Confucian Creation of Heaven* (Albany: SUNY Press, 1990), 7. Kwong-loi Shun raises some important objections to Eno's project in his review of this book, *Harvard Journal of Asiatic Studies* 52, no. 2 (December

1992): 739–56. See also P. J. Ivanhoe's brief review, *Journal of Asian Studies* 50, no. 4 (November 1991): pp. 907–8.

17. Hansen, op. cit.

18. They may also be guilty of the mistake of identifying all of "Western philosophy" with some trend or fad within it (see § 1.1). If one assumes that the paradigm for Western philosophy is something like Whitehead and Russell's *Principia Mathematica,* then Chinese thought will undeniably lack the rigor in argumentation necessary to count as philosophy. But Chinese thought may seem quite philosophical if the standard of comparison is Aristotle's *Nicomachean Ethics,* or some of Plato's dialogues.

19. An excellent collection on this topic is Kenneth Baynes, James Bohman, and Thomas McCarthy, eds., *After Philosophy: End or Transformation?* (Cambridge, Mass.: MIT Press, 1987). This is a collection of essays by seminal thinkers representing various views on the nature and future of philosophy, and includes a helpful introduction and bibliographies. Another good anthology on this topic is Avner Cohen and Marcelo Dascal, eds., *The Institution of Philosophy: A Discipline in Crisis?* (La Salle, Ill.: Open Court, 1989).

20. For a selection of Derrida's writings, see Peggy Kamuf, ed., *A Derrida Reader: Between the Blinds* (New York: Columbia University Press, 1991). Note that a special issue of the *Journal of Chinese Philosophy* has been dedicated to "Derrida and Chinese Philosophy" (*JCP* 17, no. 1 [March 1990]). For clear exegesis and penetrating criticisms of Derrida and other deconstructionists, see John M. Ellis, *Against Deconstruction* (Princeton: Princeton University Press, 1989). The work of Rorty's that has received the most general acclaim (and lays the foundation for his later criticism of Western philosophy) is *Philosophy and the Mirror of Nature* (Princeton: Princeton University Press, 1979). A recent collection of his essays is his *Philosophical Papers,* 2 vols. (New York: Cambridge University Press, 1991). For his views on comparative philosophy, see the review he published in *Philosophy East and West* 39, no. 3 (July 1989): 332–37. For informed critiques of the Rortian project, see Charles B. Guignon and David R. Hiley, "Biting the Bullet: Rorty on Private and Public Morality," in Alan R. Malachowski, ed., *Reading Rorty: Critical Responses to* Philosophy and the Mirror of Nature *(and Beyond)* (Cambridge, Mass.: Basil Blackwell, 1990), 339–64, and Charles B. Guignon, "Saving the Differences: Gadamer and Rorty," in *Proceedings of the Philosophy of Science Association* 2 (1982): 360–67. Martha Nussbaum responds (decisively, I think) to one kind of argument characteristic of several "postmodern" thinkers in "Sophistry About Conventions," in her *Love's Knowledge* (New York: Oxford University Press, 1990), 220–29. For a debate over postmodern views of textual interpretation, see Umberto Eco et al., *Interpretation and Overinterpretation* (New York: Cambridge University Press, 1992). See also Eco's brief and witty response to postmodern

criticisms of rationality in "On the Crisis of the Crisis of Reason," in his *Travels in Hyperreality*, trans. William Weaver (New York: Harcourt Brace Jovanovich, 1986; o.p. 1973), 125–32. For an ambitious attempt to respond simultaneously to many postmodern thinkers, see Alasdair MacIntyre, *Three Rival Versions of Moral Enquiry* (Notre Dame: University of Notre Dame Press, 1990), chap. 9, "Tradition against Genealogy: Who Speaks to Whom?" The foundation of MacIntyre's recent work is *After Virtue*, 2d ed. (Notre Dame: University of Notre Dame Press, 1984; 1st ed., 1981). He further develops his thought in *Whose Justice? Which Rationality?* (Notre Dame: University of Notre Dame Press, 1988), and *Three Rival Versions of Moral Enquiry* (op. cit.). MacIntyre begins to address the challenge provided by Confucianism in his "Incommensurability, Truth and the Conversation between Confucians and Aristotelians about the Virtues," in Eliot Deutsch, ed., *Culture and Modernity: East-West Philosophic Perspectives* (Honolulu: University of Hawaii Press, 1991), 104–22. For representative essays by, and bibliographies on, Derrida, Rorty and MacIntyre, see Baynes, Bohman, McCarthy, op. cit.

21. See, for example, Rorty, "Philosophy as Science, as Metaphor, and as Politics," in Cohen and Dascal, 13–33; and MacIntyre, *After Virtue*, especially chap. 9, "Nietzsche or Aristotle?" and chap. 18, "After Virtue: Nietzsche *or* Aristotle, Trotsky *and* St. Benedict."

22. "Philosophy as a Science and as a Worldview," in Cohen and Dascal, 39. Consider also the tone of a leading journal that recently celebrated its centennial with a review issue discussing developments in four areas in contemporary philosophy. Tyler Burge's "Philosophy of Language and Mind: 1950–1990" makes no reference to any crisis in philosophy at all, and (in fact) praises "the emergence of philosophical community," marked by "a sharing of philosophical concerns, vocabularies, and methods of dispute" (*The Philosophical Review* 101, no. 1 [January 1992]: 50). Philip Kitcher's review of trends in epistemology, "The Naturalists Return," dismisses Rorty, and "numerous literary theorists," in one brief footnote (ibid., 114, n. 143). "Toward *Fin de siècle* Ethics: Some Trends," by Stephen Darwall, Allan Gibbard, and Peter Railton, devotes all of three and a half pages to critics of modern moral philosophy in general (pp. 180–83), and concludes that such critics have not yet made their case. Margaret Wilson probably spends the most time responding to those who think of contemporary philosophy as being in some kind of crisis, in "History of Philosophy in Philosophy Today; and the Case of the Sensible Qualities." Although she never uses the word "crisis," among the critics of "analytical historians" to whom she responds (pp. 195–209) are Rorty and MacIntyre. She argues that the critics' charges are largely unjustified.

23. This scheme is a simplification in another sense, which I discuss below.

24. Some would say that the problem with Western philosophy is *philosophy* itself, that we have to stop doing philosophy. One who thought this about Western philosophy, and who also thought that there was no Chinese *philosophy*, might advocate adopting some practice or institution from the Chinese tradition *in place of* philosophy. I think this view is mistaken on several counts, but I do not mean to rule it out a priori. Discussing it is outside of the scope of this paper, though.

25. Of course, our beliefs about what the subtopics of philosophy *are* may be revised in the light of Chinese philosophy.

26. For the sake of simplicity, I shall not refer to this complication again, but the reader should keep it in mind. I thank Arthur Kuflik for making clear the need to be explicit on this point.

27. I suppose we could label the view that (a) we should stop practicing philosophy of any kind, and (b) we should adopt some non-philosophical Chinese institution or practice in place of philosophy, the Replacement View.

28. David L. Hall and Roger T. Ames, *Thinking Through Confucius* (Albany: SUNY Press, 1987), 325.

29. Hall and Ames, 38.

30. Hall and Ames, 39.

31. Hall and Ames, 40.

32. Hall and Ames, 331.

33. I find compelling many of the criticisms that have been made of their interpretation of Kongzi 孔子 (Confucius). See the reviews by P. J. Ivanhoe, *Philosophy East and West* 41, no. 2 (April 1991): 241–54; Joel Kupperman, *Harvard Journal of Asiatic Studies* 49, no. 1 (1989): 251–59; Michael Martin, *JCP* 17 (1990): 495–503; and Gregor Paul, "Reflections on the Usage of the Terms 'Logic' and 'Logical,'" *JCP* 18, no. 1 (March 1991): 73–87. (See also the impassioned response to Martin's and Paul's reviews by Hall and Ames, *JCP* 18, no. 3 [September 1991]: 333–47, and the surrebuttals by Martin, *JCP* 18, no. 4 [December 1991]: 489–93, and Paul, *JCP* 19 [1992]: 119–22.) For an interpretation of Kongzi closer to my own, see Herrlee G. Creel, *Confucius and the Chinese Way* (New York: Harper Torchbooks, 1960; o.p. *Confucius: The Man and the Myth*, 1949). Ames attempts to interpret Mencius in a way that brings him into line with his interpretation of Confucius, in his "The Mencian Conception of *Ren xing:* Does It Mean 'Human Nature'?" in Rosemont, 143–75. For what I think is a definitive rebuttal, see Irene Bloom, "Mencian Arguments on Human Nature (*Jen-hsing*)," *Philosophy East and West* 44, no. 1 (January 1994): 19–53.

34. Arthur Waley, *Three Ways of Thought in Ancient China* (Stanford: Stanford University Press, 1982; o.p. 1939), 145.

35. I shall be focusing on Nivison, of course, but allow me to draw special attention to Lau's "Some Logical Problems in Ancient China," *Proceedings of the Aristotelian Society*, n.s., 53 (1952/1953): 189–204; idem, "On Mencius' Use of the Method of Analogy in Argument," *Asia Major*, n.s., 10 (1963) (reprinted in idem, *Mencius* [New York: Penguin Books, 1970], appendix 5); and idem, "Theories of Human Nature in *Mencius* and *Shyuntzyy*," *Bulletin of the School of Oriental and African Studies* 15, no. 3 (1953): 541–65. Some of A. C. Graham's major papers are collected in his *Studies in Chinese Philosophy and Philosophical Literature* (Albany: SUNY Press, 1990; o.p. Singapore: Institute for East Asian Philosophies, 1986). Included in this volume is "The Background of the Mencian Theory of Human Nature," which is an excellent example of how to combine philosophy and philology. For a bibliography of A. C. Graham's work, see Rosemont, 323–28.

36. Nivison, loc. cit.

37. *Proceedings and Addresses of the American Philosophical Association* 53, no. 6 (August 1980): 739–61.

38. Kwong-loi Shun has developed many of Nivison's insights in interesting and important ways. See his "Mencius and the Mind-Inherence of Morality: Mencius' Rejection of Kao Tzu's Maxim in *Meng Tzu* 2A:2," *JCP* 18, no. 4 (December 1991): 371–86; idem, "Mencius and the Mind-Dependence of Morality: An Analysis of *Meng Tzu* 6A4-5," *JCP* 18, no. 2 (June 1991): 169–93; idem, "Mencius' Criticism of Mohism: An Analysis of *Meng Tzu* 3A:5," *Philosophy East and West* 41, no. 2 (April 1991): 203–14; and idem, "Moral Reasons in Confucian Ethics," *JCP* 16, nos. 3/4 (September/December 1989): 317–43. For critiques of this last essay, see Bryan W. Van Norden, "Kwong-loi Shun on Moral Reasons in Mencius," *JCP* 18, no. 4 (December 1991), 353–70, and David Wong, "Is There a Distinction between Reason and Emotion in Mencius?" *Philosophy East and West* 41, no. 1 (January 1991): 31–44.

39. For these issues, see the previously cited papers by Nivison, and also "Philosophical Voluntarism in Fourth-Century China," "Weakness of Will in Ancient Chinese Philosophy," "Problems in Mencius: Part I," "Two Kinds of Naturalism: Tai Chen and Chang Hsüeh-ch'eng," "The Philosophy of Wang Yangming" (In David S. Nivison, *The Ways of Confucianism: Investigations in Chinese Philosophy*, ed. Bryan W. Van Norden [Chicago and La Salle, Ill.: Open Court, 1996]), and "Hsun Tzu and Chuang Tzu," in Rosemont, 129–42.

40. See especially Yearley's *Mencius and Aquinas: Theories of Virtue and Conceptions of Courage* (Albany: SUNY Press, 1990); idem, "Recent Work on Virtue," *Religious Studies Review* 16, no. 1 (1990): 1–9; and idem, "Conflicts among Ideals of Human Flourishing," in G. Outka and J. Reeder, eds., *Prospects for a Common Morality* (Princeton: Princeton University Press, 1993),

233–53. (See also the extensive discussion of *Mencius and Aquinas* in the *Journal of Religious Ethics* 21, no. 2 (Fall 1994): 343–95.) In emphasizing Yearley's contribution in showing the relevance of Confucianism to Western virtue ethics, I do not mean to slight his contributions to our understanding of particular Chinese texts. See especially Yearley, "Hsün Tzu on the Mind: His Attempted Synthesis of Confucianism and Taoism," *Journal of Asian Studies* 39, no. 3 (May 1980): 465–80; idem, "The Perfected Person in the Radical Chuang-tzu," in Victor Mair, ed., *Experimental Essays on Chuang-tzu* (Honolulu: University of Hawaii Press, 1983), 125–39; and Yearley, "A Confucian Crisis: Mencius' Two Cosmogonies and Their Ethics," in R. Lovin and F. Reynolds, eds., *Cosmogony and Ethical Order* (Chicago: University of Chicago Press, 1985), 310–27.

41. G.E.M. Anscombe, "Modern Moral Philosophy," *Philosophy* 33 (1958): 1–19.

42. MacIntyre, op. cit. See especially chap. 1, "A Disquieting Suggestion," and chap. 5, "Why the Enlightenment Project of Justifying Morality Had to Fail."

43. See, for example, Kurt Baier, "Radical Virtue Ethics," in Peter A. French, et al., eds., *Midwest Studies in Philosophy XIII: Ethical Theory: Character and Virtue* (Notre Dame: University of Notre Dame Press, 1988), 126–35; Robert B. Louden, "On Some Vices of Virtue Ethics," *American Philosophical Quarterly* 21, no. 3 (July 1984): 227–36; and J. B. Schneewind, "The Misfortunes of Virtue," *Ethics* 101, no. 1 (October 1990): 42–63.

44. One impediment to productive comparative work is shallow misreadings or caricatures of Western virtue ethicists. For antidotes to the parody of Aristotle as intellectually arthritic and overly rationalistic, see Martha Nussbaum's brilliant *The Fragility of Goodness* (New York: Cambridge University Press, 1986), 235–394; idem, "The Discernment of Perception: An Aristotelian Conception of Private and Public Rationality," in *Love's Knowledge,* 54–105; and Stuart Hampshire's "Two Theories of Morality," *Morality and Conflict* (Cambridge, Mass.: Harvard University Press, 1983), §§ 1–12. (Nussbaum discusses comparative ethics in her "Non-Relative Virtues: An Aristotelian Approach," in French, 32–53.) For an extensive bibliography on virtue ethics, see Yearley's "Recent Work on Virtue," loc. cit.

45. Although Yearley's extensive and sophisticated work stands out, he is not the first one to discuss the relevance of Confucianism to Western virtue ethics. See, for example, Max Hamburger, "Aristotle and Confucius: A Study in Comparative Philosophy," *Philosophy* 31 (October 1956): 324–57; idem, "Aristotle and Confucius: A Comparison," *Journal of the History of Ideas* 20, no. 2 (April 1959): 236–49; George H. Mahood, "Human Nature and the Virtues in

Confucius and Aristotle," *JCP* 1 (1974): 295–312; Joel Kupperman, "The Supra-Moral in Chinese Ethics," *JCP* 1 (1974): 153–60; and idem, "Character and Ethical Theory," in French, 115–25. Much previous work has focused on treating Kongzi and Mengzi from the perspective of virtue ethics, but recently one of Yearley's students has extended the analysis to Xunzi. See Jonathan Schofer, "Virtues in Xunzi's Thought," *Journal of Religious Ethics* 21, no. 1 (Spring 1993): 117–36. (For an insightful discussion of Xunzi from a very different perspective, see Henry Rosemont, "State and Society in the *Hsün Tzu*: A Philosophical Commentary," *Monumenta Serica* 29 (1970–1971): 38–78.) Furthermore, although he has not drawn the connection between virtue ethics and Confucianism, Tu Wei-ming (one of the most influential proponents of the Confucian tradition today) offers an interpretation of the Mengzian tradition that is (I think) quite compatible with the virtue ethics approach. See Tu Wei-ming, *Humanity and Self-Cultivation: Essays in Confucian Thought* (Berkeley: Asian Humanities Press, 1979); idem, *Confucian Thought: Selfhood as Creative Transformation* (Albany: SUNY Press, 1985); and idem, *Centrality and Commonality: An Essay on Confucian Religiousness* (Albany: SUNY Press, 1989).

46. See Fingarette, op. cit.

47. Of the four cardinal virtues of Plato and Thomas Aquinas—wisdom, justice, courage and temperance—only one corresponds, even approximately, to the four cardinal virtues of Mengzi and his Neo-Confucian interpreters— benevolence, righteousness, wisdom, and ritual propriety.

48. See P. J. Ivanhoe, *Confucian Moral Self Cultivation* (New York: Peter Lang, 1993).

49. As recent scholarship has stressed, Confucianism has not been a monolithic movement since the death of Confucius. See P. J. Ivanhoe, *Ethics in the Confucian Tradition: The Thought of Mencius and Wang Yang-ming* (Atlanta: Scholars Press, 1990), and Bryan W. Van Norden, "Mengzi and Xunzi: Two Views of Human Agency," *International Philosophical Quarterly* 32, no. 2 (June 1992): 161–84.

50. See, for example, J. J. C. Smart and Bernard Williams, *Utilitarianism: For and Against* (New York: Cambridge University Press, 1973).

51. David Wong gives a promising opening to this project in his, "Universalism vs. Love with Distinctions: An Ancient Debate Revived," *JCP* 16, nos. 3-4 (September/December 1989): 251–72.

52. Chad Hansen, "A *Tao* of *Tao* in Chuang-tzu," in Mair, 24–55. (Hansen presents a different interpretation of Zhuangzi in *A Daoist Theory of Chinese Thought* [chap. 8].) For readings from Harman and Mackie, and an extensive bibliography on moral realism and anti-realism, see Geoffrey Sayre-McCord, ed., *Essays on Moral Realism* (Ithaca, N.Y.: Cornell University Press, 1988).

(Mackie does not describe himself as a relativist, but I take it that his position commits him to relativism. Interestingly, Mackie argues that the diversity of ethical beliefs across different cultures provides good evidence that there are no objective values; however, he merely asserts this without doing any comparative ethics. Another reason for doing comparative philosophy is to provide evidence for evaluating Mackie's "argument from relativity.")

53. See Graham, "Taoist Spontaneity and the Dichotomy of 'Is' and 'Ought,'" in Mair, 3–23. For criticisms of ideal observer theories similar to Graham's, see Bernard Williams, *Ethics and the Limits of Philosophy* (Cambridge, Mass.: Harvard University Press, 1985), 83–92. For criticisms directed specifically at Graham's version, see Yukio Kachi's comments, and Graham's response, in *Philosophy East and West* 40, no. 3 (July 1990): 389–98, 399 (respectively). See also Herbert Fingarette, "Reason, Spontaneity, and the *Li*—A Confucian Critique of Graham's Solution to the Problem of Fact and Value"; Henry Rosemont, "Who Chooses?"; and Graham's responses to these papers, in Rosemont, 209–25, 227–63, and 297–321 (respectively).

54. Schwartz, 192–94, 215–37.

55. Yearley, "The Perfected Person in the Radical Chuang-tzu," loc. cit.

56. Paul Kjellberg, "Skepticism, Truth, and the Good Life: A Comparison of Zhuangzi and Sextus Empiricus," *Philosophy East and West* 44, no. 1 (January 1994): 111–33.

57. Although we typically associate *wu wei* ("unselfconscious action") with Daoism, note that the phrase occurs in *Analects* 15:5. See Schwartz's insightful comments on this issue in Schwartz, 188–91.

58. For an interpretation of Zhuangzi similar to my own, see P. J. Ivanhoe, "Zhuangzi on Skepticism, Skill, and the Ineffable *Dao*," *Journal of the American Academy of Religion* 61, no. 4 (Winter 1993): 101–16. For summaries and insightful critiques of various interpretations of Zhuangzi, see Paul Kjellberg, "Zhuangzi and Skepticism" (Ph.D. dissertation, Philosophy, Stanford University, 1993).

59. This is not to rule out the possibility that one or more of the questions will someday be *aufgehoben*.

60. "The Argonauts," in *The Penguin Book of Greek Verse*, trans. Constantine A. Trypanis (New York: Penguin Books, 1971), 607 (translation slightly modified).

61. For criticisms of Derrideans and Rortians, see above, note 20. Within the Western tradition, my own sympathies lie with the hermeneutic movement, broadly construed. (For this broad sense of "hermeneutics," see Guignon and Hiley, 362, n. 41.) It seems unclear to me *why*, from either a Derridean or a Rortian perspective, one should bother to do comparative philoso-

phy at all. Many of us would say that we should study other philosophic traditions because they may have understood some truths that we have missed, or might have new insights into the nature of the world—but "post-modernists" cannot say either one of these things because they do not believe in Truth, or a perceiver-independent world. (Contrast, for example, MacIntyre, who argues that studying other philosophic traditions is an intellectual *necessity:* it is only by responding to the challenges provided by alien traditions that we can claim any justification for our own beliefs. See, e.g., *Whose Justice? Which Rationality?*, chap. 18, "The Rationality of Traditions.")

62. Williams refers to this, somewhat parochially, as "Socrates' question" (*Ethics and the Limits of Philosophy*, 1–21 and *passim*), and concludes (as the title of his book suggests) that philosophy has only a limited role in answering it.

63. My complaints about contemporary philosophy have some similarity to those of certain contemporary feminists (see, for example, Rosemarie Tong, *Feminine and Feminist Ethics* [Belmont, Calif.: Wadsworth Publishing Co., 1993], 23–24, and Annette Baier, "Doing without Moral Theory?" *Postures of the Mind: Essays on Mind and Morals* [London: Methuen, 1985], 228–45). It is perhaps significant that one of the greatest woman philosophers, Christine de Pisan, although she was quite able to engage in sophisticated theoretical philosophy (witness *The Book of the City of Ladies,* trans. E. J. Richards [New York: Persea Books, 1982]) also wrote a work that has been described by its contemporary translator as "strictly a guide to practicalities. Part etiquette book, part survival manual, it was written for women who had to live from day to day in the world as it was" (Christine de Pisan, *The Treasure of the City of Ladies, or the Book of the Three Virtues,* trans. Sarah Lawson [New York: Penguin Books, 1985]), 21).

64. In other words, too many contemporary academics philosophize like Gongsun Long 公孫龍, and not enough like Mengzi and Socrates.

"Existentialism" in the School of Wang Yangming

Philip J. Ivanhoe

Introduction

In a 1973 article, David S. Nivison analyzes and to some extent takes issue with certain aspects of Professor Okada Takehiko's use of the concept of "existentialism" to describe the thought of Wang Ji and his teacher Wang Yangming.[1] Nivison's piece is an excellent example of how to do a certain and rather rare kind of comparative philosophy. In examining the thought of these two Neo-Confucian thinkers and comparing them to existentialist thinkers in the West, he shows great sensitivity and care concerning what Lee H. Yearley refers to as "similarities within differences and differences within similarities."[2] Nivison notes where the use of the term "existentialism" appears to distort rather than make clear an analysis of Wang Ji and Wang Yangming's thought. At the same time, he seeks to identify genuinely existentialist elements in the thought of these two thinkers.

I begin this essay by providing a more complete account of Okada's original sense of the term "existentialist." I will argue that he did not mean to imply any strong resemblance to Western existentialists by his use of this term, an idea Nivison himself entertains but does not fully pursue. Nevertheless, as Nivison also points out, there are moments when one feels the force of genuinely existentialist themes animating the thought of both Wang Ji and Wang Yangming. And so, in one sense, Okada's original intent need not limit the range of our inquiry. I will work from this assumption and attempt to extend Nivison's analysis of the genuinely existential aspects of the thought of these two thinkers. In particular, I will discuss Nivison's claim that, "the notion of existential anxiety is actually incompatible with Wang Yangming's point of view."[3] I will argue that while largely correct this claim needs to be given additional nuance. For a certain kind of angst is very much a part of Wang's thought; it is a critical and perhaps necessary aspect of the beginning student's moral self-cultivation. Realizing that this is the case and understanding why it is so, not only helps us to distinguish some of the profound differences between Wang Yangming and existentialists like Kierkegaard, it also helps us to appreciate some of the dramatic differences between Wang and Mencius, the philosopher whose thought he claimed to uphold.[4]

Okada's Use of the Term

Nivison begins his article by noting that he had "particular difficulty"[5] in grasping the exact sense of the term "existentialism" intended by Professor Okada in his original essay. He further notes that the problem he raises concerning its use might well prove to be ephemeral since Okada employs the term to translate the Chinese term *xiancheng* 現成 which might easily have been rendered as "realization."[6] Nevertheless, as Nivison goes on to say, "Theodore De Bary, as editor and as a contributor to the volume, took the "existentialist" characterization quite seriously, and I do not think it absurd for me to do so. An idea may be valuable even if it occurs to us accidentally. Indeed, it may even be right."[7]

I suggest that Professor Okada uses the term "existentialism" in at least two distinct senses and that distinguishing and understanding these senses helps us to see why ascribing certain features of western existentialism to his analysis is misleading. Such an understanding will also help us to discern a major and important implication of the thought of these two thinkers, one which has a distinct and genuine existentialist flavor.

The first sense of the term is the more obvious and less interesting. In the opening lines of his essay, Okada clearly states that he is using the term to translate the *name* of one of three major schools of Wang Yangming's thought: "In the sixteenth century the Wang Yangming school developed into three main branches. The first was the Left Wing or existentialist school; the second was the Right Wing or quietist school; and the third was the Orthodox school, or cultivation school."[8] In other places, Okada uses the term to describe a type or style of thinking.[9] This is a slightly different sense, since in at least one case, it is used to describe thinkers not in the "existentialist school" but in the competing "quietist school" instead.[10] As Nivison points out, Okada also believes that this style of thinking represents a legitimate—though perhaps over-drawn—feature of Wang Yangming's original philosophy.[11]

The second sense of existentialism is less obvious though clearly present. In various places, Okada uses the term to represent a view or doctrine about the nature of reality and, as a result, about the place where one discovers the principles (*li* 理) which, according to Wang Yangming, are the mind. Nivison seems to have something close to this—at least to the latter half of this—in mind when he quotes his own review of the De Bary volume. Commenting on Professor Okada's essay he says, "I think he means by 'existentialism' the thesis that if we wish to grasp what our mind is we have to observe what it is doing; that is that the mind's 'substance,' typically in late Neo-Confucianism identified with a world-ordering 'principle,' is not something lying behind a person's play of mental act, emotion and moral effort, but that play itself."[12]

While Nivison correctly describes the epistemological side of Okada's sense of "existentialism," he does not bring out the fact that for Okada the term entails a deep metaphysical claim as well. We see the metaphysical sense in certain passages where Okada uses the expression "existential innate knowledge."[13] For example, he says, "In other words, what made Wang Yangming what he was, was the existential innate knowledge that was Nothing then and there." Note that Okada refers to, "the existential innate knowledge *that was Nothing then and there.*" He returns to this idea—that innate knowledge is Nothing—in several places. For example, in one passage Okada says, "According to Wang Ji, the Nothingness of the original substance is then and there existential; effort is substance, being is Nothing. They are in complete unity and there is no space for a hair between them."[14]

Okada is claiming that the original substance of the mind (or the mind in itself), which in its active knowing mode is innate knowledge (or pure knowing), is not so much a state or a thing but rather the *fun-*

damental character of all reality.[15] As such, it is a character one can *realize* directly only in the actual things and affairs of one's own life. Relying upon Nivison's suggested translation of *xiancheng* as "realization," we can paraphrase Wang Ji's view by saying that one has to *realize* that *liangzhi* is here at hand in all things and in every event, and at the same time one must *realize* it—i.e. bring it into play—in everything one does. The idea that *liangzhi* is the fundamental character of all reality is the more basic sense of the term, and is particularly emphasized by Wang Ji. The related sense of it being the working of the human heart-and-mind and the process wherein one becomes aware of its true nature can be seen as following from this. The parallels with Chan (as well as other forms of Chinese Buddhism) are unmistakable and deeper than is commonly acknowledged.

Existential Themes

The similarities to Chan by no means end with this point. For because of these beliefs about the nature of reality and the mind, Wang Yang-ming and Wang Ji were led to develop a distinctive and provocative method of self-cultivation. This method is the source of their existential flavor, and it is something they share with the Channists who inspired so much of their thought.

Okada sees this very clearly—as many Japanese scholars of Ming Confucianism seem to. He points out the linkage between these metaphysical views and Wang Ji's method of practice: "the original substance of the mind is right then and there, it is self-sufficient then and there, and it is existential then and there. *Therefore it stresses direct enlightenment as the sole means in learning*, in complete rejection of gradual cultivation."[16] De Bary notices this too: "if one assumes, as Ming existentialists do, that the essential mind or nature is trans-moral in its perfection, then *self-cultivation becomes a matter of true self-expression*, rather than of moral judgement or self-restraint."[17] In my own work on Ming Neo-Confucianism, I place even greater emphasis upon this point.[18] The issue of how one is to *practice* self-cultivation seems to be not merely an incidental implication of the philosophy of Wang Yang-ming and Wang Ji but rather the crux of their disagreement with members of the competing Cheng-Zhu school.

Like other Neo-Confucian thinkers, Wang Yangming and Wang Ji tended to see moral self-cultivation largely if not exclusively in terms of ridding oneself of the obscuring influences of selfish desires. But in contrast to thinkers like Zhu Xi, they believed that only a deep and persistent concern with the actual affairs of one's own life would prove efficacious in this task. This led them, like western existentialists, to pay tremendous attention to the things one did and one's awareness of and responsibility for these actions. Also like western existentialists, there was a certain anti-intellectual bias in their thought. They denied that broad learning or speculative thought could bring one closer to one's goal.[19] Instead, one was to be mentally on guard, constantly monitoring one's thoughts and actions. As Wang Yangming once put it, "One must, at all times, be like a cat catching mice—with eyes intently watching and ears intently listening."[20] Nivison is absolutely correct in pointing out that in the end this concern with one's actions proves to be a rather "thin" similarity. For unlike western existentialists, these Neo-Confucian thinkers were not forging a self by tracing a trajectory of authentic decisions. *Liangzhi* was a kind of faculty for them and they sought to relieve this faculty of the interference of selfish thoughts so that it could function freely in a seamless process of seeing-knowing-weighing-judging-doing. If one could achieve such a state, one's judgments and actions would always agree—in the main if not in every detail—with the judgments and actions of other enlightened individuals.

Western existentialists all agree that recognizing and shouldering the profound burden of an authentic life results in a persistent state of anxiety. Did Wang Yangming believe that the ever-attentive self-awareness he advocated also resulted in a state of profound anxiety?[21] The answer—and Wang would surely be pleased by this—depends on who one *is*.

If we examine the *Chuanxilu*,[22] the most complete and representative collection of Wang's teachings, we see that something like existential anxiety is very much part of a *beginner's* state of mind. I will argue that, in the end, this anxiety has more in common with the "Great Doubt" of Chan Buddhism than it does with existentialist thinkers like Kierkegaard. Nevertheless it is an important aspect of Wang's philosophy and is the source of much of his existentialist flavor.

In the introduction to the *Chuanxilu*, Wang's disciple Xu Ai testifies to the discomfort and doubt he experienced when he first encountered Wang's teachings.[23] Anyone who has read Wang's work has probably experienced similar feelings and can easily imagine how much more provocative some of his views must have been for his contemporaries. For example, when Wang argues that Qinshi Hwangdi's burning of the books was very much in the spirit of Confucius' desire to edit the classics,[24] one experiences a distinct feeling of intellectual vertigo. In addition to eliciting an initial disorienting doubt, Wang's method of teaching often produced feelings of deep tension and distress among his disciples. The interactions with his disciples were highly charged and deeply personal experiences. He often challenged them with tasks that seem clearly impossible. "This study that I speak of is the task of *creating something out of nothing*. You gentlemen must have faith. The task is simply to establish a commitment."[25] The disciples seem almost frenzied in some of their interactions with Wang. Some talk of being "frightened and sweating"[26] as they struggle to understand his teachings and generate the commitment to become a sage. There is evidence that Wang believed periods of intense emotional stress enhance one's chances of obtaining moral insight.[27] Perhaps he believed that such occasions lay bare the true nature of moral choice and throw the disciple back upon his individual resources. Wang's disciples describe their moments of enlightenment as arriving in the midst of great fear[28] and resulting in a cathartic release of profound tension.[29] Throughout the process which leads to sagehood, the disciples are urged to maintain an obsessive preoccupation with the task of moral self cultivation.

> This effort must be carried out continuously. Like eradicating robbers and thieves. One must resolve to wipe them out completely. In idle moments, one must search out and discover each and every selfish thought for sex, wealth, fame and the rest. One must resolve to pluck out and cast away the root of the sickness, so that it can never arise again. Only then may one begin to feel at ease. One must at all times, be like a cat catching mice—with eyes intently watching and ears intently listening. As soon as a single (selfish) thought begins to stir, one must conquer it and cast it out. Act as if you were cutting a nail in two or slicing through iron. Do not indulge or accommodate it in any way. Do not harbor it, and do not allow it to escape.[30]

In summary, Wang's teachings aroused an initial disorienting shock and a disquieting *doubt* among his disciples. He called upon them to generate *faith* in and make a *commitment* to the task of becoming a sage. In these ways his teachings closely resemble the three-fold system of "great doubt," "great faith," and "great commitment," described by the Chan master Gaofeng Yuanmiao (1238–1295) in his work *The Essentials of Chan*.[31]

Earlier in his life, Wang himself displayed an obsessive concern with the attainment of sagehood, a concern which Julia Ching describes as "mad ardor."[32] Tu Weiming also notes this aspect of Wang's thought in his study of Wang's early life and sees it as the primary focus of his learning.[33] But, in itself, a consuming desire and dedicated effort to find spiritual fulfillment need not lead one toward existentialism, nor does it necessarily entail an existentialist-like anxiety regarding one's thoughts and actions. What gives Wang's teaching an existential air is his faith in an innate and perfect moral mind and his belief that the only effective form of moral self-cultivation is to bring this moral faculty into play in the actual affairs of one's own life.[34] Wang rejected the orthodox view of the Cheng-Zhu School, which claimed one can improve oneself through careful study of the classics and a regimen of reflection and meditation.[35] For him, the only effective practice was to pay attention to the workings of one's own pure knowing in the actual affairs of one's own life. Only by working on one's own *real problems* could one improve oneself morally. Other methods of self-cultivation not only would fail to help, they would present a very real danger of leading one to some of the worst forms of self-deception and moral decay.

So for Wang, the crucial movement toward sagehood consisted of a break with one's past views, a commitment to become a sage, and an unwavering faith in the power of one's pure knowing. His disciples were under continuous pressure to fulfill these imperatives and their rigorous self-scrutiny colored their lives with a distinctively existential anxiety. But if they could shoulder this burden and carry it through to the point where they break free of their selfish desires, they would not only relieve this anxiety once and for all, they would realize the unparalleled joy of sagehood. For joy is a fundamental characteristic of the mind in itself.

> I said, "You said that 'joy is characteristic of the original substance of the mind.' When one's parent dies and one cries sorrowfully, is this joy still present?"
> The Teacher said, "There is real joy only if the son has cried bitterly. If not, there won't be any joy. Joy means that in spite of crying, one's mind is at peace. The original substance of the mind has not been perturbed."[36]

Here Wang's differences with existentialists begin to far outweigh his similarities. We get a better idea of the nature of these differences and how they both arise out of and inform other aspects of his thought if we compare Wang to an existentialist thinker like Kierkegaard.

Kierkegaard's ultimate ideal is the Knight of Faith, and he chooses Abraham as the paragon of this ideal. Kierkegaard thought that his contemporaries often overlooked or consciously suppressed the true character of Abraham. He sought to rectify this state of affairs by emphasizing the most important feature of Abraham's character—his incessant anxiety.

> The ethical expression of what Abraham did is that he meant to murder Issac; the religious expression is that he meant to sacrifice Issac— but precisely in this contradiction is the anxiety that can make a person sleepless, and yet *without this anxiety Abraham is not who he is.*[37]

Kierkegaard contrasts the Knight of Faith with a type he calls the Knight of Infinite Resignation. The latter make a movement toward faith but one which falls short, for their infinite resignation relieves them of the anxiety which is the *sine qua non* of genuine faith. Only one who realizes that such an appeal brings together both the infinite and the finite has a true grasp of the situation, and such a realization results in anxiety, for it is fundamentally absurd.[38] Knights of Infinite Resignation make sense out of the world by resigning themselves to a higher authority, whereas Knights of Faith embrace the absurdity of daily bringing the infinite realm into the finite world of human life. The paradoxical double-vision of the Knights of Faith is the source of their anxiety and distress. Those who are in this state are bereft of the comfort of explanations; they cannot fully account for what they do. By the very logic of their appeal, Knights of Faith must live their lives without the comfort of a reasonable and complete account.

> Abraham remains silent—but he *cannot* speak. Therein lies the distress
> and anxiety. . . . Speak he cannot; he speaks no human language. And
> even if he understood all the languages of the world, even if those he
> loved also understood them, he still could not speak—he speaks in a
> divine language, he speaks in tongues.[39]

Kierkegaard contrasts the Knight of Faith with another type called
the Tragic Hero who in many ways resembles the Knight of Infinite
Resignation. Tragic Heros are committed to a universal ethical vision.
Like Knights of Infinite Resignation they find relief from the ultimate
responsibility of their actions by relying on a higher authority, in their
case some transcendent conception of what is ethical instead of the
will of some divine being. Kierkegaard picks as one of his exemplars
for this ideal type the figure of Brutus, who is called upon to punish
his own guilty son.[40] Invoking universal morality, Brutus is able to
explain his action. It pains him terribly to punish his son, whom he
loves, but the moral imperative of justice compels him to act. With the
warrant of the ethical in hand, his action enjoys universal approba-
tion—even that of the son he punishes—and this enables him to rest
contentedly in his decision.

Kierkegaard argues that one cannot possibly explain Abraham or
his actions on the model of the Tragic Hero. For unlike Abraham, tragic Heros do not have to live within the profound contradiction
between the imperatives of the infinite realm—e.g. to kill one's son—
and the finite—to insure that he will live. An appeal to the ethical does
not allow for this; what is required is what he calls a "teleological sus-
pension of the ethical." Such a move is only available to the Knight of
Faith.

> The difference between the tragic hero and Abraham is very obvious.
> The tragic hero is still within the ethical. He allows an expression of
> the ethical to have its *telos* in a higher expression of the ethical; he
> scales down the ethical relation between father and son or daughter
> and father to a feeling that has its dialectic in its relation to the idea of
> moral conduct. Here there can be no teleological suspension of the
> ethical.[41]

Like the Knight of Infinite Resignation, the Tragic Hero does not
experience the continuous distress and anxiety of the Knight of Faith.

Tragic Heroes may feel distress and anxiety in the midst of performing their difficult tasks and in the immediate aftermath, but they come to rest, content in the knowledge that they *did the right thing*. They can appeal to the higher, universal justification of the ethical to *explain* their actions, and this removes the burden of responsibility from their shoulders. The Tragic Hero acts confidently for the sake of the knowable—the ethical. The Knight of Faith acts for the sake of the inexpressible—for God. Kierkegaard contrasts Abraham's sacrifice of Issac with the actions of a Tragic Hero.

> Abraham's situation is different. By his act he transgressed the ethical altogether and had a higher *telos* outside it, in relation to which he suspended it. For I certainly would like to know how Abraham's act can be related to the universal, whether any point of contact between what Abraham did and the universal can be found other than that Abraham transgressed it. It is not to save a nation, not to uphold the idea of the state that Abraham does it; it is not to appease the angry gods . . . Why, then does Abraham do it? For God's sake and—the two are wholly identical—for his own sake. He does it for God's sake because God demands this proof of his faith; he does it for his own sake so that he can prove it.[42]

It is possible, and potentially productive, to read Kierkegaard as a self-cultivationist, for he seems to recognize distinct stages in the process of coming to faith.[43] But if we read him as a self-cultivationist, he is a self-cultivationist who believes that one can never really attain a state of complete peace and ease, because one's ontological situation requires one to exist not between but *within* two worlds and hence always be embracing the absurd.[44] Kierkegaard's God is forever outside of him and beyond appeal ("for in the world of time God and I cannot talk with each other . . ."). There is nothing "natural" and "spontaneous" about the state of faith or the actions one performs out of faith.[45]

For Wang Yangming, the process of self-cultivation leads ultimately to enlightenment. One comes to realize fully *liangzhi,* a kind of "god within." When this innate moral faculty is brought fully into play, one's actions flow spontaneously and are without the slightest error. In such moments one not only feels no anxiety concerning one's actions, one has no strong sense of one's independent agency or existence. One "forms one body with Heaven Earth and all things." For *liangzhi* is the natural functioning of the mind itself, the active, knowing mode of principle (*li*).

Kierkegaard's views here diverge dramatically from those of Wang Yangming: his Knight of Faith parts company with Wang's Confucian sage. According to Kierkegaard, one can never be sure that one truly realizes one's own finitude and surrenders to faith. True faith ultimately is an act of grace, from our side of things we can never be certain or complacent about it. We must remain in constant anxiety about the purity and strength of our spiritual commitment. If one is not in such a state, one cannot possibly be authentic.[46]

Conclusion

In conclusion I would like to note that Wang differs not only from Kierkegaard but also from Mencius, the early Confucian philosopher whom he claimed to defend and follow.[47] But while they are alike in being different from Wang, Mencius and Kierkegaard prove to share even *less* than Wang and Kierkegaard do. For it turns out that Mencius really has no genuine existential flavor at all. The reasons for this can be traced to the profound differences between pre-Qin Confucianism and its later Neo-Confucian heirs.[48] Mencius did not share Wang's belief that all human beings possess an innate and perfect moral mind obscured by intervening selfish desires that were to be identified and dissolved by the cleansing power of one's *liangzhi*. Instead he believed human beings are endowed with fragile, nascent moral sprouts that need a great deal of protection, care, and guidance in order to grow into strong moral dispositions.

For Wang, the task of moral self-cultivation requires one to constantly monitor one's every thought in an effort to detect the selfish desires blocking the smooth operation of *liangzhi*. One is to bring every selfish thought into full awareness where it will wither away in the purifying light of *liangzhi*. In significant ways, Wang's description of moral self-cultivation resembles the task of relieving oneself of a profound and recalcitrant form of self-deception. It can only be successfully carried out by an obsessive attention to the events of one's own life. This is what gives Wang's teachings a genuine existential flavor and is the source of the distress and anxiety we see among his young disciples. Mencius required an unwavering dedication to the task of self-cultivation, but it was the dedication of a strong, calm, and patient farmer, not the frenetic self scrutiny of the self-deceived in search of a way out of a self-imposed deception.

NOTES

1. Okada's essay appeared in William Theodore De Bary, ed., *Self and Society in Ming Thought*, (New York: Columbia University Press, 1970), 121–42 (hereafter cited as *SSMT*). Nivison's article, entitled "Moral decision in Wang Yang-ming: The problem of Chinese 'existentialism,'" appeared in *Philosophy East and West*, 23 (1973): 121–38 (hereafter cited as *MD*).

2. See Lee H. Yearley, *Mencius and Aquinas: Theories of Virtue and Conceptions of Courage*, (Albany, New York: SUNY Press, 1990).

3. *MD*, 130.

4. In order to simplify the presentation of my views, I will concentrate on the thought of Wang Yangming and Søren Kierkegaard. Most of what I have to say about the role of angst in Wang Yangming applies equally to Wang Ji, though not everything I say about Kierkegaard would apply equally well to existentialist thinkers such as Sartre.

5. *MD*, 121.

6. *MD*, 121.

7. De Bary uses the term four times in his introduction to the volume (see *SSMT*, 18, 21 [2x], and 22).

8. *SSMT*, 121. For other uses with this sense, see pages 138 and 139.

9. *SSMT*, 133, 137–38.

10. *SSMT*, 133.

11. *MD*, 122.

12. *MD*, 121.

13. *SSMT*, 129, 130–31, 136.

14. *SSMT*, 135.

15. It is "Nothing" in the sense of being without any selfish thoughts, that is, any sense of being fundamentally other. At such a moment, one has realized Wang's oft-repeated ideal of "forming one body with Heaven, Earth, and all things." Cf. *MD*, 123–24.

16. *SSMT*, 130. Italics mine. See also pp. 128, 136. For a collection of essays on the distinction between "direct" or "sudden" enlightenment and

"gradual cultivation" see Peter N. Gregory, ed., *Sudden and Gradual: Approaches to Enlightenment in Chinese Thought* (Honolulu: University of Hawaii Press, 1987). Wang Ji seems to advocate a radical version of sudden enlightenment wherein one comes to a profound and transforming insight through a direct and sudden intuition. Wang Yangming believes this is only one approach and is suitable for only certain individuals. For this distinction, see the section on the so-called "Four Sentence Teaching" in Wing-tsit Chan, trans., *Instructions for Practical Living and Other Neo-Confucian Writings by Wang Yang-ming* (New York: Columbia University Press, 1963), 241–45 (hereafter cited as *IPL*). Tu Wei-ming has argued, and I agree, that Wang Ji's interpretation of the Four Sentence Teaching "comes very close to the spirit of Ch'an (Zen)." See his "An Inquiry into Wang Yang-ming's Four Sentence Teaching," in *Humanity and Self-Cultivation: Essays in Confucian Thought* (Berkeley: Asian Humanities Press, 1979), 162. I would add that the entire Four Sentence Teaching seems to be modeled on the "mind verses" competition between Huineng and Shenxiu found in the early sections of the *Platform Sutra*. See Philip B. Yampolsky, trans., *The Platform Sutra of the Sixth Patriarch* (New York: Columbia University Press, 1967), 128–31. However, the Sixth Patriarch, unlike Wang Yangming, seems clearly to favor the sudden teaching.

17. *SSMT,* 21. Italics mine.

18. I argue for this view more fully in *Confucian Moral Self Cultivation* (New York: Peter Lang Publishing, 1993) (hereafter cited as *CMSC*).

19. However, as Nivison points out (*MD*, 131), Wang did not rule out the need to think things out carefully in certain difficult situations.

20. The quote is from Wang's *Chuanxilu.* For the context of this remark and a discussion of its significance, see my *Ethics in the Confucian Tradition: The Thought of Mencius and Wang Yang-ming* (Atlanta: Scholars Press, 1990), 85 (hereafter cited as *ECT*).

21. I have benefitted from the comments and work of Teemu Ruskola on the issue of existential anxiety in Wang Yangming's thought. In particular, I found his manuscript "Existential Responsibility: *Mauvaise Foi* in Sartre and *Ch'eng* in Wang Yang-ming" very helpful.

22. For a complete translation of this work see *IPL*. For a selective translation of another collection of Wang's works, see Frederick Goodrich Henke, *The Philosophy of Wang Yang-ming* (reprint) (New York: Paragon Book Company, 1964). Nivison reviewed both translations in *Journal of the American Oriental Society* 84, no. 4 (1964): 440–41. For a study of the history of the *Chuanxilu*, see *ECT*, 115–23.

23. "I was shocked when I first heard him, then became skeptical." *IPL*, 3.

24. Wang believed that Confucius would have preferred to do away with writing altogether but settled on paring the classics down to an absolute minimum. For a discussion of this aspect of Wang's thought, see *ECT*, 103–4.

25. For this passage, see *ECT*, 88.

26. *IPL*, 216.

27. *IPL*, 38.

28. *IPL*, 75.

29. *IPL*, 224.

30. For this passage and a discussion of this aspect of Wang's thought, see *ECT*, 85.

31. The notion of the critical importance of the "great doubt" was first described by Dahui Zonggao (1089–1163). For a discussion of the evolution of this idea, see Heinrich Dumoulin, *Zen Buddhism: A History*, vol. 1 (New York: Macmillan Publishing Company, 1988), 256–59.

32. See her *To Acquire Wisdom the Way of Wang Yang-ming* (New York: Columbia 1976), 49–51. Professor Ching is careful to point out that Wang wanted "to reach beyond ardor, on to sagehood" (p. 50).

33. See his *Neo-Confucian Thought in Action: Wang Yang-ming's Youth (1472–1509)* Berkeley: University of California Press, 1976). Tu also discusses what he calls Wang's "existential choice at Yang-ming Grotto" (pp. 55–63). By this he means Wang's commitment to follow and propagate Confucianism as opposed to Daoism and Buddhism. While there is some sense to calling such a commitment "existential," such a description, as will become clear, also can obscure important aspects of Wang's philosophy.

34. For a discussion of this aspect of Wang's thought, see *ECT*, 80–88.

35. For a more complete and detailed discussion of Zhu Xi and Wang Yangming's theories of moral self cultivation, see chapters four and five in *CMSC*.

36. *IPL*, 230. For other examples, see 147–48, 216, and 280.

37. From *Fear and Trembling* in Howard V. Hong and Edna H. Hong, trans., *Fear and Trembling and Repetition* (Princeton: Princeton University Press, 1983), 30 (hereafter cited as *FT*). Italics mine. See also p. 28, "what is omitted from Abraham's story is the anxiety . . ."

38. Based upon a taxonomy of Kierkegaard's writings, believed to be necessary to reveal his true views, Alastair McKinnon argues that Kierkegaard was not an irrationalist at all. See his "Søren Kierkegaard," in *Nineteenth Century Religious Thought*, vol. 1, N. Smart, J. Clayton, S. Katz, and P. Sherry, eds.,

(Cambridge: Cambridge University Press, 1985), 181–213 (hereafter cited as *SK*). McKinnon argues that Kierkegaard's discussions of the absurd are almost all in pseudonymous works and thus present a view of faith from an outsider's perspective. From within faith, allegedly, there is no paradox. My position is that Kierkegaard believes that rationality alone cannot bring one to faith, nor can it fully provide an account of faith. He is therefore, to some extent, an anti-rationalist. This is the source of his persistent anxiety. I have benefitted greatly from the suggestions of Karen L. Carr on this and other issues concerning Kierkegaard's philosophy.

39. *FT,* 113–14. On page 35 we are told, Knights of Faith are even denied the solace of explaining themselves to God, "for in the world of time God and I cannot talk with each other, we have no language in common."

40. See *FT,* 58.

41. See *FT,* 59.

42. See *FT,* 59–60.

43. Kierkegaard seems to say that one must first be a Knight of Infinite Resignation before one can become a Knight of Faith. "Infinite resignation is the last stage before faith, so that anyone who has not made this movement does not have faith . . ." (*FT*), 46. However, given Kierkegaard's view of the self and the role that grace must play in the movement toward faith, an account of his philosophy as an ethic of self-cultivation seems highly problematic.

44. It is true that at one point Kierkegaard claims that "the Knight of Faith is the only happy man" (*FT,* 50). This seems to point to a form of faith in which one is relieved of anxiety. But given Kierkegaard's extensive and detailed description of Abraham, such an interpretation appears untenable. I am not denying that Knights of Faith enjoy a special kind of joy, I am only saying that they are still haunted by anxiety. This seems to be a necessary result of their ontological situation.

45. The situation for existentialists like Sartre seems even more dire. Kierkegaard at least has his God; Sartre makes his choice in the face of "Nothing."

46. Kierkegaard does not use the term "authenticity" but this concept seems appropriate as a description of those in faith. Cf. *SK,* 209 where McKinnon describes one not in faith as resorting "to a variety of defense mechanisms which are really *lies* or *self-deceptions* about his own nature." Italics mine.

47. For a study of some of the ways in which Mencius and Wang differ, see *ECT.*

48. For a more complete and careful study of these differences, see *ECT* and *CMSC.*

PART TWO

Replies and Comments

David S. Nivison

1. Response to K. Takashima, "Towards a New Pronominal Hypothesis of *Qi* in Shang Chinese"

1. There are two papers in this book that deal with Shang oracle inscriptions, by Shaughnessy, and by Ken-ichi Takashima (hereafter Ken). Necessarily, so do my responses, and I have also used oracle material in my response to Chad Hansen. The "general reader" is due some basic help. The inscriptions are found on shoulder blades of cattle and on turtle shells, and discoveries have been going on since 1899. The materials date to the later Shang era (ca. 1220–1040 BC), and (recent discoveries) to early Zhou (1040–). The inscriptions are short, an early type being a single test sentence (or its negation) predicting a future event (such as rain tomorrow), or announcing the king's intention to do something. The shell or bone was cracked by the application of heat against a gouge on the reverse side, and the crack was then interpreted by the king or his diviner, as meaning that the test sentence was (or was not) true, or acceptable. We call the test sentences "charges." Sometimes the king's interpretation, which we call his "prognostication," is also inscribed, and/or also a "verification" saying what actually happened later. A set of inscriptions illustrating all of these components is given by Ken in his examples (6A)–(6C). (I do not like Ken's translation of the basic sentence "qi yu": "it shall be going to rain." But I think he means simply "it is going to rain"; see what he says at the end of his section 1.2.)

1.1 For all of sixty years, all scholars working on these objects thought that the "charge" sentences were questions put to the spirits (or to the shell or bone itself). These sentences often contain the graph *qi* 凶 (其), that in later Chinese could represent a possessive pronoun or definite article, or a word giving a "modal" tone to a sentence. E.g., as a noun phrase "qi yu" could mean "the rain" or "its raining," but as a sentence "qi yu" could mean "It's sure to rain"; or "Oh for rain!" (*Odes* 62.3). For a long time, scholars in China merely called it a "particle" when they found it in Shang excavated material; i.e., they paid no attention to it (a healthy attitude, I suspect). In 1953, a certain Guan Xiechu published a book analyzing Shang Chinese grammar, and called *qi* an interrogative adverb expressing doubt. In 1956, Chen Mengjia in a book on all aspects of oracle-bone study had a chapter on grammar, in which he pronounced that Shang *qi* does not have the deictic or indicating function it would have in later Chinese (apparently Chen was referring to both pronominal and "modal" post-Shang uses of *qi*), but is a particle expressing doubt or uncertainty—thus Chen agreed more or less with Guan. (Consistently with this, but surprisingly, Chen even thought that prognostication sentences are questions; for they too often contain the word *qi*.) In 1970, Zhang Zongdong in Frankfurt published a book on oracle inscriptions, treating the charge sentences (and sometimes phrases in the prognostications) as questions, and calling *qi* an interrogative particle; but also arguing that sometimes it functions as a conditional particle.

1.2 Meanwhile, beginning in 1968 (prodded by my language students' puzzlement), I had been working on *qi* in conference papers, arguing that in Zhou (post-Shang) Chinese *qi* as "modal particle" and *qi* as possessive pronoun were "the same word," in the sense at least of having a common origin—a view rejected by almost all historical linguists, except for Søren Egerød in Denmark. (The "linguistically correct" view has been that two completely different words just happened to be homophones and got written with the same graph.) David N. Keightley introduced me to the study of oracle material in 1971: I was seeking more material on the early use of *qi*; thus began studies that led to my years of work on chronology and astronomy. Later in 1971 I wrote a long paper, unpublished and scarcely distributed (I seem rashly to have given Ken a copy), attempting to work out my "one word" idea with Shang data. In it I accepted (as did we all) the view that the divination sentences were questions. Also in 1971 Ken wrote a long research paper, never published and later repudiated, in which he too (influenced by me) tried to make sense of the "one word" idea; he too translated the charges as questions. In that paper Ken explicitly favored "perhaps" as a translation for *qi*, consistently with the "question" and "uncertainty" interpretation of Guan and Chen.

1.3 But actually, in 1959 the distinguished scholar Rao Zongyi had argued that the charges are sometimes really statements, not questions. And in 1972, two important papers in English challenged the view that the divination sentences are questions. Paul Serruys (Ken's professor) wrote a long draft review article on Zhang's book, which he published in 1974, and David Keightley wrote a long (never published) conference paper presented in Monterey, California. Both scholars, independently, came to the conclusion that the charge sentences are not, grammatically, questions at all, but are test statements. (I defended their thesis in an international conference in Hawaii in 1982, publishing in 1989.) This view led Serruys explicitly to reject the theory that *qi* was an interrogative particle or an indicator of uncertainty in the Shang language; on the contrary, he says (see Ken's quote [section 1.1] of Serruys' note 8), it is a word indicating a "definitely certain judgment."

1.4 At the same time, Serruys put forward a thesis that has gained much acceptance: He noticed that in paired divinations, one positive and one negative, *qi* was used in the test sentence stating the alternative one would expect the diviner (or the king) not to favor; and he reasoned that its meaning must be such as to indicate this disfavor. He usually did not let this guide his translations, but occasionally he did, rendering *qi* "might (*qi*: but would rather not)." He seems to have seen this as not conflicting with his "definite judgment" idea but as *being* that judgment. Ken, however, naturally took Serruys to be endorsing his own translation "perhaps." Ken now adopted the "test statement" interpretation of the "charges," but at the same time took the view that "perhaps" must be the translation of *qi* wherever *qi* occurred. (Serruys' footnote rejecting the "uncertainty" interpretation seems to have been added later than 1972.)

1.5 By 1974–1975, Ken and David Keightley were exchanging papers. Ken criticized David's mishandling of *qi* (i.e., his failure before this to translate *qi* as "perhaps"), and in 1975 their papers show that he had persuaded David that *qi* must be "perhaps." David accepted Serruys' "disfavored alternative" theory at the same time, and reasoned that the diviner indicated his disfavor by "weakening" his formulations: e.g., if you want it to rain, you say "it will rain // it (*qi*) *might* not rain," i.e., "(*qi*) *perhaps* it won't rain." The word *qi* became a window into the subtleties of the Shang world view: Good and evil in the world (and on the shell) were in paired balance; the diviner ever-so-slightly loaded the dice in his own favor by the "weakening" modality of the word *qi*. This idea caught on. Even my own work published in 1977 accepted "perhaps." But I was not thinking much about *qi*: I had set the problem aside, and was in the midst of a lively argument with Ken (and later with Serruys) on whether the verb *you* ("there is" or "has") in Shang and early Zhou Chinese had an adjectival use as (in effect) a possessive pronoun or definite article. (This is a view I still hold, and the argument still continues.)

1.6   Soon afterwards, however, I came to see clearly that the "perhaps" idea for *qi* was impossible, and was leading both Ken and David to produce grossly incorrect and unlovely translations, with forced theories about Shang language and psychology. When a book draft from David reached me in 1991, and I saw that he was heading toward publication of a major work that was going to be vitiated by this mistake, I started protesting, with letters, and then papers, going back to my suspended investigations of twenty years earlier. I remained convinced that *qi* the pronoun and *qi* the modal had a common history, that must be the key to its meaning in Shang. Presently I began to find unmistakable Shang pronominal uses of the word. Both Ken and David were swayed by the ensuing argument, Ken coming to see that in many instances *qi* could not be taken as expressing uncertainty. But he still, as his present paper shows, partly holds onto the "perhaps" idea: *qi* for him tends to express determination when used in statements of intention to act, but tends to express uncertainty in test predictions of what will happen.

2.   What is exciting in his present paper, however, is that now he too sees that Shang *qi* was referential, a sort of pronominal adverb or adjective. And he now accepts a suggestion of mine, that this explains Serruys' discovery: It is not that in using *qi* the diviner expresses an inward shudder; in whatever order he may set down his statements, he naturally *thinks* of the alternative he favors first; so *qi* when it appears tags "old information." (It should be noted that Serruys' observation works only in paired statements just one of which contains *qi*; in many such pairs, *qi* is used in both, or in neither; and the rule that it marks something disfavored fails completely in other contexts.) And Ken now accepts and adds evidence for another suggestion I have been pushing: not only that *qi* often appears in subordinate clauses, especially conditional clauses (as Zhang Zongdong and others had argued), but also that it does this not because it injects a tone of uncertainty, but because the verb phrase has become a noun phrase, and *qi* now functions as a noun modifier. This becomes especially clear when the clause is negated; because in a Shang *sentence* about what is not going to happen *qi* stands *after* the negative—which can negate adverbial *qi*; but in a sub-clause it stands *before* the negative—because the *qi* must then nominalize the whole phrase. A subject, to be sure, can be (and usually is) "exposed" in such a sub-clause; but a negative adverb cannot be: We could say, "(*wang* =) as for the king, ([*qi dian* =] his going hunting =) if he goes hunting . . .," i.e., "if the king goes hunting, . . ."; but not "(*bu* =) as for not, (*qi dian* =) if he goes hunting . . ." (in trying to say "if he does not go hunting, . . .").

2.1 Ken has offered a good example of a negated subordinate noun-clause introduced by *qi* (though I will have to improve it). But I have to reject his apparatus of scales of modality for *qi*, that allow it to "change its meaning at will," and to express either uncertainty or determination as the translator may feel is needed. No word could do this, in a "learnable" language; it would be like having a rule in English that said "yes" could mean "no," as one liked. Ken has been led to introduce this idea because he hasn't yet quite got "perhaps" out of his thinking. Nor with it, the hope that *qi* enables us to sense the subtlest modalities in Shang thinking. The oracle inscriptions are a marvellous mine of information; but they are language-poor: most of them are fragments, and most of the complete sentences display endless repetitions of a very few grammatical structures. We are never going to have the access to the mysteries of the Shang mind that Ken and David have wanted to think they can glimpse, unless the archaeologists give us materials of a quite different kind.

3. Ken's "prospective aspect" idea is right. (I will need to explain why.) But one must not suppose from this that since the future is never certain, *qi* can after all be seen as registering uncertainty. For *qi* does not have to be *absolutely* future-referring. The "prospect" may be *relative* within the past tense of a narrative, hence known with certainty to have occurred (or not). In an oracle inscription a narrative has to be in a verification, and instances of *qi* in such narratives are bound to be uncommon, but there is one in *Heji* 13399f: At the end of the verification there are four graphs, "qi ji zhu, qi" 其旣祝啓 = "about-to finish invocation, clear," = "when they were about to finish the invocation, the weather cleared." An example in an early "Classic" is found in *Shang shu* 32, "Shao Gao" 17: "Wo bu gan zhi yue, bu qi yan" 我不敢知曰, 不其延 = "We not dare know say, not going-to continue" = (said of the Mandate of Xia, and of Shang) "We do not dare to say confidently, it was not going to continue"—i.e., say that each of those dynasties ended because its fated time had run out. In neither of these contexts does *qi* convey a modality of doubt.

4. I think that Ken's analysis of the behavior of *qi* in subordinate clauses is now the same as my own: we have in these constructions an application of *qi* as adjectival (anaphoric, "pronominal") before a noun or noun-phrase, in this case a nominalized verb-phrase. But there are several pieces of unfinished business:

(1) How can one be sure that *in the Shang language itself* the "prospective aspect" *qi* and the "pronominal" *qi* are not two unrelated words, that just happen to be homophones?

(2) With Ken, I find *qi* before a negative to be key evidence for its pronominal function of creating an embedded sentence (see his 2.3). I will offer other examples, and a different analysis of his primary example.

(3) Even if there is evidence that "prospective aspect" *qi* and "pronominal" *qi* are the same word, how could one word have two such apparently different meanings in different contexts?

4.1 The "one word" hypothesis: (a) It is unlikely that this language would have both 'negative + *qi* + noun' constructions and 'negative + *qi* + verb' constructions with *qi* changing its lexical identity, especially when one notes that the negative in *both* constructions can be *wang* 亡. Moreover, (b) one can find, rarely, parallel constructions where in the one we have *qi* pre-verbal (apparently unproblematic "modal" syntax) and in the other a pre-verbal *zi* 茲, immediately recognizable as a pronominal adverb (though otherwise *qi* and *zi* behave differently). I will translate *qi* "now," = "in this case," and *zi* as "then," = "in that case" (but smooth English might omit these translations):

A. 貞：何以羌。王固曰，其以 。 Testing: He 何 will bring Qiang-[captives]. The king read the cracks, saying, "[He] will now bring [some]." (*Bingbian* 572.3, 573.2; compare *Heji* 274a–b.)

B. 癸酉卜貞：子汰逐鷹，隻。王固曰，茲隻 。 Crack on day *guiyou*, testing: Zi Da, hunting deer, will catch [some]. The king read the cracks and said, "He will then [= when hunting] catch [some]." (*Bingbian* 606.6–7; *Heji* 7075b.)

One can also have a charge "qi yu" 其雨, plus verification *zi yu* 茲雨 : "It will (now) rain"; "It (then) rained." (See Shima 469.4) One can also find in later Chinese (albeit rarely) a similar *qi*-like use of *zi*. For example, after *ning* 寧 "it would be better that . . ." one normally finds *qi* as clause-marker, e.g., in *Zuo zhuan* Xiang 26.6: 寧其利淫 "it would be better that we [risk] employ[ing] villains"; but one can find *zi*, e.g., *Zuo*, Yin 11.3: 無寧茲 . . ."would it not be better then that. . . ."

4.1.2 But I admit that *qi* "pronominal pure and simple" is very rare in the Shang language. The normal possessive construction in Shang Chinese was *you* 有（㞢）"[for . . .] there is . . ." used attributively, = "had [by . . .])"; see Nivison 1977. (But after *wang* 亡 one finds *qi*, because '*wang you* X' would mean "it is never true that there are X's.")

4.2 No one has worked on the Xiaotun corpus in *Bingbian* more thoroughly than Ken, and I hesitate to differ with one of his interpretations. I agree that *Bingbian* 76–77 and 386–87 (Ken's examples 23–25B) are about the same events (divined on the same date, though by different diviners). But the location of the king's crack-reading 77 (2) on the reverse side exactly opposite 76 (3) does not imply that "the Fang" (enemy) must be the subject of *wang gong* "not make a successful attack." The meaning of the word *gong* (connoting accomplishment), and its context in 386 (9–10), show that *wo shi,* "our emissaries," must be the ones who are "unsuccessful." The king's point is that, notwithstanding, the Shang side will suffer no injury, hence the reading *ji* = "lucky." The remainder of the king's words then must be taken rather differently. I see no reason to suppose the presence of a person named "She" (reading a problematic word as a name is often too easy a way out). If the decipherment is right, I would take 舌＝舍 "ceasing," and so in Old Chinese idiom "just," i.e., not trying to do more; compare *Mencius* 3A4, "Moreover, why doesn't Xuzi become a potter, and just get all the things he needs from his own house?" 且許子何不爲陶冶，舍皆取諸其宮中而用之，(i.e., without going out and buying them). And I would read Ken's 値 as 德, (see his note 17 on my theory about verbal *de*). The entire text of *Bingbian* 77 (2) (Ken's [23]) then reads as follows:

王固曰：吉；隹其亡攻，舍虫其德 。. The king read the cracks and said, "Lucky. It's just *that we will not make a successful attack.* (*she* 舍 =) Without trying to do that, let us just (*de* 德 =) make a show of force."

Ken's and my view is that here adjectival *qi*, in effect "that," nominalizes and embeds the sentence *wang gong*. (For a similar example, see *Bingbian* 522.4, *Heji* 14161b.)

4.2.1 Here, what followed *wei* 隹 （惟）was a noun clause *with adjectival qi preceding and nominalizing 'negative + verb'*. In an ordinary negated sentence (negative *wu* 勿 excepted), where *qi* would be adverbial (hence "modal") rather than adjectival, it would stand after the negative in Shang idiom. Understanding this point lets one read the following correctly:

C. 王固曰：吉；虫出乎，己其伐。其弗伐，不吉。
    The king read the cracks and said, "Lucky. Let there be a proclamation: we attack on *ji*-day. *If we do not attack [then], we will not be lucky."* (*Bingbian* 277, *Heji* 6461b)

In this example (provided in Nivison 1992b), a *qi*-nominalized sentence, as topic, functions as a conditional clause. For another interesting example of this conditional clause construction, see *Bingbian* 228.3 (unrecognized in *Heji* 226b):

D. 五十其不入，祀入.
    If fifty [human victims] are not sent in, we will perform the rite with those that are sent in.

Again, *qi* precedes the negative in this construction.

4.2.2 Normally (though there are exceptions) the subject or topic of a noun clause is displaced, standing before the *qi*, for example, after *gao*, "to announce":

E. 甲午貞：告妻其步。

Day *jiawu* (31) testing: We make ritual announcement that Bi will march. (*Shi duo* 418; Shima 123.4; not in *Heji*.)

If we think of *qi* in the *sentence* "Bi qi bu" as an adverbial "in this (= his-here-now) case," then the nominal transformation must be "as for Bi, his-here-now marching." As Ken points out, in such cases the *qi* is functioning, in effect, as a possessive marker (though still "prospective"), like the later *zhi* 之, which is also basically a pronominal word. We get the same thing in conditional clauses, and the *evolution* of such constructions shows clearly that the role of *qi* was pronominal: *Shang shu* 49 "Bi Shi" 4, "ma niu *qi* 其 feng, . . ." 馬牛其風 = "if horses and cattle run about in heat, . . ."; but also *Shang shu* 26 "Jin Teng" 8, "Er *zhi* xu wo, . . ." 爾之許我 = "if you grant (us =) what I request, . . ." Later on, explicit conditional particles are used, such as *ruo* 若 in the protasis and *ze* 則 in the apodosis; and still later the *zhi* nominalizing the protasis is omitted. I think Ken would agree.

4.3 Examples like A and B (and E) show that the "one word" theory works. But what could the meaning of this one *qi* be? Out of it must emerge both the ordinary "pronominal" use, and the later true "modal" uses expressing fear, hope, determination, etc.

4.3.1 I *think* what I have to say is that it is the "thisness" of the sense of *qi* (contrasting in Shang usage with *zi* 茲 "that," "then") that accounts for its "anticipatory" or "prospective" sense: Consider first the common uses of *qi* before a verb. By "in this case" I must, it seems, understand *qi* as facing both ways, meaning "in the situation in question, [it will be] thus. . . ." This must be part of the explanation of the later royal command use, e.g.: *Shang shu* 30, "Jiu Gao" 7, "Qi er dian ting zhen jiao 其爾典聽朕教, perhaps analyzable as "(I command) that you respectfully heed my instructions." Similarly *qi* is often used in test statements of intention for the future in the oracles. It seems to me likely, furthermore, that the later verb *qi* 期 "to anticipate" evolves from *qi* in this aspect of its early use.

5. It will be seen that I have been applying a form of Occam's Razor: *Do not multiply words/meanings beyond necessity*. Friends who see in *qi* two words, or *ad hoc* meanings like "perhaps," are not thinking this way. And I apply another idea in a way that eludes even Ken: Every difference in form must signal a difference in meaning, he insists in his note 2; so, one will be tempted to think, we *must* have certain translations for *qi* used wherever we find it, and not elsewhere. But the "difference" may be in *ranges* of use, not in each individual case of usage—for example, in English, in some cases of "will" vs. "is going to," but not necessarily in all, or even most cases. (In my 1992b:1 cited by Ken, I went on to develop a special case somewhat like Comrie's, where the difference between "will" and "is going to" obviously does matter.) In oracles, which are about the future anyway, the presence of "prospective" *qi* usually makes no translatable difference. If I am right, then to hunt for a perfect dictionary definition for *qi* and force it into one's translations wherever the word occurs will result in grotesque mistranslation. I have stressed this against a view of some others, who hold that a theory about a point of language needs only to account for the common cases; the rare and marginal ones are thought not to matter. Obviously, I think that in most of the common cases it doesn't matter whether *qi* is used or not, and the Chinese to this extent have been right in ignoring it. But the rare cases (such as its position in negated sub-clauses), where a difference does show up, are crucial for understanding how the word works, and what it is.

But such issues only serve to show how valuable to me have been my discussions, over decades, with alert friends like David Keightley, Paul Serruys, and Ken-ichi Takashima.

BIBLIOGRAPHY

(*This does not repeat items in Takashima's bibliography*)

Chen, Mengjia 陳夢家, *Yin-xu buci zongshu* 殷虛卜辭綜述, Peking, 1956 (see p. 88).

Guan, Xiechu 管燮初, *Yin-xu jiagu keci di yufa yanjiu* 殷虛甲骨刻辭, 的語法研究, Peking, 1953.

Keightley, David N., "*Shih Chen* 釋貞: A New Hypothesis about the Nature of Shang Divination." Paper for the conference "Asian Studies on the Pacific Coast" (ASPAC), Monterey, California, 17 June 1972, 86 pp. (unpublished).

Rao, Zongyi 饒宗頤, *Yin dai zhen-bu renwu tong-kao* 殷代貞卜人物通考, Hongkong, 1959 (see pp. 70–71).

Note: In section 2.2 (near the end) Ken argues that "wei geng qi ji"

隹庚其吉 quoted by me is a "cleft sentence"—on his analysis, predicate (VP) before subject (NP). But one should expect a conditional sentence in such a prognostication context; and I cannot, of course, accept his "maybe" interpretation of the *qi* here. In any case, the shell is a (rare) carapace (*Bingbian* 66); the inscription is unreadable from the plate, and is probably mistranscribed. It is possible that it ought to read, 隹庚其令, 吉 i.e., "(if) it is on a *geng* day that [Di] decrees [snow], this will be lucky." One does not expect inversions of this kind in the Shang oracles (which are very business-like, not "Delphic"). Sentences of this kind belong in poetry ("Many are the wonderful things. . . ."); and in fact there are three examples quoted by Ken himself from the *Odes* (his [20]–[22]).

2. Comment on E. G. Pulleyblank, "Zou and Lu and the Sinification of Shandong"

Professor Pulleyblank's article deals with problems and details so far from my own work and competence that any comment I can make is going to be a study in presumption. Modesty bids me shrink back, but temptation beckons.

Pulleyblank sets his problem thus: The traditional picture of very early China, reaffirmed even by a few archaeologists such as K. C. Chang, and others, is of a unilinear culture reaching back as far as one can see or imagine. This must yield to that archaeology that shows sharp cultural divergence in the neolithic between the west-central painted pottery cultures (Yangshao) and the northeast black pottery culture (Longshan), and more recently a multiplicity of local cultures from the north and west south to below the Yangzi. The basic division proposed sixty years ago by Fu Sinian, between an ancestral Xia culture in the west and an early Yi culture in the east is acceptable; but Keightley has argued that the eastern black pottery culture is the origin of fundamental *ur*-Chinese characteristics; that the rise of Shang culture owes a great deal to it; that "the mind-set that we think of as 'Confucian' in later times" can be discerned in black-pottery techniques. Keightley even implies that Chinese writing began in the east.

But this would require that the Yi language was a variant of proto-Chinese, Pulleyblank insists. He sets to work to show that this is impossible: From traces of Yi speech in place-names and early references to certain minor states as being "Yi" and alien, i.e., non-Xia, Pulleyblank argues that the eastern seaboard area from Shandong south to Yue and beyond was at the beginning of history non-Chinese, speaking an Austroasiatic language related to Vietnamese. As late as the Chunqiu Period this component in the North Chinese population and political order was still being assimilated; and notable among such originally Yi areas was the statelet of Zou, also called Zhulu, the native state of none other than Mencius. (Even "the name of the village in Lu from which Confucius is said to have originated," namely Zou, is a variant and homophone of this state-name Zou.)

I am happy to leave this argument to these two gentlemen, trusting that they will inform us when they settle it. Here, I content myself with noting that they almost seem to be agreeing on one startling matter. Keightley's daring suggestion that we can see a proto-Confucian "mind-set" already nascent in Longshan pottery can be set beside Pulleyblank's quite persuasive argument that the native state of Mencius was as late as 519 (when Confucius would have been in his thirties) identified as "Yi," and alien; and why not, later, the "Second Sage" himself? And (Pulleyblank doesn't make a point of it) maybe even Confucius had an "Yi" background. For that matter, what about Mozi? Said to have come from Song, and so derivatively Shang; and what about Shang? Perhaps we are to see the whole of Eastern Zhou classical Chinese philosophy as a revolutionary surfacing of a persisting residual *non*-Chinese outlook, breaking through an overlay of aristocratic hierarchy to press pragmatic, even relatively egalitarian, philosophies of individual worth.

I leave such delicious thoughts to ferment in the minds of my readers, or to evaporate, as may be best. (But one must not forget that Mencius himself (3A4) said, to Chen Xiang, follower of the egalitarian Xu Xing, "I have heard of the Xia converting the Yi to their ways, but not of the Xia being converted to Yi ways." Mencius, however, consistently uses the term "Yi" of all "barbarians," not just of the "Eastern Yi.") In trying to look deeply—perhaps too deeply—into the Chinese past, I have had my own problems. In my case, it has not been a matter of taking the side of archaeology against a "traditional" picture, but (to my surprise and unease) the reverse. We pursue the lines of evidence we feel we know how to handle. I will sometimes take a shot at a linguistic guess or theory—see my response to Kenichi Takashima—but I must admit to being at best a linguist without a licence. When I turn away from philosophy to amuse myself (philosophy and cultural themes don't give you tight evidence), I read bone and bronze inscriptions ("archaeology," to be sure), and line them up with details I extract from old historical texts.

This diversion has led me to reconstruct an exact chronology of the simplest political events, such as successions of kings and beginnings of "dynasties," back much farther into the past than any respectable "dirt" archaeologist would for an instant allow to be possible. In doing this, I owe a large debt to David W. Pankenier. In an article written in 1984 (appearing in *Early China* 9–10 [1983–1985]), Pankenier showed, I think convincingly, that a dramatic conjunction of planets in February 1953 B.C. marked the first year of power of Yu, the first ruler of the Xia Dynasty. An article I co-authored (with K. Pang) six years later continued his work, again using astronomical evidence, to argue for a precise dating of Xia reigns down to 1876 B.C. Since then, in conference papers, I have worked out exact dates forward and backward, and I would now argue that the first year of Yao was 2026 B.C. (I take 1953 B.C. as Yu year 1, = Shun 14 in the *Bamboo Annals,* and suppose that Yao 58, when the *Annals* says Yao's son was exiled, was Yao's last year.)

One trouble with this is that like most of my colleagues I have all my life believed that Yao (Shun and Yu too) never existed, and is mere myth. (The *name* "Yao" I continue to think is mythical. Mencius twice refers to him as "Fang Xun," his real name: 3A4, quoting him, and 5A4.) But the real trouble is that I am recognizing Chinese "emperors" at a time when the entire fraternity-and-sorority of archaeologists sees no possibility of there having been anything for such rulers to rule over, and probably centuries before there was any writing, or any readily conceivable way for such events to be recorded and remembered long enough to get into the written chronicles and histories that we have. Yet I am unable to find a flaw in the line of argument that leads me to my conclusions.

One thing to notice is that these findings (if so they be) are not quite inconsistent with the picture given us by Professor Pulleyblank and the archaeologists, of a China around 2000 B.C. that was a welter of small communities probably speaking different languages, only a few of which could be "Chinese," in the sense of being the ancestor-communities of the later culture and polity the historians describe. We think of the "Tu Fang" and the "Gong Fang" as barbarians, because the Shang royal oracle inscriptions call them "fang," hence (presumably) other and alien, and we think of the Shang as "Chinese," and "civilized." But this is because it was the Shang who happened to be the community that not only had writing, but also happened to win out in the struggle for survival, and that therefore happen to get into what we call "history." As far as we know, only one writing system developed in China. If the Tu Fang had defeated King Wu Ding of Shang in the late thirteenth century B.C. and the diviners and scribes had fallen to them, they would have been the ones who used it, and it might be they, and their accounts of the "Shang Fang," that we would know about.

In the same way, perhaps, we know about Yao, or Fang Xun (if we do know about anyone with one of these names), because it is he who happened to be in the memory-line, however that worked, which we may never know. (The *Yijing* appendices do speak of "knotted cords" before writing.) We need make no assumptions about a pan-Chinese "state" at such a time: It may very well be that every large village around 2000 B.C. thought of itself collectively as the center of the world, and would have passed on that kind of account of itself, had the luck of time not meted out oblivion.

Yao, a.k.a. Fang Xun, *is* possible as of 2026 B.C., however, even as more than headman of a large village: The earliest levels of the urban site Erlitou could probably accommodate him. (For dates of sites, I am following M. Matsumaru and H. Nagata, *Chugoku Bummei no Seiritsu* [Tokyo: Kodansha 1985], 30.) So let me try something I *can't* believe.

The *Bamboo Annals* ("modern" text) dates Yao to 2145. If two-year completion-of-mourning intervals are posited after deaths of rulers in the preceding *Annals* account, then Zhuanxu 13, when a calendar is said to have been invented, becomes 2287. But if 2026 is accepted for Yao and the same two-year intervals are posited, then 2287 turns out to be the first year of Huang Di, i.e., the opening date in the *Annals*. I do not think this is coincidence, and I assume an early stage of the text that did make 2287 the first year of recorded history. (I also think that the date is fictional, and was adopted for calendar-makers' convenience.)

The chronicle for Huang Di says that in his fiftieth year he performed certain important rites on the banks of the Luo River, on day *gengshen* (57), in the seventh month. Strangely precise. It is reasonable (and in accord with *Annals* usage elsewhere) to understand the first day of the month to be intended; and if Huang Di 1 was 2287, then Huang Di 50 was 2238. If the current calendar was the one that in a later stage of the *Annals* is ascribed to Zhuanxu, one must at least look at the calendar that was known as the "Zhuanxu Calendar" in classical times. This was the calendar used in Qin and in Early Han, and it began the year with the first lunar month of winter, i.e., the month before the month containing the winter solstice. If this was the calendar in use in 2238 (if even the concept of a calendar existed then), then the first of the seventh lunar month was the first day of "summer," i.e., the first day of the month preceding the month containing the summer solstice. In 2238 that day was 3 June, i.e., Julian Day 90 4147. One now must divide by 60, and modify the remainder by subtracting 10 or adding 50, to get the sixty-day cycle number—discovering (try it!) that 3 June 2238 B.C. *was* in fact a *gengshen* day.

So I cannot throw my notes away, but must retain them guiltily in my "agnostic" file. And agnosticism is the attitude that in some degree seems to me appropriate for a great deal of what we try to be able to say about so early an "Early China" as Professor Pulleyblank and I, in our different ways, are saying. We must watch and wait, and be very careful what we either accept or scoff at. Our methods, meanwhile, must be rigorous, guessing clearly labeled as guessing.

But why must I be "agnostic"? For it seems obvious that I put together a reasonable theory, that yielded deductively—to my own surprise—a successful "prediction," that is, a precise datum confirmed by independent data previously unknown to me. What more do I want?

My answer is suggested by David Hume's famous critique of miracles (see my "Response" to critics in *Early China* 15, for a different application of this idea). Briefly, an account of a miracle is believable only if its being invented is even more unlikely than its being true. If the *Annals* had implied a date in the thirtieth millennium B.C. rather than in the late third, I would without hesitation have dismissed a "successful" result as a bizarre accident. How far back is too far back? I don't know; and it seems to *me* that 2238 B.C. is neither here nor there.

We all have agnostic files, and we all have waste-baskets. I would have to respect a person who reaches for the latter receptacle, in this case. I myself said—precisely—that this is something I *can't* believe; I did not say I *dis*believe it.

3.   Critique of E. L. Shaughnessy, "Micro-Periodization and the Calendar of a Shang Military Campaign"

Fifteen years ago, having been introduced by David N. Keightley to the mysteries of ancient Chinese oracular and bronze inscriptions, I was conducting a seminar that drew a handful of addicts from Stanford and Berkeley. Edward L. Shaughnessy and David W. Pankenier were in the group—both now professors in Eastern universities—as well as Professor Keightley himself. At one of the meetings, responding to a challenge from Keightley, I spent all of my time on the recently discovered bronzes from Fufeng, Shaanxi, cast and inscribed in the tenth and ninth centuries B.C. by persons of the Wei lineage. While preparing myself, I attacked the presumably hopeless problem of determining the absolute dates for some of them. Almost by chance, I reached for James Legge's text and translation of the supposedly fake "modern text" *Bamboo Annals,* and began to get interesting results.

Shaughnessy and Pankenier took up the scent like bloodhounds, and in the years since then, using inscriptions together with astronomical evidence and clues in the *Annals,* we have worked in different directions, with many disagreements, trying to reconstruct exact dating far back into the Chinese past. (Pankenier has gotten the most spectacular results, having pinned down the exact dates of the beginnings of both the Xia and the Shang Dynasties.) Shaughnessy's paper in this volume continues this interest, making use of important work by Keightley, who (in his *Sources of Shang History:* see Shaughnessy's note 10) considers four lunar eclipses mentioned in oracle inscriptions of the reign of Wu Ding of Shang. Keightley dates these to the years 1198, 1192, 1189, and 1180 B.C. Shaughnessy and I would date the last to 1201 (see below); but as a whole this set of dates late in Wu Ding's tenure is consistent with our results from work on the *Bamboo Annals.*

This background explains Professor Shaughnessy's interest in the problems he addresses in this paper, and shows how he is able confidently to focus his attention on just a few decades.

Shaughnessy offers a fine-tuned analysis of two groups of oracle inscriptions. One group, all from the same bone, to demonstrate his method, seems securely dated to 1181. The second is made up of inscriptions that seem to be about a set of related military campaigns that one can assume occurred some years earlier in the same few months. Here he applies his method to the task of substantive historical reconstruction and tentatively dates them to 1211–1210, in the reign of Wu Ding. It is a pleasure to be the first to examine critically the work of a master at this craft. I have learned important things from this effort.

The first group, of five routine ten-day "no misfortune" inscriptions, is of special interest because the last one contains a mention, dated to the month and sixty-day cycle day, of a lunar eclipse. Shaughnessy shows how to triangulate the day-cycle and month dates in the five to determine exactly what the cycle number for the first day of the year has to be, then uses this information to single out four possible years within what he (and I) believe to be the possible range of inscriptions of this type, viz. 1225–1175. One of those four years is a year when there was a lunar eclipse visible in China, and this confirms his triangulation analysis.

In proceeding this way Shaughnessy is perhaps being a bit theatrical. One would think that he could have by-passed the demonstration of method by going directly to the eclipse, dated to day *yi-you* (22) in the eighth month. In the entire fifty-year period, Mucker and Meeus list only one lunar eclipse visible in China and on a Julian Day that is equivalent to an *yi-you* day, and it was on 25 November 1181. In not bringing in the full detail of the eclipse, Shaughnessy has inadvertently dodged a fascinating difficulty: For if 25 November is to count as the middle of the "eighth month," then the current Shang year must have begun on 19 April, a full season later than a Shang year is supposed to begin. I myself have never seen evidence of such a calendar.

Let me cautiously propose a solution: Shaughnessy in note 6 calls attention to the word "*wen*," "It was heard," after the record of the eclipse, and to D. N. Keightley's caution that this may indicate that the eclipse was not visible in the Shang capital (the night could have been heavily overcast), so that the notation may be a mistake. I suspect this is true, but in a very limited sense: The fragment Shaughnessy is using (*Heji* 11485, fig. 1) shows the eclipse inscription in heavy bold and large graphs, against a background of inscriptions in relatively much smaller graphs. This looks like a so-called "display" inscription, suggesting to me that it may have been carved on an already inscribed shell several months later. So perhaps by the time of inscribing, a report had come in of a lunar eclipse "on day *yi-you,*" and the inscriber thought it to have been in month 8 rather than in month 10. The inscriber's "8th month" then would begin with *xin-wei* (8), 12 Sept (we can assume a different distribution of long and short months from that conjectured by Dong Zuobin). This gives the day *yi-si* (42), as required, being now 19 February, as the first day of the "natural" *tian zheng* year beginning with the pre-spring-equinox month; and it is quite possible that such a calendar was being used.

In the second part of Professor Shaughnessy's article, there is more variety of content and richer language in the inscriptions. Perhaps inevitably here and there I would have translated differently. (Each scholar working on these materials tends to develop his own private language of translation.) I use Professor Shaughnessy's enumeration in the following examples:

2a. In the "prognostication" the line "On *ding si* we ought not to harm them" does not make sense to me. I would prefer "strike a (successful) blow" to "harm." But it is "ought" that I balk at. The graph is the rare *wu* 冊 rather than the common *wu* 勿, and I do not think they were synonyms in the Shang language. The difference, I propose (using the philosopher R. M. Hare's useful distinction), is between a *prescriptive* "ought not" (unproblematic for the latter common *wu*) and a *descriptive* "ought not," which is going to be almost the same as "will not." The king is not saying "we ought not to try to score a blow on *ding si,*" sending out orders accordingly; he is predicting failure on that day; the divine Powers have willed that we *are not to* succeed on *ding-si.* (The name Zhu, incidentally, mystifies me; why an unknown and previously unmentioned commander at this point in the text? I have always thought the word, which is *hapax,* must be an adverb; "repeatedly" would make sense, but one can only guess.)

2c. "Que will not expect to capture Fou": It is not likely that we should have a divination predicting the future state of mind of Que. For my views on *qi,* here rendered "expect," see my comment on Professor Takashima's article. I think it is a particle indicating simple future time here, in reference to an already understood topic; Shaughnessy here and elsewhere follows the view of Paul L-M Serruys. Oddly, if Shaughnessy had, consistently, rendered *wu qi bo* in 2a "we ought not to expect to" make a successful strike, he would have at least given us sense.

4b. "Fou will not gather our legions." Desiring to understand this, I scrutinised usage of the verb *se,* "gather" (said of a harvest), in other oracle texts. It is used both as a verb and as a noun in hunting contexts, apparently meaning "corral." The meaning here surely is "Fou will not surround our legions," or "Fou will not draw our legions into a trap."

11c. The translation I would have given is "(we will) command Lin to march on ahead, taking the archer-lord (with him)."

12a-b. I agree completely with Shaughnessy's solution to this puzzle. As to translation, I have two small suggestions: (1) I probably would have rendered ". . . strike a blow at *his* legions at [You] . . .," taking *you* before *lu* not as *right* but as the quasi-possessive pronominal use of the verb *you* (see my article on this use in *Early China* 3). But I do not fault Shaughnessy here; it is quite possible that the meaning is "strike at the enemy's right flank." (2) In 12b, I doubt that the verb *pei* 配 can mean here that the king is going to "accompany" Lin. The hierarchic implication of *pei* is the opposite: the king can *pei* Heaven, or *pei*-sacrifice to his ancestors; a wife is said to *pei* her husband, etc. So, take *pei* causatively: "the king will have Lin *lend support,* and attack . . ." etc. This makes better sense: the king himself is making the main attack against the enemy in Shu; he is also having Lin make a supporting strike against enemy forces in You—an after-thought, at a later date, as Shaughnessy's analysis would suggest.

I come finally to larger questions of absolute dating. Professor David Keightley in his *Sources of Shang History* has expressed the view that Wu Ding's reign probably was about twenty years, comprising the two decades 1200–1181 (p. 203, table 14). He relies on the astronomical evidence I have already described in support of this dating: four Period I lunar eclipse records, all from the same pit (YH127), which should be Wu Ding material, appear to him to be datable to the years 1198, 1192, 1189, and 1180. But I—and I believe Shaughnessy concurs—would redate the eclipse Keightley assigns to 1180: I think it belongs in 1201. (The latter is a partial eclipse, and the 1180 eclipse is total; but the eclipses of 1198 and 1189 are also partial.) And I do not believe that Wu Ding was still alive in 1180. In note 5, on his demonstration set, presumably 1181, Shaughnessy gives arguments for putting the set in Period II, which is post Wu Ding, and I agree. I believe that Wu Ding's last year was 1189, his reign thus just including Keightley's four eclipses. I do not suppose that Keightley would confine Wu Ding to 1201–1189, even if he thinks of YH127 as *the* Wu Ding pit; the practice of inscribing bone-and-shell divination material may well have started only at the end of a much longer reign. It is plain that Shaughnessy doesn't limit Wu Ding to 1200 and later, for he dates the campaign complex that he examines to 1211–1210. I have no complaint with this date, and obviously with Shaughnessy I reject 1179. I do not know how to choose between 1215 and 1210.

But I lean to the view that Wu Ding began a long reign long before this. All early secondary sources (there is no primary-source testimony) say that Wu Ding reigned fifty-nine years. It is reasonable enough to be suspicious about so long a span; and all the sources could derive from a single source, which could well be wrong.

But there is an important reason for taking fifty-nine years seriously: It is the reign-length found in the "Current Text" *Bamboo Annals* (*Jin ben Zhu shu ji nian*), a chronicle pretending to cover over two thousand years of history to 299 B.C., that was reported to have been discovered in a burial site in 281 A.D. This document has been thought by most scholars for centuries to be a fake, but has been shown by much work by Shaughnessy, D. Pankenier, and myself over more than a dozen years to be either a genuine Warring States text (my view now) or closely based on such a text. Shaughnessy himself has made the most important single contribution to this scholarship in his article in *HJAS* in 1986, showing that the chronicle for Wu Wang of Zhou has been lengthened three years, by having transposed into it a bamboo strip of graphs taken from the chronicle for Cheng Wang; his result shows that these two parts of the *Annals,* at least, are almost certainly word for word the text as it read in the late fourth century B.C. Proof of the authenticity of a small part of the text does not establish the rest of it; but it does reverse the field: Anyone who scoffs at or simply disregards other parts of the "modern text" *Bamboo Annals* now owes us some reasons. And if *any* independent reason can be advanced for taking some other part of the text seriously, the skeptic owes us very powerful reasons for rejecting that part.

Is there any independent reason for giving Wu Ding a fifty-nine-year reign? I will briefly outline mine: In my article in *HJAS* in 1983 (p. 558, note 87), I mention research of mine showing from late Shang inscriptions that the Di Yi reign (next to the last) began in 1105. The winter-solstice month in that year began with day *yi-you* (22). The idea occurred to me that the "yi" of Di Yi" comes from the "*yi*" of this first day. But this way of accounting for the *gan* terms that always terminate the (posthumous?) name of a Shang king did not seem to work in other cases, so I set the idea aside. But recently I noticed that when one takes (with Pankenier) 1555 as the date of the Shang victory over the preceding power (traditionally Xia)—there are various ways of confirming this—one gets a *jia* day as the first day of the reign of the founder's successor Tai Jia, *if* one posits that the reign must be preceded by three years of mourning.

I then turned back to the end of the dynasty, to Di Xin, whose beginning date 1086 is firmly established by some of Shaughnessy's early research. 1086 begins with an *yi* day or a *jia* day, so it can't explain "Di Xin"; but three years earlier, in 1089, the post-winter-solstice month, which often begins a Shang year, began with *xin-si* (18), 23 January. Then I turned to Wenwu Ding, before Di Yi. The *Annals* chronicle gives him thirteen years, so the actual first year ought to be 1118; and a conference paper of mine presented in Anyang in 1987 ("A New Study of *Jia Bian* 2416") shows that this date is right. That year began with a *geng* or *ji* day; but three years earlier, in 1121, the post-solstice month begins with *ding-hai* (24), 17 January, nicely explaining "Wenwu Ding."

The theory had to be taken seriously, and I tried working out exact dates for every king in the dynasty, using *Annals* reign lengths. In doing this, I assumed that (just as in the Western Zhou part of the text) the compilers had not known about mourning periods and had left them out. (In Zhou the mourning calendar-gap was two years; in Shang it seems usually to have been three.) So they were forced to introduce compensating distortions. One of these distortions must be the dating of Wu Ding, which in the *Annals* is 1274–1216. If Wu Ding, as inscriptions and astronomy show, must have lived at least twenty-seven years longer, one does not suppose that his reign was twenty-seven years longer; fifty-nine years seems enough to choke on. So I assumed that dropping mourning periods had led compilers to suppose that a long preceding period of time was at least twenty-seven years shorter than it actually was. Accordingly, I looked for a year beginning with a *ding* day, about a quarter century after 1274. I found that 1250 is such a year, the post-solstice month beginning with *ding-si* (54) 4 January. If Wu Ding's fifty-nine years too were preceded by a three-year mourning interval, then his dates are 1250/47–1189. I cannot pretend that I am sure of these dates, but I have been able to work out a complete Shang chronology that is consistent with them. And one that explains, furthermore, some other puzzles: why the fifth-generation king Tai Wu was given seventy-five years when he couldn't have reigned that long, and why his brother Yong Ji is made to precede him rather than to follow him, as the oracle inscriptions show he did; why the twenty-fifth king Feng Xin (a.k.a. Lin Xin) is sometimes recognized as a king and sometimes not; and why the same is true of the *Annals'* second and third kings Wai Bing and Zhong Ren. (Normally the *gan*-name year is the king's succession year; but it is never the case that two successive kings have the same *gan*; so if the succession year yielded the same *gan* as that of the predecessor, the *gan* of the accession (post-mourning) year had to be used instead.) I omit much; a full presentation of these matters belongs in another publication.

But the nature of the present book lends itself to another not inappropriate observation: There are (this is a horrible thing for a philosopher to say) different tastes in epistemology. There are some scholars who are most comfortable when working with a "solid" body of "concrete" material, things like pots and vessels that you can bounce or

scratch. I like these things too, and so does Shaughnessy; but sometimes I see colleagues (other than Shaughnessy) who seem to me to be
meditating on such materials until they see all sorts of meanings in
them, which to me seem highly speculative, and then mentally trans-
ferring the security of the solid detail of these physical objects they
started with to their own speculations. And this makes me uneasy.

I imagine that they see me often doing things that make them just
as uneasy. I am fond of numbers (Shaughnessy too is like this, to a
point), and I am drawn to things that have numbers that I can play
with, even if these materials are quite disreputable—such, indeed, was
the *Bamboo Annals*. Then I stumble around putting various things
together experimentally, and if I hit on something that "fits" I get very
excited, and hunt for a theory that might explain it, in a precise way.
(Precision is my own epistemological refuge.) And if I find one that
seems to explain more and more, I become happier and happier. I am
sure that some of my "solid detail" colleagues look at me in alarm, and
see me so to speak going off into space with nothing under my feet. I
try to tell them, "Look, what I am doing is just applying basic scientific
method." And they try to tell me, "No, you are treading air; what we
are doing is just applying basic scientific method."

Perhaps we need each other.

4.   Comment on Kanaya Osamu, "The Mean in Original Confucianism"

I am much honored to have Professor Kanaya's elegant essay before
me. Reading it has shown me more of the great richness of early Confucian ethics, which is only what I should have expected from a scholar
like himself.

My first reaction to his paper was to say to myself, "Here at least is
one contribution on a problem that has never engaged me." On reading him a second time, I hope more thoughtfully, I saw that the problem is one that engages everyone. Let me try to sneak up to the point
without being noticed.

First, a philological detail, on which I am less than sure: Kanaya
quotes an example of the *zhong* ("mean") idea from the *Zhongyong*

(VI), where Confucius is represented as praising the Emperor Shun for "employing the middle" or "mean." I will repeat Kanaya's translation, and then think about it:

> Shun loved to question others, and he carefully considered what was said within his hearing. He praised what he thought to be good, and concealed what he thought to be bad, and grasping these two extremes employed the middle in governing the people.

Grasping what "two extremes" *liang duan*? The immediately preceding phrase must give the answer, for here we have paired concepts that are obviously antithetical: *yin e er yang shan*—verbs *yin* and *yang*, the familiar words, but here "conceal" and "praise"; and their objects *e* and *shan*, "bad" and "good." But only rhetorically are "concealing the bad" and "praising the good" describable as "two extremes," if by "extremes" we mean incompatible alternatives. And one might think that this is what the expression *liang duan* must mean. Consider its use in the *Shiji*, biography of the Prince of Wei (*juan* 77, "liezhuan" 17): The Qin army has massacred the Zhao army at Changping, and has invested the Zhao capital Handan, which is on the verge of surrender. The Prince's sister, married to the Prince of Zhao, appeals to him; he pleads with the king of Wei, who sends his army to the border, commanded by his general Jin Pi. But then Qin threatens action against Wei, and the king is afraid, sending out orders to his general, who "kept the army back, fortifying Ye, and while ostensibly aiding Zhao, in fact grasped the two alternatives *chi liang duan* and looked on from a distance."

So just what does *liang duan* mean? Literally "two ends," e.g., of a stick, in the *Shiji* example necessarily two courses of action—attack, or hold off—only one of which can be followed, so that "holding two ends" becomes a metaphor for paralyzing indecision. But in the *Zhongyong* example it has to be "giving due consideration to two possible courses," both of which were things Shun could always have done, at the same time, if he so chose. Are they properly thought of as "extremes"? I suppose they might be: Shun might have made it his way always to deal with bad advice or with a despicable idea by silence; and this might well not be good: sometimes you have to call a spade a spade, if you have a principle that is important. And he might also have always praised a good idea, and again this might not be a good policy, for there are situations where implementing a good idea requires a bit of finesse.

But looking at the text again, I doubt that this is just what it means, if it says that he *did* "conceal the bad and praise the good" and *then* "grasped the two ends," "employing the mean." So is the meaning that Shun employed government policies that mixed the "good" and the "bad" together judiciously? I somehow doubt that we are invited to think this either. What seems to be going on is just smooth rhetoric: we are given two contrasting ideas; then the idea of weighing alternatives, which seems naturally to follow; and then the idea that again seems naturally to follow, of pursuing a reasonable "middle" course. If you cut into this with a logician's scalpel, as I did, insisting on getting rigorous sense out of it, you get into trouble. And similarly if you apply the philologist's bag of tricks, again as I did, insisting that a striking metaphor has got to have consistent meanings in different contexts, again you get into trouble.

So I was going a bit too far. Should I then learn not to be so keen on rendering an idea clear and precise? And surrender my *metier,* my very *raison d'etre?* Apparently one has to use the wisdom of an ancient uncle of mine, when he instructed me in my early youth on the art of making pancakes. He had no recipe: "You just have to get it about right," he told me. I thought of him at once when I read about Yanzi's directions for making a good soup. One blends things together; but of course it is supposed to be a *good* blend; one isn't supposed to put poison in the soup.

Let me indulge my wrongheadedness and look more closely at this matter. On the one hand, we can ask if the "mean" is supposed to mean "moderation." Professor Kanaya would accept this, e.g., "If one pays close attention to this aspect of everyday moderation," etc. He goes on to discuss Aristotle and Mencius, not unhelpfully. But I find myself remembering a novel that I read many years ago, *Lost Horizon;* an arch line stuck in my mind (why?): The ladies of Shangri-La, it said, had "happily applied the principle of moderation to their own chastity." It would seem that if we give the notion of the "mean" *any* positive content, we can imagine a situation in which it negates itself, at a higher (or lower) level: even moderation can be carried to extremes.

But that means that (with my old uncle) there is just no getting away from "just knowing" what it is to "get it about right." *That*—sensing, finding, putting one's finger on the *right* course, on the way it is *good* to follow, obviously can't be carried to extremes, if carrying something "to extremes" just *means* getting it wrong. Surely this is what Mencius meant when he said that grasping the "middle" without *quan*—judicious "weighing"—is no better than grasping "one" thing, i.e., grasping an injudicious extreme. But what is Mencius' "weighing" if not just sensing, among alternative possibilities, what the *best* choice or blend is?

And now, it seems to me, we have something truly admirable, but hardly helpful. For I had thought that I was being told, by Confucius and his followers and by the early part of the *Zhongyong*, that following the "mean" is the way to do what is right and good. But it begins to seem that I cannot even grasp what the "mean" *means* unless I already *know* what is right and good.

But again, I've gone too far. I've treated the *zhong-yong* principle as a piece of advice for the moral connoisseur, who as connoisseur needs no advice. For the rest of us, it is generally speaking a *good idea* to bear in the back of our minds that choosing the right course is often going to require caution, judicious weighing, a "nothing too much" attitude, not just mechanically or insensitively going ahead to apply a rule or principle: that following even a *prima facie* correct policy "come hell or high water" can be disastrous. It has long seemed to me that this explains why, through the long evolution of our moral make-up, we humans still retain the philosophically obnoxious capacity at times to deliberately back away from a course we "know" to be the best—a characteristic of humans pejoratively called "weakness of will." The answer surely is that this capacity has survival value, for human kind and for humane society. Granted, too often it lets loose the cowardice in us. But there will be times when it is going to save us from behaving like lemmings. Or like unfeeling brutes.

5. Comment on Susan Mann, "Women in the Life and Thought of Zhang Xuecheng"

Anyone who has read Zhang Xuecheng will have come to admire and marvel at the breadth and penetration of his intellect. But one also finds in the writings of his last years angry explosions on the subject of women. Their place is in the home, says Zhang. Their education should be in morals and the rules of proper conduct, and only after that (if at all) in literary arts such as poetry. He argues for the strictest interpretation of traditional "ritual" rules binding women to what we now would think of as a second-class life, subservient to male domination. In the late twentieth century, one does not want to find this kind of material in a writer one has other reasons to admire. And indeed, for a long time, this side of Zhang, and especially his diatribes against the recently deceased "liberated" poet Yuan Mei, were all that most readers who knew anything about him knew about.

I had had to deal with this side of Zhang, of course, and I tried, almost out of a sense of duty to my subject, to find ways to understand and excuse him, while confessing difficulty. His attacks on Wang Zhong and on Yuan Mei were not limited to their views on women and customs governing women's lives; and some of his criticisms are philosophically acute. He found Yuan Mei at times elegantly coarse, and fawning on the favor of powerful and visibly corrupt officials, including at least one who had done harm to Zhang's own enterprises.

Curiously (less in Zhang's favor), we can see both men intellectually close to Zhang himself. Qian Mu with good reason analyzes the three together in his history of Qing thought; both play variations on themes close to Zhang's "Classics are history" idea. One suspects that Zhang may have seen them as dabbling in ideas about intellectual history in which he felt himself to have a much sounder understanding, and even a proprietary interest. In Yuan's case, there was the successful poet, basking in praise, affluent through his literary skill, contrasting with the socially awkward Zhang, who simply couldn't write poetry, always strapped for money. And for all of his "advanced" ideas about women's education, Yuan's letters reveal him to be a person who could regard females as mere animals (and, interestingly, as one who also defended upper-class homosexuality). We may think Zhang backward, but he respected women, always.

Zhang's views about women that make me wince are not simple, and are found in a matrix of his thinking that is far from simple or (all told) repellent. Professor Susan Mann has taken up the problem of his

attitudes toward women, at several levels: his criticisms of Wang and
Yuan, of course; also the very broad-minded treatment of women in his
local historical writing. Her discussion of Zhang's late-in-life identification of himself as in an "Eastern Zhejiang" intellectual tradition uncov-
ers a genuinely new perspective on that problem, which should be
read in conjunction with the important things that Professor Yü has to
say about it. But it is her exploration of Zhang's extraordinarily
nuanced writings about women close to him in his own life that both
rescues Zhang for us as a humane and sensitive man, and requires me
to recognize in this paper a valuable new kind of history.

Almost two-thirds of Mann's article is taken up with a careful review
of Zhang Xuecheng's writings on women he knew—sisters, cousins,
wives or mothers of friends, together with his teacher Zhu Yun's
"Funeral Ode" on Zhang's mother. The scholarship here is extraordinarily fine (as is the writing: no reader will be able to put it down). My
own book on Zhang would have been far better if I had not left this
work to be done by a successor; but I doubt that I could have begun to
do it as well. I did, of course, include some of this rich material, generated by the Chinese convention of semi-formal short biographical
sketches and memoirs that a scholar-writer is normally called on to
write, or volunteers to write, for friends and family members who have
passed on. This literary institution is one of the most graceful and
admirable features of the older Chinese way of life; and the volume of
this kind of matter, for the last imperial dynastic period alone, and
even just for women, waiting to be explored by scholars like Mann is
enormous.

Like anyone bringing much new material to bear on an old subject,
Susan Mann has in part resolved some old questions and has in part
suggested new ones. One of the old questions is a problem that I
raised, without (I now think) knowing just how I ought to deal with it:
In 1800, the year before his death, Zhang wrote the last of the essays
that make up the present collection we (following his wish) call the
Wenshi tongyi: his "Zhedong Xueshu," "The Eastern Chekiang Tradition
of Learning." The puzzle is that this essay naturally has led scholars,
like Lynn Struve in the United States, and others before her in China,
to talk of an "Eastern Chekiang School" of learning, particularly of historiography. But no filiation of teachers and disciples leading to Zhang

can be got from this essay (nor did Zhang himself have successors); and a study of his life and work points in another direction, showing us a man whose intellectual direction comes partly from the "Tongcheng" group (Fang Bao, Yao Nai, etc.) but is largely his own; indeed he was sometimes critical of "Zhedong" scholars like Quan Zuwang. I marked down the usual way of talking as a simple mistake: Zhang's self-identification in 1800 was, I said, a "lifetime's afterthought." Professor Yü Yingshih in his own book on Zhang and Dai Zhen has nodded agreement, and in fact gently (and justly) chides me for neglecting more evidence for this judgment, that was at my fingertips.

But the many scholars who have accepted the "Eastern Chekiang School" way of talking are hardly fools. Zhang obviously did feel, keenly, in that last essay that there was something unique and important in his own local background; and though perhaps he forces the idea a bit, we ought not hastily to mark his statement down to senility. What Susan Mann has done, by sensitively probing the roles of generations of nameless women in educated families east of the Qiantang River, as contrasted with their sisters to the west, is to enable us to see this matter, I am persuaded, in part as Zhang himself felt it: one did breathe a different air, feel a distinct moral and intellectual tone, when one crossed that river. Intangible, in a sense; but good history cannot ignore such intangibles. Professor Yü in this volume develops an entirely different argument that complements and supports Professor Mann's: in the "Zhe-dong" essay Zhang was trying to fill a logical gap in his definition of his own position as contrasted with Dai Zhen. One can still say as I did, and with good evidence, that Zhang in that 1800 essay gives us a "lifetime's afterthought"; but to say no more would be misleading.

Another matter comes to mind after my reading this paper, that had bothered me for years. Susan Mann, I think, resolves it: I am speaking of the use, in the Hu-Yao *nianpu* of Zhang, of the obviously derogatory expression "Shaoxing shiye," apparently of Zhang, when we find him delivering an opinion on the role of women that displeases us. There is, Mann says, scholarship (new to me) that establishes our word "shyster" as the meaning of "shiye," in this phrase at least, as applied to Shaoxing-trained legal yamen clerks. The matter is touched on cautiously by Mann in note 56, where she suggests interestingly that the high tradition of learning represented by Huang Zongxi and his kind may have interacted with commonplace legal-clerk picky-ness so as to contribute to the old-fashioned moralistic tenor of the area.

The problem is that Hu Shi and Yao Mingda, while willing enough to criticize Zhang fairly, also obviously admired him, and I have sensed nothing in their attitude that would prepare me for their saying of him that he was a "shyster." The English word has an inescapable meaning, of a *characteristic* dishonesty. And there can be no question that Hu Shi knew this, and knew just what he was saying to *us*, if *shiye* just means "shyster." What, then, is going on? I seem not to have touched this in my book, though I did notice the phrase with surprise.

As Professor Mann notes, the Hu-Yao biography does not say that Zhang was a "Shaoxing shiye," exactly. What the authors do is to quote a few sentences from Zhang's essay "Fu Xue" ("studies for women"), one of the handful of his writings criticizing the poet Yuan Mei, proba- bly written in 1798, the year of Yuan's death. I paraphrase: In the pre- sent dynasty, music by female entertainers is banned from the Palace precincts, and the Office of Entertainment has been eliminated; and so improper contact between the sexes cannot get a foothold. As for the doings of singing girls and prostitutes, and panderers, these activi- ties are most severely forbidden by law. To be sure, such things exist, and officials regulate them; but this is merely a matter of coping with failings in conduct, and doesn't give them legal status. Even though a big fish may slip through the net, in the most serious cases the law still stands. So it is absurd for a *"junzi* who cherishes legal restraints" (*Lunyu* 4.11) to appeal to the letter of such lapses in the law. Zhang is implying that Yuan Mei is justifying his accepting female students of poetry on the specious (Zhang says) ground that the law recognizes a status for female entertainers. So the authors comment, "This is entire- ly the twisted talk (*kou-wu*) of a *Shaoxing shiye*," i.e., this is the sort of argument that a "Shaoxing shyster" might have used. The comment is a criticism, and an appropriate one, for Zhang's reasoning is both legalistic and tortured, and prejudice-driven. We may want to say that Zhang is self-deceived; but it is not implied that Zhang himself is dis- honest, or is here being dishonest, or is himself a "shyster."

Susan Mann in this paper puts a new kind of history before us, that enriches the historian's craft. Her concept of Zhang Xuecheng's "moral imagination" points to something of first importance that historians neglect: Men may have dominated the world of events on which historians focus; but the moral sensibilities and intuitions of justice that guide many (one hopes, most) of them are learned as children in a domestic world of women, their mothers, and mothers of their friends. (A matter stressed by Susan Okin, as P. J. Ivanhoe pointed out to me.) In her study of Zhang and the women he cared about, through his own words, she has shown an aspect of Zhang Xuecheng that we need to appreciate if we are to "understand him as a man," fully, as was my own aim.

6. Comment on Professor Yü Ying-shih, "Zhang Xuecheng Versus Dai Zhen: A Study in Intellectual Challenge and Response in Eighteenth-Century China."

Professor Yü Ying-shih's article examines the entire range of the relationship between Zhang Xuecheng and his older and already famous contemporary Dai Zhen. When they met in 1766, at Zhang's initiative, Zhang was under thirty, Dai over forty; when Dai died in 1777 Zhang, almost forty, was still to do his most important writing, over the next twenty-five years, writing that I have argued, and Yü has now shown more clearly, lets us see the still little known Zhang again and again confronting the problem of this older and famous man whom he both admired and resisted intellectually.

Professor Yü first, using material that I neglected or didn't have, lays bare the full story of their first encounter in Beijing. The important aspect of this is its effect on the younger "unknown" man. Zhang excitedly recognizes that Dai is really a philosopher, behind his admired public figure as a classical philologist, and he is encouraged: Dai is like himself, and no one else sees this. But Zhang is at the same time staggered by Dai's erudition, and shamed by his own recognition that he himself still lacks a solid base in learning. Gradually Zhang comes to see that where Dai's basis for understanding *li*, philosophical truth, is (with the earlier Gu Yanwu) the study of the Classics, his own is to be the study of history. But it will be a study of a very special kind,

which Zhang sometimes calls *wenshi*, literally "literature-history," sometimes *jiaochou,* which at first seems to mean to us simply dry library science, but really for Zhang is the historical analysis of the whole range
of all kinds of writing, closer to what we call intellectual history. Zhang
gradually persuades himself that this is a matter that Dai really didn't
understand at all, and that virtually no one really understands save
Zhang himself. Here Zhang finds his "basis," his *yong,* one might say,
thus justifying himself by both admiring and condemning the great
scholar of his age.

This enduring challenge-response relation Zhang has to Dai, living
and later dead, is what leads him to the formulation of his most
famous Big Idea: The Classics are History. A great deal has been written about what Zhang meant by this, as Zhang's philosophical stature
has gradually been recognized during the past century. (I myself have
said part of it; I think I would want people to read with special care
what I say on pp. 201–4 of my own book on Zhang.) In his article in
the present volume Professor Yü makes a persuasive case that, as he
says, "had it not been for Dai's challenge, almost surely Zhang would
not have formulated and argued his thesis in the way he actually does
in the *Wenshi Tongyi.*"

I will return to this matter. But first, I want to look at two
theses that Professor Yü argues in this exploration of Zhang's reaction
to Dai.

One is the theme that Dai's learning, and his scorn for people who
talk abstractly and speculatively without a basis in "real" learning, is
what first shaped Zhang's intellectual course: He would establish his
own basis in *jiaochou.* This leads Professor Yü to a discovery that excites
him: Early references in Zhang's writings to his work on *wenshi,* or on a
"Wenshi tongyi," are really references to his investigations and writing
that shortly, in 1779, became what we now have as the *Jiaochou tongyi.*
I.e., we err in supposing that Zhang was working on two books at the
same time; he was merely using two names for the same thing. The
writings that became the real "Wenshi tongyi" came later, Professor Yü
argues, beginning in 1783 and continuing to the last essay he wrote,
the "Intellectual Tradition of Eastern Zhejiang," in 1800. (And there
actually was a printed edition of this book in 1796, obviously without
the last item.)

The second thesis involves an admirable examination of what Zhang was trying to say in the "Zhejiang" essay, considered together with earlier writings such as his "Zhu and Lu" (perhaps 1777: I have thought that I find in the "Zhu Lu" echoes of themes, even phrases, from Dai's last book, *Mengzi ziyi shuzheng,* finished shortly before he died; see my "Two Kinds of Naturalism," for the Asilomar conference of 1977, to appear in Bryan Van Norden's collection of my papers). Yü picks apart the intellectual lines of "descent" that Zhang gives in these essays, showing that he is trying to argue in the earlier that Dai's own "ancestry" stems from Zhu Xi, though Dai didn't see this and disparaged Zhu; and that in the later Zhang is filling a vital gap in the argument by giving his own descent line as stemming from Lu Jiuyuan, by way of scholar-philosophers over centuries in Eastern Zhejiang. (Zhang himself respected both Zhu and Lu, Zhu's philosophical opponent, but thought of himself as adhering to the former.) Yü accepts my judgment that Zhang's identifying himself in an "Eastern Zhejiang tradition" was a "lifetime's afterthought" (as he has said earlier, in his invaluable book, *Lun Dai Zhen yu Zhang Xuecheng,* 1976, p. 56); but the argument here, coupled with Susan Mann's analysis, must persuade anyone that the matter cannot be left at that: Zhang was serious, had thought carefully, and had his reasons.

Further, this review of Zhang's review of the Neo-Confucian era shows again that Zhang saw what is surely right, that the Qing world of scholarship was not the sharp change from an earlier age of self-cultivationist moral philosophy that it is often thought to have been. Professor Yü has seen an "intellectualization," but not a discontinuity. I of course agree. In my first article in 1953 ("The Problem of Knowledge and Action in Chinese thought since Wang Yang-ming," in A. F. Wright, *Studies in Chinese Thought*), I—guided by Zhang, actually—saw the change as being from the Ming view, that the person who merely talks about moral concepts cannot be said to understand them unless he "realizes" them in his conduct, to a formally similar view, that talking ("emptily") about moral and other "principles" is unsatisfactory unless one demonstrates their "reality" through ("solid") scholarship, research into "actual facts." This is precisely the structure of Zhang's anxiety about his own lack of an adequate "basis," which was his first reaction to Dai Zhen and his impressive learning.

The corollary, it seems, is that the original root motivation of Qing "philology" was not empiricist at all; though as it got going and picked up speed, impressive and exciting discoveries were achieved, stimulating investigations of a kind all of us prize. The "search for evidence" became exactly that. And surely, no analysis of this intellectual turn in terms of the logical development of thought (my way of looking at it forty years ago) can be complete unless it includes the economic and institutional bases studied by Benjamin Elman and others, in particular the suppression of private academies that had been the nurseries of moral philosophy (and Ming political ferment), and the rising prominence of wealthy patrons of scholarship, government projects, and government academies, important in the careers of both Dai and Zhang.

But what shall I say about the *Jiaochou tongyi,* and Professor Yü's discovery that Zhang's early references to his work on a *wenshi tongyi* really are about the former book, which he finished in 1779? I am puzzled. Unless I committed some gross error (which is entirely possible), it still seems to me that the case stands as I saw it in my book in 1966. Zhang did complete a book of some sort in 1779. But here is what I said:

> The *Jiaochou tongyi* has an unusual history. It is likely from indications in Zhang's correspondence that the book had been developing in his mind and in his notes for half a dozen years. Many of its central ideas appear, even to the exact words, in his Hezhou history, in the long series of prefaces to the chapter on bibliography. Originally it had four chapters rather than the present three and was entitled "Jiaochou lüe" ("Summary on the Study of Books") after a chapter in Zheng Qiao's *Tong Zhi,* which Zhang much admired. The book, in its original form, was stolen, then partly reconstructed from other copies, and in 1788 completely revised. In that year Zhang asked his friends to return all existing partial copies—apparently he had given little thought to the book for almost a decade—and set about to restore a continuous text, only to find that his friends' copies often contradicted one another. Unable to reconcile these contradictions, he proceeded to edit freely, so that the final result was "quite different" from the varied originals. (*Life and Thought,* p. 57.)

The theft occurred in the summer of 1781, when Zhang was returning to Beijing from a half-year stay in Henan: He was waylaid by bandits, who took everything, even his clothes, and the manuscripts of all his previous writings—so that what survives from his earlier life are mostly occasional pieces such as biographical sketches and letters of the sort friends would have copies of. The last chapter of the *Jiaochou tongyi*, or whatever it was, had apparently been sent to no one.

As for the supposed 1796 first edition of the *Wenshi tongyi*, Zhang makes clear enough that it was merely a small (and now long lost) printing up—remember that printing was very much a "cottage industry"—of a selected few essays and letters, a sampling of Zhang's *oeuvre*, obviously designed to be used as bait for badly needed support. The real first edition of what we know as the *Wenshi tongyi* and *Jiaochou tongyi* is the Kaifeng edition of 1832, still only a fraction of his work, based on posthumous editing. It remains possible that he never intended the *Jiaochou tongyi* as more than a "wai-bian" component of his *wenshi tongyi*, which was to be everything; and that he saw it in 1788 as an earlier stage of his intellectual journey that turned out, when he got back to it, to be more or less salvageable.

Taking this view of the *Jiaochou tongyi* makes it less easy to see it simply as Zhang's *yong* (concrete application of principles)—the "solid scholarship" component of his *oeuvre* complementing the "philosophical" *Wenshi tongyi*. That role is at least shared not only by his enormous *Shi ji kao* (never completed and now lost) but also by his massive (and largely lost) work on local historiography, that continued through all stages of his life. The *Jiaochou tongyi*, at least the first part of it, we must see as a stage in his philosophical thinking.

This is at once what it looks like: At the very beginning is a short and packed three-part "Yuan Dao," which states in a nutshell the essential idea developed in the philosophically rich second *juan* of the present *Wenshi tongyi*, where we also find a much longer monograph-length "Yuan Dao." The first writing that emerged in human life was the anonymous product of the functional parts of the archaic political order, ruler, offices, and functionaries with their responsibilities, encompassing the whole of human society; always first a concrete need before something is written, writings gradually accumulating and used as needed by officials who were also teachers, training their successors and instructing the people. Eventually the Golden Bowl broke, the ancient state fell apart, the traditions of learning carried on in government offices floated free and became schools of learning and philosophy, genres of writing, carried on by "private" authors who wrote their own books, to establish their own fame, the long history of human vanity. This is the one Big Idea that Zhang drew out of Liu Xin, and transformed into intellectual history. (Whenever Zhang mentions Liu Xin, e.g. in his letter to Qian Dian in 1778, I think we must see this idea in his mind.)

And the Classics: What are they, in this scheme, this vision of Zhang's? Explaining *that* is the vision's function; and the explanation gives Zhang his *raison d'etre*. Dai Zhen, following Gu Yanwu, saw the Classics as *zai dao zhi shu*, books written by the "sages" that *tell* us what the "Way" is. The study of philosophical truth must, therefore, be the study of the Classics. To understand what the Classics are telling us, we must understand their language, technical terms, cultural detail. And to do this we need philologists like Dai Zhen. But this is not what the Classics are. The Classics are the residues of the accumulated writing and wisdom in the offices of the ancient state; they are, Zhang says, the anonymous "documents of the ancient kings." As such, they do not *tell* us what is true, but *show* us how the Dao, the "Way," gradually took form in human institutions: how it became embodied in the existential detail of human history. They are a synthesis of *dao* and *qi*. Only a historian—such as Zhang—can grasp this and *see* what they show us. The Classics are, then, metaphysically considered, history.

As a true "hedgehog," Zhang was fated to keep writing and re-writing this vision all his life—once it had hit him, at least as early as 1770 (though, of course, there was development). So, yes, Professor Yü is right: When we find Zhang in surviving letters prior to about 1780 mentioning *wenshi* and *jiaochou*, he *is* probably talking about what we have in the *jiaochou tongyi*, more or less. But perhaps one can *ask* the question "What book is he talking about?" only if one is not looking at what was going on in Zhang's developing thought, and simply reads back into his life the point of view of his posthumous publishers.

Professor Yü's careful research on the actual course of Zhang's and Dai's early encounters is illuminating and essential for a full understanding of the two men. While I have here suggested slightly different accounts of Zhang's published works, I fully agree with Professor Yü's characterization of Qing philosophical thought as an "intellectualization" of earlier trends. It is precisely this that enables us to see and appreciate Zhang and Dai as philosophers, and that structured their views of themselves and of each other.

7.   Comment on Henry Rosemont, "Beyond Post-Modernism"

Behind and informing this essay is a philosophical *and* political attitude pressed with the utmost sincerity, and with considerable passion. I think that I would be dishonoring its author if I were to pretend to ignore this, thus ducking the question whether I do or can share his point of view. To a very large extent I do share it; but without all of the passion; and in some matters of detail he sees me as more of an ally than I am. I proceed cautiously: Henry's essay is deep, and he may find my understanding not complete. He relates his argument to early work of mine that was important to me personally, and my discussion is going to be, deliberately, partly autobiographical.

The argument: There is something called "post-Modernist relativism" (Rorty and Derrida are mentioned herein; we are referred to Rosemont's other writings for a full list). And this relativism is very bad: It holds at least by implication that we cannot understand other persons in other times and cultures, and perhaps even other minds in other bodies (if minds are "in" bodies), because what humans are able to think is constrained by their culture or conceptual framework. This of course makes impossible our own *métier*—Rosemont's and mine—in arguing (sometimes with each other) about what the Chinese have thought in the past and think now; so guns must be spiked. This "post-modernism" seems to me to be a trendy idea dressed in new jargon, argued by people with short memories. (When I was much younger I got intoxicated by Benjamin Whorf, Karl Mannheim, and Ruth Benedict, to more or less the same effect; I got over it.)

Rosemont offers analysis: There are two relativistic claims he wishes to distinguish, analyze critically, and evaluate: First, the "cultural dependency claim," that people's basic beliefs, values, etc., are dependent on their times, culture, language. Second, the "impassible barriers claim," that people of diverse languages and cultures are separated by "incommensurable conceptual frameworks" that prevent them from understanding one another; at most they can believe falsely that they do so. Rosemont argues that these two claims are logically independent.

In the balance of his essay, he argues that these claims have contrary effects: The "cultural dependency claim" is at least potentially enlightening and liberating, because it opens our minds to the great diversity of the ways of being human, and so is a valuable counter to the cultural jingoism of the high imperialist stage of Western history. On the other hand, the "impassible barriers claim" is constricting and conservative, because at the extreme it licenses its believers in regarding "others" as so radically other as to be beyond the reach of our moral sensibilities, indeed hardly human. (One is reminded of the perfectly sincere debates carried on among the Spanish clergy as to whether the natives of "New Spain" they were enslaving and slaughtering were actually human beings.)

I sympathize with a lot of this, but I think Rosemont's analysis is flawed, sometimes trivially, at times not. Perhaps trivially, it is a mistake to say that the "impassible barriers claim" and the "domino effect" argument used during the Vietnam War are both empirical generalizations based on zero instances. The "domino effect" concept is a commonplace truth of intuitive dynamics, illustrated by phenomena as diverse as the spread of the Chinese tribute system, the "Medizing" of Greek cities on the approach of the hosts of Persia, the believed and therefore effective influence of the New Hampshire primary on the selection of presidential candidates, and for that matter, dominoes. The argument was whether the effect would be instantiated in Southeast Asia; so to demand an instance *of that* as proof would be to commit a category mistake. A single instance would have to be the result that *established* the prediction. On the other hand, the "impassible barriers claim," as Rosemont correctly points out, is a paradox in the strict sense, because to produce an instance and *show* it to be an instance would be to pierce the barrier and thus to *defeat* the claim. But, not so trivially, the indicated conclusion, it seems to me, is not that the claim is false *tout court*, but (disturbingly) that if it is true *or false* it must be logically impossible for us ever to know it to be true *or false*. So we may as well peddle along, hopefully. And humbly.

And why *not* humbly? It is not obvious to me that what occasions Henry's philosophical exasperation necessarily has any connection with what arouses his political-humanist indignation (which I share). Americans who failed to reflect that bereaved grandmothers in Baghdad must be weeping were not committing a philosophical fallacy leading them to dismiss the Iraqis as in effect non-human. They were, surely, simply failing to reflect, in their excitement over the demonstration of American military power. Chingis Khan, hearing sweet music in the wailing of women whose sons and husbands his armies had slaughtered, understood perfectly well what he was listening to. On the other hand, animal lovers are quite aware that the objects of their affection would have to cross an "impassible barrier" to have any inkling of the wonders of Shakespeare or Beethoven. The savagery that was part of the imperialist expansion of Europe might have been tempered (it sometimes *was* tempered) if conquerors (and "missionaries") had reflected that the peoples they were beating down might live in their own "worlds" of values beyond the reach of "our" understanding. To entertain *that* idea (even if it is wrong) seems to require rather than to preclude a boundary-transcending human sympathy. It is surely no accident that more typical objections to "post-modernist" relativism are by deep-dyed conservatives, complaining that the foundations of civilization (meaning Western Civilization) are being eroded by it.

It seems implausible that post-modern inhumanity can be blamed on post-modernist philosophers having committed a logical fallacy, thereafter inducing everyone to accept it. (For inhumanity comes all too easily to humankind, without any such philosophical help.) Surely Henry would agree, and perhaps would rather say that without our realizing it this fallacy has seeped into our thinking. But what could ever count against such a claim? If it isn't just obvious, as perhaps it is for Henry, one will look in vain for evidence that would clearly put it to the test. I am suspicious of claims like that.

And while I see Henry's logical point, that the two "claims" are logically distinct, it does seem to me that both are too vague to sustain this kind of analysis. If one is dependent on one's culture for the way one thinks, and if there is such a thing as a conceptual scheme, perhaps embedded in one's very language, surely the scheme and the language are parts of what we call the culture. If this is right, then it seems to follow that the "impassible barriers claim" is simply a logically irresponsible extreme form of the "cultural dependency claim." I would suppose that this is what some of the "relativists" Rosemont inveighs against intend, i.e., that for them the point of cultural dependency is to float the idea of impassible barriers.

To suggest this is to suggest, and I now draw near to Professor Rosemont again, that if we entertain the idea of cultural dependency sensibly—applying to it, with Professor Kanaya, the *zhong-yong* concept—we may find it to be an idea that has both validity and value. But notice that Rosemont speaks mainly of what I may be led to notice about *others,* by being aware of the ways in which *their* values and beliefs may be dependent on *their* culture, and of how I am going to be inclined to dehumanize others, if I teach myself that there are impenetrable fences around *their* thought-worlds. Surely someone like Derrida, telling me that everything must be "deconstructed," and then my deconstruction itself must be deconstructed, is telling me that I must point the finger back at myself: It is *I* who am culturally dependent, in such a way that anything that I come to think about the other's world is bound to be self-deception.

I agree with Rosemont that this won't do. But the challenge must be met head-on. The fallacy, it seems to me, is the idea that there is a completely describable pure given out there that I would just see, fully, if only my dirty bifocals didn't mess up my vision, as they inevitably must. But it is a philosophical commonplace that nothing in the real world is ever completely described; there is always something more that can be truly said about it—even another doctoral dissertation waiting to be written (don't despair, oh grad students). One does not need to lament with the Zhuangzi of the "Tianxia pian" that a person's limitations condemn that person to an incomplete grasp of the truth. The way to look at this matter of "dependency" is the other way around: It is just because I've *got* that pair of glasses that I can see at all. I, being the unique person that I am, have a point of view that may enable me alone to be the one who notices what I notice, discovers what I discover. And in due course it will be your turn. The task of our communicating our insights, weighing and adjudicating our findings, may well be frustratingly hard (so may be the task of writing a good dissertation); but to say that it is in principle impossible is precisely to commit the "impassible barriers" fallacy in an extreme form.

Let me try a perhaps entertaining example: When I was writing my book on Zhang Xuecheng, I was at that stage of academic life that involves, as part of the process of surviving, frequently writing project proposals addressed to some foundation or government agency, usually without success. Or one can find oneself expected to contribute ideas to a group effort of this kind. Just at this point, I was examining what Zhang was doing in 1787. In that year he obtained a letter of introduction to Bi Yuan, a wealthy high official:

> They met in 1787, when Bi was still governor of Henan. Zhang, armed with an introduction from Zhou Zhen-rong, visited Bi Yuan in Kaifeng and tried to enlist his support for an ambitious project, which Zhang had thought might interest Bi—a *Critique of Historical Writings (Shiji kao)*, a massive study of historical bibliography that would require the extended labors of a number of scholars. (*The Life and Thought of Chang Hsüeh-ch'eng*, p. 97)

Reading over the document that Zhang apparently presented to Bi at this time—"Essential Considerations in Compiling a Critique of Historical Writings" ("Lun Xiu Shiji Kao Yaolue"), I had a shock of recognition. There was I! An eighteenth-century Chinese "foundation pitch"! At once I reflected that something like this had occurred in 1772–1773. At that time Zhang's teacher Zhu Yun had submitted a memorial to the emperor with a proposal that was adopted, leading to the creation of a board of scholars to compile the famous *Siku Quanshu*. There is ample evidence in Zhang's writings at this time of his interest in this project, and of ideas of his like those the project embodied. Putting this together with accounts of gatherings of Zhu's students at Zhu's house, and with what I knew of the careers of others in the group, it became obvious to me that in part what Zhu was doing was pooling ideas, many of them Zhang's, into a proposal to the throne designed to create job opportunities for his students and friends. I began to notice Zhang involved in this kind of activity again and again—familiar to me, yet dressed in very Chinese Qianlong era clothing.

Surely there is nothing mysterious in this. Yet notice that what was happening was not that I was confined or misled by my own "culture," but that I was led to a better understanding by it. Caution, of course, is always needed.

But let me return with Professor Rosemont to the vicious kind of non-thinking that characterized attitudes at the onset of the "Cold War." The subject needs no analysis of post-modernist fallacies; it is more than rich enough as it is. Obviously most of the public was gripped by mindless fear, with politicians feeding it, telling their people what they wanted to hear. Henry has said very kind things about my article "Communist Ethics and Chinese Tradition," written near this time, as being in a quite different tone.

But I did not completely recognize myself in his account of what I was doing in that piece of writing. He would have me arguing "that although neither Confucianism nor Maoist communism were democratic in anything resembling the Western sense of the term, they nevertheless advanced similar moral principles which, when contextualized, were deserving of everyone's moral reflection." And that in so doing I was trying for a detached scholarly sympathy at a time when in general "the scholarly voices were very quiet." (But "scholarly voices" were not completely mute. It was not for nothing that John Fairbank was called before a Congressional committee, and had his travel plans "inconvenienced," as he generously wrote later.)

This praise of me may not be fully deserved. A few years later I was still disposed to write—accurately, I continue to think—that Neo-Confucian idealists of Song and Ming were yearning unrealistically for "a utopian totalitarianism, minus the trappings and sinews, the harsh reality, of power" (*Confucianism in Action*, p. 24). My attitude at the time toward both Maoism and Confucianism was rather hostile. I *was* trying in this article the experiment of looking at Mainland Communist *xuexi* pamphlets (called to my attention by my long-dead friend Mary Wright) analytically and reflectively, deliberately avoiding polemics. But I was less sympathetic than Henry Rosemont suggests. At that time I was fascinated and a bit frightened by the "totalitarian" implications I sensed in *Confucian* self-cultivation ethics; so my detecting Confucian-Maoist continuities was a *criticism* of both. I think the experience of working through the problem led me gradually to see more clearly that, granted the frightening aspects of "coercive persuasion," and the coercive enlistment of the individual's conscience in the process of that person's own "remolding," it still had to be admitted that one *can* have a *moral* responsibility for the shaping of one's own attitudes; and I sensed that contemporary moral philosophy shied away from this as being almost dishonest—as indeed I had.

There were several consequences: A few years later, I developed an undergraduate course on "Marxist Ethics," partly to educate myself on the European background. So I found myself exploring the "Paris Manuscripts" and other early works of Marx dealing with "alienation," on to Bernstein, Kautsky (fascinating but simple-minded), Trotsky ("Their Morals and Ours"), the "mechanist" vs. "dialectical materialist" controversy, the weird intricacies of "cadre" training, and so on. This led to friendships with Robert Tucker (too short; he was briefly at Stanford), and (enduring) with Sidney Hook. The intriguing problem was how Marxism, which seems to embody in extreme form the two "claims" Rosemont talks about, could engender a moral philosophy at all. Eventually I discontinued the course, realizing that I was never going to write anything more on the problem, and coming more and more to feel that the subject was, intellectually, hopelessly sterile.

The Cheshire cat's grin was the lingering realization that one must take seriously the idea, evident even in otherwise repellent Stalinism, that there is an inescapable voluntaristic aspect of our moral life: We are blameworthy if we think out our obligations wrongly; and we are also blameworthy if we try to reject responsibility for our moral dispositions. And if there is the possibility of blameworthiness, there has to be the possibility of doing something about it. So, a *person* is fascinatingly complex: We have dispositions, and dispositions about our dispositions. I can want to do something, and even do it, deliberately, while wanting not to want to do it. And while trying, meaningfully, to do something about the shape of my wanting. Confucian self-cultivation philosophy began to look more interesting, and along with it universal philosophical puzzles like weakness of will (which Bryan Van Norden fingers as my "favorite" topic) and its first cousin self-deception.

Questions like this were coming under scrutiny more and more by philosophers who often were, or were to become, acquaintances: Harry Frankfurt, whom I have merely heard and read; Donald Davidson, a long-time friend and mentor; Richard Jeffrey, once at Stanford; and (later) Michael Bratman and Herbert Fingarette. As I pursued later Confucian ethics in my teaching, the existence of suitable undergraduate texts (such as Wing-tsit Chan's translation of the *Chuanxi lu*) induced me to try a course on Wang Yangming. And around 1972, Henry Rosemont, then review editor for *Philosophy East and West,* asked me to do a review article on translations of the *Mencius.* By 1973, heading into a Guggenheim year partly at Oxford, working on "weakness of will" in Chinese philosophy, I readied a paper on that topic for the international Congress of Orientalists in Paris in July, and meanwhile tried to come to terms with Wang Yangming in a paper still dear to me, that I used around the country, also offering a study at the annual meeting of the Association for Asian Studies in Chicago, on "voluntarism" as a feature of the moral philosophies of Mozi and of Mencius. (All three, unpublished at this writing, will be included in a volume of my papers that Bryan Van Norden is editing, *The Ways of Confucianism* [forthcoming from Open Court].)

The Wang course was my first association with P. J. Ivanhoe, and in time led to our—mostly his—four-volume computer-generated *Stanford Chinese Concordance Series.* And I take this opportunity to thank Henry for asking for the *Mencius* review (and for his eight years of patience after having generously given me six months for it); for this task led me deep into that most rewarding of Chinese minds. Meanwhile another dimension of my work, teaching old Chinese, had led me into studies of ancient Chinese grammar, leading soon, with the help of David Keightley from 1971 on, to the study of archaic Shang oracle inscriptions; and from there (because Keightley himself had been working on the problem) to Shang antecedents to the concept of "virtue" (if that is what the word *de* means), with more papers and lectures.

In doing this I can see myself as having turned back to the beginning of the story I was trying to tell in the "Communist Ethics" essay. That paper, as I wrote it, I had conceived as a continuation of my first published article, "The Problem of 'Knowledge' and 'Action' in Chinese Thought since Wang Yang-ming"—quite naturally: the latter was my contribution to the first intimate conference of the "Committee on Chinese Thought" in Aspen, Colorado in 1952; and I had no sooner turned in the revised manuscript in the spring of 1953 (while finishing my dissertation on Zhang Xuecheng at Harvard) than I put this same manuscript to use to induce Walt Rostow of the MIT Center for International Studies to engage me to do a study of recent Chinese Communist thinking; the "knowledge-action" theme was the subject of one of Mao's essays that had been a starting point for much more writing on the Mainland. (A longer version of my later "Communist Ethics" resulted in 1954, which I also submitted to the second "Chinese Thought" conference organized by John Fairbank in Franconia, New Hampshire, *in absentia,* because by that time I was on my way to Kyoto as a Fulbright Fellow.)

The theme of these papers had been pressed upon me by Zhang Xuecheng's always visible unease about "empty words," a form of the common "knowledge-action" anxiety in later Neo-Confucianism, and a theme I came to see growing out of the ancient virtue paradox (virtue can be taught only to the student who is disposed to take the lesson to heart, this disposition being itself a criterion of virtue). The virtueless person knows what it is but evades the reality—content with an undeserved reputation; or protests lack of ability when what is lacking is resolve; or (the *xiang yuan*) pretends to wisdom without demonstrating it or really living it. (Much of this is nicely worked out by Tom Metzger, without benefit of my "knowledge and action" paper: he admitted to me in 1977 that he hadn't read me—while inscribing a copy of his book *Escape from Predicament* as a gift; this encourages me to think that we're both right.)

That was the beginning of much more work on the "virtue" problem, some of it soon to be published in Bryan Van Norden's collection. So my wayward "oracle-bone" adventures have been to a significant extent a coming home. My great regret is that I have been unable to share this with my friend and early mentor and protector Arthur Wright, who would have been fascinated. At a conference at Harvard in the summer of 1976 (organized by none other than Henry Rosemont, together with Benjamin Schwartz), where I offered a first long paper on *"de"* ("Can These Bones Live?"—which may not live), I was stunned when Ben Schwartz announced to us that Arthur had just dropped dead. I owe him much that I can never repay.

8.   Comment on Chad Hansen, *"Dao and Duty"*

Professor Hansen summarizes two broad alternative views of ethics in "Western" thinking: concentration on what one ought to *do* ("duty") if one is to do right; and concentration on what qualities one should have: what one should *be* ("virtue"), if one is to be moral. The former is exemplified by utilitarianism; the latter notably by current interest in Aristotle. Hansen asks whether there is something similar to this "dialectic" visible in the ancient Chinese scene, and he argues that there is, with telling differences: It is not accidental that the standard term for "morality" has come to be *dao-de: de,* commonly translated "virtue," does mean "virtue" but with a difference; and *dao,* not commonly translated "duty," is nonetheless the "counterpart" of "duty," in the Chinese balance. These ideas are worked out in the author's recent book *A Daoist Theory of Chinese Thought,* after a long development through books and articles over two decades. (For ideas conspicuous in the present paper, see p. 20 in that book, especially.)

Salient features of Hansen's position seen from this long *oeuvre* are these:

(1)   While decrying the view that Chinese philosophers exhibit a "special logic" requiring one to "think like a Chinese" in order to understand them, Hansen goes on to ascribe to Chinese thinking extraordinary "special" qualities: metaphysically it is "mereological," i.e., language consists of names, of wholes (quasi-stuffs), individuals being parts of those wholes (like Quine's "rabbit" *qua* part of the "rabbit-fusion"); accordingly reasoning is the relating of names to names; function-words become invisible and thus there is no clear concept of the sentence; and also (more startling) no concept corresponding to the Western concept of truth, since for us it is sentences that are true.

(2)   If philosophical language does not identify and state truths, it must be doing something else. Hansen argues that what it does is guide action. The word *dao,* "way," as a noun, is used to refer to a way things go or are done or should be done; and as a verb to indicate a *dao* in the noun sense (probably Hansen feels the verbal sense to be primary); i.e., it is used to guide action. Philosophies are *daos,* guides to action.

(3)   Since language is "action-guiding" rather than truth-stating, moral talk tends to lack auxiliaries like Chinese counterparts to our "ought to," etc. I assume that Hansen means that, e.g., one tends to say that "a son is filial," rather than that "a son ought to be filial."

(4)   As for the word *de,* it refers to the state of the hearer of a *dao* that orients that hearer to the satisfactory or smooth or skillful performance

of a *dao*-guiding, in a correct *dao*-as-way of acting. Accordingly Hansen finds that a better sense for *de* is "virtuosity." A "virtue" for him is like the developed skill of an athlete or musician. The connotation of "power" that some translators have felt in the word *de* is accounted for by the fact that if one has the appropriate virtuosity, one has a sense of effortless command over the desired result, be it some gymnastic feat or the knack of catching cicadas.

(5) We all have our leanings. As Hansen leans into Chinese philosophy, he favors Daoist ethics over other kinds, especially over Confucian kinds, and as he looks at the polyphony of Daoism, he sees one kind as quintessential (exemplified especially in the first verse of the *Daodejing*, he thinks), and he has his own idiosyncratic description for it: it takes *dao* as (action-guiding) *discourse;* it is meta-ethical; and it is skeptical. All characterizations of the real Daoism as "mystical" (a bad word for Hansen, connoting denial of reasoning) are mistaken; the "mystical" characterization of Daoism is a bum rap foisted on the Daoists by the Confucians, especially those of the Mencian stripe, who are the real mystics.

Most of this point of view is close to the surface in the present article, if not always explicit in it. It enables Hansen to say at the end that, yes, there is a "duty"–"virtue" pairing of concepts in old China, in a way, except that *dao,* as what we should do, is not quite "duty," and *de,* as what we should be, is not quite "virtue."

My perhaps over-long summary may make Chad Hansen uneasy, for he will sense that it is intended as criticism, not mere description. I have been trying to sharpen up what I think are the salient features of his thought, so as to present to myself as clearly as I can what I find that I can't accept, while at the same time trying to be fair. The great value, to myself, of having his essay in front of me is its boiling down the issues for definitive evaluation. I am grateful.

Let me begin with this "action-guiding" business. Other philosophers who speak of moral statements as "action-guiding" are saying that their *meaning* is such that one cannot "brush them off." If one really understands a statement saying that X is right, and if one accepts that statement, one will necessarily be moved to or toward doing X: one will choose to do X if one can. These are going to be the philosophers who think that "weakness of will" is impossible. The sentence "a scout ought to be loyal," accepted by a scout, will move him to be loyal.

But: In Hansen's analysis, the "action-guiding" aspect of old Chinese as conceived by its users is not part of the *semantics* of "ought" expressions, but is a matter of the *psychological impact* of any form of language, poetry, for example, or standardized technical terminology. Whether this difference in the sense of "action-guiding" makes a difference I am not sure; but in any case, it seems to me that neither sense, the semantic nor the psychological, is either necessary or sufficient as an explanation of the frequent use of the "a scout is loyal" or "a son is filial" type of expression, for such usage occurs in all languages.

Further, old Chinese, in its earliest examinable stage, has remarkably fine-grained resources for expressing and distinguishing modes of obligation. As Takashima has shown, in the oracle language of the late thirteenth century B.C. there is a rigid distinction between "controllable-action" and "non-controllable-action" verbs, marked, in a divination, by different negatives, the negation of the former being necessarily a test of the proposition "we ought not to do X": 勿 X," "*mjet* X." Moreover, in this language one seems to be able to distinguish, by the choice of a negative particle (as one cannot in English) between what R. M. Hare would call a "prescriptive" vs. a "descriptive" ought-not usage: "毋 X," "*mjeq* X," seems to mean "one is not to X," or "it is not allowed (by the spirits) that X." (For an oracle inscription example, see my response to Professor E. L. Shaughnessy.) This distinction perhaps even survives in the old Chinese of the *Lun yu:* Thus we will recall Confucius' "Golden Rule," "*ji suo bu yu wu* 勿 *shi yu ren,*" "What you do not wish for yourself, you should not do to others" (12.2, 15.24). But also, "*Zi jue si: wu yi, wu bi, wu qu, wu wo*" (9.4), where *wu* is 毋, and the sense is descriptive: "The Master had four prohibitions: do not merely guess, do not be too sure, do not be stubborn, do not be egotistical." Old Chinese is not obligation-idiom poor.

The *Guanzi* (13.36), "Xin shu" part I says, "*De* 德, 'virtue,' is the localization of *dao* 道, the 'Way'; it is what a thing gets *de* 得 [from *dao*] to come into existence." I would liken this to the relation between *xing,* the "nature" of a thing, and *tian,* "heaven," as expressed in the opening line of the *Zhongyong* and as implied in Mencius; but this relation is nonetheless Daoist, as in *Zhuangzi* 12 (paraphrasing): in the Great Beginning there was Non-being, from which came the One, from which things "get" that by which they come to be what they are.

Comparison with the *Laozi* enables us to identify this "non-being" as *Dao*. Appallingly, the mental-set of seeing inner essential "nature" as identical with a transcendent reality seems to be Daoism itself, and alive and well in China long before that land had acquired its Indian "stain."

Hansen will be led to say either that this isn't really Daoism, or isn't his kind of Daoism, or that its real (esoteric?) meaning is obtained only when we take *dao* as really "(action-guiding) discourse," the "input", *de* as the "programmed state" of a person who then, as dancer or athlete, is capable of an "output" which is the appropriate performance or *dao*-"way." One may be forgiven for feeling that Hansen systematically rids his position of the inconvenience of refutation conditions. (As well as, perhaps, reaches for a way to find ancient Chinese (namely, "Daoist") thinking to be philosophically healthy, as misguided Western thinking is not.) Be that as it may, given the texts available to Hansen's opponents (which I merely sample), and given Hansen's dazzling skill as a talker, I do not expect the argument to be settled soon, and will not try here to settle it myself.

But forgive me for looking, now, more closely at the core of his interpretation of *dao* and *de*. As *A Daoist Theory* makes clear, Hansen is claiming more than just to have tagged a Late Warring States concept; he is getting at a pervasive difference between a fundamental mode of Western thinking (Indian, Greek, Roman, and later) and all of Chinese thinking prior to its "contamination" by Buddhism from India: There was no mind-body dualism, and none of the thought-world that goes with it; only this *dao* = discourse, *de* = state = virtuosity, *dao* = performance business. I think I am justified in noting two things:

(1) The *de*-concept is here made parasitic on the *dao* concept; we must first understand *dao* as Hansen does, before we can understand *de*.

(2) The notion of *de* as "power" is purely and at most an overtone or derivative of *de* as "virtuosity." Hansen might accept Munro's concept of *de* as resulting from "imitation of models," of correct *li*, or of physical skill, with concomitant sensed subjective command over performance. But not the mysterious mana-like "inner power" that Waley for example talks about.

Why am I uneasy? For one thing, the term *de* with a recognizable religious or philosophical meaning is far older than the term *dao* with such a meaning. The oracle language does (I think) contain both "words" (but one wonders what a word is, if one must see its meaning as changing). Articles by Rao Zongyi and by myself have shown that already in the Shang language of the late Wu Ding era (ca. 1200 B.C.) there is a word written with a graph ancestral to the graph that represents the word *de* "virtue" in early Zhou and later. And its identity is hardly in doubt, for it occurs in fixed expressions that turn up in early literary material, such as *"jing de,"* "reverence [one's] virtue," *"nuo de,"* "[Heaven-]approved virtue," *"de xing,"* "fragrance of virtue," etc. Also, I have found what appears to be the idiom "A *you de yu* B," literally "person A has 'virtue' from person B" (is "virtued" by B), i.e., A has by some act earned B's gratitude, placing B under an obligation to favor A. This social "logic" of the gift relation (one recalls the researches of Mauss and Granet) appears to be the basis of the "virtue" that persons of prominence such as rulers, parents, and teachers are felt to have: the compulsion that the recipient B of a favor feels toward the giver A, to return the benefit in some way, gets to be perceived by B as a psychic power emanating from A, this power being A's *de*. Thus we can think of A's *de* as being essentially a generalized sort of "gratitude credit." As the "gift" drama proceeds, A enhances his or her *de* by declining the favor that is urged in return.

Accordingly, one important way in which a person acquires more *de* is by an act ostensibly in the public interest in which one displays noteworthy restraint or unselfishness. (Noteworthy: not necessarily conspicuous, as Confucius points out about Wu Tai Bo.) This is why a dynastic founder (or usurper) has to decline repeatedly the (usually carefully orchestrated) pleas of his followers that he take the throne, before finally yielding. The phenomenon is not unique to China; it is pan-human: George Washington, for example, was expected (especially abroad) to use his position as victor-general to make himself the head of the new nation, perhaps even king. Instead, he retired to private life; and it was probably only in this way that he acquired the prestige that enabled him later to function as the country's first president. Similarly, Senator Rudman has enhanced his political effectiveness by renouncing his Senate seat in order to devote himself to campaigning for Federal fiscal responsibility. *De* is both "virtue" (generosity, self-sacrifice) and power. Turning again to China, where the felt social force of a favor given, or restraint exercised, or sacrifice made, has always been especially strong (at all levels of society, and even in trivial transactions), note that *de* has an interesting military dimension: In 656 B.C., Duke Huan of Qi led the combined forces of Qi and his allies in a confrontation with the forces of Chu. (The date magnified the drama: it was four hundred years after King Wen had claimed the Mandate of Heaven, and three hundred years after the succession of King Mu, following the destruction of the Zhou armies and the death of King Zhao in his campaign against Chu.) As the story is told in the *Zuozhuan,* there is a parley: the Chu envoy voices defiance; if Huan uses his forces, the very mountains and rivers will be Chu's ramparts and moats; but if he seeks to prevail by using his *de*—i.e., holding his hand—then who could refuse his leadership? There is an accommodation, and Chu ritually acknowledges Zhou authority. I have argued that just this sort of maneuver—gaining prestige, awe, and compliance through dispaying (and risking) but holding back one's forces, is what is referred to in Wu Ding-era Shang inscriptions about the Shang king's going on a "*de*-campaign" *(de fa)* against this or that enemy border people. Again *de* is both "virtue" (in this case restraint) and power. (For another example, see my response to Professor Takashima, section 4.2.) Here there is indeed a similarity to the "mana" of the shaman (who gets his "power" through his ascetic mode of life and self-sacrificial practice and/or the austerities of initiation). But there is not a hint of "power" by way of "virtuosity." One does find such a connection in the sort of "skill" examples in *Zhuangzi* that Hansen probably has in mind: e.g., the cook whose knife never dulls, the marvelous craft of the maker of bell-stands, or the keen skill of the catcher of cicadas. Nor would I object that the word *de* does not actually occur in these accounts. There is another memorable story, however, in which the word does occur: the fighting cocks that are trained to utter perfection, so that "their *de* is complete." This is said of them only when they are as though carved out of wood, terrifyingly showing not the slightest sign of arousal or aggressiveness at the sight of their opponents. In this picture, precisely because "their *de* is complete" in this sense, there can be no hint of Hansen's "power" as efficaciousness in the exercise of a skill; but we do sense (read down into the animal world by Zhuangzi's humor) an echo of the *de* of the warrior. What about *dao?* Hansen needs *dao* in the sense of "discourse," or "showing the correct way," in order to generate the meaning he argues we should assign to *de,* i.e., enabling state (as of a computer). There is no doubt that the word *dao* eventually acquires the meanings "talk," "explain," "guide" (though in the last meaning the graph will often be distinguished by an added element: 導, suggesting that it is felt to be a different word). But let us see what the earliest discoverable examples look like.

The word probably is to be discerned in the oracle language, though only in a very few inscriptions. Here are two examples:

(1)   *Yibian* 3401, Shima 86.3 (*Heji* 6032z):

Jiaxu bu, Que zhen: Yi yihai wang tu shou, wang huo.

甲戌卜, 殼貞：翌乙亥王途首, 亡禍

(2)   *Yibian* 6419, Shima 86.3 (*Heji* 6037z):

Zhen: Yi gengshen wo fa; yi ri. Gengshen ming wu; wang lai tu shou, yu xiao.

貞：翌庚申我伐；易日。庚申明霧；王來途首, 雨小。

The graphs I here transcribe "tu shou" 途首 (using the apparent modern forms and sounds) probably should be read "chu dao" 除道 (using the same phonetic elements), "to perform a rite clearing the road ahead of evil influences." Thus (1) becomes "Crack on day *jiaxu* (11), Que divining: Next day *yihai* (12), the king will clear the way; there will be no misfortune." And (2) becomes, "Divining: On the next *gengshen* (57) day, we offer a beheaded victim; [the weather] will change to sunshine. [Verification:] On day *gengshen* (57) in the morning it was foggy; when the king came back from clearing the way, it rained a little." (The verification is actually the verification of the king's "crack-reading" on the reverse of the shell (*Heji* 6037b):

〔王〕固曰：易日；其明雨, 不其夜囗。

"[The king] read the cracks and said: [The weather] will change to sunshine; while it will rain in the morning, it will not [. . .] at night.")

In these examples *shou* "head" may be the etymonic root (rather than or as well as the phonetic) for the (later) graph *dao;* if so, the meaning may be not simply "way" but "route," or "the way one is head-ed." This would be consistent with the figurative sense the word acquires in philosophy: a *dao* is a "way" that (normally) can be traveled forward but not backward. But clearly, in this earliest identifiable use, *dao* is literally a "way" or "road."

The assumption that this is its primary meaning is also consistent with the earliest uses of the graph in the *Shangshu*. Of thirty-six occur-rences, only twelve are in pre-Han chapters. We find the senses (1) to guide rivers into their proper courses ("Yu Gong," four cases); (2) the way of the king ("Hong Fan" 24.14, four cases); (3) to confess [what they did]: said of criminals ("Kang Gao" 29.9); (4) correct policy ("Jun Shi" 36.6); (5) to declare [the way to be followed] ("Gu Ming" 42.24); (6) way followed ("Kang Wang zhi Gao" 43.5). Two of these do begin to suggest Hansen's "discourse," but there is no ground here for taking his meaning as the basic meaning of the word.

I hope that Professor Hansen will not want to reply that he was "doing philosophy," and that I am "doing philology," and am therefore simply talking past him. This is a distinction that I do not recognize: When a piece of philosophical analysis has philological implications, those implications must be heeded; and the exercise of doing this is part of the philosopher's job, if he does all of his job. This is part of what Zi Xia was trying to say, as I quote him in my response to Bryan Van Norden.

When all's said, however, I think Chad Hansen is right in seeing both "duty ethics" and "virtue ethics" as so to speak two recog-nizable wings of ancient Chinese moral philosophy. We can see this in philosophers' reflections that do not even mention *"dao"* and *"de."* I quote another ancient philosopher who is not one of Hansen's favorites:

> *Ren* (benevolence) is man's heart; *yi* (duty) is man's path. Sad indeed
> it is when one neglects one's path and fails to follow it, or loses one's
> heart and does not know enough to seek it. (*Mencius* 6A11)

We need no "computer" analogy to understand this. We under-stand it (whether we agree or not) because it is a natural way for us as human beings to think about ourselves and the lives we lead.

In responding vigorously to Professor Hansen's argument, I wish not to be misunderstood. Were he allowed a counter-response, the matter would appear far from one-sided, and the argument would go on. We, his friends, need his provocation, to force us to think more clearly. Without it, we would be like Zhuangzi after he lost his friend Huizi.

9. Critique of Donald Munro, "A Villain in the *Xunzi*"

Professor Munro argues that our habitual assessment of Xunzi, as the rival of Mencius who argued that "man's nature is evil," is a mistake: Not that he did not do this, but that "the *statement* that human nature is evil" is found only in the "Xing E" chapter; whereas "the *theme* of the imbalance of goods and desires" and its disordering effect on state and society is found throughout Xunzi's work. The incidental fact that later ages came to see Xunzi and Mencius as arch opponents on the issue of human nature has led us to miss the real Xunzi, who is best revealed not in his attack on Mencius but in his many attacks on Mozi, whose egalitarian asceticism and disparagement of rites would exacerbate the problem. So Mozi is Xunzi's "villain." Xunzi's solution to human ills is (1) to recognize that hierarchy is a feature of all nature, including human society; and (2) to teach men to desire only what is appropriate to their status. This will become increasingly clear, Munro suggests, as we take better into account the parts of Xunzi, such as the "Fu Guo" chapter, that are fully available now in John Knoblock's translation.

As for human nature, Munro notes that remarks and implications throughout the book add up to a very mixed picture: humans "have innately positive traits," even "an innate moral sense (*yi*)" ("Wang Zhi"); "they love the virtues of ritual propriety, duty, loyalty, trustworthiness" ("Qiang Guo"); and (right in the "Xing E") "they possess the endowment . . . that enables them to practice" virtue. Munro writes, "Had developing a theory of human nature been his interest, I doubt that Xunzi would have left it in such a mess." There, surely, is a one-liner that graduate students will be quoting in their orals for the next generation.

I find much of this very easy to agree with. But perhaps the profs will ask a few more questions; so let me try. It seems true that Xunzi did not write a book. The book got made later, by putting together things that he wrote over a long life of thought; and when he wrote the essay on human nature, he was making certain points, not wrapping the subject up. And it is true, I think, that even if he thought that humans begin without any explicit moral sensibilities, and are motivated only by nonmoral desires, and by seeing that to optimize satisfactions, one must adopt the Confucian "way" (Xunzi's position at the end of the "Zheng Ming"), one must still suppose him to be, at least implicitly, allowing that we are the sort of beings that can somehow come to apprehend a prudential "ought" as a *moral* "ought," and honor it as such.

Call this an "innately positive trait" if you like. *This* much has to be assumed by any analysis of morality that admits there is such a thing as morality to analyze. Can we go on, and see Xunzi in the "Wang Zhi" chapter's famous "ladder" as saying "that people are born with an innate moral sense (*yi*)"? Animals have *zhi*: "knowledge," but here apparently just "consciousness"; whereas humans also have *yi*, and thus are capable of "distinctions" (*fen*) of social status, and can form and live in social groups. We need not, here, think of Xunzi as talking about the structure of your nature and mine as individuals, more than what I have just granted he must be assuming. Human*kind* is like this: humans form themselves into societies, which come to be cemented by a unique kind of mental *artifact*, "rites and right," *li-yi*. It is important to see that this often-used expression in Xunzi means *li and yi*, with Knoblock and Dubs (and contra Watson's "ritual principles"). So we find Xunzi saying (in "Yi Bing," HY 54.15.21),

> The country of one who makes rites (*li*) splendid and honors right (*yi*) is well governed; the country of one who makes rites (*li*) mean and cheapens right (*yi*) is in disorder.

Xunzi constantly speaks of "*li yi*," unanalyzed, as created by the sages of old; we must therefore, take him as holding the same for *yi* considered *simpliciter*. In the "Wang Zhi" "ladder," *yi* for Xunzi is natural for man, in that it is consistent with the order of nature that man should come to have concepts of what is right, and in that the race of humans, unlike the race of horses, had sages who could work this out; but it is man-made, for all that. The position is difficult, and Xunzi tries to face the difficulty in "Xing E," perhaps not quite successfully.

At most we can say that for Xunzi man has innately an unfilled and undetermined capacity to think morally. Probably Xunzi would allow me to extend the paired definitions he gives near the beginning of the "Zheng Ming" chapter; e.g., *zhi*, "knowledge," means both the unfilled capacity to know, and (a second meaning) that capacity realized in our coming to know things. So too with *yi;* but in the second "filled" sense (just as, he would have to add, in the case of *zhi*) *yi* is not really *yi* unless it is filled in the right way (for Xunzi is not a relativist). But *yi* as sheer capacity can get filled in a wrong way, so that we end up doing wrong and thinking it to be right, as he says clearly at the beginning of the "Jie Bi" chapter.

I came to understand Xunzi better as I read Munro on the "theme" he sees Xunzi developing against Mozi—that man's desires are naturally unlimited and the supply of satisfactions limited; and so desires must be structured to conform to hierarchy if disorder is to be avoided. But I hesitate when asked to *contrast* this "theme" with the "statement" in the "Xing E" that "human nature is evil" (or whatever *e* is to mean). For statements *express* themes. Is it not better to see the "Xing E" as another *expression* of Xunzi's dominant theme, or a part of it?

I hesitate also when asked to see Mozi purely as "villain." Xunzi owes a lot to Mozi: his consequentialism, his severely rational approach to ethics, his stress on the importance of order, and hierarchy too, and his no-nonsense authoritarianism, epistemological and political. Indeed, also, his picture of humans as endlessly wanting and squabbling, unless harnessed in a structured political order.

He also receives from Mozi, as well as from Mencius, his most difficult problem, how through thinking consequentially we can come to be moral. Mozi "solved" the problem by, in effect, ascribing unbelievable powers to our rational will: we can simply choose to *be* moral, committedly, once we see it to be in our interest. Mencius sensed this wouldn't do, and posited a moral nature, that we can learn to recognize and cultivate. Xunzi saw this solution as undermining authority, as well as being hard to believe, but he had great difficulty in thinking out what to put in its place. Somehow it has to be that "*li* and *yi*" were made by the sages and are available to us only though education (and if necessary are enforced by judges and rulers); but how could the sages have made them (a vexing problem in "Xing E"), and how can we learn them in the right way? This is precisely what makes Xunzi fascinating, as David Wong's paper shows, and as all have sensed.

Nonetheless, Professor Munro's putting the finger on Mozi is right, it seems to me, in this sense: The fundamental problem, for ancient Chinese moralists, was not finding an "independent bottom" for ethics. That's *our* problem, due to our historical need, as modern ethical analysis has developed, to replace the surety of revelation. The problem engaging virtually every moralist of consequence in ancient China was how to put the world back together, to end violence, to make an ordered life possible. This was Mozi's problem too, indeed especially, and we should expect Xunzi to have looked at him carefully. But it is also true that Xunzi found Mozi's solutions dangerously wrong-headed. Munro's paper quite properly reminds us of that.

10.   Critique of David B. Wong, "Xunzi on Moral Motivation"

Professor Wong's argues that Xunzi and Hobbes are similar in constructing a political-social philosophy on the premise that human nature is inherently selfish. Human selfishness will lead to a condition in which all are insecure, in conflict and in want, unless a state comes into being, enforcing moral and legal rules of behavior on all, curbing otherwise untamed desires. Hobbes' program has the defect that his state is run by humans who are no more morally motivated than the rest of humanity, and being in control are not subject to control, and are therefore corruptible. In Xunzi's scheme, however, rulers and elite, at least (and ideally all members of society), are to be educated so as to love morality for its own sake. This would solve the problem that Hobbes neglects; but it leaves Xunzi with the problem of explaining how such a moral and political order could ever get started, and even if started, how education and sanctions could ever transform an essentially selfish people so that they become genuinely moral—so that, for example, in the extreme case of my being forced to choose between a moral course of action at the expense of life itself, and an immoral course that would bring me obvious material benefit, I would choose the moral course and give up life.

Wong searches Xunzi for hints of a solution. The solution cannot be that of Mencius (who directly addresses this problem in 6A10): For Xunzi, there is no core of "goodness" in human nature that can be nurtured into virtue. Virtue is necessary, but somehow it must be gotten to emerge through education out of non-virtue or worse; and even if we suppose that our teachers and rulers could do this for us, the problem remains how the moral and "ritual" order itself could ever have come into being. For Xunzi, "Heaven" is impersonal and uncaring, and cannot be supposed to have created morality or moral-tending dispositions in even the most outstanding individuals, the "sage-kings" at the beginning of the human story. The "sage-kings" created morality, seeing the need for it if human life is to be bearable. But this creation must have required them to make themselves moral, and it is hard to see how they could have done this if, as Xunzi insists, they had the same lamentable nature as the rest of us.

Wong in the end finds a solution in a creative reinterpretation of Xunzi, starting with an observation he finds in one of my own unpublished papers. In the "Wang Zhi" chapter, Xunzi says that "birds and beasts" have *zhi*, literally "knowledge," but here (in contrast to plant life) apparently the capacity for conscious intentional action; whereas "man" has more than this, having *yi*—Xunzi uses the same word that Mencius uses for an innate incipient sense of duty. But if Xunzi is consistent, and also says (in the "Xing E" chapter) that human nature is "bad," in the course of a drum-beat criticism of Mencius, then he must mean something else: perhaps, a bare capacity that enables men to form societies with hierarchical social distinctions and to apprehend an obligation as a *moral* obligation; yet a capacity that has no positive *content*. And since there is no content, a Mencian cannot say, "See! Xunzi admits a crucial element of goodness in human nature after all!" For it is obviously possible for this disposition to be filled out in a duty-like commitment to some *immoral* end (as Xunzi points out at the beginning of the "Jie Bi" chapter); thus Xunzi's *yi*, in the "Wang zhi" chapter, if not "bad" is in any case *non*moral.

As to the further question, how can this unfilled capacity to sense an obligation as a moral one come to be realized in me, or in a sage-king, as a genuine commitment to and love of morality, Wong has a suggestion that is the novel contribution of this essay. Xunzi's answer ought to be, and in effect is, that humans, especially in crisis points in life, have emotional needs that are best satisfied by what come to be conventional ritual practices. Most obvious are the rites of mourning, satisfying humans' love of their own deceased kind and kin (a tendency humans share with animals; they just have more of it). This tension-relieving function of rites is given greater impact by music; and man's capacity to be "transformed" in this way by music is also nonmoral in itself, for it can as easily lead to moral corruption and licentiousness. So the way is open for ancient surpassingly intelligent sages to have invented the "rites," which all (including the sages themselves) come in time to love; and this is the origin of morality and of our commitment to it.

I hope that Professor Wong will find my rephrasing of his thought acceptable. It is (I hope obviously) a sympathetic one. If I've got it right, his is not far from a suggestion that I made at the end of my inaugural lecture for the Evens-Wentz Professorship at Stanford in 1984, "Golden Rule Arguments in Chinese Philosophy." Acknowledging Herbert Fingarette, I said,

> *Li* (rite) involves countless gestures and acts that . . . serve as signals to you and invite response from you in such a way as to reassure both of us that you and I are "we"; and of course it serves this function effectively best when these acts are expected and "traditional." As such it is pre-moral . . .
>
> *Shu* ("reciprocity") was the articulation of the ideal attitude that should be expressed in this kind of behavior . . . The golden rule . . . is not an affirmation of one's particular mores, . . . neither is it the basic principle of morality. It is something more basic than this: It is the very ground of community, without which no morality could develop at all. It is the attitude that the other person is not just a physical object, or a (possibly hostile) animal, that I might use or manipulate, and that might shove back or bite, but a person like myself, whom I should treat accordingly even in trivial ways, thereby reassuring him or her and myself of our common humanity.

I could stop here, and Professor Wong and I after fine-tuning our analyses could find that we see Xunzi just about the same way. But

Xunzi himself is too interesting to let me neglect an opportunity to ponder him more carefully.

When one looks at Xunzi, there are various ways of taking the first step. Usually, in China, it has been to fix on his criticism of Mencius' conception of "human nature" as "good," obvious enough, when one reads the pounding administered in the "Xing E" chapter. But maybe taking "human nature is evil" simply as Xunzi's axiom is a point of view that really belongs to the later Confucian anti-Buddhist phase of Chinese thinking: The enemy was the threatening Buddhist conception of morality itself as illusion, and of a highest truth as trans-moral. The defense was the claim that morality is built into our very essence. And then there's Xunzi: embarrassing.

Or one can begin with the question how morality gets going: how one can reason one's way to there being some things that are really right or good, given where we seem to have to start, i.e., with some things that we just want, and then seeing that certain ways of acting are more or less useful for attaining what we want. The question can be split: In a natural world, how can we (and how did Xunzi, if he did) justify our intuition that some things and qualities are really good, and some ways really right. And how do we, obviously appetitive creatures (whatever else), come to have believed this: come to have traditional rules and standards, and come to appropriate them subjectively through education? How is our moral life possible, and what is its basis, if it has one? I think Xunzi did feel such teasing questions, and inevitably we do, as we read him. But the questions are suspiciously Western ones. Once we had answers given by religious revelation and dogma. We lost that, and moral philosophy struggles to fill the gap.

Now let's look at the problem that confronted one moralist after another in Eastern Zhou and Warring States China: Political and social anarchy were becoming more and more destructive. Historical memory reached back to a time (people thought, at least) when it wasn't so, when the world was one, life was ordered and livable. The problem: how to put the world back together again. Of course there were many answers (including the answer that the best thing to do is to leave things alone). But how must we expect the Magistrate of Lanling to have viewed the matter? All the old questions about Xunzi will reappear as we ask this, but not in the same order; and some not yet dwelt on will stand out.

It will seem reasonable that magistrates, etc., must be upright, and therefore "cultivated"; and dangerous not to admit that the run of mankind as one encounters them are a sorry lot. It was just as Mencius himself had put it: it is only the cultivated gentleman who is capable of moral constancy even if he lacks a "constant livelihood"; the ordinary person, driven by want, will stop at nothing. The thesis that "human nature is evil" now functions not as an axiom but as an explanation, and as a key as to how to go ahead with dealing with a practical problem. Part of the solution is that those in command must arrange things so as to make life possible for the mass of men and women. And part of the solution has to be that the masses must be got to obey, and to respect the rules. But the rules are not going to be respected just because they are rules; they must have a basis, and that must be respected; the authority of the rules rests on the authority of teachers and magistrates, which in turn rests on their teachers and magistrates, and ultimately on the authority of the "sage-kings" of old. So the unique authority of the sage kings of old, as the originators of the rules of civilized behavior, must be defended, by any acceptable philosophy. It will not do to allow the possibility that I, or you, or the next person, might reasonably claim to be as well qualified as a sage to originate "rites" and laws. This would be as dangerous as to license the (rhetorical) question "Why should I obey the law?"

But this, Xunzi thinks, is just what Mencius does, implicitly; for did he not say (M6A7) that the sages are like me in having the same "taste," the same kind of love, for "order and right"? They merely happened to be there first. So what is to prevent me now from claiming the sensibility that would enable me to play the sage myself? Why do we need sages? The solution seemed to be to deny that the sages had any moral sense denied the rest of us; we're all humans, and all ornery, essentially. What made the sages sages was their superior intelligence; and we all are aware enough that there are great differences in intelligence among human beings.

This move creates for Xunzi the problem of explaining how the sages could ever have lifted themselves (and the rest of us) off the "moral ground," so to speak. Professor Wong's solution seems to me to be a neat one: rites develop, non-moral at first, that appeal to us and comfort us in psychological crisis points in life. But notice that Xunzi's move does not really resolve the problem of the prior authority of the sages: Simply shifting from morally good nature to intelligence won't do, because I or you might reasonably claim to have the *intelligence* of a sage. Xunzi needs something else.

And I think—I'm not sure—that he has something else; but if he has, he doesn't talk about it as much as I would wish. In the "Xing E" chapter, about half way through, we have a challenge to Xunzi's position on the sages posed and answered:

> Someone may ask whether the accumulation of [the result of] conscious activity as to rites and norms, *li yi ji wei* 禮義積僞, is not [a part of] man's nature, so that for that reason the sage is capable of producing [them =] rites and norms. But I would answer that this is not so. A potter may mold clay and produce an earthen pot, but surely molding pots out of clay is not a part of the potter's human nature.

The meaning wanted for the word *wei* 僞 here is the second meaning given at the beginning of the "Zheng Ming" chapter; i.e., *wei*, "conscious activity" as "realized," cumulatively, over time. The hypothetical objector is asking why we may not say that even if a sage cannot be said to invent rites and norms *tout court* on the basis of a special "nature," can we not argue that the fact that the sages do it *over time,* gradually, but in the end *do* it, shows that the rites and norms come from something special in the sage's nature? But no, Xunzi insists: the making of a pot, too, is a process, and the potter must use material at hand, following or adapting a given process for a given purpose; the material, the process, the purpose, and the resulting pot were not "in" him.

The implication—and note that this is *not* part of what Xunzi is rejecting here—is that the "manufacture" of "rites and norms" *takes time.* One would suppose that just as it is with the potter, so it is with the sage: he must see a need, and then must mold simple rules, or make simple adjustments in existing rules. Conceivably this sage may not himself see the finished "product," or even have intended to "produce" it. Xunzi's easy use of this way of speaking shows, I would argue, that he does not need to have an "individual genius" concept of "sagehood"; the development of institutions under the fashioning hand of the sages may well take ages. And if that is the case, then the authority of the sages is secure, for obviously I cannot, now, step forward and say "I'm a sage, and I say we're now and henceforth going to do thus and so." For that just isn't the way it was done: respect for the sages is respect for the *accumulated* wisdom of the past.

So a would-be innovator is blocked, even if all humans, including both the sages and me, are alike: because while I might claim that I can do something if sage S could, I cannot claim that I can duplicate a creative *process* that may have taken innumerable piecemeal decisions over centuries by many "sages."

Several things now need to be noted:

(1) Xunzi did not get what he needed by shifting from moral "taste" to intelligence as the ingredient that makes a sage a sage. Whatever his needs to reject Mencius' doctrine of the goodness of human nature, his need to defend the unique authority of the sages is not one of these needs. Because to do that, he needed something else: namely, the notion of the creation of civilization—of "rites and norms"—as gradual and cumulative over historical time.

(2) Further, *this* defense of the authority of the sages works just as well even if one *grants* Mencius' doctrine of the goodness of all natures: Babbette's feast owed incalculably much to the nameless culinary sages of Medieval and Renaissance France and Italy. Similarly, the perfect moral cookbook is not something that I could hope to create *de novo* if the traditions of the past were to be erased. At most, I could only begin the process again.

(3) Although I find Xunzi in the "Xing E" using language that reveals this way of looking at the origin of "rites and norms," it is still, I think, the case that Xunzi never develops this idea of historical process as part of his philosophy. What he *says* is notably two things:

(a) In the "Xiu Shen" chapter, we read that in learning the rules of civilized life, to distinguish between what is valid and what is invalid one must rely on a qualified teacher; and recursively it follows that for all of us ultimately it is the sages who are our teachers. (Contrast the ultimate Mencian, Wang Yangming in the sixteenth century: "The thousand sages are all passing shadows; *liangzhi*—my own moral intuition—is my real teacher.")

(b) And in the "Fei Xiang" chapter he addresses the commonplace challenge of his time, that the "sages" are all different,
and so one cannot tell which one should be followed. This,
he says, is not true: It appears to be so only because of the
erosion of time. There was "good government" even in
remote ages when records are almost nonexistent. Therefore the answer to the question "which to follow" is the latest ones, the sages of early Zhou, when surviving institutional records are most complete (an argument already
suggested by Confucius). A "process" argument would have
led him to the same conclusion: we should follow the sages
who represent the culmination of the process of development of civilized order.

(4) Appearance to the contrary, Xunzi is *not* a relativist: Our customs
and ceremonials, laws, even "language" (in the sense of terms
used in formulated rules) may have been "made" by the sages;
but the authority of the sages would not be secure if Xunzi were
to grant even implicitly that the sages might have done these
things differently. What they did was in essence the only thing
they could do, to meet the needs of the human situation given by
the natural order of things, metaphorically by "heaven." This has
the implication that if we call the historically given civilized order
the "Way," we have to see this "Way" as an expression of an anteri-
or "Way" that is indescribable—since any description would be an
expression, in historical time. This is probably what Dong Zhongshu meant by saying that "the great source of *Dao* is Heaven," i.e.,
the explicit *Dao* of man has as its basis the implicit Dao of Heav-
en.

My final suggestion here is that Zhang Xuecheng, in the eighteenth century, is the one who in effect adds all of this up, notably in
his monograph-essay "Yuan Dao." Zhang is a "Mencian," in the mere
sense of accepting and using things he finds in Mencius as part of his
tradition, but without getting into the "human nature" tangle. He does
cite Dong Zhongshu, but doesn't do more than that with Dong. But he
doesn't appeal to Xunzi. Zhang just tries to think the whole thing out
for himself: In the beginning, "man had his *dao* in himself without

realizing it"; the most basic human needs in simple social groupings led to rules and customs, then to leaders who as needed made simple adjustments, which were the basis of further adjustments in later generations by their successors, without any of these "sages" who in this way were giving expression in growing historical institutions to the *Dao,* the "Way," ever consciously trying to invent anything. It was in this way that the "sages" created "rites and norms," and in this way that they and we came to accept them as right.

To go on with Professor Wong's fine suggestions for a creative interpretation of Xunzi, perhaps we should look again at Zhang Xuecheng. As I do this, the suggested comparisons are less obviously with the authoritarian Hobbes and more with the conservative traditionalist Edmund Burke—a point that P. J. Ivanhoe has made nicely in a forthcoming article on Xunzi. But if the authority of the sages and Classics is now shielded from radical challenge, all change cannot be blocked without a new logical difficulty: If the institutions of human civilization are the product of piecemeal human innovation over time, no step in the process can be supposed to be purely arbitrary, for it is ultimately the needs of the basic human situation that justified everything that the "ancient kings" did; they did what they had to do. So if Xunzi thought that the "Way" of the "sages" was final and perfect, he must suppose that this human situation does not really change over historical time, and is not altered even by the events of history. It seems to me that Xunzi did tend to think this; but others in his day, such as the Legalists and the Daoists, would have none of it; and even Confucius seems to be ambivalent on the matter. In later centuries this problem was to become more insistent, intensifying into a tension that would shape a civilization.

11. Comment on Bryan Van Norden, "What Should Western Philosophy Learn from Chinese Philosophy?"

Three years ago, nudged by the urging of my friend Admiral James B. Stockdale, I spent an evening with a small book long unopened. It was a fine copy, given me in 1942 by Laura E. Richards, a family friend in my home town Gardiner, Maine, of the works of Epictetus. Near the end of it (section LI of the *Enchiridion*), I found the following:

> The first and most necessary topic in philosophy is the practical appli-cation of principles, as, *We ought not to lie;* the second is that of demon-stration, as, *Why is it that we ought not to lie;* the third, that which gives strength and logical connection to the other two, as, *Why this is a demonstration.* For what is demonstration? What is a consequence; what a contradiction; what truth; what falsehood? The third point is then necessary on account of the second; and the second on account of the first. But the most necessary, and that whereon we ought to rest, is the first. But we do just the contrary. For we spend all our time on the third point, and employ all our diligence about that, and entirely neglect the first. Therefore, at the same time that we lie, we are very ready to show how it is demonstrated that lying is wrong.

(*The Works of Epictetus,* trans. Thomas Wentworth Higginson [New York, prefaces dated 1865 and 1890], 243.) It seems that the complaint against a philosophy that neglects how we ought to live is an ancient theme in *Western* philosophy. But this was not quite Epictetus' point: He grants that analysis has its value, but complains about a fixation on it that neglects what it is for. (I wrote to Henry Rosemont, 20 March 1991, quoting this text in my reflections on a talk he had given in Berkeley, with the comment, "I have long been fascinated with the problem of *akrasia,* but had never seen the matter looked at in quite this way.") Epictetus would have been pleased with Confucian ethics, which includes within itself the problem of self-change, of effective commitment to valued principles.

On the other hand, philosophy does not have to be explicitly *about* how we ought to live if it is to be effectively relevant to that project. Consider Zi Xia, a prominent disciple of Confucius:

> One who studies widely and with set purpose, who questions earnestly, then thinks for himself about what he has heard—such a one will inci-dentally achieve goodness. (*Lunyu* 19.6, in Arthur Wayley, *The Analects of Confucius* [New York: Random House, 1938], 225.)

Ren zai qi zhong, what is really valuable will be *there,* and you will obtain it, even if it is not the explicit object of what you may be searching for. Here is an ancient *Chinese* apparently saying something we do not expect: The important thing in philosophy (as in anything) is to take what you do absolutely seriously. If you do *that*, then the criticism that your philosophy is not explicitly directed toward what the critic deems important is out of place.

Zi Xia is right, and the increasingly familiar complaint against contemporary "Western" philosophers that they are not helping their students to "learn how to live" needs reflective reexamination.

Bryan Van Norden's essay opens with Bernard Williams' distinction between a "notional option" and a "real option," in ideas that can come to our attention in examining the thought of others. (How "other"? Is there a special difficulty for us in confronting Chinese philosophy, in contrast for example to Greek philosophy? Van Norden says in so many words that the difference is at most one of degree, not of kind.) A notional option is an idea we can understand, only to see that we cannot engage ourselves; too much of what it fits into just isn't ours. On the other hand, a real option is an idea one could adopt without losing one's "hold on reality," after careful and reasoned comparison. Confucius, I take it, has unintentionally offered us examples of each in the same breath:

> To sacrifice to a spirit that does not belong to one is flattery; to see what is right and not do it is lack of courage. (*Lunyu* 2.24)

Yong, the fortitude of the warrior; Confucius extends two familiar notions to contexts meant to be a little surprising. In the latter case we get it; in the former, *we* just blink.

Van Norden goes on to distinguish three possible views of what value Chinese philosophy might have: (1) None, for the person who thinks Western philosophy is "triumphant," so that any idea in Chinese philosophy either duplicates something the West already has, or is wrong. (2) Some, for the person who thinks Western philosophers have at least some problems they could use some help with, perhaps from the Chinese if the Chinese are not utterly different from us. And (3) salvation, for the person who thinks that Western philosophy is utterly wrong-headed, and that the Chinese have just what we need. The last ("radical") view he ascribes to Hall and Ames, and (the "West has failed" part of it) to such as Derrida and Rorty. The middle ("moderate") view is Van Norden's, and is said to be mine, and Yearley's. Van

Norden concludes that we *could* use some help: "contemporary philosophy" has "to a great extent abdicated answering" the question that
has in the past guided much of Western philosophy and has always
been foremost in Chinese philosophy: How can we live better lives?

I am delighted to find myself in such good company. But do I
deserve this commendation? After all, there are many who would
describe me first of all as an intellectual historian (perhaps not quite
accurately); and they would be likely to be persons who think that any
kind of historian ought to try not to let his own values color his
description and analysis. In a very large part of my work, I think I have
taken this ideal for granted. What I have gradually come to see is that a
historian cannot do everything; he must select his projects. And he is
morally responsible for the choices he makes as to how he will spend
his time; for we all have this responsibility for everything we do. Two of
the things he must always consider are, (a) what he himself is best able
to do; and (b) the intrinsic importance of what he attends to. I think
that I have also gradually come to see, especially as I came to be working among philosophers, that as I study the enormous range of detail
in the history of Chinese philosophy, what Williams and Van Norden
call the "real options" are likely to be the most worthwhile things to
look at; and further, that when one does this one simply is not doing
the whole job if one does not also do it *critically*. This is what I like
about Zi Xia's maxim: you have to be absolutely serious.

But this does *not* mean that we should be always anxiously looking
for what advice the Chinese can give us as to how we should "live our
lives," surely not if we always take this to mean how we should live our
personal lives, important though this may be. Just as important is how
we should live our social, economic, and political lives; or our lives as
scholars: how we should choose our projects and frame our investigations. And when we ask these questions, it may not be what the Chinese have said that is useful, but what they reveal, perhaps without
intending to, and perhaps without getting it right.

Van Norden suggests (correctly I think) that contemporary philosophy is notably enamored with "paradoxes," and (perhaps not correctly) that this is characteristic of what is supposed to ail us. I have felt
this fascination, and I think it is indeed a mark of our century. Further,
while I am intrigued and pleased with how following this trail has led,

e.g., to the proof of the surprising fact that no axiomatized system of arithmetic can be both consistent and complete, I will grant that it is not immediately obvious how this insight helps me or anyone to live a better life. But wait: Let's look again at that ancient chestnut, "All Cretans are liars," said by a Cretan. As one mulls over this, sooner or later it will occur to one that there can be *forms* of the paradox that are stated not in the indicative mood but in the imperative. ("Disregard all my orders!") Karl Popper, seeing this, is led to his incisive (and surely not irrelevant) criticisms of concepts of political sovereignty, all of them, including democracy, as being ultimately paradoxical, in a sense that could be fatal.

I myself, bitten by this bug, look at ancient Chinese so-called "Legalist" philosophers, and find them saying in effect, to their ruler-advisees, "Be suspicious of all advice." It then becomes less surprising that the most prominent of them is in the end drawn and quartered, and the most memorable literary image of one of them ends up with both feet cut off. The flip side of this puzzle is the completely "virtuous" figure who adopts a stance of utter selfless loyalty, to the death if it so be, thereby attaining a moral stature of independence: the Duke of Zhou is the paradigm. (The tale of his offering himself in place of his brother and king is fiction; but some ideas in a civilization are so central that they cannot be trusted to mere historical chance for their enactment.) In an early paper I tried to show, accurately, I think, that Liu Shaoqi cast himself in the same mold.

This is only one of the "paradoxes of virtue": what of the moral teacher who tries to show her student how to live a better life? He understands her, and sees that she is offering him a "real option"; but it's one thing to see, and another to be moved. Or is it? Wang Yang-ming thought not. Confucius (and perhaps Mencius) did not know how to deal with the student who to the end just said "I can't." Mozi seemed to think that it was enough to show that a moral way of life is in one's interest; Xunzi at least noticed that even if approval necessarily leads to action, it need not be moral action, without quite a bit of work; whereas Mencius "solves" the problem by supposing that the seeds of moral-making motivation are in all of us. Bryan Van Norden, reviewing this tangle, notices that the seemingly profound, and basic, difference between Mencius and Xunzi on "human nature" can be resolved into a still deeper difference in their almost unstated concepts of *agency*. His argument is one of the most impressive demonstrations I have seen, of what we can learn from Chinese philosophy by approaching it in Zi Xia's way. What we get, if we are serious, is a deeper grasp of humanity.

And we need it: for we are human ourselves.

12. Comment on P. J. Ivanhoe's paper, "'Existentialism' in the School of Wang Yangming"

Starbuck hesitates. In horror at the thought that forces itself into his mind, he stands outside Ahab's cabin. There is a rack of muskets on the wall, loaded. Ahab had once actually threatened him with one of them. Starbuck takes it in his hand, checks the load. He could, really could, do it. The Law is half a world away; this mad captain on his mad course will in effect murder the entire crew. If he acts, Starbuck will see his wife again, his son; if he does not . . .

He doesn't, and we realize that he has told himself he cannot, he the law-abiding first mate. Perhaps we should say that he "chooses" the lesser anxiety, but anxiety can't be escaped. He knows he was free to choose, really, frighteningly, free. He cannot escape responsibility for his action or inaction.

P. J. Ivanhoe presents a reexamination of my own tortured attempt in 1972 to assess uses of the word "existentialist" to describe aspects of the thought of Wang Yangming and his "left school" disciples. And in doing this, Ivanhoe gives us a far more careful and nuanced analysis of Kierkegaard than was within my own reach. I had tried to look especially at the concept of existential anxiety. Did we find something like this in Wang? Yes, there are moments of a kind of agonizing, when Wang reflects on how crazy "normal" people must think him. But the basis is different. Ultimately Wang is *sure:* it is he who really knows what it is to be human. At the time, I was much influenced by Frederick Olafson's *Principles and Persons* (he had been a visitor at Stanford, and we had become friends).

What Ivanhoe does is to focus on the psychic experience of Wang's students, at the beginning of their remaking of themselves, pointing out that to get them started on the quest for sagehood Wang has to put such stress on sheer will power—the "task" is to "create something out of *nothing*"—that his students sweat with fright at their own sensed helplessness. *They,* under Wang's touch, feel themselves to have no adequate inner resource to fall back on, in seeking what they desperately want. Deliberately engendered anxiety, to serve the teacher's purpose, but (we feel) anxiety nonetheless. Ivanhoe makes an important point, and makes it well.

But, of course, there is a difference. The psychic content of distress felt by the disciples may look like *angst.* But they are trying to do something they feel and fear they *can't* do, or might do wrong; and it is not something we ordinarily think of as *act* at all, but taking an impossible boot-strapping step in *thought.* They are not looking at something, perhaps shocking, that they could *do,* thinking about it, appalled by their own sensed *freedom* to *do* the thing. For that perspective requires a perception of thought and act as radically distinct. Even though a true-blue existentialist ("Do what you are." "Essence is existence.") may bridle at my sticking this to him (her?). One can hardly suffer (savor?) *angst* before the Act without being, even if simultaneously, both actor and spectator.

And it is just here that we must see how utterly different Wang's thought-world is. Over and over he stresses that thought and act are *not* separate: They are a seamless whole, thought being incipient action. In this Wang grasps the real point and implication of the philosophy of self-cultivation that had been evolving in China for millennia: self-change must focus on the ultimate springs of action in dispositions the student will need help in noticing, and if the self-monitoring and self-correcting isn't done right disaster may be the end result.

Consider, if you will, two mountain climbers. I myself am not a mountain climber, unless the mountain is carefully selected and safe: I have climbed Mt. Fuji, with its simple switch-back trail studded with "stations," and Mt. Tai, with its ancient stone steps beset with shrines, and I shall not try another. I want for my example two daring types, risking real danger. One of them, George, stands on a perilous craig, a sheer cliff beneath him. He takes the wind, excitement rising in his blood. He looks. So far down! Yes, he could do it! Rowena would weep, if not for long. An attention-catching if perhaps not glorious end to a life otherwise unmarked. Absurd, yes; but what isn't? *He* would have *done* it! Giddy with this realization of his terrifying freedom, he steps back involuntarily, lest his very excitement pitch him into the abyss . . . George, the existentialist (and the child of nineteenth-century romanticism).

Contrast Rowena herself, carefully and painstakingly picking her way up a treacherous scree-strewn trail hugging the face of the steep mountainside. (Why? To improve her skill? To get to the longed-for top? To enact, in the climbing, a metaphor for accomplishment?) She half-slips on a loose stone, catches herself, looks down, gasps in horror, recovers. With sheer will power she sets her mind and attention grimly to the Task, inches forward, "like a cat watching a mouse." One misstep could . . . Watch out! Rowena is the candidate-Sage, pursuing the life of unceasing *gongfu*.

Is my point valid? Here are two experimental objections:

(1) Anxiety is anxiety. The existentialist's hocus-pocus of saying it in German does not make it anything else. There are of course different *causes* of anxiety, just as there are different *causes* of death. But what gets caused is in the end the same. To argue the contrary—that there are "anxieties" of different tones or kinds, each "internally related" to its own particular matrix, would be like arguing—as one commentator to *Mencius* in fact did—that there are "whites" of different kinds: Is the white of white feathers like the white of white snow, and the white of white snow like the white of white jade? So asked the Philosopher of his rival Gaozi, thinking to trap him. One *might* answer, no: there *is* a dry fluffy white, and a wet sticky white, etc. But (it will be objected) this is sophistry; white is white, and anxiety is anxiety. Wang Yangming did have ways of making his beginning students desperately anxious.

But the tone of the sophist is harder to hear in Rowena, who insists that the tense worry she feels as she watches a thunder storm building—with all else she has to contend with on that mountain side—is after all utterly different, and perhaps indeed insignificant, compared with what she went through when she finally decided to send George packing. *That* changed her life; and sometimes, as one poet said, death itself is less than change. And in making such a life-changing, life-shaping, self-shaping decision, one is, it seems, as radically free to choose as one is radically bound to the full responsibility for the consequences. It was not for nothing that Marjorie Grene characterized existentialism as "dreadful freedom." Show us, if you can, in Wang Yangming anything like what Ivanhoe deftly describes as "forging a self by tracing a trajectory of authentic decisions." Rowena is not doing *that* on that mountain.

(2)   So what I am demanding, if Wang is to be seen as having an existentialist *nioi,* is something typical of his way of thinking that involves anxiety about making a radically important life-shaping decision. Something like the tension experienced (as I put it once) by "the mod new-leftist throwing his first rock." In a philosopher who "assimilates decision to perception" (again as I put it once)—in the kind of life that he means to teach us to live—this requires looking (Ivanhoe's instinct is true here) at the *beginning* of the Wang experience. But perhaps just looking at the way Wang reduces a group of neophytes to a state of desperate "sweating" is not looking back quite far enough to see what is going on, even there. True enough, those students do seem just to be anxious about whether they *can* in the end do what Wang demands—pursue the road of self-watching that leads to "sagehood." But let us look again at the description Wang has given of his own experience. On reflection he is sure that he is right, and the reflection may have been immediate. But in his committing himself to a life of moral teaching, synonymous (for him) with a "determination to become a sage" himself, he at the same time knows that he is marking himself as "insane" in the eyes of all "gentlemen" whom normal persons seek to be approved by, deliberately stepping outside the mold that the ubiquitous weight of social approval presses upon him. *That* part of the experience, even if his reflective philosophy at once brings comfort, does seem "authentic" in the existential sense.

Now, the students: We can suppose that just to become a student of such a master, not just experimentally but really committing oneself, required just that resolve to step out of line, to cut oneself completely loose from all social pressures that pushed one, even sub-consciously, to weigh personal advantage at every social turn—to be, if so it must be, "insane." "You must make up your minds," Wang tells them. "But

we *want* to make up our minds," they plead; "we don't know how."
Wang replies, "If there is the least trace of selfishness in your thinking,
this is not yet the 'mind to become a sage'." Wang implies, You *say* you
can't; but the real trouble is that you have not yet *really* committed
yourselves. The students' distress, as they half sense this implication,
does begin to look more like *angst.*

Commitment has another shape in Wang Yangming. We are tempted to see his *liangzhi,* "pure knowing," as Ivanhoe says as a kind of
"God within." Wang says that "pure knowing, rather than the 'sages' of
old, is his real teacher. He and his students write poems about it that
have the tone of religious hymns. The adept, by purging the "obscura-
tions" of selfish thoughts in himself, is to let this inner light shine,
learn to recognize it, to trust it, and to have the courage to act on it.

And it can't be resolved into rules: Wang's ethics is unflinchingly
situational. Often-used paradigms are the stories of ancient sages acting contrary to standing rules of conduct: Shun marrying without
informing his parents; Wu Wang attacking Shang before completing
mourning for his dead father. They just *knew* that in their situations
their actions were right. We smile at this, because we do not live in a
moral (and legal) world dominated, as Wang's was, by filial obligation.
But if Wang means what he says, he is telling his students that what is
in effect the voice of God may well command something that normal
morality explicitly forbids, and that this voice must be obeyed.

The examples are not bloody ones: we do not have a father hearing
a Command to apply the sacrificial knife to his own son. Further, one
must agree with De Bary that it is impossible to see Wang himself imag-
ining that the Inner Voice honestly heeded would ever dictate doing
something immoral, or even something radically morally novel.
Nonetheless, the logical shape of his teaching cannot fail to suggest
the lesson that Kierkegaard drew from the story of Abraham: the really
good person is the "knight of faith," in Wang's case, faith in *liangzhi.*
Wang himself may have been reassured by the reflection, suggestive of
Mencius, that "the minds of all people are the same as mine." But a
student must sometimes have been troubled. Here too, then, is the
possibility of recognizable existential anxiety. At some times, and for
some persons, at least.

There is a traditional story that resembles the story of Abraham more closely (developed by Robert Lifton in his book *Thought Reform and the Psychology of Totalism*): A destitute couple have a little boy, and must also support the aged mother of one of them. If they stretch their means this far, they face starvation. They reason, "We can have another son, but we will never have another mother." So they decide to do away with the boy and commence to dig his grave (first, fortunately). Not far down, they strike a hard object, which turns out to be a pot of gold, even bearing an inscription with their names, praising their filial piety. But of course, in this story there is at least a principle (other than sheer faith) being honored, whatever we may think of it; so I suppose Kierkegaard would dismiss it as uninteresting.

PUBLISHED WORKS OF DAVID S. NIVISON

BOOKS:

1. *Confucianism in Action.* David S. Nivison and Arthur F. Wright, eds. Reprint, Stanford: Stanford University Press, 1959.
2. *The Life and Thought of Chang Hsüeh-ch'eng (1738–1801).* Stanford: Stanford University Press, 1966.
3. *The Stanford Chinese Concordance Series.* Editor and co-compiler. San Francisco and Taipei: The Chinese Materials Center, 1979.
4. *The Ways of Confucianism: Investigations in Chinese Philosophy.* Bryan W. Van Norden, ed. La Salle, Ill.: Open Court. (Papers by Nivison on Chinese philosophical problems; expected 1996).

ARTICLES:

1. "The Problem of 'Knowledge' and 'Action' in Chinese Thought since Wang Yang-ming." In Arthur F. Wright, ed., *Studies in Chinese Thought,* Chicago: University of Chicago Press, 1953.
2. "The Philosophy of Chang Hsüeh-ch'eng." Kansai Asiatic Society, *Occasional Papers* III (Kyoto, August 1955). To appear in *The Ways of Confucianism.* See above, *Books,* #4.
3. "Bukkyo ni taisuru Sho Gakusei no Taido" ("Chang Hsüeh-ch'eng's Attitude toward Buddhism"). *Indogaku Bukkyogaku Kenkyū* 4, no. 2 (30 March 1956).
4. "Communist Ethics and Chinese Tradition." *The Journal of Asian Studies* 16, no. 1 (November 1956). Partial reprint in Ralph C. Croisier, ed., *China's Cultural Legacy and Communism.* New York: Praeger Publishers, 1970. Full reprint in John A. Harrison, ed., *China: Enduring Scholarship Selected from the Far Eastern Quarterly—The Journal of Asian Studies, 1941–1979.* Tucson: The University of Arizona Press, 1972. A longer version of this article was published as a project monograph by The Center for International Studies, Massachusetts Institute of Technology, 1954.
5. "Chinese Philosophy for the Undergraduate." Arthur F. Wright in collaboration with David S. Nivison. In H. G. Creel, ed., *Conference*

on Chinese Civilization in Liberal Education. Chicago: University of Chicago Press, 1958.

6. "Protest Against Conventions and Conventions of Protest." In Arthur F. Wright, ed., *The Confucian Persuasion.* Stanford, 1960. Partially reprinted in Johanna M. Menzel, ed., *The Chinese Civil Service: Career Open to Talent?* Boston: D. C. Heath, 1963, under the title "The Criteria of Excellence." Reprinted in full in Arthur F. Wright ed., *Confucianism and Chinese Civilization.* Stanford: Stanford University Press, 1964.

7. "Does It Matter How Annandale Went Out?" *Colby Library Quarterly* 5, no. 8 (December 1960). Reprinted in Richard Cary, ed., *Appreciation of Edwin Arlington Robinson,* Waterville, Maine: Colby College Press, 1969.

8. "Aspects of Traditional Chinese Biography." *The Journal of Asian Studies* 21, no. 4 (August 1962).

9. "Ho-shen and His Accusers: Ideology and Political Behavior in the Eighteenth Century." In David S. Nivison and Arthur F. Wright, eds., *Confucianism in Action.* Reprint, Stanford: Stanford University Press, 1959.

10. Introduction to *Confucianism in Action,* ed. David S. Nivison and Arthur F. Wright. Reprint, Stanford: Stanford University Press, 1969.

11. "Moral Decision in Wang Yang-ming: The problem of Chinese 'existentialism'," *Philosophy East and West* 23, nos. 1–2 (1973). To appear in *The Ways of Confucianism.* See above, *Books,* #4.

12. "The Pronominal Use of the Verb *Yu* (*GIUG: 出, 入, 有, 有)* in Early Archaic Chinese." *Early China* 3 (1977).

13. "Royal 'Virtue' in Shang Oracle Inscriptions." *Early China* 4 (1978–1979).

14. "Reply to Professor Takashima." *Early China* 4 (1978–1979).

15. "Mencius and Motivation." *Journal of the American Academy of Religion* 47, no. 3, Thematic Issue S (September 1979).

16. "Two Roots or One?" *Proceedings and Addresses of the American Philosophical Association* 53, no. 6 (August 1980). To appear in *The Ways of Confucianism.* See above, *Books,* #4.

17. "Western Chou History Reconstructed from Bronze Inscriptions." In George Kuwuyama, ed., *The Great Bronze Age of China: A Symposium.* Seattle, 1983.

18. "The Dates of Western Chou." *Harvard Journal of Asiatic Studies* 43, no. 2 (December 1983).

19. "Was 1040 the Date of the Chou Conquest?" (research note). *Early China* 8 (1984).

20. Formal addresses of greeting and closing at the opening of the Fourth Annual Conference of the Chinese Paleography Society (in Chinese). *Guwenzi yanjiu* 9 (1984).

21. "*Guoyu* 'Wu Wang fa Yin' tian xiang bian wei" ("A Study of the forged description of the heavens 'when King Wu attacked Yin' in the *Records of the States*"). *Guwenzi yanjiu* (October 1985).

22. "Chinese Philosophy." In Mircea Eliade, editor-in-chief, *Encyclopedia of Religion*. New York: The Macmillan Publishing Company, 1987.

23. "Chang Hsüeh-ch'eng." In *Encyclopedia of Religion*, vol. 3. New York: The Macmillan Publishing Company, 1987.

24. "Hsin." In *Encyclopedia of Religion*, vol. 6. New York: The Macmillan Publishing Company, 1987.

25. "Jen and Yi." In *Encyclopedia of Religion*, vol. 7, New York: The Macmillan Publishing Company, 1987.

26. "Li." In *Encyclopedia of Religion*, vol. 8. New York: The Macmillan Publishing Company, 1987.

27. "Meng Tzu." In *Encyclopedia of Religion*, vol. 9. New York: The Macmillan Publishing Company, 1987.

28. "Tao and Te." In *Encyclopedia of Religion*, vol. 14. New York: The Macmillan Publishing Company, 1987.

29. "The 'Question' Question." *Early China* 14 (1989).

30. "Forum" response to Qiu Xigui. *Early China* 14 (1989).

31. "The Origin of the Chinese Lunar Lodge System." In A. F. Aveni, ed., *World Archeoastronomy*. Cambridge University Press, 1989.

32. "Astronomical Evidence for the Bamboo Annals' Chronicle of Early Xia," with Kevin D. Pang. Early China Forum, *Early China* 15 (1990).

33. "Response: David S. Nivison," Early China Forum, *Early China* 15 (1990).

34. "Hsun Tzu and Chuang Tzu." In Henry Rosemont, Jr., *Chinese Texts and Philosophical Contexts: Essays Dedicated to Angus C. Graham*. La Salle, Ill.: Open Court, 1991.

35. Memoir on John K. Fairbank as "Teacher and Mentor." In P. Cohen and M. Goldman, compilers, *Fairbank Remembered*, 73–76. Cambridge: The John K. Fairbank Center for East Asian Research, 1992.

36. "The *Bamboo Annals* (*Zhushujinian*)." In M. Loewe and E. L. Shaughnessy, eds., *Handbook on Early Chinese Texts of the Zhou and Han Periods*. Berkeley: Institute for East Asian Studies, University of California, 1993.
37. "A New Interpretation of the 'Shao Gao'," *Early China* 20 (1996).

REVIEWS AND REVIEW ARTICLES:

1. Henri Maspero. *Melanges Posthumes sur les Religions et l'Histoire de la Chine*. *The Far Eastern Quarterly* 11 (1952).
2. H. G. Creel. *Chinese Thought: from Confucius to Mao Tse-tung*. *The Far Eastern Quarterly* 14 (1955).
3. Liu Wu-chi. *A Short History of Confucian Philosophy*. *The Far Eastern Quarterly* 15 (1956).
4. O. Briere, S. J. *Fifty Years of Chinese Philosophy, 1898–1950*. Trans. Lawrence G. Thompson. *The Journal of Asian Studies* 20 (1960).
5. Liang Ch'i-ch'ao. *Intellectual Trends in the Ch'ing Period*. Trans. Immanual C. Y. Hsu. *The Journal of Asian Studies* 20 (1960).
6. Wolfgang Franke. *The Reform and Abolition of the Traditional Chinese Examination System*. *The Journal of Asian Studies* 21 (1961).
7. Wing-tsit Chan, trans. *Instructions for Practical Living and Other Neo-Confucian Writings by Wang Yang-ming;* and Frederick G. Henke, trans. *The Philosophy of Wang Yang-ming. Journal of the American Oriental Society* 84 (1964).
8. D. C. Lau, trans. *Lao Tzu: Tao Te Ching*. *Bulletin of the School of Oriental and African Studies* 28 (1965).
9. Wm. Theodore deBary, ed. *Self and Society in Ming Thought*. *American Historical Review* (October 1971).
10. "On Translating Mencius." *Philosophy East and West* 30, no. 1 (1980). A survey of translations of the *Mencius*. To appear in *The Ways of Confucianism*. See above, *Books*, #4.
11. "Emperor of Chinese Studies." Review article on John K. Fairbank, *Chinabound: A Fifty-year Memoir*. *The New York Review of Books* 29, no. 8 (13 May 1982).
12. Wm. Theodore deBary. *Neo-Confucian Orthodoxy and the Learning of the Mind and Heart*. New York: Columbia University Press, 1983.
13. Benjamin I. Schwartz. *The World of Thought in Ancient China*. *Philosophy East and West* 38, no. 4 (October 1988).

FORTHCOMING:

1. "Philosophical Voluntarism in Fourth-Century (B.C.) China," (1973). To appear in *The Ways of Confucianism*. See above, *Books*, #4.
2. "The Philosophy of Wang Yangming," (1973). To appear in *The Ways of Confucianism*. See above, *Books*, #4.
3. "Weakness of Will in Ancient Chinese Philosophy," (1973). To appear in *The Ways of Confucianism*. See above, *Books*, #4.
4. "Problems in the *Mencius:* 6A1-5," (1975). To appear in *The Ways of Confucianism*. See above, *Books*, #4.
5. "Problems in the *Mencius:* 7A17," (1975). To appear in *The Ways of Confucianism*. See above, *Books*, #4.
6. "Motivation and Moral Action in Mencius," (1975–1976). A longer version of "Mencius and Motivation." (See above, *Articles*, #15). To appear in *The Ways of Confucianism*. See above, *Books*, #4.
7. "Hsun Tzu on Human Nature," (1976). To appear in *The Ways of Confucianism*. See above, *Books*, #4.
8. "Two Kinds of Naturalism—Tai Chen and Chang Hsüeh-ch'eng," (1977). To appear in *The Ways of Confucianism*. See above, *Books*, #4.
9. "The Grammar and Theology of the Shang King's Crack-Reading," (1978). To appear in a planned collection *Studies on the Three Dynasties*.
10. "Shang Oracle Inscriptions Concerning Illness," (1978). To appear in *Studies on the Three Dynasties*.
11. "Was the Shang King a Shamen?" (1978). To appear in *Studies on the Three Dynasties*.
12. "Chugoku ni okeru Kodai 'Toku' no Kannen" ("The Concept of 'virtue' in China in Antiquity"), (1979). To appear in *Kokotsugaku*. English version to appear in *Studies on the Three Dynasties*.
13. "The 'He *zun*' Inscription and the Beginning of Zhou," (1980). To appear in *Studies on the Three Dynasties*.
14. "Virtue' in Bone and Bronze," (1980). To appear in *The Ways of Confucianism*. See above, *Books*, #4.
15. "The Paradox of Virtue," (1980). To appear in *The Ways of Confucianism*. See above, *Books*, #4.
16. "Can Virtue be Self-Taught?" (1980). To appear in *The Ways of Confucianism*. See above, *Books*, #4.

17. "The Genealogical Inscriptions in the British Museum and Library," (1982). A supplement to "The 'Question' Question." (See above, *Articles*, #30). To appear in *Studies on the Three Dynasties*.
18. "The Date of the Brundage Rhinoceros," (1983). To appear in *Studies on the Three Dynasties*.
19. "The King and the Bird," (1984). To appear in *Studies on the Three Dynasties*.
20. "Golden Rule Arguments in Chinese Philosophy," (1984). To appear in *The Ways of Confucianism*. See above, *Books*, #4.
21. "The Chinese Lunar Lodge System: Chinese Origins and Mesoamerican Parallels," (1985). To appear in *Studies on the Three Dynasties*.
22. "The Hampers of Zeng," (1985). To appear in *Studies on the Three Dynasties*.
23. "A New Examination of Inscription #2416, in *Xiaotun Yinxu wenzi*, 'Jiabian'," (1987). To appear in *Studies on the Three Dynasties*.
24. "Di Yi, Di Xin and the Late Shang Ritual Calendar," (1987). To appear in *Studies on the Three Dynasties*.
25. "An Analysis of the *Bamboo Annals*," (1988). To appear in *Studies on the Three Dynasties*.
26. "A Tell-Tale Mistake in the *Lushi chunqiu*," (1989). To appear in *Studies on the Three Dynasties*.
27. "The Authenticity of the 'Mao Kung *ting*' Inscription," (1989). To appear in a symposium volume honoring the retirement of Noel Barnard.
28. "A Chronology of China to the End of Xia," (1990). To appear in *Studies on the Three Dynasties*.
29. "The Origin of Liu Xin's *chao-chen* Rule for the Jupiter Cycle," (1991). To appear in *Studies on the Three Dynasties*.
30. "Standard Time," (1991). To appear in a volume of papers on problems in the philosophy of science, being edited by Professor Nancy Cartwright, University of London, forthcoming.
31. "Qingming Day, 1040 B.C.," (1991). To appear in *Studies on the Three Dynasties*.
32. "Notes on 'Notes': A Response to Professor Serruys," (1991). To appear in *Studies on the Three Dynasties*.

33. "So-called 'Modal *Qi*' in Old Chinese," (1992). To appear in *Studies on the Three Dynasties*.

34. "The Chinese Callippic Cycle and the *Guoyu* Astrological Text for the Zhou Conquest," (1992). To appear in *Studies on the Three Dynasties*.

35. "Names into Dates: An Explanation of the *gan*-Names of the Shang Kings," (1993). To appear in *Studies on the Three Dynasties*.

36. "Kong Jia of Xia, 1577–1569 BC," (1994). To appear in *Studies on the Three Dynasties*.

37. "The Classical Philosophical Texts." To be chapter 9 of the forthcoming *Cambridge History of Ancient China*. Michael Loewe and E. L. Shaughnessy, eds. Cambridge: Cambridge University Press.

38. "*Te* ('virtue')." *Encyclopedia of Chinese Philosophy*. Antonio S. Cua, ed. New York: Garland Publishing, Inc.

39. "*Chung* and *Shu*." *Encyclopedia of Chinese Philosophy*. Antonio S. Cua, ed. New York: Garland Publishing, Inc.

40. "Chang Hsüeh-ch'eng." *Encyclopedia of Chinese Philosophy*. Antonio S. Cua, ed. New York: Garland Publishing, Inc.

41. "Chinese Philosophy of History." *Encyclopedia of Chinese Philosophy*. Antonio S. Cua, ed. New York: Garland Publishing, Inc.

INDEX

Abraham (biblical), 257–59, 340
absolutism, 159–60
American Pragmatists, 231
Ames, Roger T., 234, 235
The Analects, 83, 86, 87, 89, 90
Anscombe, G. E. M., 236
Anyang, excavation pit at, 62, 64
Aquinas, Thomas, 224, 237
Aristotle, 85, 173, 174, 231, 237
aspectual character, of a verb
    Chinese progressive, 11
    classical Chinese, 11
    English progressive, 11
    English prospective, 12
    grammaticalized, 11
    lexicalized, 11
Austroasiatic language family, 45, 52

Ba Shu script, 53
Bamboo Annals, 279, 280, 281, 286, 287,
    288, 289
Ban Gu, 132, 136, 140
Ban Zhao, 104
Becker, Lawrence, 218
Beethoven, Ludwig van, 162
belief systems, non-Western, 167, 168
Benedict, Ruth, 303
Berlin, Isaiah, 126
Bi Yuan, 137, 138
black pottery culture. *See* China,
    prehistoric: Longshan pottery
    culture
The Book of Changes (Classic of
    Changes), 87, 125, 128
Book of Documents, (Shangshu), 12, 21,
    22, 196

Book of Odes, (the Odes) (Shijing), 21–22,
    46, 49, 196.
Book of Rites (Record of Rites) (Liji), 43,
    88, 108
bronze inscriptions, 22–23, 279, 282
Burke, Edmund, 331

Canon of Dao De, 175, 186
Cartesian tradition, 159. *See also*
    Descartes.
Castañeda, Hector-Neri, 231
Chan(nists), 253, 254, 256
Chang, K. C. *See* Chang Kwang-chih.
Chang Kwang-chih (K. C. Chang), 40,
    277
Chang Tsung-tung
    on *qi*, 17–18, 19
Chen Mengjia, 268, 269
Chen Xiang, 278
Cheng-Zhu School, 253, 256
Chiang K'ai-shek, 161
China, historic
    cultural uniformity of, 39, 40
    isolation of, 40
China, prehistoric
    and archaeological discoveries, 39,
        41, 278, 279
    and Austroasiatic language family, 45,
        52, 53
    bronze age, 53, 54
    diversity of, 39, 40
    eastern, 40, 41–42, 52, 53
        as "Confucian," 41, 54
        as source of Chinese writing, 42
    east-west division of, 40–43, 52
    Hua, as name, 42

and language, spoken, 42, 45
and language, written, 42, 52, 53–54
Longshan pottery culture of, 40, 41
and Tibeto-Burman language family,
　52
traditional picture of, 39
transition of, into history, 54
and Vietnamese language, 45, 52, 53
western, 40, 41, 42
　as source of Chinese spoken
　　language, 42
　as source of Chinese written
　　language, 52, 53–54
Yangshao pottery culture of, 40, 41,
　52
Chinese Buddhism, 253
Chinese dynasties
Eastern Zhou, 278, 326
Han, 40, 45, 281
　intellectual tradition of, 83, 141,
　　142, 146, 149, 150
Ming
　Confucianism of, 253, 308
Qin, 45
　calendar of, 281
　intellectual tradition of, 83
Qing
　intellectual tradition of, 122,
　　127–29, 131, 138–39, 141, 145,
　　146, 148–50, 279, 300, 302–3
Shang, 39, 42, 50, 53, 143, 148, 316
　calendar of, 59, 60, 283
　dating of, 282
　enemies of, 44
　in history, 280
　and human sacrifice, 48
　King Wu Ding (see Wu Ding)
　kings of, 287–88
　military campaign, reconstruction
　　of, 58–72
　and mourning calendar-gap, 288
　oracle bone inscriptions (see oracle
　　bone inscriptions, Shang)

royal house of, 48, 49
　script of, 53
　and surname Zi, 49, 51
　and the Yi, 42, 44, 48
Song, 96, 278
　intellectual tradition of, 146, 148,
　　149, 150, 308
　and surname Zi, 51
Western Zhou
　and bronze inscriptions, 22–23, 58
　calendars of, 70
　and mourning calendar-gap, 288
Xia, 42, 48, 50, 143, 148
　dating of, 282
　founding of, 39
　rulers of, 279, 280, 281
Zhou, 42, 48, 53, 98, 132, 143, 316
　clan exogamy in, 50
　enemies of, 44
　and *fuyong* states, 46–47
　in history, 39
　marriage politics in, 47, 49, 50–51
　and mourning calendar-gap, 288
　oracle bones in, 267
　surnames, system of, 50–51
Chinese language, characteristics of, 314
Chinese language roots
　and Austroasiatic language family, 45,
　　52, 53
　spoken, 42, 45
　and Tibeto-Burman language family,
　　52, 53
　and Vietnamese, 45, 52, 53
　written, 42, 45, 48, 52, 53–54
Chinese periods
　Chunqiu, 43, 50, 51
　　and genealogies, creation of, 51
　Spring and Autumn, 42, 43, 44
　Warring States, 43, 53, 88, 98, 286,
　　315, 326
Chinese states
　Jin, 47, 49
　Little Zhu(lü) (Ni), 43, 50, 51

Lu, 43, 46, 47, 48, 50, 54
    as home of Confucius, 43
Qi, 46, 47, 49, 90
Zhou, 91
Zhu(lǔ) (Zou), 43, 44, 46, 47, 51, 54
    as home of Mencius, 43
    marriage politics in, 49
    political status of, 46–48
    sinicization of, 47, 49, 54
Ching, Julia, 256
Chomsky, Noam, 14
Chuanxilu, 254–55
Chunqiu. See Spring and Autumn Annals
Communism (ists), 161
Comrie, Bernard, 11, 12, 276
Confucianism, Confucians, 51, 126,
        143, 144, 146–49, 161, 187, 230,
        238, 253, 260, 308, 309, 326, 332
    Cheng-Zhu school, 128
    on the concept of *ren* (humanity), 181
    and Dai Zhen, 124, 125, 127, 139, 149
    and the *Dao (dao)*, 126–28, 135, 139,
        140, 142, 175, 180, 186 (*see also*
        Confucius: and the *Dao* [*dao*])
        of discourse, 182, 184
        of performance, 182
    dao wenxue, 128, 129, 150
    and family roles, 104, 110
    and interpretation of code, 182
    and *li* (ritual), 110, 227 (*see also*
        Confucius: and the *li*)
    Lu-Wang school, 128
    and the Mean, 83, 91 (*see also*
        Confucius: and the Mean)
    and Mohism, disagreement between,
        180–81, 237
    and philology, 121, 126–29, 136, 137,
        139
    transformation of, into monistic
        philosophy, 83
    transition of, to intellectualism,
        128–29, 131
    and virtue, 181, 236, 237

    and Xunzi, 193, 204
    and Zhang Xuecheng, 122, 126, 135,
        140–42, 144, 146–51
    zun dexing, 128, 129, 150
Confucius (Kongzi), 43, 90, 139, 143,
        185, 234, 236, 255, 316, 331, 333,
        335
    and the *Dao (dao)*, 139, 178 (*see also*
        Confucianism: and the *Dao*
        [*dao*])
        of discourse, 179
        linguistic, 179
        of performance, 181
    on interpretation
    and the *li*, 178, 181 (*see also*
        Confucianism: and *li*)
    on the Mean, 85, 86–87, 292 (*see also*
        Confucianism: and the Mean)
    personality of, 86–87
Conversations of the States. See Guoyu
Creel, Herrlee G., 46
Cua, Antonio, 212

Dai Zhen, 236, 302
    and the *Dao*, 141, 142, 143, 147
    as methodological individualist, 131
    as philologist, 121, 123–25, 127, 129,
        130, 135, 136, 137, 139, 141, 149,
        302
    as philosopher, 123, 124, 125, 127
    Yuan Shan, 123, 125
    and Zhang Xuecheng
        influence on, 122, 131, 137, 143,
        299
        differences between, 121, 129–31,
        135, 139, 144–45
Dalai Lama, 163
dao. See the Dao
the *Dao (dao)* (the Way), 184, 186, 189,
        315, 317, 330
    and Confucianism, 126–28, 135, 139,
        150, 178–79
    and Dai Zhen, 141, 142, 147

of discourse, 177, 179, 181, 182, 184,
186–88
linguistic, 179
and Mencius, 139, 185
and Mozi, 179–81
of performance, 177, 181, 182,
184–88
and the Six Classics, 139, 141, 142
as a term, early use of, 318–19
and Xunzi, 199, 203
and Zhang Xuechang, 140, 141, 142,
147, 149, 150
dao-de (Dao-de), 175, 177, 189, 312
dao-ethics
as duty ethics, 174, 188, 312
and *de*, relation between, 176–77
and discourse *dao*, 177
and performance *dao*, 177
Daoism (ists), 175, 180, 181, 185,
186–89, 205, 227, 237, 314–15,
331
as moral skepticism, 186–87, 189
and Xunzi, 205–6
and Zhuangzi, 193, 205
de, as virtue, 174–75, 183, 187, 204, 312,
315–17. *See also* virtue ethics
and *dao*, relation between, 176–77,
184, 188, 314–16
De Bary, Theodore, 251, 252
Derrida, Jacques, 158, 231, 239, 306
Descartes, René, 225. *See also* Cartesian
tradition
Meditations, 161
Dong Zhongshu, 330
Dong Zuobin, 284
duty ethics. *See also dao*-ethics
in Chinese thought, 174, 184, 188, 189
in Western thought, 173–74
Du Yu, 46
Duan Yucai, 139

Eastern Chekiang School. *See* Eastern
Zhejiang tradition

Eastern Zhejiang tradition (Eastern
Chekiang School), 143–45,
146–49, 151, 294
Egerød, Søren, 268
Elman, Benjamin, 300
the Enlightenment, 162, 165
Eno, Robert, 230
Epictetus
the *Enchiridion*, 331–32
existentialism
in Kierkegaard, 254, 257–59
in Wang Ji and Wang Yangming,
250–52, 254–57

Fairbank, John, 308
Fang Bao, 196, 295
Feng Youlan, 83, 214, 215
Fingarette, Herbert, 227, 237, 325
Four Books (Classic of the Four Books),
97, 125
Freud, Sigmund, 219
Fu Sheng, 142
Fu Sinian, 40, 41, 42
fuyong states, 46–47

Gaofeng Yuanmiao
The Essentials of Chan, 256
Gaozi, 236
Gauthier, David, 204
Gong Zizhen, 127, 128
Gongyangzhuan, 43
Graham, Angus C., 11, 188, 212–13,
215, 235, 237–38
Disputers of the Tao, 224
Grene, Marjorie, 338
Gu Yanwu, 103, 105, 129, 139, 144, 146,
147, 148, 149, 302
Guan Xiechu, 268, 269
Guliangzhuan, 43
Guoyu (Conversations of the States), 44, 51,
90, 91

Hall, David L., 234, 235

Han Yu, 140
Hansen, Chad, 229–30, 237
    on Chinese language as action-
        guiding, 312–13, 314
    on Daoism and *dao*, 313, 315, 317
    A Daoist Theory of Chinese Thought,
        230, 312, 315
    Nivison's response to, 311–19
Hare, R. M., 284, 314
Harman, Gilbert, 237
harmony, nature of, 88–91
He Shen, 155
Hegelianism, 159
Heidegger, Martin, 231
Heraclitus, 239
Ho Ping-ti, 40, 44
    The Cradle of the East, 40
Hobbes, Thomas, 203–5, 206, 232, 331
Hong Liangji, 138
Hsu Chin-hsiung, 70, 71
Hu Shi, 95, 109, 122, 296
Huang Zongxi, 105, 145, 146, 147, 296
Huber, Elizabeth, 41
Hume, David, 208, 281
the Hundred Schools, 194

Ivanhoe, Philip J., 297, 310
    Nivison's response to, 336–41
    on Xunzi, 210–11, 331

Jacoby, Annalee
    Thunder Out of China, 161
Jia Kui, 140, 142

Kanaya Osamu, 195, 306
    Nivison's response to, 289–92
Kant, Immanuel, 174, 208, 209, 225
Kantian deontology, 173
Keightley, David, 41, 268, 269, 276, 282,
        283, 310
    on origins of Chinese civilization,
        41–42, 52, 278
    on *qi*, 5, 7, 15, 16

Sources of Shang History, 282, 286
Kierkegaard, Søren, 251, 254, 257–60,
        340–41
Knoblock, John
    *Xunzi: A Translation and Study of the
        Complete Works*, 194
Kong Anguo, 142
Kong Yingda, 140
Kongzi. *See* Confucius
Kropotkin, Peter, 163
Kuomintang, 161

Laozi, 175, 186–88
Laozi (Lao Zi), 88, 315
Lau, D. C., 235
Legalism (ists), 143, 331, 335
Legge, James, 282
li (ritual), 182, 227, 252, 260
    in Confucianism, 110, 227
    in Confucius, 178, 181
    in Mencius, 185
    in Xunzi, 196, 198, 199, 203
Li Xueqin, 44
liangzhi (liang zhi), 253, 254, 259–60,
        329, 340
Lifton, Robert
    *Thought Reform and the Psychology of
        Totalism*, 340
Liji. See Book of Rites
Ling Tingkan, 138
Liu Shaoqi, 335
Liu Xiang, 104, 132, 136
Liu Xin, 132, 136, 302
Liu Zongyuan, 140
Liu Zongzhou, 148
Longshan pottery culture. *See* China,
        prehistoric: Longshan pottery
        culture
Lu Jiuyuan, 106, 299
Lu school. *See* Eastern Zhejiang
        tradition
Lu Xiangshan, 128, 143, 144, 146, 147,
        148, 150

Lū Zhangcheng, 103, 104
Luo Qinshun, 128
Lyons, John, 9

Ma Rong, 140
MacIntyre, Alisdair, 231
　After Virtue, 231
Mackie, J. L., 237
Mann, Susan
　Nivison's response to, 292–97
Mannheim, Karl, 303
Mao Tse-tung, 161
Maoist Communism, 308
Marxism, 309
Marxist totalitarianism, 161
Maspero, Henri, 44, 46
McCarthy, Senator Joseph, 161
the Mean, 83–92
　as approximate and elastic, 85–86
　and differentiation, 89, 90
　and extremes, 84, 86, 87, 90, 91
　and harmony, 88, 89, 90, 91
　as the "middle," 83–84, 86, 87, 90
　and music, role of, 88, 89
　as the ordinary, 84–85
　problems for interpretation of,
　　290–92
　and rites, role of, 88–90
The Mean (Zhongyong), 83–86, 292
Mencius (Mengzi), 43, 139, 150, 155,
　184–85, 227, 229, 235, 236, 278,
　279, 326, 335
　and existentialism, contrast between,
　　251, 260–61
　and Laozi, 187–89
　and virtue ethics, 175, 184–85, 188,
　　189
　and Xunzi, contrast with, 202, 207,
　　209, 211, 212, 213, 217–18, 322,
　　327
the *Mencius (Mengzi)*, 86, 128, 236
Mengzi. *See* Mencius
Metzger, Tom

Escape from Predicament, 311
microperiodization
　application of
　　to Bin-group inscriptions, 58–60,
　　　62–68
　　to calendar of Shang Military
　　　Campaign, 59–72
　　to Li-group inscriptions, 58, 59,
　　　68–72
　　and lunar eclipse record, 61, 62,
　　　283–84
　methodology of
　　common month standard,
　　　conversion to, 60–61
　　and *ganzhi* cycle, 59, 61, 62, 72
　　and intercalary months, 59, 67–68
　　and lunar month, 60–61
　　parameters, setting of, 60–62
Mill, John Stuart, 214, 232
modernism, 162
　responses to critiques of, 165–66
Mohism, 143, 186, 187, 194, 227, 237
　and Confucianism, disagreement
　　between, 180–81
Mozi, 178–80, 184, 185, 186, 188, 232,
　236, 278, 335
　and *dao*, 179–81
　on human desire, solutions to, 194
　and *li*, 179
　and Xunzi, 193–96, 199–200, 322–23
Munro, Donald, 230, 315
　Nivison's response to, 320–23
the *Music*, 196

naming practices, significance of,
　106–7
Neo-Confucianism, Neo-Confucians,
　150, 227, 228, 229, 250, 252–54,
　260, 299, 308, 311
　and Mencius, 175
　Zhang's genealogical reconstruction
　　of, 143–45, 149
Nietzsche, Friedrich, 231

Nivison, David S., 3, 69, 71, 122, 131,
    155–56, 168–69, 213, 218
  and Chinese philosophy, 224, 235
  and chronology studies, 58, 69, 70,
    279–82, 286–88
  on Communist ethics and Chinese
    tradition, 161, 308, 310
  on "existentialism" in Wang Ji and
    Wang Yangming, 250–53, 254
  on Mencius, 202, 236
  on *qi*, 4–5, 7, 8, 13–15, 16, 18, 22, 23,
    24, 25, 28
  on Xunzi, 193, 194, 202, 203, 205,
    206, 215
  on Zhang Xuecheng, 95, 106, 112,
    122, 126, 129, 132, 133, 134, 137,
    141, 145, 146, 156

the Odes. *See Book of Odes*
Okada Takehiko,
  on "existentialism" in Wangji and
    Wang Yangming, 250–52
Okin, Susan, 297
Olafson, Frederick
  Principles and Persons, 336
One Hundred Family Names, 95
options, real and notional, 226, 227, 229
oracle-bone inscriptions, Shang (OBI).
    3–28, 52–53, 267–77. *See also*
    bronze inscriptions
  of the Bin group, 58–60, 62–68
  and calendar reconstruction, 58–72
  divination sentences, nature of,
    267–69
  divinatory charges
    context of, 5
    order of, 16
  ganzhi cycle, use of, 59, 61, 62
  general background on, 267
  intercalary months, use of, 59, 67–68
  of the Li group, 58, 59, 68–72
  and microperiodization, 59–72
  and military campaign inscriptions,
    58–60, 63–72
  and periodization, 59
  placement, role of, 5–7, 17
  and same-piece relationship, 60,
    62–63
  and semantic charges, positive and
    negative, 5–6
  and the Shang calendar, 59–60
oracle-bone linguistic aspect, Shang
    (OBL), 3, 7, 12, 13, 15, 21, 23,
    24, 25, 28
  and non-stative/non-eventive verbs,
    12
  and stative/eventive verbs, 12

painted pottery culture. *See* China,
    prehistoric: Yangshao pottery
    culture
Pankenier, David W., 279, 282, 286
Parfit, Derek, 179
philology, in Chinese intellectual
    history, 121–22, 126, 128, 129,
    131, 136, 137, 139, 141, 149
philosophy, as a concept, 225. *See also*
    Western philosophy
philosophy of "sincerity," 83, 85
Plato, 225
Pol Pot, 163
postmodernism, 155
  and relativism, 155, 156, 162
Pulleyblank, Edwin G.
  Nivison's response to, 277–82
Pythagoras, 239

qi
  as adjective, 23, 28, 270, 272, 274
  as adverbial particle, 4, 15, 270, 274,
    275
  as anaphoric pronoun, 3, 13–17, 19,
    20, 28, 272
    of a genitive nature, 21–22, 23, 24,
    26–27
  as aspectual particle, 3, 4, 11, 13, 16,

19, 20, 23, 27, 28
anticipative, 11, 16, 28, 275
lexicalizing, 11
prospective, 11–12, 16, 28, 271,
    272, 275
as delimiting "old information,"
    16–17, 270
and desirable semantic charges,
    relation to, 8–10, 17
and *fu,* relation to, 12
as genitive-pronominal, 21–22, 23,
    24, 26–27, 28
historical changes in meaning of, 227
history of debate over meaning of,
    268
as interrogative, 268–69
as modal particle, 3, 4–10, 13, 14, 16,
    19, 20, 23, 27, 28, 268–71, 275
    degree of force of, 16
    and human will, role of, 7–8
    intention/wish scale, 7–8, 10, 16
    possibility/certainty scale, 5, 6–8,
        10, 16, 28
    presupposition theory of, 9–10, 13,
        16, 26
Neo-Confucian sense of, 227–29
the "one-word" hypothesis of, 13,
    268, 270, 272, 275
pronominal hypothesis of, 4, 13–28,
    268, 270, 272, 273, 275
    and divinatory charges, order of,
        16–17
as "subjunctive mood," 3, 24–28
as subordinate sentence marker, 3,
    17–24, 28, 271
as verb, 18–19, 28
and verbs, relation to, 7
Qian Daxin, 123, 124, 125, 132, 134,
    136
Qian Dian (Zi Xianchi), 136, 302
Qian Mu, 139, 293
Qinshi Hwangdi, 255
Quan Zuwang, 146, 295

Qui Xigui, 68
Quine, W. V. O., 158

Rao Zongyi, 268, 316
relativism, 155–56
    and culture dependency claim,
        156–57, 305–6
    moral value of, 159–62, 164
    impassable barriers claim, 156–57,
        304–6
    problems of, 157–59, 162–65,
        166–67
Remaining Writings of Zhang Xuecheng,
    122
Rorty, Richard, 231, 239
Rosemont, Henry, 332
    Nivison's response to, 303–11
Russell, Bertrand, 225

sage-kings, sages
    and Confucians, Confucius, 128, 129,
        178
    and the *Dao (dao),* 139, 141, 178
    and the Mean, 86, 88
    Shun, 86, 238
    in Xunzi, 197, 198, 199, 206, 213,
        214–15, 217, 327–31
    in Zhang Xuecheng, 330–31
Schiller, Friedrich von, 162
Schwartz, Benjamin, 238
    The World of Thought in Ancient China,
        224
Seferis, George, 238
Serruys, Paul L-M, 276, 285
    on *qi,* 4–5, 6, 16, 17–18, 269, 270
Shang oracle-bone inscriptions. *See*
        oracle-bone inscriptions, Shang
Shangshu. See Book of Documents
Shao Jinhan, 121, 123, 125, 146
Shao, Tincai, 146
Shaughnessy, Edward L.
    Nivison's response to, 282–89
Shen Pei

on *qi*, 14, 25
Shi Tong, 132
Shibo, 91
Shijing. See Book of Odes
Shuijing Zhu, 130
Sima Qian, 39, 140
  Shi Ji, 130
the Six Classics, 138–39, 141, 143, 148, 149
Snow, Edgar
  Red Star Over China, 161
Socrates, 173, 237
Spring and Autumn Annals, 43–48, 97
Stalin, Josef, 163
Sun Baoxuan, 121
Sun Xingyan, 137

Takashima, Ken-ichi, 314
  Nivison's response to, 267–77
Takeuchi Yoshio, 83
the Three Dynasties, 143, 148
Tibeto-Burman language family, 52, 53
Tongcheng writers, 106
Tu Weiming, 256

utilitarianism, 173

Van Norden, Bryan
  on Mencius and Xunzi, 207, 209
  Nivison's response to, 331–35
Vandermeersch, Leon, 50–51
Vienna Circle, 165
virtue ethics. *See also de*, as virtue
  in Chinese thought, 174, 175, 180, 188–89, 236
  in Western thought, 173, 174, 236–37

Waley, Arthur, 235, 315
Wan Sida, 148
Wan Sitong, 148
Wang Huizu, 97, 135
Wang Ji
  as "existentialist," 250, 252–53, 254

on moral self-cultivation, 253–54
Wang Yangming, 106, 128, 145, 148, 150, 236, 329, 335
  and "existentialism," 338–40
  similarities to, 250–53, 254–56, 260
  differences from, 251, 257, 260
  on moral self-cultivation, 253–54, 255–56, 259–60, 337
  and sagehood, commitment to, 255–56, 339
Wang Zhong, 293
Watson, Rubie, 107
the Way. *See* the *Dao*
Western philosophy, 224, 225, 238
  and Chinese philosophy, differences between
    in context, 225–30
    in methodology, 230
  degree of success of, dispute over, 231–32
  value of Chinese thought for, 231, 232–33, 334
    Moderate View, 233, 235–36
    Radical View, 233, 234–35
Western Zhejiang tradition, 148
White, Theodore
  Thunder Out of China, 161
Whorf, Benjamin, 303
Williams, Bernard, 226
Wollheim, Richard, 219
Wong, David B.
  Nivison's response to, 323–31
Wu Ding, 58, 67, 72, 280, 282, 283, 286
  dating reign of, 286–87
Wu Hung, 41

the Xia, 40, 42, 53, 278
the Xia-Zhou (Xia-Chinese) polity, 49, 51
Xie An, 96
Xu Ai, 255
Xu Xing, 278
Xunzi, 335

and Confucianism, 193, 204, 321
and Daoism, the *dao,* 199, 205–6, 331
on force, the role of, 204
on hierarchies, role of, 194–98,
    204–5
and Hobbes, 203–5, 206, 232, 331
on human desires, and their
    solution, 194, 196–99, 203–5,
    206–12, 213, 214, 219–20
on human nature, 195, 196, 198, 199,
    200, 202–3, 205–6, 210–12, 213,
    215–16, 218–20, 320–21, 325,
    327, 330
and Mencius, contrast between, 202,
    207, 209, 211, 212, 213, 217–18,
    325, 327
metaphysical position of, 195, 197
moral transformation, problem of,
    202, 205–7, 210–12, 214–15,
    216–19, 326–27
reaction of, to Mozi, 193, 194–97,
    200, 322–23
on ritual and music, the role of, 203,
    206, 211, 216–17, 219, 327–28
on social chaos, 193, 195, 197, 199,
    200, 203, 205–6
Xunzi, 88, 175, 194
Xunzi, school of, 88

Yan Dongyu, 132, 133
Yangshao pottery culture. *See* China,
    prehistoric: Yangshao pottery
    culture
Yanzi (Yan Zi), 90, 291
Yao Mingda, 296
Yao Nai, 295
Yearley, Lee H., 236, 237, 238, 250
the Yi, 40, 46, 53, 278
    as alien people, 42, 44, 47
    assimilation of, 48–49, 54
    and human sacrifice, 48
    language of, 44–45
    and Shang rulers, 48

Yi Zhi, 236
yin and *yang,* 87
Yu Weichao, 48
Yu Min, 22
Yü Ying-shih
    Nivison's response to, 297–303
Yuan Mei, 106, 107–8, 110, 293, 296
    Poetry Talks, 107
the Yue, 44, 45
    language of, 45

Zhang Runan, 124, 126, 129
Zhang Xuecheng, 155, 156, 292–93,
    295–97, 307, 311, 331
    on the classics as history, 138, 139,
        141, 142, 143, 146, 148, 298, 302
    and Confucianism, 122, 126, 135,
        140–42, 144, 146–51
    and Dai Zhen
        first meeting between, 123–27,
            136, 297
        influence of, 122, 131, 137, 143,
            299
        intellectual differences between,
            121, 129–31, 135, 136, 139,
            140–46, 149, 295, 298
    and the *Dao,* 140, 141, 142, 143, 147,
        149, 150, 151, 302, 330
    and Eastern Zhejiang tradition,
        143–49, 151, 294–95
    and female relatives, role of, 95–98
        Lady Shi, 96–97
        Zhang's wife, 97
    Hezhou Zhi Yu (History of Hezhou), 133,
        137
    and *jiaochou,* 132, 133, 135, 136, 137,
        298
    Jiaochou Lue, 134
    Jiaochou Tongyi, 131–35, 137, 298,
        300–301
    and local culture, influence of, 105–7
    as methodological holist, 131, 141,
        142, 150

and philology, 126, 127, 129, 131,
  135, 136, 139, 141, 149
and reconstruction of intellectual
  genealogies, 143–45
Shiji Kao, 137–38
and surrogate mothers and sisters,
  role of, 98–105
  Lady Xun and daughters, 98–103
  Lady Yuan, 98, 103–4, 105, 112
Wang Zhong, criticism of, 108
and *wenshi,* 131, 132, 133, 135, 137,
  140, 141, 298
and *wenshi jiaochou,* 133, 135, 136
Wenshi Tongyi, 121, 131–39, 141–43,
  146–49, 294, 298, 300–301
on women in the historical record,
  111–12
on women's place and virtues, 94, 97,
  104, 106, 110, 111–12, 293
Yuan Mei, criticism of, 107–8, 293, 296
Zhang Zongdong, 268, 269, 271
Zhexi culture, 105–6
Zhedong culture, 105–6, 108

Zheng Hewen (Chengzhai), 123, 124,
  125
Zheng Qiao
  Tong Zhi, 130
Zheng Xuan, 140, 142
Zhongyong. See The Mean
Zhu Gui, 141
Zhu Xi, 227, 254
  intellectual lineage from, 143–50,
  299
  on the Mean, 83, 84, 85
  and Zhexi school, 105–6
the Zhu Xia, 42, 44, 47, 50, 51
Zhu Xigeng, 146
Zhu Yun, 96, 98, 121, 123–26, 307
Zhuangzi, 188, 193, 205, 227, 229, 237,
  238
Zhuangzi, 175, 238
zhuhou states, 46, 47, 49
Zi Xia, 332, 334, 335
Zuozhuan (The Zuo Commentary), 43, 44,
  46, 48, 90